Eurafricans in Western Africa

Western African Studies

Willing Migrants
Soninke Labor Diasporas, 1848–1960
FRANÇOIS MANCHUELLE

El Dorado in West Africa
The Gold-Mining Frontier, African Labor, and Colonial Capitalism in the Gold Coast, 1875–1900
RAYMOND E. DUMETT

Nkrumah & the Chiefs
The Politics of Chieftaincy in Ghana, 1951–60
RICHARD RATHBONE

Ghanaian Popular Fiction
'Thrilling Discoveries in Conjugal Life' & Other Tales
STEPHANIE NEWELL

Paths of Accommodation
Muslim Societies and French Colonial Authorities in Senegal and Mauritania, 1880–1920
DAVID ROBINSON

West African Challenge to Empire
Culture and History in the Volta-Bani Anticolonial War
MAHIR ŞAUL AND PATRICK ROYER

Between the Sea & the Lagoon
An Eco-social History of the Anlo of Southeastern Ghana, c. 1850 to Recent Times
EMMANUEL AKYEAMPONG

'Civil Disorder is the Disease of Ibadan'
Chieftaincy and Civic Culture in a Colonial City
RUTH WATSON

Smugglers, Secessionists, and Loyal Citizens on the Ghana-Togo Frontier
PAUL NUGENT

Eurafricans in Western Africa
Commerce, Social Status, Gender, and Religious Observance from the Sixteenth to the Eighteenth Century
GEORGE E. BROOKS

*Lineages of State Fragility**
Rural Civil Society in Guinea-Bissau
JOSHUA B. FORREST

*'Kola is God's Gift'**
Agricultural Production, Export Initiatives & the Kola Industry in Asante & and the Gold Coast, c. 1820–1950
EDMUND ABAKA

*forthcoming

Eurafricans in Western Africa

Commerce, Social Status, Gender, and Religious Observance from the Sixteenth to the Eighteenth Century

George E. Brooks

Ohio University Press
ATHENS

James Currey
OXFORD

Ohio University Press
Scott Quadrangle
Athens, Ohio 45701

James Currey Ltd
73 Botley Road
Oxford OX2 0BS

First published 2003

Ohio University Press books are printed on acid-free paper ∞

10 09 08 07 06 05 04 03 5 4 3 2 1

Published in the United States of America by Ohio University Press,
Athens, Ohio 45701

Cover photograph depicting Rufisque, Senegal, is from Jean Barbot, *A Description of the Coasts of North and South Guinea, In Six Books* (London, 1732), volume V, plate 2, after page 20. It appears courtesy of the Lilly Library, Indiana University, Bloomington, Indiana.

British Library Cataloging in Publication Data is available
ISBN-0-85255-489-3 (James Currey, paper)
ISBN-0-85255-499-0 (James Currey, cloth)

Library of Congress Cataloging-in-Publication Data

Brooks, George E., 1933–
Eurafricans in western Africa : commerce, social status, gender, and religious observance from the sixteenth to the eighteenth century / George E. Brooks.
p. cm. — (Western African studies)
Includes bibliographical references (p.) and index.
ISBN 0-8214-1485-2 (acid-free paper) — ISBN 0-8214-1486-0 (pbk. : acid-free paper)
1. Africa, West—Ethnic relations. 2. Racially mixed people—Africa, West—History. 3. Europeans—Africa, West—History. 4. Africa, West—History—To 1884. 5. Europe—Colonies—Africa—History. 6. Africa, West—Commerce—Europe. 7. Europe—Commerce—Africa, West. 8. Slave-trade—Africa, West—History. I. Title. II. Series.

DT474.5.B758 2003
966'.004034—dc21

2002192965

For Elaine

Rufisque, Senegal (detail). From Jean Barbot, *A Description of the Coasts of North and South Guinea, In Six Books* (London, 1732), volume V, plate 2, after page 20. Barbot's panoramic depiction of Rufisque shows Senhora Catarina's African-type dwelling (C) with a large cross raised over the front gate of the compound. (Barbot's visit is described on p. 134.) Courtesy of the Lilly Library, Indiana University, Bloomington, Indiana.

Contents

Maps

Preface and Acknowledgments

An attempt to describe and analyze the activities of Eurafricans for a period of three centuries is a daunting undertaking at the present stage of historical scholarship. Eurafricans were dispersed across an area covering fifteen hundred kilometers along the western African littoral from Senegal to Sierra Leone, equivalent to the distance from Maine to Florida, and they participated in commercial networks that extended into the interior of the continent for more than one thousand kilometers. Documentation on the lives of these individuals is sparse. The few Eurafricans who were literate were reticent concerning their commercial activities and their circumstances generally. European traders, missionaries, colonial officials, and ship-borne visitors provided the bulk of available information on Eurafricans during those centuries, but much of what they recorded was misinformed, self-serving, and imbued with racial prejudice. African traders living in the interior made strategic decisions concerning where to dispatch caravans to the Atlantic littoral, but little information is available about their relations with Eurafricans.

With the exception of the letters written by the redoubtable Anna Maria Falconbridge, all the sources cited in this volume were written by men—despite the fact that many African and Eurafrican women were protagonists in western African commerce. Only the most successful women—that is, those who were most helpful or most challenging to male interests—were mentioned in the sources. Little is known about kinship relationships, including those of individuals bearing the same surnames. European and Eurafrican men rarely concluded Christian marriages with the women in Africa, nor did they record the names of the mothers of their children or register their children's births. And even when an individual's father was identified, the common practice of having multiple sexual partners precluded the possibility of identifying full or half siblings. In addition, European and Eurafrican slavers routinely victimized slave women under their power, and the offspring that resulted were given—or took—their masters' names. Complicating matters still further, Africans hired by Europeans and Eurafricans as seamen and compradors frequently adopted the names of their employers.

Additional complexities regarding western African social and cultural relationships are exemplified by the instance of a young Mandinka trader named Gaspar Vaz who lived at Kassang along the Gambia River. He had formerly been a slave in the Cape Verde Islands, owned by a tailor named Francisco Vaz. His success as an interpreter and broker derived from the fact that he was the nephew and heir of Kassang's *satigi* (governor). Living in a Mandinka community whose residents included Muslims, Vaz wore a rosary concealed in his garments (Mota and Hair 1977, 146–49).

Eurafrican names may be spelled differently in European sources according to their pronunciation in African languages. For instance, there is no *v* sound in Mande languages, and hence, Englishmen trading along the Gambia River recorded "Boss" for Eurafricans named Vaz. Alternatively, Vaz was rendered "Vos." In like manner, English clerks recorded "Beares" and "Beers" for Luso-Africans named Vieira. Portuguese conventions included the use of "Roiz" as the shorthand for Rodriguez, "Sa" for Souza, and "Va" for Vasconcellos. In this light, Donald R. Wright remarked on the "off-hand fashion" of Royal African Company account books: "For every such entry of gifts to 'Sra. Terezia Giar, wife of Valentine Mendez,' or to 'the Senhoras of Niumi on their going to the cry of Sr. Antonio Vos,' an obscure company writer recorded twenty more gifts to Eurafricans without including any suggestion as to their relations, their position in Gambian society, or their place of residence" (Wright 1976, 195–96).

Records concerning Eurafricans became more extensive and detailed during the latter part of the eighteenth century. Eurafricans living at Saint-Louis, Gorée, Ziguinchor, and Cacheu found it advantageous to register property, contract Christian marriages, and record the births of their children. Over time, reckoning by patrilineal descent supplanted the matrilineal practice among groups living south of the Gambia River, a social transformation influenced both by Europeans and by Muslim traders and clerics.

A word on place names. To avoid confusion between Cape Verde, Senegal, the westernmost point in Africa, and the Cape Verde archipelago some five hundred kilometers westward in the Atlantic Ocean, the archipelago is cited as Cabo Verde (as the modern-day nation is titled), and the inhabitants are Cabo Verdeans. I follow Portuguese and Luso-Africans in using "Serra Leoa" to refer to the littoral between Cape Verga and the Sherbro River to avoid confusion with the modern-day nation of Sierra Leone and the Sierra Leone River and estuary. English traders referred to the littoral east of Cape Palmas as the "Ivory Coast," while the French used "Côte d'Ivoire," which latter became the name of the modern-day state. Since place names have changed over the centuries, the text includes double citations such as Kassang/Caçao to record that the Gambia River port of Kassang was recorded as Caçao in Portuguese sources.

Many sources used in this study are available only in specialized research libraries—hence, the extensive use of quotations from sources that, in many instances, would be traduced by paraphrasing. In the course of this study, I became increasingly appreciative of the contributions of the scholars who edited and annotated primary sources. Regarding Portuguese archival materials, Christiano José de Senna Barcellos's seven-part *Subsídios para a história de Cabo Verde e Guiné* (1899–1913) is indispensable for research on Luso-Africans. A half century after Barcellos's work was published—but still in the days before copiers and word processors—Padre António Brásio undertook the stupendous task of editing numerous volumes of documents deposited in Portuguese archives. And Elizabeth Donnan deserves special mention: her four-volume *Documents Illustrative of the Slave Trade to America* was published in 1930 when few U.S. scholars were interested in African history.

While pursing a distinguished naval career that culminated in a promotion to vice admiral, Avelino Teixeira da Mota edited collections of Portuguese documents and maps along with numerous publications that addressed a remarkable range of historical, geographic, and cultural issues. Complementing Mota's scholarship on many topics are the publications of António Carreira, a Cabo Verdean who spent many decades in Portuguese Guiné working for the colonial administration and commercial firms. Carreira published extensively on history, ethnography, and textiles, and he compiled and edited numerous documents concerning Guiné and Cabo Verde. Both Teixeira da Mota and Carreira generously shared their scholarship and experiences with me and numerous other researchers. I am also grateful for a long-standing friendship with Padre Henrique Pinto Rema, a former editor of the *Boletim Cultural da Guiné Portuguesa* and the chronicler of Portuguese Franciscan missionaries worldwide, who has provided me with much information and advice in my research on Luso-Africans.

Of immense importance for historians, linguists, and anthropologists is the scholarship of Paul Edward Hedley Hair, doyen of British scholars specializing in the history of European involvement with Africa. Hair published an immense corpus of books and articles, including many documents in Portuguese and other European languages presented in translation with meticulous annotations—as attested by the numerous publications listed in the References section at the end of this book.

Scholarship concerning French involvement with western Africans was greatly expedited by J. Machat's *Documents sur les établissements français de l'Afrique occidentale au XVIII siècle* (1906) and Pierre Cultru's *Histoire du Sénégal du XV siècle à 1870* (1910), followed in 1913 by Cultru's *Premier voyage du Sieur de la Courbe fait à la coste d'Afrique en 1685,* which delineated Père Jean-Baptiste Labat's plagiarism of Michel Jajolet de la Courbe published in 1728 to the advantage of André Brüe and the confusion of generations of readers. A half century later, Raymond Mauny transformed historians' viewpoints with the interior-coastal perspectives delineated in *Tableau géographique de l'ouest Africain au moyen age* (1961). Léonce Jore incorporated numerous quotations from documentary sources in *Les établissements français sur la côte occidentale d'Afrique de 1758 à 1809* (1965), and John Hargreaves translated and edited a well-chosen selection of French sources for *France and West Africa: An Anthology of Historical Documents* (1969). Subsequently, Guy Thilmans and Nize Izabel Moraes transcribed, translated, and edited numerous European documents, with their scholarly endeavors culminating in Moraes's indispensable four-volume collection, *A la découverte de la Petite Côte au XVII siècle (Sénégal et Gambie)* (1993, 1995, 1998). Beginning in the 1970s, the study of Senegambian history was transformed by new works of synthesis—notably, Marie-Hélène Knight's research on Gorée and Saint-Louis and the work of Christian Roche on the history of the Casamance region. Senegambian history in large perspective was treated in Philip Curtin's *Economic Change in Precolonial Africa: Senegambia in the Era of the Slave Trade* (1975), Boubacar Barry's *La Sénégambie du XV au XIX siècle* (1988), and numerous contributions by Jean Boulègue and Martin A. Klein.

Three historians "anchor" English scholarship on western Africa—north, south, and comprehensively. Sir John Gray's magisterial *History of the Gambia* (1940) is unsurpassed; so too is Christopher Fyfe's *History of Sierra Leone* (1962). And Walter Rodney's synthesis of Portuguese, French, and English sources in his *History of the Upper Guinea Coast, 1545–1800* (1970) greatly influenced subsequent historical studies, including the present volume. Because few Scots or Irish were involved in western African commerce during the period covered in this study, *English* is the collective noun used here, except for references to Britain and British involvement in European affairs following the union of England and Scotland in 1707 (Hair and Law 1998, 243 n. 2).

Many of the topics treated in Gray's volume were supplemented and updated by David Gamble's pathbreaking anthropological and bibliographic studies and by oral data collected by Bakari Sidibe, Winifred Galloway, and Donald Wright that delineate commercial, social, and cultural linkages between the inhabitants of The Gambia and groups living in many areas of western Africa. Wright's *The World and a Very Small Place in Africa* admirably demonstrated how western African polities were inextricably drawn into the world economy. Following publication of his monumental *History of Sierra Leone,* Christopher Fyfe compiled the documents printed in *Sierra Leone Inheritance.* He has since published a number of studies relating to historical topics subsequent to the time period covered in this book, and he has mentored generations of researchers. Peter Kup followed *A History of Sierra Leone, 1400–1787* (1961) with the meticulously transcribed and edited *Adam Afzelius: Sierra Leone Journal, 1795–1796* (1967). Bruce L. Mouser's numerous contributions delineated Serra Leoa commercial networks and chronicled the activities of Eurafrican families, and the value of his publications was enhanced by expertly prepared maps. Mouser has, for many years, generously shared research from numerous archives.

Three reference works deserve special accolades: E. Joucla's exhaustive *Bibliographie de l'Afrique Occidentale Française* (1937), J. D. Fage's *Guide to Original Sources for Precolonial Western Africa Published in European Languages* (1987), and Adam Jones's *Raw, Medium, Well Done: A Critical Review of Editorial and Quasi-Editorial Work on Pre-1885 European Sources for Sub-Saharan Africa, 1960–1986* (1987). For Portuguese sources, Alexandre Marques Pereira merits special recognition. The longtime librarian at the Sociedade Geografia de Lisboa, Pereira generously shared with researchers his unrivaled knowledge of out-of-print journals and rare publications.

I first undertook research in Europe and West Africa in 1960–61, supported by a Ford Foundation Training Fellowship. Subsequent research funding included a Social Science Research Council grant (1971–72), travel funds from the Indiana University African Studies Program (1974), a Summer Faculty Fellowship (1975), and a National Endowment for the Humanities grant (1976–77). Two Indiana University travel grants for conferences in Africa enabled me to conduct research: the President's Council on International Programs grant (1978) and the Arts and Sciences grant (1988). I visited western Africa in 1988 as a member of the U.S. presidential delegation to Guinea-Bissau to attend the celebration and conference commemorating the four-hundredth anniversary of the founding of Cacheu, and I returned in 1990 on a grant from the American Council of Learned Societies.

During research trips to Senegambia, I benefited from the expertise of Jean-François Maurel and Saliou Mbaye, successive directors of the Archives Nationales. Boubacar Barry and his wife, Aissoutou Sow; François and Jacqueline Zuccarelli; and Mireille Jacques and her daughter and son-in-law, Paule and Hans

Zandvoort, offered generous hospitality and shared their knowledge of Senegal. Mamadou Diagne and Astou Talla taught me about Wolof and Lébou traditions. Philip Curtin, Roger Pasquier, Pierre Cariou, Marie-Hélène Knight, and Christian Roche generously shared publications and unpublished manuscripts. (I have long been out of contact with Knight and Roche and would appreciate information concerning their whereabouts.) During visits to The Gambia, I enjoyed the memorable hospitality of Kebba and Marion Foon, Bakari Sidibe and his wives Ayo and Binta, Winifred Galloway, and Hassan Farage and his family.

In May 1977, my first research visit to newly independent Guinea-Bissau was facilitated by José Blanco of the Gulbenkian Foundation. At a time when there were few vehicles available, José Araújo offered his own vehicle, and, with Boubacar Barry as guide, I visited the old trading centers at Cacheu, Farim, Geba, and Bafatá. Fr. Angelo Bianchi and Fr. Henrique Cazzaniga of the Pontifício Instituto das Missões Estrangeiras (PIME) arranged for typists to make copies of mission records. On this and subsequent trips to Guinea-Bissau, I added to my genealogical files by photographing tombstones in cemeteries. During visits to Guinea-Bissau, I have received generous hospitality from PIME fathers and brothers. Thanks to Fr. Luigi Scantamburlo and the crews of the *Anumba* and other pirogues, I have visited many of the Bissagos Islands and learned much about the history and current circumstances of Bijago and other groups living on the neighboring mainland. Mina Höhener provided gourmet meals and accommodation on the island of Orangozinho. Foremost among the pleasures of visiting Bissau was associating with the dynamic group of scholars at the Instituto Nacional de Estudos e Pesquisa (INEP). Tragically, INEP's archives and library were destroyed during the conflict that devastated Bissau in 1998 and 1999.

It was my good fortune to be hired at Indiana University in 1962, when J. Gus Liebenow was attracting a remarkable group of faculty members and graduate students to participate in the newly established African Studies Program. Over the years, I have received much assistance and informed advice from extraordinarily gifted Africana bibliographers. Alan Taylor, Jean Meeh Gosebrink, David Easterbrook, Nancy Schmidt, and Marion Frank-Wilson have been, successively, the "most valuable players" of the African Studies Program, ably seconded, to be sure, by their colleagues in Serials, Reference, Inter-Library Loan, and the Lilly Library. Indiana University colleagues who have contributed their expertise include Quentin Hope and Darlene Sadlier, who assisted in translating arcane French and Portuguese sources; Irving Katz, who elucidated issues regarding Jewish history and genealogies; Ann Carmichael, who explained the etiology of diseases; and Paul Newman, who advised me on linguistic matters. John

Hollingsworth, master cartographer, created the maps that are invaluable complements to the text.

When this manuscript was nearing completion, it was read by Christopher Fyfe, Paul Hair, Bruce Mouser, Dan McCall, and Don Wright. I am immensely grateful to them for their numerous contributions. I also wish to thank the Ohio University Press reader for informed comments and recommendations. The text was greatly improved by Joan W. Sherman's skillful and judicious copyediting. Gillian Berchowitz, Nancy Basmajian, Sharon Arnold, and Sharon Rose of Ohio University Press provided much good advice and professional expertise. Computer glitches were overcome with insouciant, can-do expertise and good-humored tolerance by Douglas Brooks and by Francis Flavin, the Indiana University History Department's first Web master, and by their apt pupils, my daughters Claire and Anne Rivron. Invaluable in this and all my endeavors is my multitalented wife, Elaine Rivron, to whom this book is dedicated.

GEORGE E. BROOKS

Introduction

THE GEOGRAPHIC SCOPE OF THIS BOOK was essentially determined by Eurafricans and their African landlords, while many of the chronological chapter breaks derived from the disruptions to trade caused by European wars and commerce raiding. Western Africa, depicted on Map 1.1, extends some three thousand kilometers from the Senegal River in the north to the Bandama River in the south and fifteen hundred kilometers east from the Atlantic littoral to the bend of the Niger River, equivalent to the part of the United States that lies east of the Mississippi River. The great majority of the inhabitants of this vast and geographically diverse territory speak languages belonging to two principal families — West Atlantic and Mande, the former principally in coastal regions, the latter mainly in the interior.

The peoples of western Africa have been linked by commercial networks since ancient times. Mande-speaking traders and smiths pioneered caravan routes from the interior that connected the riverine networks of West Atlantic–speaking groups, promoting long-distance trade in salt, gold, iron, kola, malaguetta pepper, and numerous other commodities. By the third century A.D., western Africa's trade networks connected trans-Saharan routes, and exchanges with North Africa multiplied over the centuries. The huge profit that Maghrebian middlemen exacted from Europeans for gold, ivory, malaguetta pepper, and other western African commodities was a principal factor promoting Portuguese reconnaissance voyages along the coast of western Africa during the fifteenth century.

When Portuguese mariners arrived in western Africa, they were constrained to accommodate to centuries-old landlord-stranger reciprocities concerning the host societies' treatment of itinerant traders, hunters, migrants, and other travelers. Portuguese had to use African modes of barter commerce, pay tolls and taxes, visit only where they were invited by African hosts, and adhere to local customs and practices while ashore. *Lançados*—venturesome Portuguese and Luso-African inhabitants of the Cape Verde Islands, who were allowed to reside in African

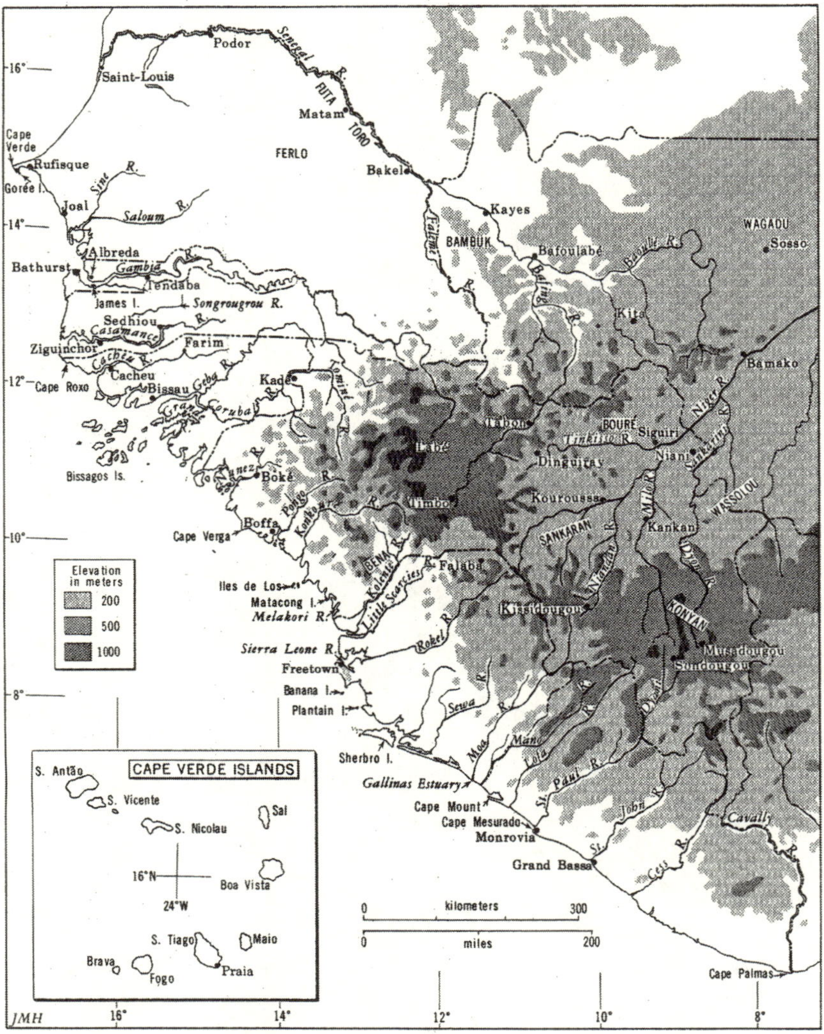

Map 1.1 Western Africa

communities — were subject to numerous constraints. African landlords refused to rent lançados more land than needed for dwellings and stores, rendering them dependent on indigenous communities for food, water, and other necessities. Of inestimable consequence for the lançados, however, they, like African strangers, were permitted to cohabit with local women, usually relatives or dependents of influential members of communities who sought the advantages that came with affiliation with foreign traders. Wives were invaluable to the lançados as interpreters of languages and cultures and as collaborators in commercial exchanges — roles subsequently undertaken by many of their Luso-African children.

Luso-Africans, the children of Portuguese traders and African women, represented a new and unprecedented element in western African societies. In social and cultural terms, these children, raised in African communities, acquired much more of the heritage of their mothers than of their Portuguese fathers, many of whom died or departed after a brief stay. This imbalance is conveyed in the word *Luso-African* itself, in which the short prefix *Luso* (derived from *Lusitania,* the Roman name for the area of Portugal) is combined with the longer *African.* The same can be said for the words *Anglo-African* and *Franco-African,* as well. *Eurafrican* serves as a generic term.

Raised in African societies, Eurafricans' lifeways were chiefly determined by the social status of their mothers. But there were significant differences in this regard between stratified and acephalous societies. The stratified and patrilineal societies of Senegambia — Wolof, Serer, and Mandinka — excluded Portuguese and Luso-Africans from marrying free persons. Luso-African children were denied membership in the "power associations" that educated youths and conferred adult status in these societies. Social outcasts, Luso-Africans lacked the rights and privileges of other members of their age sets, including the right to cultivate land. Luso-African males in these societies sought employment as sailors, interpreters, and compradors working for Portuguese and fellow Luso-Africans, with the bleak prospect that whatever wealth and possessions they acquired would be expropriated by rulers and other elites. Female Luso-Africans shared the same disabilities and became interpreters and intermediaries for European traders and African elites. Luso-African men and women contested their pariah status. They wore European-style garments, displayed crucifixes and rosaries attesting their adherence to Catholicism, spoke Crioulo (which derived from Portuguese and West Atlantic languages), and asserted that they were "Portuguese," "whites," and "Christians" — claims derided by Portuguese and other Europeans.

Circumstances were significantly different among acephalous and matrilineal societies south of the Gambia River, such as the Papel, Landuman, Temne, and

Bullom. In these societies, elders and community leaders generally allowed lançados to marry daughters and female dependents in order to derive commercial opportunities from kinship affiliations. Luso-African children in acephalous societies shared the same socialization and opportunities as all other children, including membership in Simo, Poro, Sande, and Bundu—the male and female power associations whose leaders appointed village heads, monitored trade routes, and exercised other transsocietal powers. Luso-Africans could participate in their parents' commercial undertakings, using to advantage their kinship affiliations and membership in power associations; alternatively, they might follow the same lifeways as their African peers, intermarry with them, and become assimilated into their societies. Many Luso-African women prospered in commerce, owning numerous slaves that served them as sailors, domestic servants, blacksmiths, boatbuilders, and other skilled artisans. These female entrepreneurs were known as *nharas,* from the Portuguese word *senhora,* meaning a woman of property and status.

The principal arenas of Luso-African commerce and settlement were the Petite Côte of Senegal and along the Gambia, Cacheu, Geba, Grande, Nunez, Pongo, and Sierra Leone Rivers where riverine and caravan networks linked numerous African groups. Luso-Africans and *grumetes* (hired African mariners, navigators, and compradors) monopolized coastwise trade in kola, iron bars, *panos* (cloth strips), indigo, and other commodities that were exchanged for slaves, gold, ivory, and other African products sought by European traders. Besides spreading the use of Crioulo wherever they traded and settled, Luso-Africans disseminated numerous European, Asian, and American plants and animals, and they developed a cuisine adopted by both Africans and Europeans. Luso-Africans' whitewashed, rectangular dwellings—ventilated by spaces between walls and thatch roofs and featuring front verandas—were widely adopted by African elites and European traders.

When English, French, and Dutch traders arrived in western Africa, they were constrained by African societies to accommodate to the same circumstances as Portuguese and Luso-Africans, and any Eurafrican children they might father with African women would live under similar constraints. Dutch commerce was expedited by Sephardic Jews established in Amsterdam affiliated with Portuguese "New Christians" who reverted to Judaism while living in western Africa. Dutch trade with western Africa was limited to the last years of the seventeenth century and early decades of the eighteenth century, after which the descendants of Dutch traders assimilated with Luso-Africans. Frenchmen employed by a succession of Senegal trading companies flouted regulations by collaborating in illicit commerce with African and Eurafrican women. So also did English traders during the interludes when the British occupied Saint-Louis and Gorée, and likewise those living along the Gambia and other rivers.

Eurafricans' circumstances significantly changed in Senegambia during the second half of the eighteenth century. French and British colonial officials at Saint-Louis and Gorée introduced European legal codes that enabled Eurafricans to acquire freehold property, bequeath dwellings and other possessions to descendants, and exercise civic responsibilities. Eurafricans procured schooling for their children and promoted marriages that combined families' commercial assets. Similar developments occurred in the colony English philanthropists founded along the Sierra Leone River in 1787 for destitute "Black Poor." Destroyed by local Temne in 1789 and refounded in 1791, this colony, called "Freetown," throve following the 1792 arrival of some eleven hundred "Nova Scotians"—slaves freed by British forces during the American War of Independence. European and Eurafrican traders established along rivers neighboring the colony opportunistically dispatched their children to Freetown for schooling, with consequences similar to the developments at Saint-Louis and Gorée.

While Eurafricans are the focus of this study, their fortunes were inextricably linked to the vicissitudes of western African societies, which experienced far-reaching changes during the period treated here. Increased European demands for slaves promoted warfare and slave raiding by predatory warrior groups. During the seventeenth and eighteenth centuries, Mandinka of the Kaabu Empire pillaged numerous groups dwelling between the Gambia River and the Futa Jallon highlands, selling their captives to Eurafrican and European slavers. The Fula state founded in Futa Jallon during the 1720s conquered neighboring societies and sold more and more captives into transatlantic slavery. During the second half of the eighteenth century, predatory warrior groups victimized members of their own societies. Meanwhile, Eurafrican and European slavers living in acephalous societies manipulated kinship affiliations and membership in power associations to gain dominance over their landlords, and they used retinues of armed slaves to pillage their societies.

The volume concludes with the onset of the French Revolution and the Napoleonic Wars, which contributed to extensive changes across the globe, western Africa not excepted. Eurafricans' experiences during the era that followed—which saw the suppression of the Atlantic slave trade, an increasing commerce in agricultural and forest products, and the expansion of European imperialism—will be treated in a subsequent work.

Eurafricans in Western Africa

Chapter 1
Western Africa
Ecological Zones and Human Geography

> People were always more important than land. Order was frequently ensured by spiritual and magical forces, as much as through military strength. Power did not always rest with a single authority. A diverse range of institutions—such as age sets and secret societies—cut across family, clan and lineage loyalties that survived from earlier times. They met the need to integrate people who shared no ties of blood into a single community.
>
> —Garlake 1990, vi

Western Africa, depicted on Map 1.1, extends three thousand kilometers from the Senegal River in the north to the Bandama River in the south and fifteen hundred kilometers east from the Atlantic littoral to the bend of the Niger River. The great majority of the people living in this vast and geographically diverse territory speak languages belonging to two principal families: West Atlantic and Mande. The exceptions are Kruan-speakers living along the littoral of Liberia and western Côte d'Ivoire and groups living in the interior of Côte d'Ivoire that speak Gur languages. Western Africa's geographic and ecological patterns are diverse—ranging from desert in the north to rain forest in the south and encompassing the Futa Jallon highlands that give rise to numerous rivers, including the Senegal, Gambia, and Niger and many of their tributaries.

The inhabitants of western Africa have been linked by commercial networks since ancient times. Mande-speaking traders and smiths pioneered caravan routes intersecting West Atlantic and Kruan coastwise and riverine relay networks, promoting long-distance trade in salt, gold, iron, kola, malaguetta pepper, and numerous other commodities. By the third century A.D., western Africa's trade matrix was connected to trans-Saharan routes, and commerce with North Africa expanded over the centuries. The profit Maghrebian middlemen extracted from Europeans for gold, pepper, ivory, and other western African commodities was a primary factor promoting Portuguese reconnaissance voyages along the coast of western Africa during the fifteenth century.

Map 1.2 depicts a provisional reconstruction of rainfall patterns and ecological zones during the past two millennia. Ecological changes determined by rainfall patterns have had such profound consequences in West Africa that alternating wet and dry phases may be used to demarcate historical periods (Brooks 1998, 139). For expository purposes, it is convenient to distinguish five ecological zones extending across western Africa: desert, sahel, savanna, savanna-woodland, and forest (the coastal-riverine areas of Senegambia and the Upper Guinea Coast will be discussed separately). Rainfall isohyets are depicted as straight lines on Map 1.2, but the ecological "zones" imperceptibly merge, and isohyets oscillate north or south depending on altitude, the presence of lakes and rivers, prevailing winds, and other factors that contribute to variations in rainfall and distinctive microclimate areas. Sylvan, agricultural, and pastoral resources vary significantly in different environments, promoting commercial exchanges between ecological zones —opportunities the peoples of western Africa have exploited from time immemorial. When Portuguese mariners inaugurated trade in the fifteenth century, they soon learned the coastwise and riverine commercial patterns that Luso-Africans subsequently exploited.

Rainfall—the amount and duration of precipitation—is the most significant factor influencing the livelihoods of the inhabitants of western Africa. The climate of western Africa is marked by two distinct seasons, wet and dry. The rainy season coincides with the Sun's south-to-north passage, with rains earliest and most prolonged in the south. Rains begin in Liberia and southern Sierra Leone as early as March and continue until late October or early November. Areas to the north receive progressively shorter periods of rainfall: in Senegal, sporadic rains may (or may not) begin in June, become frequent in July, and last until September. Prevailing patterns are discerned in the average annual amount of precipitation—roughly four thousand or more millimeters of rainfall in the Cape Mount area, two thousand to one thousand millimeters in the interior as far north as the Gambia River, six hundred millimeters at Cape Verde, and only four hundred millimeters at the mouth of the Senegal River. Beyond that point lie the southern fringes of the Sahara.

As depicted on Map 1.2, rainfall isohyets "bend" around the Futa Jallon massif

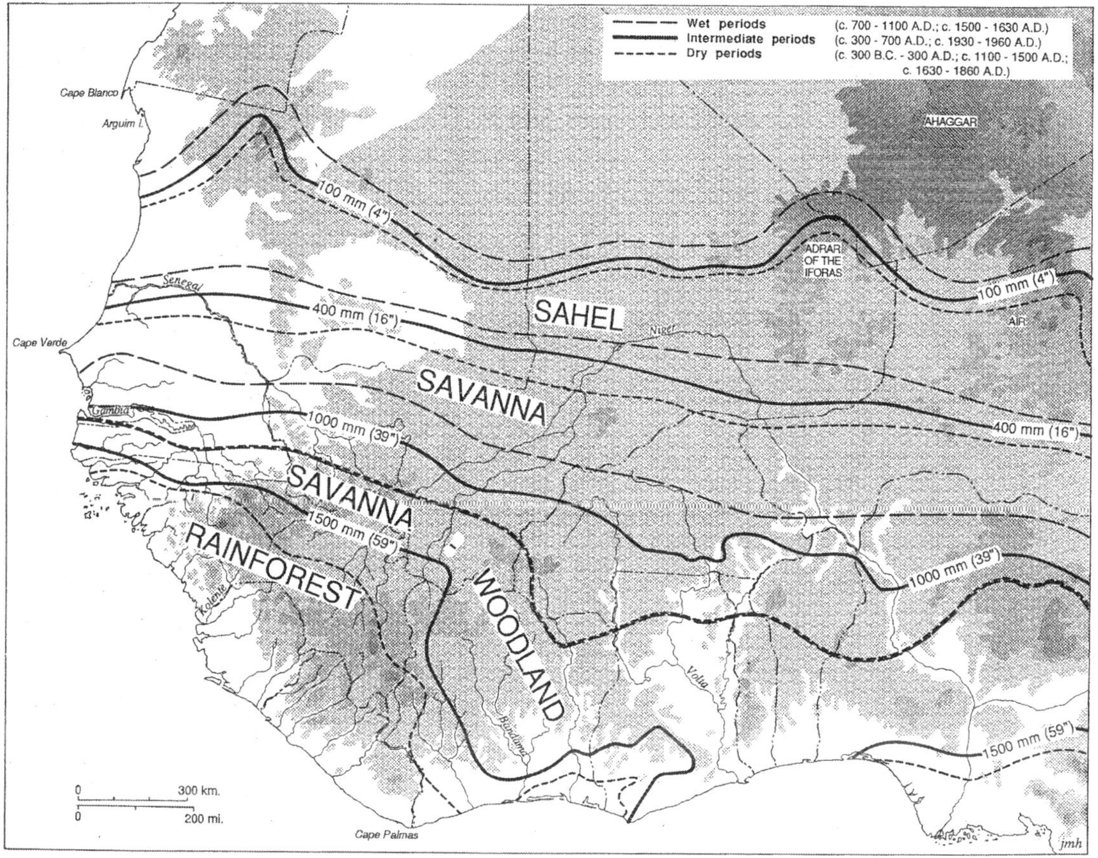

Map 1.2 Rainfall patterns and ecological zones

and extend southward parallel to the coast, following the highlands that cleave the region into two watersheds, with streams flowing north-northeast and south-southwest. Futa Jallon is the fountainhead of West Africa, source of the Niger, Senegal, Gambia, Casamance, Geba, Corubal, Nunez, Scarcies, and Moa Rivers, as well as numerous other rivers and streams. Of special historical importance are the northern outliers of Futa Jallon, which separate the tributaries of the Senegal and Niger Rivers; this north-south "divide" has had significant ramifications for trade routes, settlement patterns, language distributions, and other social and cultural phenomena.

The savanna-woodland zone encompassing Futa Jallon receives rainfall between May or June and September or October and supports a diverse vegetation of grasses, shrubs, and trees, the latter growing larger and more numerous approaching the forest zone. Soils in the savanna-woodland zone are of poor quality and strongly impregnated with iron and alumina oxides. Farmers practice swidden, or recurrent, agriculture in these ferruginous soils, cultivating land for only a few years before leaving plots fallow for a number of years to regain marginal fertility. Soils that have been depleted of nutrients by excessive cultivation, burn-offs by herders, and exposure to the elements—leaching by rains and baking by the sun—develop an almost impenetrable lateritic crust that sustains only sparse vegetation. Depending on rainfall and soil fertility, cultivators grow sorghum, millet, upland rice, cotton, vegetables, and condiments and safeguard *karité* (shea butter), oil palm, kola, and other trees, skillfully employing intercropping and crop rotation (Church 1980, 76–90; Richards 1985, 21–24, 55–61; Nyerges 1996).

The western Africa littoral has distinctive environmental conditions due to Atlantic winds and currents, especially with respect to greater rainfall along the seaboard and the penetration of tides up rivers for considerable distances. Geographers have delineated two coastal-riverine zones that elucidate what African and European mariners learned from experience. The Senegambian coastal zone is less than twenty-five kilometers wide and extends from the Senegal River to the Sine-Saloum estuary, a distance of three hundred kilometers. The Upper Guinea Coast zone stretches one thousand kilometers from the mouth of the Gambia River to Cape Mount and generally extends less than fifty kilometers into the interior.

The Senegambian Coastal Zone

Though there are fewer than three hundred kilometers between the mouths of the Senegal and Sine-Saloum Rivers as the blue-and-white Senegambian crows fly, there is a remarkable increase in average annual rainfall, from some four hundred millimeters in the north, six hundred millimeters around Cape Verde, and nine hundred millimeters around the mouth of the Sine-Saloum estuary. Of great significance for ameliorating the climate of coastal Mauritania and Senegambia (but less so for the coastal-riverine areas of the Upper Guinea Coast) is the Canary Current (Map 1.3). Its cold waters nourish plankton and are rich in commercially valuable species of fish, especially tuna. The Canary Current flows southward at a rate varying from sixteen to fifty-five kilometers a day, following the straight and almost unbroken coastlines of Mauritania and northern Senegal to the Cape Verde peninsula, where the current divides. With the onset of the rainy season (May to October), the winds and currents change. Prevailing winds shift from the northeast to the south-southwest, and the flow of the Canary Current diminishes.

The long and straight coastline from the Senegal River to the Cape Verde peninsula, known as the Grande Côte, is pounded by heavy surfs and swept by strong northeast-to-southwest winds blowing from the Sahara that increase the velocity of the Canary Current. There are no safe roadsteads, and few people inhabit the barren littoral. Seemingly, even the skilled and courageous Lébou fishermen living at the mouth of the Senegal River were too daunted by the hazards of the Grande Côte to venture south until they acquired sail-driven pirogues that enabled them to make return voyages during the rainy season when winds prevail from the south-southwest.

There are a few coves and anchorages on the northern shore of the Cape Verde peninsula, and the principal ships' haven along the Senegambian coast is the anchorage formed by the cradling arm of the cape and the small volcanic islet of Gorée, which deflect ocean currents and offer protection against Atlantic storms (the modern-day port of Dakar was created by the construction of breakwaters extending from the Cape Verde peninsula). During the June to September rainy season in Senegambia, when winds shift to the south and southwest, even this anchorage can be dangerous, for during storms, vessels exposed to the combined force of winds and currents may drag their anchors and wreck on the shore. At Cape Verde, the greater part of the Canary Current is deflected out into the Atlantic Ocean. The lesser branch of the Canary Current, known as the Guinea Current, flows southward following the configuration of the Upper Guinea Coast and the Malaguetta Coast to Cape Palmas and east along the Gulf of Guinea.

The Petite Côte, extending between Cape Verde and the Saloum River, is the arena of Niominka mariners, who live on the Djomboss Islands in the Sine-Saloum estuary and neighboring communities. Niominka have long exploited

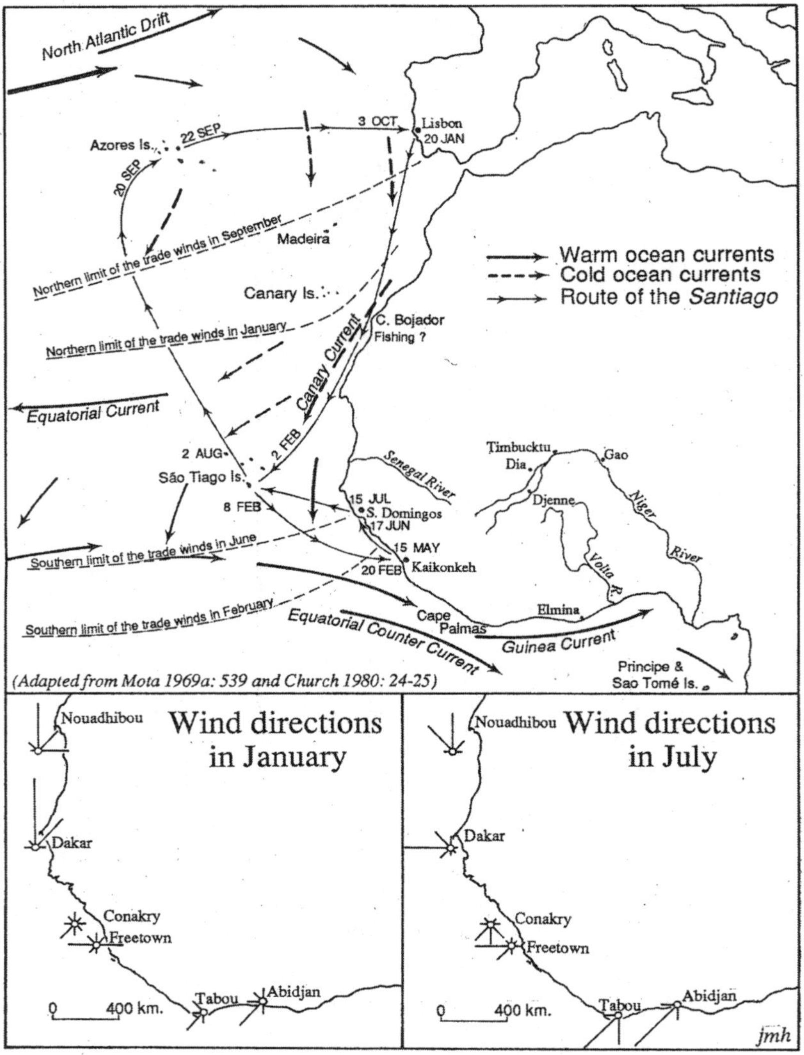

Map 1.3 Ocean currents and prevailing winds; voyage of the caravel *Santiago* in 1526

some of the richest fishing grounds in West Africa. Hydrologic conditions are particularly favorable for marine life along the Petite Côte, with upwellings to the surface throughout the year of cold, oxygen- and mineral-rich waters that sustain great quantities of plankton. There is a threefold changing of offshore waters, as the equatorial countercurrent that keeps to the depths from November to May rises to the surface from May to October. To these riches are added the organic matter in the alluvium carried to the seacoast by Senegambian rivers during the rainy season (Gruvel 1908, 104–119; Van-Chi-Bonnardel 1967, 740–42).

Together with other Serer groups, Niominka employ solar evaporation to produce sea salt of excellent quality along the coast north of the Saloum River. Salt was—and is—a commodity of commanding importance in western Africa's markets. Except for deposits in the Sahara, there are few inland salt sources and only a few plants that yield vegetable salts. Freighted with salt, dried fish, and dried oysters, Niominka dugout craft once carried on an extensive coastwise and riverine commerce that extended from Cape Verde to the Casamance River. Niominka networks along the lower Gambia River connected with those of Banyun traders who expedited the northward passage of malaguetta pepper and kola from the Cacheu River. Networks along the middle and upper Gambia River linked with Mande traders who brought gold to exchange for salt, malaguetta pepper, and kola.

Niominka communities along the Petite Côte were most likely the place of origin and refinement of the pirogue, a composite craft that revolutionized patterns of coastwise and riverine trade and greatly increased the quantities of bulk commodities such as kola and iron bars transported between markets. Portuguese mariners introduced the use of sails, rudders, and European tools that were modified to Africans' needs. Pirogues are constructed in different sizes for different purposes, but their basic features are similar. The lower part of the hull comprises a single hollowed-out log, to which is added planking reinforced by crosspieces to build up the sides of the craft. Wave breakers fore and aft make the craft more seaworthy in ocean swells. Small pirogues have sails attached to poles and are maneuvered with an oar by a seaman sitting in the stern. Large pirogues, some of which are capable of carrying tons of cargo, are steered by means of European-style rudders. Pirogue hulls are fitted to accommodate masts rigged with one or more sails (Gamble 1967, 94; Van-Chi-Bonnardel 1969, 38–39; Chauveau 1986, 202–6).

The inhabitants of the Senegambian coastal zone, seafarers in particular, have long adapted their lives to the daily pattern of wind changes: during the daylight hours, the land heats faster than the sea, resulting in a land-to-sea breeze that decreases ocean swells and surfs; toward evening, however, the land cools faster than the sea, causing a sea-to-land breeze. Thus, mariners depart in the early morning to fish offshore banks or travel along the coast, using the onshore winds that begin in late afternoon to make port for the night. A variety of magical devices are believed to protect sailors from the dangers of the sea and ensure abundant catches of fish. Portuguese and other European mariners in the past shared similar beliefs and consequently adopted those of African pilots and seamen, their tutors regarding the navigation of the waters of western Africa. Luso-Africans contributed to disseminating both European and African beliefs and practices wherever they ventured in western Africa.

During the dry season from October to March, the Guinea Current is accompanied along the Senegambian and Upper Guinea Coast by winds blowing from the north-northeast. During the rainy season from May to October, the prevailing north-northeast winds diminish, to be supplanted by winds blowing from the south-southwest; meanwhile, the velocity of the southward-flowing Guinea Current diminishes significantly, braked by the intrusive warmer waters of the equatorial countercurrent. During these months, mariners in sailing vessels are able to navigate from south to north along the Upper Guinea Coast and Senegambia, though only with considerable difficulty and often prolonged voyages (Van-Chi-Bonnardel 1967, 740–46).

The onset of the rainy season is presaged along the coast of western Africa by "tornadoes" (from the Portuguese *trovoadas,* meaning thunderstorm) — tumultuous line squalls with spectacular thunder and lightning and sheets of rain that rend the heavens and drench the land. These storms dissipate the heat and humidity that have become increasingly oppressive during the final weeks of the dry season. In the quiet aftermath of an hour-long tempest, the atmosphere is purged, and for a day or two, one can see great distances in the clear, almost bracing air before the humidity and overcast gradually return. Fierce as tornadoes are, they are welcomed by sailors no less than landsmen. Experienced mariners readily identify the unmistakable signs indicating the onset of a tornado. Fishermen and small craft make for shore, while larger vessels stand under reduced sail, their crews confident in the knowledge that a tornado's winds invariably blow offshore; when the storm has passed, vessels return to their previous anchorages, taking advantage of the onshore winds that invariably follow the tempest.

Western African cultivators clear land and plant crops at the outset of the rainy season. The staples of the savanna zone and northern areas of the savanna-woodland zone are millet, sorghum, and upland (or "dry") rice. These crops are harvested during November and December. The beginning of a year is reckoned from the time of harvest in November, and the cycle of planting, cultivating, and gathering crops is everywhere linked with religious ceremonies and festivals of thanksgiving. Portuguese and Luso-Africans introduced Christian beliefs and festivals that became syncretized with local practices and evolved into distinctive Luso-African folkways.

A notable feature of the dry season is the harmattan, a cold, dry, dust-laden wind that blows south from the Sahara from November to February and blocks off sunshine, cools the atmosphere, and reduces humidity. Temperatures drop considerably, especially at night. The arid winds help dry standing waters left from the rainy season that serve as breeding pools for mosquitoes. The harmattan winds scorch vegetation and facilitate the clearing of land by burning in preparation for planting at the onset of the rainy season. However, cleared land left unprotected from the harmattan winds is desiccated, contributing to the formation of infertile, lateritic hardpan soils. Dust particles from the Sahara are widely distributed at the height of the harmattan, often extending miles out to sea, where the haze they produce poses an additional danger to navigators. After February, when the harmattan ceases to blow, heat and humidity progressively build to oppressive levels, not to be broken until tornadoes herald the onset of the rainy season.

The Gambia River constitutes one of western Africa's ecological, social, and cultural frontiers. Sorghum, millet, and upland rice are the staple crops of the mostly stratified societies living north and east of the Gambia, while paddy rice is the staple of the acephalous societies living south of the river along the Upper Guinea Coast. For centuries, the Gambia River has been approximately coterminous with the one-thousand-millimeter rainfall isohyet, the "tsetse fly line" demarcating the northern range of tsetse flies bearing trypanosomes (the organisms that spread trypanosomiasis, or "sleeping sickness"), which are lethal to camels, horses, donkeys, sheep, and zebu cattle. Tsetse disdain to fly any great distance across open spaces—hence, the correlation between approximately one thousand millimeters of rainfall and the presence of tsetse. Fula practicing independent pastoralism must herd zebu in tsetse-free areas of the Sahel and savanna zones; in modern times, they can also safeguard their cattle with inoculations. The smaller ndama breed of cattle is resistant to trypanosomes, and Fula and other groups living in the savanna-woodland zone keep ndama as part of mixed farming regimes, but they do not milk them (Richard-Molard 1956, 53–55; Curtin 1975, 218–19). Goats and sheep are raised in Senegambia and thrive in the neighboring savanna and savanna-woodland zones but do not flourish in the coastal-riverine environment extending southward.

In contrast to the narrow, tubular mouths of the Sine-Saloum and Senegal Rivers opening to the south, the westward-facing mouth of the Gambia River extends more than 20 kilometers across and is easily entered by vessels of any size. The Gambia River provides a magnificent waterway connecting the Atlantic coast and the heartland of western Africa. The river can be navigated by large seagoing sailing vessels as far as Kassang/Caçao, some 300 kilometers upriver; smaller vessels that can tack more easily in the narrowing river are able to sail to Barracounda Falls, about 170 kilometers farther, and during months of high water, small craft drawing less than a meter can cross the ledges of laterite rocks and continue many kilometers farther still along the river and its upper tributaries (Gray 1940/1966, 1–3; Wright 1997, 3).

The principal groups trading along the Gambia River prior to the arrival of Europeans were Niominka mariners and Banyun middlemen, the latter belonging to the Banyun-Bak network that linked the Cacheu, Casamance, Gambia, and Sine-Saloum Rivers. Apparently, Niominka seafarers did not venture south of the Casamance River, being deterred by the reefs and shoal waters off Cape Roxo and by the difficulties of making return passages against the southward flow of the Guinea Current and the prevailing northerly winds during the dry season. Instead, the Banyun trade network linked the Gambia, Casamance, and Cacheu Rivers via streams, *marigots* (tidal river channels), and portages.

The Upper Guinea Coast Monsoonal Zone

This coastal-riverine zone extends from the Gambia River south to Cape Mount, which is geographically coterminous with the southernmost extension of West Atlantic–speaking groups and the beginning of settlements of Kruan-speakers. The most distinctive feature of the zone is its *ria* (sunken) coastline (Map 1.4). Geologic activity has caused a submerging of the littoral from the Saloum River to northern Liberia, enabling the ocean to flood coastal areas and invade the lower reaches of rivers, transforming them into estuaries. As the modern air traveler can observe, there is no true coastline between the Sine-Saloum estuary and Cape Mount but only an irregular succession of drowned river estuaries and marshy lowlands interspersed with innumerable low-lying islands and islets, many barely rising above the surface of the sea. The ria coast has the highest tides in western Africa. These tides sweep up the estuaries and penetrate many kilometers up rivers and tributary streams. Tidal bores may reach five and seven meters in the Grande and Geba Rivers, respectively (Mota

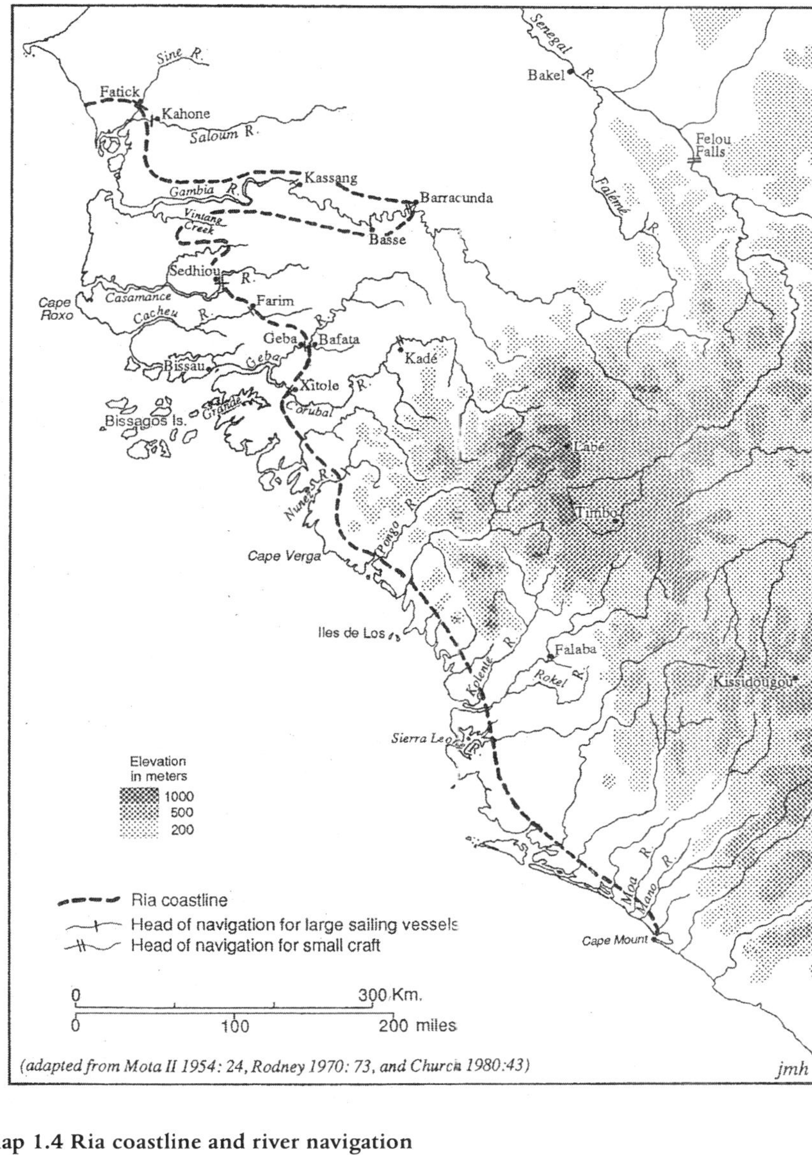

Map 1.4 Ria coastline and river navigation

1954, 1:369). Experienced mariners use tidal flows to ascend rivers, taking precautions to avoid the onset of the tidal bores.

When Portuguese seafarers learned from African mariners how to navigate the Upper Guinea Coast, they measured distances along rivers on navigational charts as "so many tides" upriver. During the rainy season, the force of the descending water made rivers more difficult to ascend, but this was the off-season for commerce, when paths were made impassible by swollen streams and there was the risk of merchandise being ruined by rains during conveyance by trading craft.

The tidal reach depicted in Map 1.4 effectively delineates an ecological, social, and cultural boundary between the coastal-riverine peoples and those living in the savanna-woodland zone. Bafatá, located along the Geba River and only one hundred kilometers to the east and north of Bissau, has 25 percent less rainfall—about1,500 mm versus 2,000 mm (Mota 1954, 1:33). Humidity is likewise much lower in the interior, dramatically so from December to February when the harmattan winds blow southward from the Sahara to desiccate woodlands and parch grasslands. In the coastal areas, by contrast, vegetation remains verdant year-round because it is sustained by high water tables, rivers, marigots, and swamplands and freshened by nighttime dew and the onshore breezes that significantly lower temperatures from late afternoon through the night. The numerous tidal estuaries are fringed by mangrove swamps bordered by forest.

During the rainy season, there is considerable erosion along the banks of rivers and their tributaries, which carry large quantities of soil in solution. Silt is deposited along the lower reaches of rivers and streams by the ebb and flow of tidal action, some to be reclaimed for agricultural use by diking to enclose rice paddies. The inhabitants of the Upper Guinea Coast are some of the world's most skillful rice cultivators. Their principal method is to dike floodplains, swamps, and land along rivers, streams, and marigots in order to utilize alluvial soils deposited by tidal action. Rice growing in *bolons* (swamp paddies) is highly productive, but the techniques employed are arduous and require much cooperation for diking to enclose land, besides planting, cultivating, and harvesting. Many varieties of rice are cultivated according to soils, water salinity, length of growing season, and other considerations. Paddy rice is harvested from November to February as different varieties mature.

The dietary staple among coastal-riverine groups, rice is served with a variety of sauces and stews prepared from vegetables, wild fruits, leaves, roots, and berries. It is seasoned with rich and highly nutritious palm oil, peppers, and other condiments and garnished according to circumstances with game or meat from the ndama breed of cattle and goats, as well as fish, shellfish, and (since European times) chicken. Such was the reputation of the rice growers living along the Upper Guinea Coast that they were expressly sought by slaveholders in the American colonies. It was western Africans who created the prosperity of coastal South Carolina, and Luso-African and Anglo-African slavers long competed to profit from the demand for slaves from the "Rice Coast" (Morgan and Pugh 1969, 81–83, 122; Linares 1981, 560–65; Opala 1987; Carney 1996).

The Casamance River demarcates a change in the fishing economy, for along its banks and extending southward, the increasing humidity and the progressively longer rainy season require that fish be either smoked or smoked and sun dried to ensure preservation. Such is also the case with salt making: increasing humidity, cloud cover, and rainfall along the Upper Guinea Coast make solar evaporation less efficient, causing people in many areas to employ the time-consuming and labor-intensive process of boiling seawater (Gruvel 1908, 126, 129; Wright 1977, 21–22). Over the centuries, river discharges, tidal flux, and ocean currents have combined to expand the continental shelf. The Bissagos Islands, which extend more than one hundred kilometers seaward, are formed by alluvial deposits that have become stabilized around volcanic outcrops anchored by mangroves and other vegetation. These low-lying islands are surrounded by mud banks and separated by shallow channels studded with sharp-edged volcanic outcrops, making navigation difficult and dangerous, especially during the rapid ebb and flow of tides.

The Malaguetta Coast

Cape Mount marks the southern limit of the Upper Guinea Coast. South of Cape Mount, the ria coastline gives way to a relatively straight and forested coast framed with heavy surfs and studded with offshore reefs that are hazardous to mariners. Seafaring groups live in the lee of coastal promontories, the most notable being Capes Mesurado and Palmas, and along numerous coves and rivers. The mouths of rivers are blocked by sandbars, and navigating them during storms and heavy seas daunts even the most experienced Kruan seamen. Rainfall is highest along the northern part of the Malaguetta Coast, being in excess of 4,800 mm at the mouth of the Saint Paul River and diminishing to about 2,800 mm at Cape Palmas. The amount of precipitation decreases from coast to interior approximately 500 mm for every fifteen kilometers inland (Massing 1980, 15).

Portuguese mariners and traders termed the five hundred kilometers of

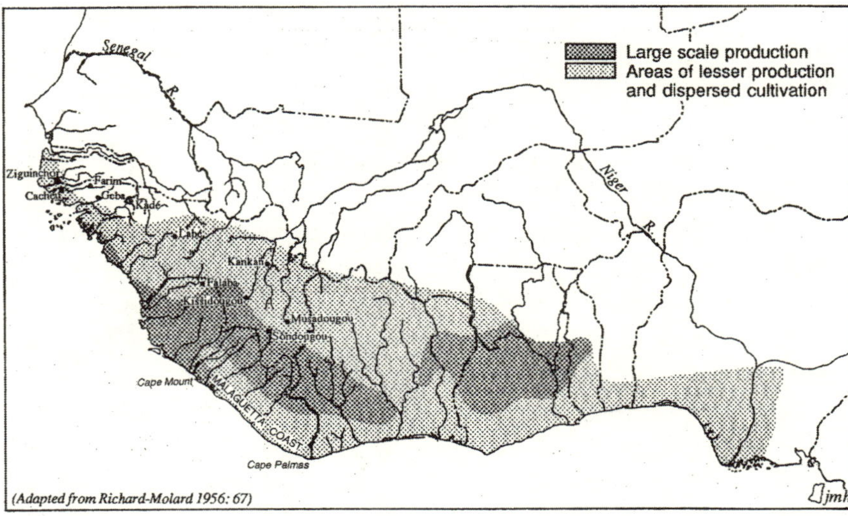

(Adapted from Richard-Molard 1956: 67)

Map 1.5 Principal areas of kola production

forested coastline between Cape Mount and Cape Palmas the "Grain Coast" or "Malaguetta Coast," named for the prized pepper that Portuguese sought on their reconnaissance voyages. The dense vegetation in this area testifies to bountiful rains that fall for more than seven months, from April to November, with a variable "middle dry season" in July or August. The forest zone was sparsely populated until recent times, due to the paucity of suitable food crops and the difficulty of clearing land with few and inadequate iron tools. During the past five centuries, African and Asian varieties of rice were introduced into many areas, as was maize and manioc brought from the Americas.

The area neighboring Cape Mount between the lower reaches of the Moa and Lofa Rivers has some of the most productive stands of kola trees in western Africa (Map 1.5). These trees, along with malaguetta pepper and sea salt, induced Mande-speaking traders to venture hundreds of kilometers through rain forest to settle among West Atlantic–speaking groups living in the Cape Mount area, beginning sometime during the c. 1100–c. 1500 dry period. It was also during this period that Kruan seafaring groups settled along the Malaguetta Coast to engage in coastwise and riverine commerce, linking West Atlantic and Mande traders with Kwa-speaking groups living to the east along the Gulf of Guinea.

Luso-Africans never settled along the Malaguetta Coast, but the highly remunerative commerce of that region was undertaken exclusively as a shipboard trade by vessels dispatched from Portugal. During the sixteenth century, French and

English interlopers challenged the Portuguese monopoly until the commerce was gradually abandoned due to the competition of the more pungent Asian peppercorns that supplanted malaguetta in European markets (Brooks 1993b, 282–86).

The Cabo Verde Archipelago

The Cape Verde Islands were uninhabited when European mariners arrived there in the 1460s (Map 1.6). The archipelago was quickly settled, and Ribeira Grande, São Tiago became the entrepôt for Portuguese trade with western Africa. Slaves purchased in Senegambia and along the Upper Guinea Coast cultivated sugarcane and other crops and herded livestock. The islands' microclimates proved suitable to grow a variety of exotic plants, making the archipelago a way station and nursery for acclimatizing European and American plants and animals that Portuguese and Luso-Africans introduced to western Africa. Orange, lemon, and lime trees are "trace elements" associated with places of trade in western Africa, as are diminutive, long-snouted pigs (where

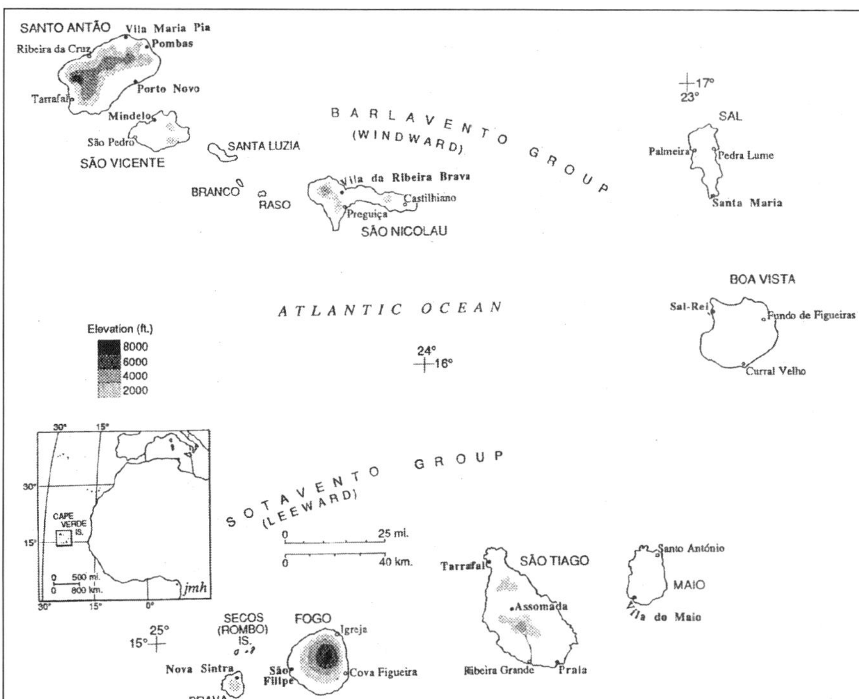

Map 1.6 The Cabo Verde archipelago

they have not been extirpated by the spread of Islam). American imports widely disseminated among the peoples of western Africa include maize, manioc, chilies (which largely supplanted malaguetta pepper in cooking), pineapples, papayas, peanuts, pumpkins, guavas, and tobacco (Murdock 1959, 233–35; Duncan 1972, 168–72). Ironically, Portuguese and Luso-Africans benefited only marginally from their introduction of new cultigens, inasmuch as African landlords generally denied them land to cultivate.

Ecological and Epidemiological Factors

Climate, ecology, and human patterns of livelihood combine to create epidemiological conditions that are exceptionally challenging for the peoples of western Africa, particularly those living in the Upper Guinea Coast. High rainfall and high relative humidity, slowly flowing rivers and streams, large expanses of swampland, rice paddies, and pools of stagnant water following the rainy season create environments favorable to the prolific breeding of insects, many of which are vectors for diseases harmful to both humans and domestic animals. Endemic tropical diseases result in high morbidity and mortality rates, especially among infants and young children.

The most redoubtable vector for human infection is the anopheles mosquito, bearer of falciprium malaria. Malaria is especially prevalent during the rainy season, when mosquitoes breed in puddles, swamps, and creeks and in the ditches and rows of tilled land. Infant mortality is extremely high among children born in the disease environment, but survivors acquire some degree of immunity. Repeated infections are debilitating, however, leaving individuals lacking in stamina an easier prey to other diseases and infections. Yellow fever, also mosquito-borne (by *Aedes aegypti*), is likewise endemic, but children gain immunity from mild attacks during childhood, and African populations were only marginally affected by the periodic epidemics that, until recent times, scourged the coast of Europeans. Other endemic diseases afflicting residents of western Africans are yaws and dysenteries. In years past, Portuguese and other first-time European visitors to western Africa were soon stricken with malaria and other endemic diseases, and many died, to the consternation of survivors. Philip Curtin estimated that somewhere between 25 and 75 percent of any group of Europeans died during the first year in Africa. Survivors acquired some immunities, and the death rate eventually declined to perhaps only 10 percent per annum (Curtin 1964, 71–87).

Europeans who were nursed by wives and received sufficient medical treatment from skilled African practitioners to survive initial malarial attacks and acquire some immunity might later reside in western Africa for long periods. And Luso-Africans, Franco-Africans, and Anglo-Africans born in western Africa acquired immunities that conferred a significant survival advantage vis-à-vis European visitors. Nonetheless, the lives of Eurafricans and Africans alike were punctuated by numerous infections, illnesses, and convalescences, especially during the latter years. It is not surprising, then, that for European mariners, voyages to western Africa were undertaken with much trepidation. One English seaman who had lost many shipmates attributed their deaths to "the violent Heats occasion'd by the near Neighbourhood of the Sun, . . . the Pestilent Air of that Incultivated and Woody Continent, the heavy Rains, and the Vexatious Troops of restless Muskitoes which at every Sting draw Blood, and devour Men Alive" (Wilkinson 1690, 18–19).

Language Groups and Commercial Relationships

The peoples of western Africa define themselves principally according to kinship and occupational affiliations and only secondarily in linguistic terms. In fact, individuals and families change languages and modify social and cultural patterns in ways that are often perplexing to outsiders. For instance, they may change their family names in order to assert their affiliation with elite families (as domestic slaves in past times did by adopting "slave-master" names); to indicate client relationships, apprenticeships, and religious affiliations; and for various other reasons. This practice makes it difficult, in many cases, to differentiate between Eurafricans, *grumetes* (hired African seamen), and domestic slaves in historical sources. Remote and even fictive kinship ties, "joking relationships" between groups, and indeed any social or cultural purchase one can claim or contrive have, for centuries, facilitated human relationships and expedited trade, travel, migration, and settlement in western Africa (W. Azevedo 1989, 99; Amselle 1998, xi–xiii).

Groups in western Africa defined by linguistic ascriptions may differ significantly in social and cultural attributes from one area to another. And what "identities" individuals and groups may have asserted in past times is a matter of speculation, inasmuch as European colonial administrators and ethnographers were as compulsive as they were expedient in establishing categories of ethnic groups from what, in all probability, were congeries of extended families and clans sparsely inhabiting the vast expanses of western Africa. Seemingly, group identities developed among people sharing ecological areas and pursuing the same livelihoods—circumstances that could be altered by environmental changes, migrations, and conquests. Some groups were relatively fixed in their abodes, some moved seasonally, and others migrated considerable distances as circumstances dictated. Nonetheless, language serves as the principal criterion for defining groups in western Africa and is so employed in this study. Language is the principal vehicle for communicating social and cultural attributes, and the language an individual speaks may be considered a "primary" identity. But it is not the only important one: *nyamakalaw* (blacksmiths, bards, and leather workers who possess special skills and reputed magical powers) have "identities" that transcend language groups, as do hunters, fisherfolk, and traders.

Regarding the principal groups discussed in this study, those speaking West Atlantic and Mande languages are especially salient, whereas Kruan-speaking groups receive only passing mention. Mande-speakers are widely dispersed, from the margins of the Sahara to the Gulf of Guinea. Of special note are Mandekan languages, which were widely diffused from the thirteenth century onward by traders and horse warriors who conquered large areas of western Africa.

West Atlantic–speakers, except for those in the diaspora of Fula pastoralists across West Africa, live along the Atlantic seaboard from the Senegal River to Cape Mount, whence Kruan-speaking groups extend eastward along the coast. Linguists classify West Atlantic languages as belonging to two branches, Northern and Southern, with the line of demarcation extending approximately where the western outliers of Futa Jallon most closely approach the Atlantic seaboard; this area has, for centuries, generally coincided with the northern fringes of the rain forest (Map 1.2). The Bijago are relegated to the limbo of an "isolated" group. The southernmost group, the Gola, are neighbors of the Dei, the westernmost of the Kruan language groups that extend southeast along the Malaguetta Coast.

One significant characteristic of West Atlantic languages is the fact that, despite great divergence in vocabulary, they are strikingly similar in their systems of sound, grammar, and semantics. This enables bi- or multilingual individuals to switch from one vocabulary to another without extensive adjustments in the overall linguistic systems involved—a key factor in facilitating communication and coastwise and riverine commerce. Crioulo, an amalgam of West Atlantic languages and Portuguese, diffused widely in western Africa as a commercial lingua franca and became the language of the inhabitants of the Cabo Verde archipelago.

Kruan-speaking groups are settled from Cape Mount south and east to the lagoons extending beyond the Sassandra River, an area that was thickly forested and sparsely inhabited until recent times. Kruan maritime groups probably did not venture westward past Cape Palmas until the c. 1100–c. 1500 dry period, their migrations associated with coastwise exchanges of malaguetta pepper, kola, salt, iron, beads, cloth, and other commodities with the Gulf of Guinea trading complex. Of particular importance regarding commerce were the Kru seafarers who, from the seventeenth century forward, sought employment aboard European trading vessels (Greenberg 1963; Bird 1970; Brooks 1993b, 29–33).

Trade Diasporas

Language groups were considerably smaller in past times, and many were widely scattered. Large expanses of western Africa were unpopulated or sparsely inhabited until iron tools became widely available with the Mande smiths' migrations into western Africa that began in the early centuries A.D. Mande smiths and traders probably first entered Senegambia and the hinterland of the Upper Guinea Coast along the upper Senegal River and its tributaries, perhaps following routes already established by the West Atlantic–speaking groups with whom they settled and intermarried. The principal exchanges were likely iron, iron manufactures, and gold, which were bartered for salt, kola, and malaguetta pepper.

The growth and articulation of Mande trade networks linking coastal-riverine groups expanded along with the southward shift of ecological zones during the c. 1100–c. 1500 dry period. Spurred by an increasingly lucrative trans-Saharan trade and the development of states with affluent elites, Mandinka-speakers penetrated progressively deeper in to the savanna-woodland and forest zones to acquire gold, kola, malaguetta pepper, and other commodities. Smiths accompanied or preceded the traders, moving south to prospect gold deposits and exploit new markets for their manufactures. Mandinka smiths and traders were constrained to settle along the upper reaches of rivers navigated by West Atlantic– and Kruan-speakers who were middlemen with coastal groups. Vai/Kono traders were the only Mande-speakers to reach the Atlantic coast for hundreds of kilometers to the north or south, their success perhaps due to the fact that the Cape Mount area was the junction of the West Atlantic and Kruan language groups. Wherever Mande settled among West Atlantic– and Kruan-speaking host societies, they married local women and introduced Mande social and cultural practices. They also founded branches of the Komo, Simo, Poro, Sande and Bundu power associations to ensure the socialization of their children, encourage and enforce appropriate behavior, expedite commerce, and otherwise advance their interests among host societies. Another Mande trading group, the Soninke-speaking Jahanke/Diahanke traders, followed caravan routes across the savanna from the cotton-producing areas around Jahaba on the Bafing River to exchange textiles for sea salt. Jahanke traders were renowned for their nonmilitant Islamic beliefs and tolerant accommodation to existing non-Muslim customs and practices (Brooks 1993b, 44–47, 60–61, 68–69).

Two trade diasporas pioneered by West Atlantic–speakers engaged in coastwise and riverine trade along the forest, savanna-woodland, and savanna zones between the Futa Jallon massif and the Gambia River. Biafada-Sapi dugout craft transported kola, malaguetta pepper, and other forest zone products northward. Banyun-Bak mariners traded salt, dried fish, and dried mollusks from coastal-riverine areas. Biafada-Sapi and Banyun-Bak networks connected with Mande caravan routes at the heads of navigation of rivers along the Upper Guinea Coast and Senegambia. Mande traders exchanged iron and iron manufactures fabricated in the savanna-woodland zone, cotton textiles produced in the savanna zone, and North African cloth and other luxury goods obtained via trans-Saharan commerce. Other western African commodities involved in short- and medium-range exchanges between groups included gold, artisanal manufactures, medicinal products, and foodstuffs. With the arrival of Portuguese caravels in the 1440s, western African trading groups seized the chance to exploit new commercial opportunities.

Another Mande penetration of western Africa began during the c. 1100–c. 1500 dry period while tsetse-infested areas receded southward. Horsemen speaking Mandekan languages conquered extensive territories in the savanna and savanna-woodland zones and founded numerous states. In most instances, West Atlantic groups were not dislodged from the areas they inhabited but were progressively assimilated to Mande linguistic, social, and cultural patterns. Also migrating southward as tsetse-infested areas receded were Fula pastoralists, a West Atlantic group. Numerous Fula began pasturing their livestock south of the Gambia River, some advancing into the northern outliers of the Futa Jallon massif. These areas, once savanna-woodland and forest, had been cleared by Mande smiths and cultivators and by West Atlantic groups using tools made by Mande smiths, thereby opening the way for occupation by Fula herders. Mandinka cultivators and Fula herders intermingled with West Atlantic–speaking Tenda-Jaad-Nun groups; the latter became increasingly fragmented, with many people assimilating to the intrusive Mandinka and Fula, resulting in a mosaic of populations scattered over many hundred square kilometers (Brooks 1985, 59–60, 81–82).

Social Organizations and Cultural Paradigms

Two political systems predominated in past times. Coastal-riverine groups along the Upper Guinea Coast—for example, Diola, Balanta, Bijago, Baga, and Bullom/Sherbro—were acephalous (or stateless and decentralized) and segmentary, that is, their systems of authority seldom extended beyond a village or cluster of villages. Two exceptions to this segmentary organization were the often transitory clan affiliations and short-lived polities forged by successful war leaders, both of which could create supralocal ties. By contrast, Mandinka dwelling in the savanna and savanna-woodland zone to the east and Serer and Wolof living in the savanna zone to the north of the Gambia River possessed tripartite, hierarchical social structures comprising ruling elites and free people, endogamous occupational groups, and slaves—institutions derived from states founded by Mandekan-speaking horse warriors. Numerous groups that in past times had matrilineal descent patterns changed to the patrilineal principle through the influence of blacksmiths, Mande conquests and state building, and the spread of Islam (McCall 1971a, 51–53).

Whether a group was acephalous or stratified, the fundamental social unit was the extended lineage, with clan affiliations established by patterns of descent and marriage. A hamlet comprised one extended family, while a village had several. The oldest male of the founding family was its nominal leader, in consultation with other family elders. There was no private ownership of the land; rather, it belonged to all members of a community and was allocated to lineages and families according to precedence, numbers, and needs. The test of leadership—whether of an extended family, of a village comprising several lineages, or of a state—was a leader's ability to engage in skillful consultation, mediate conflicts, make alliances, extort tribute from strangers and subject groups, display wisdom in judicial processes, be evenhanded in the distribution of resources, and otherwise command admiration and respect. If a leader lacked these skills, his people would move away and seek other associations, which was almost always a feasible option given the expanses of western Africa and the low population densities that existed until recent centuries.

Extended families and their dependents constituted the building blocks of western African societies—modules that might be transferred from one polity to another by their own volition or by conquest. Lucie C. Colvin's assessment of the exercise of power in the stratified Wolof society of Senegambia parallels Carol P. MacCormack's description of how strong-minded men and women might augment their power in acephalous Bullom/Sherbro groups one thousand kilometers distant. Colvin remarked, "Accumulating people was a major goal of socio-economic and political life. Households sought to accumulate people, just as they did food, clothing and animals. Ruling families sought to win the allegiance of people, as well as control over the land, trade, and mineral wealth. The ultimate recourse that people had, when they felt that they were abused by their sovereign, was to threaten collectively to withdraw their allegiance and go into exile. People were exchanged for goods and given as gifts—not just slaves, but also women, children and young men clients" (Colvin 1986, 61).

MacCormack reported the same social dynamics relevant to accumulating people and power: " Precolonially, the area was a loosely organized system of polities headed by the notable persons, often descendants of a founding or conquering historical personage. Heads of chiefdoms, heads of towns, and even heads of residential compounds attempted then and now to build up the number of their dependents and followers by marrying them, begetting them, attracting them through clientage, and, in the past, capturing or buying them" (MacCormack 1980, 97). In the absence of private landownership in both acephalous and stratified societies, slaves were the most important means of accumulating private wealth. In addition to the economic contributions made by slaves in agriculture, artisansal pursuits, and numerous other activities, children born of female slaves added to the numbers and importance of families and lineages (Thornton 1992, 74–76, 84–86; Wright 1997, 50–52).

Portuguese and Luso-Africans who prospered in commerce emulated African rulers in their acquisition of dependents, both free and unfree. Luso-African households and compounds were inhabited by the children of Luso-African women and slave concubines; grumetes and their families; and free and captive smiths, woodworkers, boatbuilders, weavers, and other artisans and their families. Visitors residing in Luso-Africans' compounds for varying periods of time included relatives and hangers-on, traders attracted from near or far, sons of rulers and traders entrusted to learn the ways of Luso-Africans, hunters, fisherfolk, bards, traditional religious specialists, and Muslim clergy.

Of inestimable importance concerning the integration of Luso-Africans into western African societies were similarities and compatibilities in religious beliefs. Examples of the similarities linking Africans and Luso-Africans include their comparable beliefs and practices associated with harvest festivals; their supplications directed to ancestors; their beliefs concerning the pervasiveness of spirits and their capacities to be either helpful or harmful; and their wearing of protective amulets incorporating vegetation, minerals, and other substances.

Community-focused religious practices are broadly similar among all the peoples of western Africa. Beliefs concerning the spirit world and its manifestations incorporate four concepts or categories of supernatural phenomena, interacting with each other and with humankind (Parrinder 1969, chap. 2–6; Crowley 1990, chap. 5). The first is an omniscient creator god considered almost completely inaccessible and consequently disassociated from humans' ordinary affairs. The name of the high god differs from society to society; for example, the god is known as Emítay to Diola, Nali Bati to Papel, Nindo to Bijago, and Ouré-Kan to Susu. This concept of the high god may have had a significant if indirect impact on human affairs by predisposing the peoples of western Africa to accept the assertions of Muslim clerics and Christian missionaries concerning the existence of Allah and God (Brooks 1984, 13).

A second category of supernatural phenomena comprises spirits dwelling in the soil, waters, flora, and fauna. These spirits are generally considered capricious and amoral, with arbitrary powers to protect or injure humans. Their assistance or noninterference in human affairs may be invoked by prayers and offerings and by the mediating influences of ancestor spirits. Trees are a favored abode of spirits, the most powerful of which are thought to reside in an area's tallest trees. Villagers shelter under large trees for the protection afforded by resident spirits. Stones commemorating ancestors placed at the base of the trunks synergistically bond the community, the living dead, and the resident spirits.

MacCormack's description of a Bullom/Sherbro village might, with minor differences regarding locales, represent innumerable communities across western Africa in times past and present.

> It is in the protective shadow of two groves of virgin forest, each containing several towering cotton trees. One is the sacred grove of the Thoma society, the other is the sacred grove of the Poro society. The two sodalities do not exist in conflict, but in a relationship of respect for each other. When one holds its initiation season the other constitutes part of the respectful audience. The swept space of the village ends abruptly at the edge of the forest. During an initiation season this margin is marked by a screen of palm fronds, and a portal through which the candidates for initiation, and members of the society, pass. The sacred grove functions as burial ground, as a site for communication with ancestral spirits, and as sacred space for rites of passage and other congregations. The cotton trees act as a focus for communication with extraordinary powers. They form a vertical axis, between the sky of an ultimate creator, and the deep earth/ground water of ancestral abode (MacCormack 1980, 99).

It is incumbent on a group founding a new community to establish links with the spirits living there, and the ties that are established are subsequently maintained by religious ceremonies and offerings. When groups move, some bring stones to establish links between ancestor spirits and the spirits residing in the new area of residence. For this reason, former village sites are readily identifiable by groves of trees that remain unmolested long after the inhabitants have moved away. Portuguese were familiar with beliefs regarding spirits residing in trees, springs, and other sacred places from pre-Christian traditions surviving in the Iberian Peninsula, but other Europeans, ignorant of such beliefs, found their ignorance costly when they attempted to fell trees sheltering local communities.

Portuguese shared similar beliefs concerning spirits, derived from ancient traditions pervasive in Europe. But Christian clergy found it especially difficult to suppress pagan festivals linked to the change of seasons and the agricultural cycle, nor could they supplant beliefs concerning the dead. In the ninth century, finding the latter impossible to extirpate, church authorities established November 1 as a day of obligation honoring all saints, known and unknown. Over the centuries, the day was transformed into Halloween (All Hallows' Eve), celebrated on October 31 as an outlet for youthful exuberance, pranks, and merrymaking of all sorts . During the eleventh century, the church established November 2 as All Souls' Day, a day of supplication for souls in purgatory. At death, souls of the faithful that have not been cleansed from venial sins or atoned for past transgressions can be helped to attain heaven by prayer and the sacrifice of the mass (*Encyclopedia Britannica* 1926, 1:709).

The celebration of All Souls' Day held particular significance with respect to pagan survivals in Europe, for many Catholics retained the belief that the dead return to partake of food left on graves or on kitchen tables. Portuguese and other Europeans believed each tree possessed a spirit (Gallop 1936, 122), which was congruent with the beliefs of western Africans that trees are a favored abode of spirits. In Europe, just as in western Africa, stones, streams, springs, and other bodies of water were thought to be dwelling places of spirits. Rodney Gallop remarked on pilgrimages to Iberian shrines that date to pre-Christian times: "Everywhere, traces of a cult of stones and rocks survive in the nomenclature of holy images. Senhoras da Rocha, da Penha, do Penedo, da Serra, da Lapa, and so on, abound. These shrines of Our Lady are usually situated on some crag or rock, or near some cave or 'rocking' stone, which struck the imagination of the ancient Lusitanians and was worshipped or populated with Mouras Encantadas" (Gallop 1936, 127). *Mouras encatadas* (enchanted mooresses) are believed to be beautiful maidens who have a snake's tail instead of legs, are guardians of treasurers, and possess other marvelous attributes.

Western Africans share with Europeans numerous legends recounting versions of the snake/dragon, young man, and maiden "triangle," with one of the three usually perishing in their encounter. Specific to serpents, Africans believe the python (*Python sebae*) has remarkable attributes. It is associated with the powerful spirit Ningiri, which dwells in the earth, in water, and in trees; consumes iron and excretes it as gold; links the sky as the rainbow; and controls rain. Among Diola, the python is believed to be a blacksmith. The python is also the totem of one of the most redoubtable power associations in western Africa (Appia 1965, 322 and n. 1; Parrinder 1969, 50–53; Sapir 1981, 528; McCall 1989; Crowley 1990, 334–36).

In the Guinea-Bissau region, spirits are known as *irans* in Crioulo (also *tchina, china, hatsychyna,* and so forth). People create statues and other objects as temporary dwelling places for spirits, which serve as the foci of religious ceremonies and places of offerings. These are likewise referred to as irans and are mentioned in European accounts as "idols" and "fetishes" (Scantamburlo 1981, 172; Hair 1967b, 45; Carreira 1961). Much as saints' images are treated in Portugal, among societies in western Africa sacred objects are sometimes verbally abused or knocked about when spirits appear indifferent to petitions for assistance (Gallop 1936, 133–35; Hair 1990, pt. 2, chap. 5: 6–7; Brooks 1984, 31 n. 37).

A third category of supernatural phenomena in western Africa comprises ancestors, or the living dead. At death, humans are believed to become inhabitants of the spirit world, where they may intercede with other spirits on behalf of their descendants and the community at large. Conversely, if displeased with the actions or neglect of their living kin, ancestor spirits may deny them assistance or inflict harm on them. Such concepts parallel the Catholic belief in the communion of saints, whereby the dead inspire and intercede for the living. Western Africans believe in reincarnation and regard life and death as a continuum—there must be deaths for there to be births—and thus, the living constitute a minority of the members of a society. Coastal-riverine groups in the Guinea-Bissau region are extremely solicitious concerning ancestors. Their deceased are interred nearby (in some societies, underneath the floors of dwellings) except for individuals guilty of witchcraft, murder, or other serious antisocial behavior, in which case their bodies are disposed of away from the village. Gravesites are marked by stones, posts, strips of cloth, or other means. Food offerings are periodically placed by the graves, where descendants hold family rites and religious ceremonies communicating with the spirits at the time of planting and at other important periods in the life cycle (Carreira 1947, 90–92 and photographs facing pp. 64 and 80; Mota 1954, 1:245–50).

The Dutch mariner Dierick Ruiters related what he learned about western Africans' practices and beliefs concerning burials and the afterlife. He did not identify his informants (and translators?), nor did he describe the circumstances under which he gathered this information.

> They believe in another world ruled in its entirety by a great monarch: If a man dies in this world posssessing a thousand guilders, he will have a thousand pounds in the other, and if a man is a captain in this life he will be a governor in the next. . . . The prayer they say before the image is addressed to the friend in the grave whom they think now holds high office and will be able to forward their request at court. They beseech the friend to go to the all high monarch with the request that the person praying may, while he lives in this world, become great, live long, and collect many treasures, so that he may arrive as a rich man in the next world. . . . All sorts of things are buried with the dead. They put gold rings on the dead person's fingers: Articles of iron, steel, copper, and tin are all buried with the deceased. For the living friend does all he can to equip his dead friend generously so that when he arrives in the other world he will be respected and be of good position. Then, when the living pray to him, their wishes are more likely to be fulfilled. They firmly believe that friends buried with many treasures become great captains in the other world, so that when they appear before the monarch they obtain audience immediately, and speak to him, and their requests are readily accepted. (Hair 1975b, 64–66)

Of particular significance for Luso-African traders was the practice of wrapping the bodies of deceased elites in numerous prestige cloths. As commerce developed, these were primarily *panos* (cloth strips) woven in Cabo Verde. The Jesuit missionary Fr. Balthasar Barreira compiled an extensive account concerning what he learned about the cohesive social functions of funerary rituals (Hair 1978c, 94–97), and he contended that western Africans' "ignorance" of the afterlife was a significant obstacle to their conversion to Christianity: "They evaluate all points about the next world in terms of things of this world, believing that the former are also material, and hence that they will employ in the other life what they used in this one. They cannot be persuaded of the existence of hell, believing only that all who die go to where God is; and the greater they were here, the more they are valued when they are with Him. So in their troubles they commend themselves to the dead, . . . and make them offerings in order that the dead may plead with God to release the living from their troubles" (Hair 1983, 62).

It is noteworthy that when Fr. Manuel Alvares, a fellow Jesuit residing in Serra Leoa, learned of Father Barreira's death, he wrote: "I commended myself to the holy exercise of prayer to his pure soul, seeking that it would intercede (for me) before the Lord" (Hair 1990, pt. 2, chap. 26: 18). Such congruences of beliefs were conducive to syncretism, whether disputed or acknowledged. Portuguese and other Europeans who held the dead in awe and fear, who communed with ancestors about crops and while dining in graveyards on All Souls' Day and May Day, and who dreaded ghosts and other spiritual manifestations doubtless found western Africans' beliefs and practices concerning death and the afterlife compatible. Such was the dual heritage of Luso-Africans.

A fourth category of supernatural phenomena comprises forces and powers immanent in vegetable, animal, and mineral substances. Individuals adept in these matters may encapsulate such forces in the horns of wild or domestic animals, in leather pouches, and in other containers that function as "power generators" by increasing the strength of the substances manyfold. Such amulets or talismans—known by the term *gris-gris* (or *gree-grees*) in popular usage—are sought to protect individuals and their possessions from sickness and harm; alternatively, it is believed that they may possess "offensive" powers to attract and win the affections of another person or to weaken or kill an adversary or enemy. Such talismans are especially valued by hunters, traders, and others who venture far from their communities and thereby leave the protection afforded them by propitiatory spirits and the shades of ancestors. These talismans may be substituted—or supplemented—by Muslim amulets enclosing verses from the Koran and by Christian crucifixes and rosaries, the latter objects, along with European garments, comprising part of the "identity" of Luso-Africans and grumetes.

Western Africans' beliefs and cultural patterns, especially among acephalous groups in the Guinea-Bissau region, became syncretized with those of the *lançados*—the venturesome Portuguese who were permitted to live ashore in African communities—and their Luso-African descendants. The resulting amalgam remained largely unchanged into the twentieth century. Both Muslim Africans and Christian Europeans evinced great respect and indeed often fear and awe for the magical powers attributed to members of coastal-riverine groups (Luso-Africans included), and they frequently turned to their religious specialists for a variety of purposes, such as establishing social relations, ratifying commercial agreements, mediation with local spirits, and medical and psychological healing.

Sociocultural Paradigms

Three sociocultural paradigms of immeasurable significance were of fundamental importance regarding the peoples of western Africa. The first paradigm involved "landlord-stranger reciprocities" that promoted safety of movement and hospitality for travelers; the second concerned endogamous craft specialists, or *nyamakalaw;* and the third involved power associations—in which blacksmiths and their wives exercised leadership roles—that socialized children, monitored adult behavior, and resolved conflicts among groups.

The origins of landlord-stranger reciprocities are lost in antiquity, but they have been incorporated into the fundaments of western African societies. Historically, travelers were provided food, lodging, and security of possessions. Hospitality and appropriate behavior toward visitors derived from the obligations of kinship affiliations, real and fictive, including the "joking relationships" shared by some groups; from customary law supported by divine sanctions and reinforced by long usage; from the socialization of children; and from oft-repeated sayings, proverbs, and heuristic stories. Concomitantly, the behavior of strangers was conditioned by all of the foregoing; by the dread of spending a night in the bush bereft of the protection of a community; by dependence on hosts for food, shelter, access to commercial networks, land, and other resources; and by respect for the occult powers wielded by landlords through their associations with the spirits of an area, especially through the mediation of ancestors.

Landlord-stranger reciprocities mediated social intercourse and promoted safe passage for travelers of every kind: traders; pastoralists; hunters; artisans; envoys of rulers; specialists in traditional medicine; uprooted migrants; sick or troubled people seeking healers and oracles; marabouts (Muslim clerics) and pilgrims; musicians; and adventurous young people visiting other communities during the slack period between harvests and the renewal of the agricultural cycle for sport, recreation, and dalliance. Visitors brought welcome news from near and far concerning absent members of the communities, commerce and commodities, remarkable events, and many other matters of general interest. Visitors adept in storytelling and bard-musicians who recounted Mande oral epics were especially welcome, as were the ministrations of gifted herbalists and healers.

Inducements to break a journey were accorded strangers who brought wealth in the form of trade goods, livestock, or other possessions; those who had special powers and skills, such as hunters, smiths, wood-carvers, oracles, and marabouts; and members of elite groups from neighboring communities or other societies. The privilege of extending hospitality to them was arrogated by community leaders, elders, and other influential persons who anticipated benefits such as receiving gifts, fostering alliances, collecting tariffs, sharing the profits of commercial exchanges, and acting as middlemen in trade with local and neighboring groups. Valued male strangers were offered female consorts for the duration of their stay. Rulers, village leaders, and lineage heads promoted marriages with favored strangers as a means of binding them to family and community—even as they attempted to restrict the strangers' reciprocal demands on them. These practices were extended to Portuguese traders and to their Luso-African descendants.

Long-distance commerce in western Africa was expedited by permanent alliances between lineages known as *jonu* in Soninke. These alliances initiated from an inviolable oath sworn between families (Curtin 1975, 73). One practice about which little is known because it involves a confidential bonding between individuals is the secret "blood pact." Blood pacts gave strangers additional protections in the territories of their blood brothers. Such protections provided unconditional support beyond normal obligations of hospitality, including judicial proceedings, mediation of disputes with authorities, assistance with funerals, reprisals for homicides, and other matters (Paulme 1968, 12, 15, 27). To what extent Luso-Africans belonged to jonu or participated in blood pacts is unknown, but such linkages may have been significant in terms of Luso-African involvement in commercial networks, judicial processes, and other activities.

Nyamakalaw

The presence of occupational specialists set apart by their craft skills, knowledge of occult powers, and endogamous marriage patterns has had numerous ramifications in western African society. Smiths, bards, leather workers, and woodcarvers are prominent members of Mandinka, Fula, Wolof, and Serer societies and frequent visitors among other groups. Endogamy protects professional secrets by imparting skills only to family members and adopted apprentices, and the awesome powers attributed to members of these groups serve no less to distinguish them from other social elements (Tamari 1997, chap. 1). Mande refer to members of the smith, leather worker, and bard ("griot") groups as *nyamakalaw* (the singular is *nyamakala*). Patrick McNaughton drew on Charles Bird's description of *nyama* as "the energy of action" in translating the prefix *nyama-* as "occult energy" and the suffix *-kala* as "handle," as in the handle of a tool or implement. *Nyamakala* thus translates as "handle of power," and it identifies people controlling potent services who are consequently set apart from the rest of society (McNaughton 1988, 18–19; cf. Dupire 1985, 89).

Historically, people throughout western Africa believed smiths possessed redoubtable skills and powers. Only they knew the secrets of iron making and could secure the permission of the spirits of land, water, and forest to mine ores; only they could fell appropriate trees for charcoal making; and only they could invoke the spirits' cooperation in the smelting and forging of iron. Successful iron working required the application of the smiths' considerable technological expertise, together with unremitting attention to requisite rituals. Smiths alone possessed the expertise to make farm implements, tools, and weapons, and the most proficient among them crafted gold and silver jewelry. Wood-carvers and woodworkers were generally smiths, for ritual protections were needed to propitiate the spirits disturbed by the hewing of a living tree and to ingratiate those represented in wood carvings. Smiths created masks, compounded the ingredients of amulets, and performed the circumcisions that marked the passage of boys into adulthood. In the daily life of their communities, they intervened to halt conflicts and mediate disputes, for no one presumed to challenge their authority.

Female smiths likewise exercised great influence. They were often potters who, like their husbands, transformed the basic elements of earth, fire, and water. As their male counterparts did with boys, they participated in socializing young females and presided at rites of passage, performing excisions on girls.

Everywhere in western Africa the clan names Camara, Koroma, and Kante signal smith families, though not exclusively, and snakes are frequently the totems of smith clans. Even if smiths had exercised no other social role than presiding at the ceremonies marking the passage from childhood to adulthood, that role, together with their professional powers and secrets, would have assured them a greater authority than any other social group. There is, however, much evidence of the smiths' great and quasi-secret importance in another sphere as well, stemming from their control over the power associations that, until recently, had unrivaled influence in many parts of western Africa. Captive smiths were especially sought and highly valued by Portuguese and Luso-Africans, since their skills were requisite for building and repairing ships and other fabrications. How masters coped with domestic slaves who possessed such prestige and reputed power was not revealed in the sources.

Like smiths, leather workers were considered to possess special powers to deal with dangerous substances—in their case, the powerful nyama released from slain animals. Leather workers may have come from both hunter and smith groups, becoming recognized as a separate nyamakala group as they applied their skills in the entourages of horse warriors, at the courts of rulers, and in the compounds of trading centers. The expansion of cavalry warfare during the c. 1100–c. 1500 dry period greatly increased the demand for saddles, bridles, and other horse tack, in addition to the scabbards, knife sheaths, garments, sandals, pouches for amulets, and other items also used by other members of society.

European purchases of animal pelts and hides stimulated the activities of leather-working groups in western Africa. Commerce in cowhides increased greatly during the latter part of the sixteenth century, when French and Dutch vessels purchased large numbers along the Petite Côte of Senegal; the trade shifted southward during the latter part of the c. 1630–c. 1860 dry period, when hides from the growing Fula herds in Futa Jallon were transported to the coast for sale. Europeans also purchased a variety of wild animal pelts, which stimulated the hunting of many animals for their skins, besides elephants for their ivory. The nyama of dangerous wild animals is considered immeasurably more potent than that of domestic animals, and the spiritual dangers involved, plus the premium paid for high-quality pelts, encouraged hunters to leave the curing of feral hides to experts thought to possess both occult and professional skills (Brooks 1985, 129–30).

Male and female bards are highly visible members of Mande groups and of the Wolof and Serer societies of Senegambia. They have traditionally had distinctive societal roles as historians, genealogists, musicians, singers, and dancers. In terms of their special powers, breath is deemed the essence of a being, as is spittle. After all, what is more problematic than the human voice, which can convey curses or praises, denigrate or uplift, and arouse or mediate conflict? Spoken words explain, educate, and convey the heritage of a people.

In past times, bards were invaluable allies of Mandekalu warriors and rulers. They were attached to elite families as praise-singers, keepers of family histories and genealogies, and educators of youths. Their praise poetry and captivating musical accompaniments celebrated the deeds of elites and served to explain and rationalize the social and cultural patterns those elites imposed on subjugated peoples. Before battles, bards employed their music and exhortations to galvanize the courage of warriors. They also served as emissaries between rulers, claiming diplomatic immunities. Bards have often been derisively characterized in European accounts as presumptious and venal, but Luso-Africans appreciated their music and benefited from the information the bards acquired in the course of their association with the elites. Bardic women attached to elite families were frequently hairdressers and thereby had an intimate association with others that reputedly allowed them to cast magical spells as well as purvey gossip (Bodiel 1950, 9; Ames 1956, 156–57; Gamble 1967, 45–46).

Few members of nyamakalaw groups practiced their specializations on a full-time basis. Smiths living at commercial centers might work at their craft year-round, but elsewhere, smiths smelted and worked iron during the dry season and farmed during the rainy season. Bards farmed during the wet season, and some were weavers during the dry season. Such patterns were similar for other groups as well. Many fishermen cultivated during the rainy season. Traders did likewise, awaiting the dry season when commodities would not be damaged by rainfall, rivers and streams could be safely crossed, and the paths of trade were open.

Power Associations

Numerous scholars have sought to describe and analyze the organizations that socialize children, monitor community behavior, and exercise numerous other functions in western African society, but much remains unknown and speculative in this regard. However, the salient elements of the purview and influence of the power associations are evident. In times past, all or almost all members of African groups became members of these groups; conversely, many Europeans defamed the associations as "secret societies" because they themselves were denied admittance to meetings and ceremonies and because their inquiries were put off with misleading or confusing responses.

Children inducted into power associations are said to "die" and be symbolically "reborn" in a new life; the old life comprises the family and the lineage, while in the new life, the prime allegiance is to the community as a whole. Robin Horton observesd, "By plunging the adolescent into an intense attachment to the guardian spirit of the society, the rituals . . . help to wean him away from deep emotional ties with parents and lineage members" (Horton 1985, 111). The secrecy for which the associations are renowned contrasts with the openness of the age-grade assemblies of village life. Horton explicated: "This secrecy counters the influence of lineage rivalries in two ways. On the one hand, it protects those engaged in deliberations against pressure from their various lineages. This makes it easier for them to consider any situation on its merits, and to avoid taking-up positions inspired by purely sectional interests. On the other hand, it enables the society to announce its decisions to the public at large as things collective and unanimous" (Horton 1985, 111–12).

Leaders of power associations or their executive agents often appear in public disguised by masks, raffia, and cloth garments. Their anonymity and their "possession" by spirit forces that protect the community also compel obedience.

As explained by William Siegmann, "Masks are part of a total costume which conceals the wearer's identity and depersonalizes his actions much as do the wigs and robes of western judges. They thus establish the idea that no mere man has the right to judge others. Thus all authority is believed to be held and all judgment given in the name and place of the spirits" (Siegmann 1980, 17).

The Komo, Simo, and Poro mens' associations and the Sande and Bundu women's associations exercised great influence among host societies, much to the benefit of Mande traders, smiths, and other strangers. Wherever Mande smiths and traders settled among West Atlantic and Kruan groups, they founded chapters of power associations that exercised the same functions as in their home areas: generating spiritual protections, providing leadership to communities, mediating disputes, inculcating and monitoring social norms, eradicating witchcraft, punishing transgressors, educating and socializing children, and in general maintaining and disseminating Mande social and cultural patterns (Brooks 1993, 44–46).

The awesome powers attributed to Komo, Poro, Simo, Sande, and Bundu enabled them to acquire surpassing influence in host societies. Children of landlord groups whose education was entrusted to power associations were inducted as members, enabling Mande leaders to exercise a growing influence over wide regions of western Africa. Luso-African children growing up in acephalous societies who were socialized together with their age mates subsequently benefited from the prerogatives and protections afforded by membership in power associations, adding to the linguistic, social, and cultural advantages they possessed in competition with Portuguese and other Europeans. Luso-Africans capitalized on these affiliations, and in addition, some Luso-Africans reputedly commanded occult powers.

Mandekalu Horse Warriors and the Imposition of Tripartite Social Stratification

The latter part of the c. 1100–c. 1500 dry period marked a second phase of Mande expansion. Mandekan-speaking horsemen raided along the southward-receding fringes of the savanna-woodland zone and founded states that transformed many aspects of the lives of those they conquered. Horse warriors and their retinues followed the caravan routes pioneered by Mande traders and smiths to pillage communities and enslave their inhabitants, establishing conquest states that acknowledged (nominal) tributary relationships to the Mali

Empire (in the thirteenth through fifteenth centuries). Mandekan languages—that is, Mandinka, Maninka, and Bamana—supplanted other Mande languages and those of West Atlantic–speaking groups across a broad swath of western Africa's Sahel, savanna, and savanna-woodland ecological zones. Many of the Southwestern Mande, Southeastern Mande, West Atlantic, and Kruan groups that survived are located in areas south of the tsetse fly line, beyond the control of Mandekan-speaking horse warriors. Members of conquered groups were constrained by circumstances to learn Mandekan dialects. This was particularly the case for the large numbers of captives taken in war or purchased by Mandekan-speakers, who comprised more than half the population in many areas and constituted the primary economic producers.

The bulking and artisanal centers founded by Mande traders and smiths among West Atlantic host communities were attractive prizes for Mandekalu horsemen, who used them as administrative headquarters from which they could rule conquered territories and impose taxes on trading communities. Mandekalu imposed linguistic, social, and cultural changes on subjugated groups. These changes derived from the Mali Empire, where, from the thirteenth century on, a consolidation and elaboration of ongoing political and social developments took place among Northern Mande groups and their subject populations. Political institutions were characterized by a stratified, tripartite social structure comprising: (1) elites and free persons; (2) nyamakalaw groups, made up of smiths, leather workers, and bards; and (3) the large population of slaves, who were either captured during conquests or obtained through commerce.

Wherever Mandekalu cavalry conquered, nyamakalaw groups were subordinated to their interests—and, to a considerable extent, at mutual advantage. Smiths and leather workers manufactured the weapons and horse tack required by Mandekalu warriors, while bards played an important role as publicists for Mandekalu elites with the praise poetry and music they created to glorify rulers and warriors. Smiths continued to be held in respect and awe by all elements of society, elites included, and they exercised significant influence for two reasons: first, because they had a unique capacity to smelt iron and manufacture tools and weapons as well as create magically empowered staffs for rulers and amulets that protected individuals, and second, because they and their wives were the leaders of power associations. Mandekalu tripartite institutions were adopted by other horse-warrior groups—notably, the Wolof and Serer elites who founded states in Senegambia.

During their ongoing depredations, Mandekalu horsemen enslaved great numbers of people, many of whom were sold into trans-Saharan slavery and, increasingly as time passed, into transatlantic slavery. Many captives, especially women, were retained as domestic slaves to cultivate land and serve as house slaves and concubines. Male slaves were extensively used as soldiers and caravan porters, the latter of whom might be sold at river ports or other markets, or loaded with returns as opportunities might warrant. Traders and caravan porters were probably the principal diffusers of Mandekan dialects outside the Mandekan "core area" (Bird 1970, 154–55; Klein and Lovejoy 1979; Brooks 1989).

Historical sources offer only glimpses of the struggles for ascendancy that took place between horsemen and their entourages and the leaders of power associations and their members. Doubtless, there were protracted struggles for influence among West Atlantic and Kruan groups where Mande smiths and traders had lived for generations and founded power associations that gained increasing control over host societies. In some areas, contests may have extended over long periods of time and witnessed many reversals of fortune, especially during the relatively brief c. 1500–c. 1630 wet period when the tsetse fly line advanced northward (Map 1.2) and compelled horse warriors to withdraw from some of the areas they had conquered. During the c. 1630–c. 1860 dry period, ecological zones again moved south, perhaps hundreds of kilometers in some areas, and Mandekalu horse warriors opportunistically renewed their raiding along the receding borderlands of the savanna-woodland zone, selling captives into the rapidly growing Atlantic slave trade during the seventeenth and eighteenth centuries. Most notable was the expansion of the Kaabu Empire, which incorporated Mandinka states south of the Gambia River. Kaabu's rulers and those of the Wolof and Serer states in Senegambia expanded their entourages of slave warriors, known as *nyanchos* in Mande states and *ceddo* in Senegambia, whose behavior became increasingly profligate and unpredictable, making them as feared by the inhabitants of their own states as by neighboring groups (Boulègue 1989, 23–24; Brooks 1993b, 99–113, 256–57).

As areas of tsetse infestation receded south during the long c. 1630–c. 1860 dry period, Fula herders moved southward with their livestock. In many areas, including the Kaabu Empire, Fula groups became more and more interspersed among Mandinka cultivators, engendering conflict. In contrast to the situation during the c. 1100–c. 1500 dry period, Fula bowmen and horsemen, not Mande forces, dominated the battlefields of western Africa. Inspired and led by Torodbe marabouts, Fula conquered vast areas across the savanna and savanna-woodland zones. In the wake of their victories, Torodbe leaders founded *almamates*, that is, states committed to Islamic principles—in Bundu in the 1690s, in Futa Jallon in the 1720s, in Futa Toro in 1776, and along the upper Niger and upper Senegal valleys beginning in 1852. After protracted warfare dating from the close of the eighteenth century, the Fula almamate of Futa Jallon destroyed the Kaabu Empire during the 1860s. Had colonial powers not intervened in the last quarter of the nineteenth century, Muslim Fula might have established hegemony over most of western Africa (Brooks 1985, 208–13).

Chapter 2
Commercial Networks
Biafada-Sapi, Banyun-Bak, and Cabo Verdean–Lançado

> An evil custom exists throughout Guinea, except in the Rio de São Domingos. In all other places, if our people do not take refuge at sea when they are ill, so as to die aboard their ships, and instead die on the land, the kings of the place inherit all their property.
>
> —Almada c. 1594 (Hair 1984a, 117)

Coastwise, riverine, and caravan routes that had existed for centuries before the arrival of European mariners linked the peoples of Senegambia and the Upper Guinea Coast with markets along the Senegal and Niger Rivers and their tributaries. The Guinea-Bissau region extending between the Gambia River and the northwestern outliers of the Futa Jallon highlands was the nexus of Biafada-Sapi, Banyun-Bak, and Mande commercial networks that expedited trade between ecological zones and coastal-riverine areas. Prior to the arrival of Portuguese vessels in the fifteenth century, cabotage—or coast-hugging trade—was undertaken in dugouts ranging in size from craft a few meters in length to vessels tens of meters long carved from the tallest available trees. Navigation in small craft along the ria coastline was facilitated by estuaries, lagoons, and linking waterways shielded from the sea and by the Bissagos archipelago, which diminished the force of the southward-flowing Guinea Current.

The Biafada-Sapi Network

The Biafada-Sapi coastwise and riverine network (Map 2.1) had a principal role in the systems of exchanges in western Africa. Biafada mariners living along the

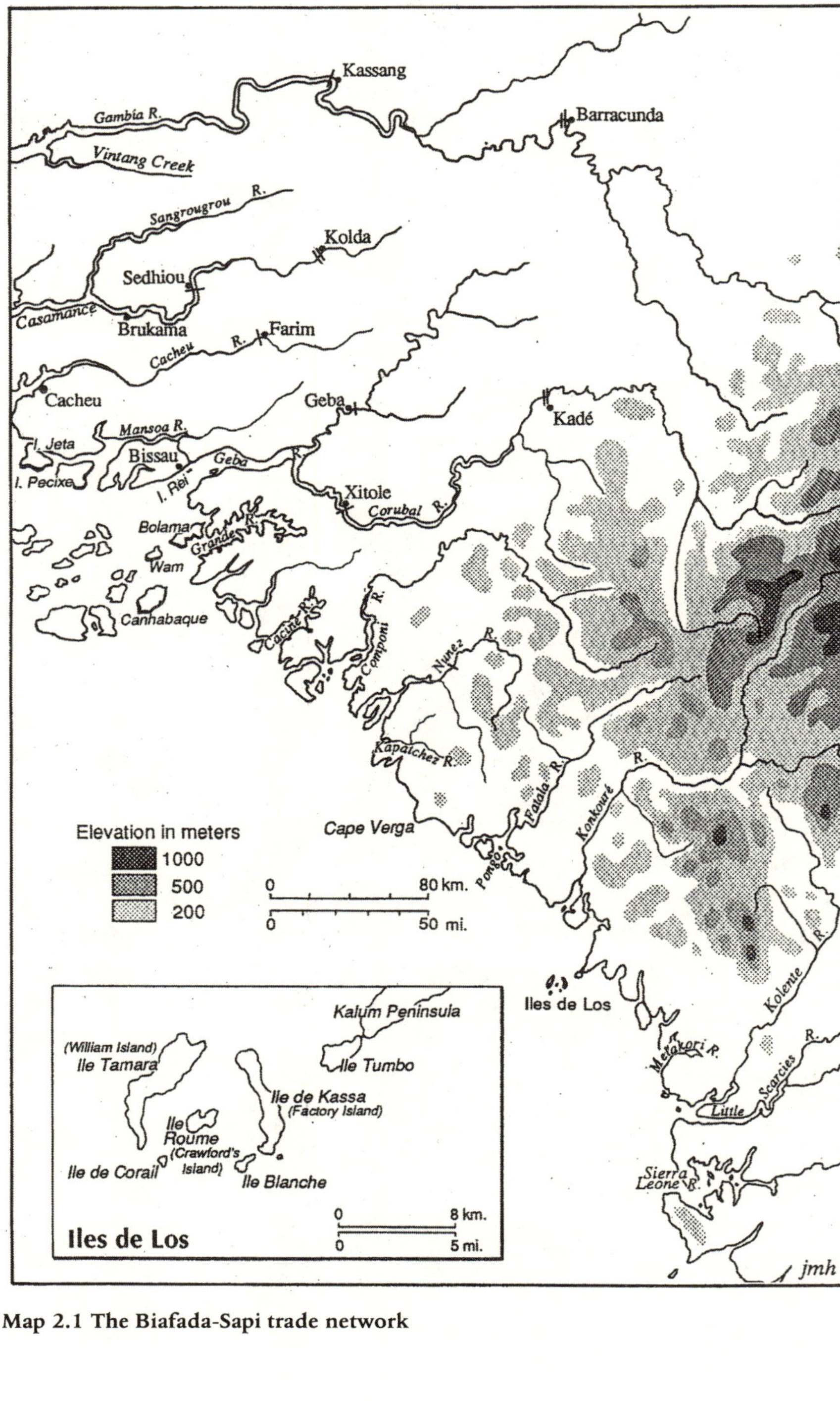

Map 2.1 The Biafada-Sapi trade network

Grande, Geba, and Corubal Rivers ventured southward along the coast of western Africa in large dugouts to obtain kola, malaguetta pepper, and other commodities from Landuma, Baga, Temne, and Bullom/Sherbro groups that harvested and traded forest products. These Sapi groups belong to the Mel subgroup of the southern branch of West Atlantic languages. The close relationships between Mel dialects made them mutually intelligible, facilitating commercial and social relationships (Hair 1984a, 126; Mota and Hair, 1977, 98–99, 244–45 n. 127). Sapi disseminated early on as a commercial lingua franca, a diffusion accelerated from the fifteenth century on by Portuguese employing Landuma as interpreters and compradors in commerce southward along the Upper Guinea Coast.

Kola trees flourish in the forests extending south of the Nunez River, and kola (*Cola nitida*) has been western Africans' most popular indulgence since time immemorial and the forest zone's principal article of commerce (Map 1.5). Kola "nuts" (which actually are seeds) contain caffeine, kolatine, and theobromine; consuming kola diminishes hunger and thirst, and the nuts are alleged to have numerous medicinal and physiological attributes. Consumption of kola is part of the social and cultural fabric of western Africans' lives and is integrated into numerous rituals bonding human relations (Person 1968, 101–4; Lovejoy 1981; Brooks 1980b and 1993b, 52–54).

Malaguetta pepper (*Aframomum melegueta*) was a second forest product widely traded in western Africa and across the Sahara until it was supplanted in trans-Saharan and European markets by peppercorns from South Asia and in western Africa by the introduction of chilies from the Americas (Mauny 1961, 249–50). Pepper bushes grow sparsely in the savanna-woodland zone and flourish in the forest zone; like kola, malaguetta pepper was prized for its variety of uses as a spice, stimulant, and medication. During the c. 1100–c. 1500 dry period, Kruan seafarers settled along the Malaguetta Coast to engage in coastwise and riverine commerce, linking West Atlantic and Mande traders with Kwa-speaking groups living to the east along the Gulf of Guinea.

The expansion of the Biafada-Sapi network was promoted by interacting developments during the c. 1100–c. 1500 dry period: the southward shift of ecological zones and of Mande trade networks; the growth of long-distance commerce promoted by increasing trans-Saharan trade; the expansion of the Mali Empire and satellite states; and the ongoing development of communities inhabited by affluent elites who could afford kola, malaguetta pepper, and other luxuries. Biafada mariners possessed huge dugouts, the largest of which were capable of transporting more than a hundred people, cattle, and large quantities of merchandise (Hair 1984a, 93). These vessels provided an economical means of transporting such bulk commodities as kola, malaguetta pepper, iron bars, and cloth between ecological zones, bypassing the forested wilderness of the Futa Jallon massif. The force of the southward-flowing Guinea Current is negligible south of the Bissagos archipelago, which diverts and diminishes the impetus of the current. Tidal flows excepted, river estuaries, lagoons, and connecting waterways shielded by bars, reefs, and islands have calm and easily navigable waters protected from surfs and heavy seas.

Biafada probably traded as far south as the Kolente River, a principal area of kola harvesting and salt production and the home of Bullom mariners engaged in commerce as far south as Koya in the Cape Mount area, where they exchanged salt for gold (Mauny 1956, 82–85, 88–89). The Geba and Corubal Rivers provided Biafada access to Mande caravan routes connecting the rivers at their heads of navigation and numerous points along their courses and tributary streams. Along their lower reaches, the Geba and Corubal are bordered by mangroves and marshy land infested with anopheles mosquitoes and tsetse flies, but their upper courses flow through savanna-woodland relatively free of both disease vectors. Donkeys supplemented human porterage.

Biafada lands constituted an extensive territory along both banks of the Grande River, extending north to the Geba and east along the Corubal (Map 2.2). The Grande River is navigable by vessels for only some fifty kilometers; it is a sea-flooded estuary into which several small streams flow. Biafada states included Guinala, which controlled trade at Guinala port and Xitole at the head of navigation for large craft on the Corubal River; Degola, which controlled the Geba ports of Geba and Bafatá; and Biguba and Balola at the head of navigation of the Grande River, which bordered Nalu and Landuma territory. All the Biafada communities and their leaders were subject to the ruler of the state of Guinala, who lived at Bruco on one of the principal channels of the Grande estuary.

Biafada territory was separated from that of Papel and Balanta by the broad Geba estuary, which is more than ten kilometers wide for most of the sixty kilometers extending from Bissau to its confluence with the Corubal River. The Impernal Channel on the east side of Ilha do Bissau divided Papel from Balanta. Biafada called the land along the north bank of the Geba River above the confluence of the Corubal River "Degola" or "Degoula," names derived from the word *kola* and testifying to the importance of trade in that commodity. Large, oceangoing dugouts unloaded their cargoes at Geba and Bafatá, and smaller craft continued upriver. At some time during the latter part of the c. 1100–c. 1500 dry period, Mandinka horse warriors conquered Degola, renaming the area Badour (Brooks 1980b, 16–17).

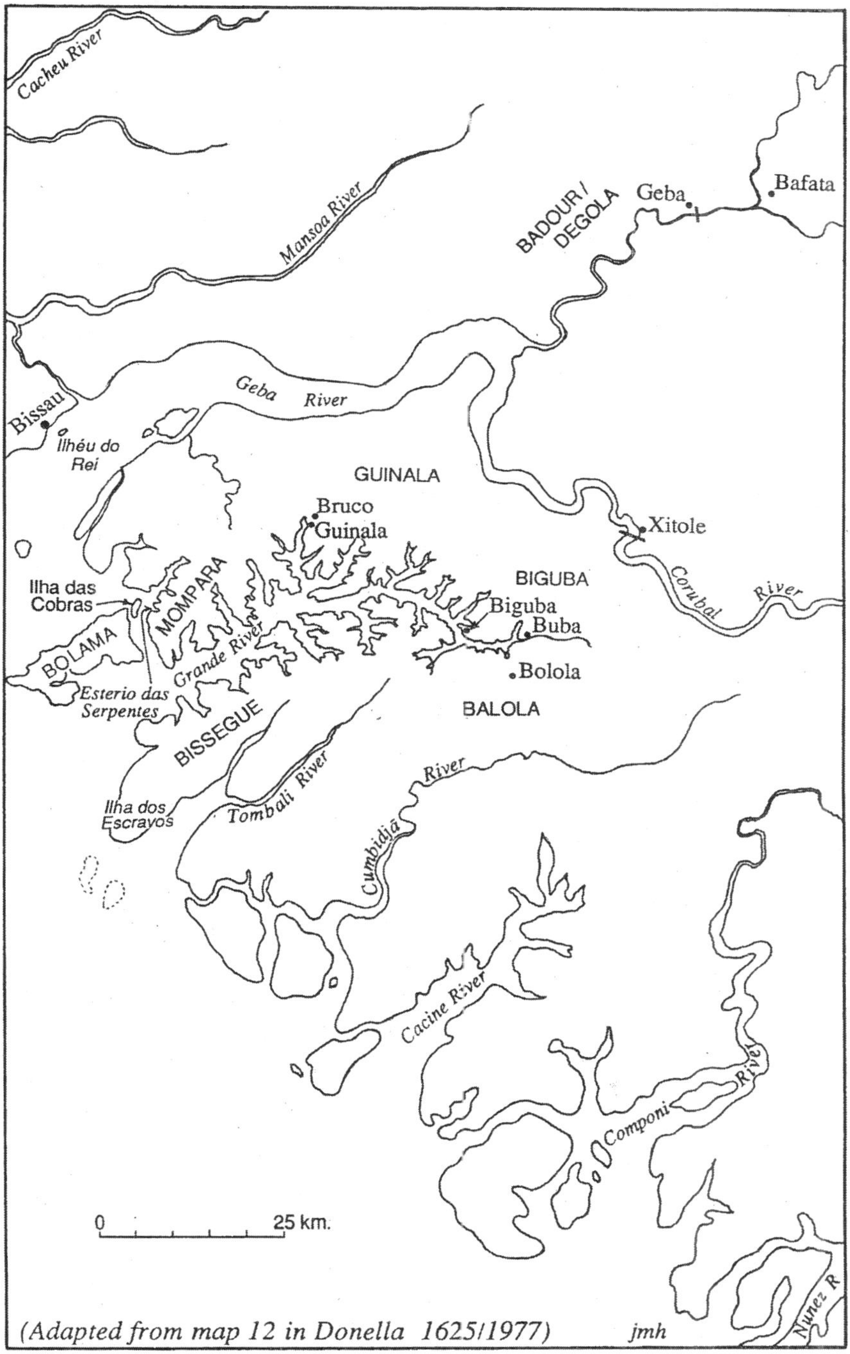

Map 2.2 The Grande and Geba Rivers

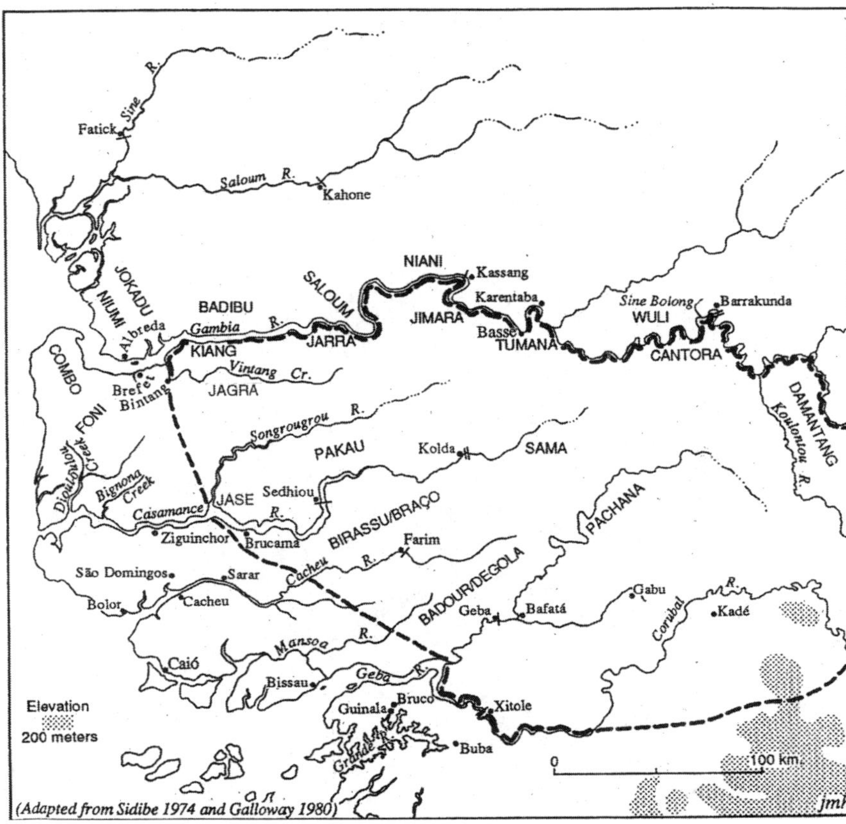

Map 2.3 The Kaabu Empire in the seventeenth century

During the sixteenth century, a number of Mandinka states in the Guinea-Bissau region between the Gambia River and northern outliers of Futa Jallon became incorporated into a loose federation called Kaabu, governed by *mansas* (rulers) selected on a rotating basis from eligible members of the Sane and Mane clans of the states of Sama, Jimara, and Pachana (Map 2.3). With territorial aggrandizement between Mandinka states precluded, the combative energies of Mandinka warriors and aspiring state builders were concentrated on pillaging West Atlantic–speaking groups. Mandinka conquests deprived Biafada of lands in the savanna-woodland zone, but Biafada retained control over the tsetse-infested lower reaches of the Geba and Corubal Rivers and coastal-riverine areas. Their territorial losses notwithstanding, Biafada continued to carry on an extensive commerce with Mande-speaking traders, many of whom were permitted to reside in Biafada communities along the Corubal and Grande Rivers.

Based on what can be learned from Portuguese sources and what can be surmised, it seems that commerce between the Geba River and Cacheu River was expedited by Papel mariners living on Bissau and Pecixe Islands, operating under the direction of Biafada traders. Coastwise navigation against the prevailing north-to-south currents and winds was practically impossible for heavily laden dugout craft, so traders probably used one of three routes to transport commodities between the Geba and Cacheu Rivers: either the Impernal Channel, the Mansoa River, or the Jeta Channel (Rio das Ancoras), together with their tributary streams, marigots, and overland portages.

Biafada long exercised a religious and political hegemony over Papel groups dwelling along the north bank of the Geba estuary. Papel rulers of Ilha da Bissau acknowledged the suzerainty of the Biafada ruler of Guinala, a subordination that continued until colonial times (Rodney 1970, 146, 148; Barcellos 1911, 5:38). The nature of the ascendancy remains to be ascertained, but the *xina* (shrine) located on Ilhéu do Rei/"Islet of the King," also known as Ile Sorcière/"Sorcerers Islet," in the Geba estuary opposite the port of Bissau was affiliated with the iran of Bruco/Buduco, the village of the ruler of the Biafada state of Guinala (Mota 1950, 148–49; 1970, 272 n. 10). A grove of trees on the island was the site of annual ceremonies of surpassing importance for Papel groups meeting together with Biafada from Guinala, and Biafada asserted that blood from offerings would show in Bruco (Frinsel 1990). Fr. Manuel Alvares and Fr. André de Faro related numerous details concerning the purported origins and practices associated with annual or biennial ceremonies (Hair 1982, 25; 1990, chap. 11: 3–4). Fr. Francisco de Santiago, who lived in Bissau in the eighteenth century, described an important festival convened every December (Dias 1945, 164), and Francisco Travassos Valdez, who visited Bissau in 1852, reported on ceremonies held in March: "[Papel] devotedly repair by thousands every year, during the full moon of the month of March, to celebrate certain rites and ceremonies, and consult the oracles respecting their agriculture, and concerning matters connected with the interests of their nation. It is there that they also perform the usual obsequies of their kings, and elect the successors to the crown" (Valdez 1861, 1:239).

The Impernal Channel on the eastern shore of Ilha da Bissau marks the boundary between Papel and Balanta. Papel lands extended north to the lower Cacheu River and west to the Atlantic; Balanta territory ran to the end of the Geba estuary and northward across the middle reaches of the Cacheu River to the Casamance River. Unlike Papel and Biafada, Balanta permitted no trade routes to cross their territory, and they limited their commerce to bartering salt produced along creeks flowing into the Geba estuary. Daunted by Balanta intransigence and bellicosity, Portuguese and Luso-Africans adopted Mandinka usage: the word *balanto* means refuse or resist (Van der Drift 2000, 152 n. 6; Hawthorne 2001, 5).

The Banyun-Bak Network

Commerce from the Cacheu River northward to the Casamance River, Gambia River, and along the Petite Côte to the Cape Verde peninsula was controlled by the Banyun-Bak trade network comprising Banyun, who speak a Nun language, Bak-speaking groups, and Serer-speaking Niominka (Map 2.4). Bak-speaking groups included Papel, who were intermediaries with the Biafada-Sapi network, and Diola groups living between the north bank of the Cacheu River and the south bank of the Gambia River, notably, those dwelling along streams, marigots, and portages. Banyun trade links between the Cacheu and Gambia Rivers comprised a riverine-portage network because the unimpeded flow of the Guinea Current, combined with the force of prevailing northeast winds, precluded south-to-north navigation along the Atlantic coast from the Cacheu River to the Casamance River. Niominka in dugout craft traded with Banyun along streams and marigots flowing northward into the Gambia River, and they engaged in commerce the length of the Gambia River and along the Petite Côte as far north as Cape Verde.

The origins of the Banyun-Bak trade networks probably derived from exchanges of surplus grains, salt, dried fish, dried mollusks, and other foodstuffs between groups dwelling north and south of the Gambia River. Sorghum and millet thrive in the savanna zone, as does rice in the better-watered lands south of the Gambia, although the productivity of harvests is subject to droughts, ravages of locust swarms, warfare, and other disasters. Banyun prospered by exchanging iron manufactures, cotton textiles, and other commodities obtained from Mande trade networks with Biafada-Sapi groups for kola, malaguetta pepper, and other products of the forest zone. Weekly markets held in villages between the Casamance and Cacheu Rivers attracted thousands of people from surrounding areas, expediting the exchange of commodities of local and long-distance origins. Papel crossed the Cacheu River to attend Banyun markets and had their own markets that Banyun visited (Monod, Mota, and Mauny 1951, 68–75, 164 n. 132, 164–65 n. 138).

The name *Banyun* is attributed to Portuguese, who derived the word from Mandinka and applied it as a collective name for a number of different groups settled at strategic sites along rivers, streams, marigots, portages, and trade paths

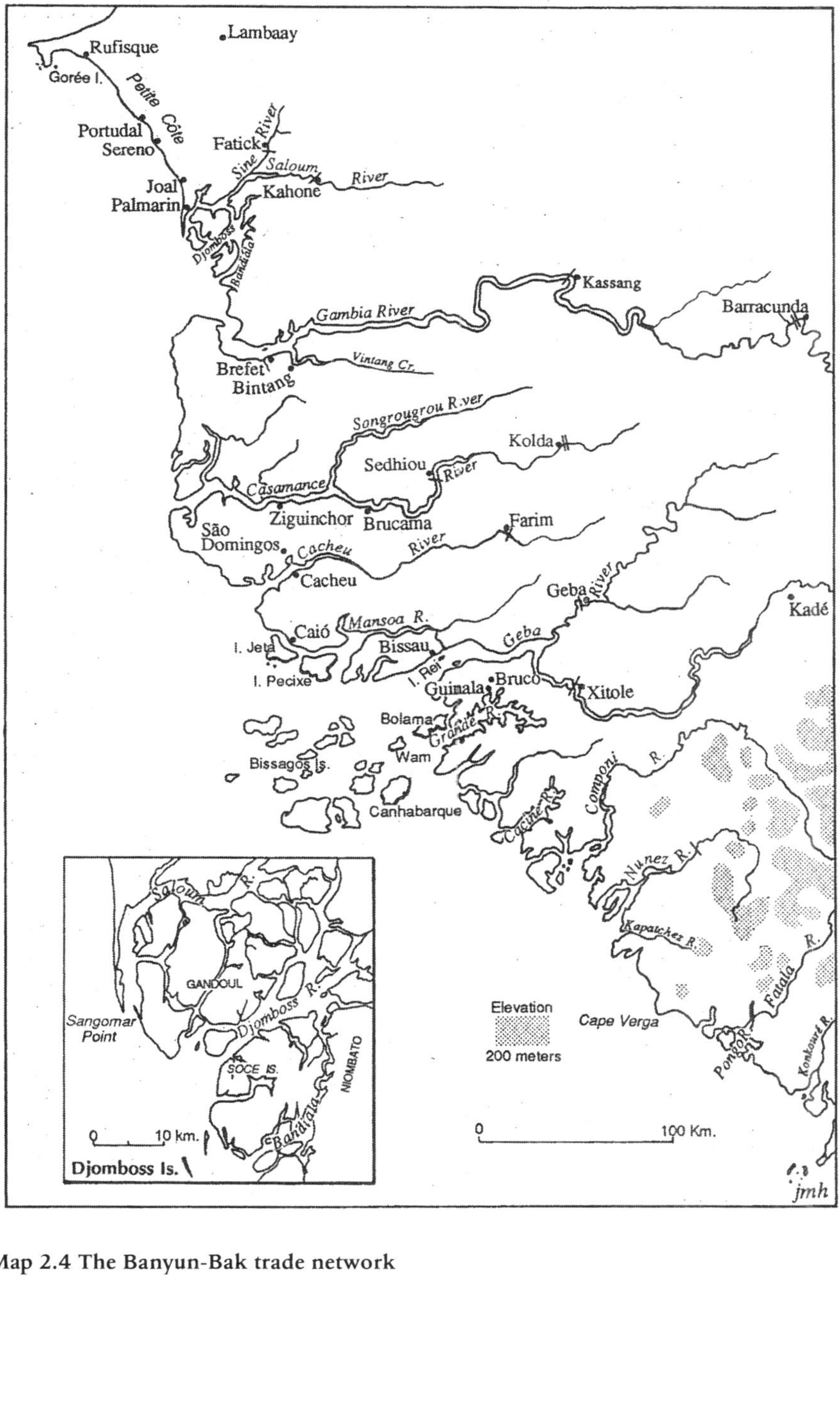

Map 2.4 The Banyun-Bak trade network

between the Gambia and Cacheu Rivers (Mota 1954, 1:144–45; Rodney 1970, 7; Lespinay 1996, 2000). Banyun elites, or *jagara,* wore red caps and struck iron clappers to announce their presence, and they used iron hatchets in awesome rites that bound contracts and imposed obedience—ceremonies that lançados and Luso-Africans found advantageous with respect to their commercial activities.

> Banyun worship a stick of wood which they call *hatichira,* which they consecrate in the following way. They take a forked stick of wood which must be cut with a new hatchet with a new handle—neither part having previously been used for any other purpose, and then they make a hole in the earth into which they pour a calabash of palm wine, some five or six litres, another with the same quantity of palm oil, and a basket of unhusked rice containing about one-fourth of an alqueire. They bring a live dog, and when they have poured the wine, oil, and rice into the hole, they kill the dog with the new hatchet, splitting open its head to let the blood flow into the hole onto the wine, oil, and rice. Then they cast the axe into the hole and implant the forked stick in the mixture, fill up the hole with earth, and hang herbs collected from the forest on the fork of the stick which extends above the ground. This ceremony is presided over by the most highly respected elders of the entire region, and afterwards they prepare the sacrificed dog with great solemnity and eat it. Thus consecrated the stick is believed to possess such powers that no one will touch it nor take anything put around it, for fear of dying forthwith. And when one wants someone to give surety that he will honor a contract, one takes him to the stick where he swears, and he will be very careful not to forswear because he believes that he will immediately die. They swear thus in their language: *hatichira hor no temrab,* which means "may the *china* kill me descending from the palm tree," for all of them climb palm trees to tap wine. And they swear in other ways, saying "may the serpent kill me, or the crocodile, etc.," and women also swear invoking as witness the same *hatichira.* (Monod, Mota, and Mauny 1951, 70–73)

Writing of his trading experiences in the 1570s, the Cabo Verdean André Alvares de Almada related that lançados were careful to protect themselves and their property by recourse to traditional religious sanctions practiced by Banyun and Papel groups. Lançados insisted that their landlords hold special feasts during which dogs were eaten and their blood offered to *chinas* (deities or spirits, from the Banyun word for tree), two or more chickens were sunk to the bottom of the river with rocks tied to their legs, and solemn oaths were sworn—ceremonies that lançados insisted be repeated every year (Hair 1984a, 89; cf. Hair 1990, chap. 4: 7; Lespinay 2000, 208).

A half dozen Banyun states extending between the Cacheu and Gambia Rivers were mentioned in European sources. The southernmost Banyun state was Buguendo, located on the north bank of the lower Cacheu River. In Portuguese times, if not earlier, Buguendo's ruler lived at Guinguim (Beguingue) at the head of the two marigots known in Portuguese times as the Rio Grande de São Domingos and the Rio Pequeno de São Domingos, thereby strategically located so that the ruler could oversee commerce passing along creeks and portages between the Cacheu and Casamance Rivers (Map 2.5). Cacheu in the Papel state of Cacanda was the bridgehead for the Banyun trade southward that linked the Biafada-Sapi network along the Mansoa and Geba Rivers. Cacheu is located on rising ground some twenty kilometers from the river mouth, midway between the Rio Grande de São Domingos and the Rio Pequeno de São Domingos on the opposite riverbank. The site is part of a long ridge of land extending southward, the only well-drained location fronting the Cacheu River for some kilometers in either direction. The brackish water of the lower Cacheu River is unsuitable for human consumption and most domestic uses, hence, the potable water of the spring-fed Bouganbor streamlet was a crucial determinant in human settlement.

North of Buguendo was the Banyun state of Bichangor. Its territory included Banyun and Diola (Bak-speakers) living along the south bank of the Casamance River. Ziguinchor, sited at the narrowest crossing point along the middle Casamance, was the locale of a weekly market that attracted thousands of people. The Mande-ruled Casa state extended to the east of Buguendo and Bichangor along the south bank of the Casamance River. Formerly a Banyun state, it was captured by Mandinka probably not long after the arrival of Portuguese mariners, for early Portuguese accounts mentioned a ruler called Jagara who was greatly feared due to the severity of his reign (Monod, Mota, and Mauny 1951, 70–71).

Later sources related that Casa's ruler had the Mande title of mansa and that his capital was at Brucama (modern-day Brikama) some fifty kilometers to the east of Ziguinchor (Mota and Hair 1977, 166–67). The word *Casa* evidently derived from the Arabic *kasa* (garment), a loanword adopted by Mandinka-speakers (Nicholas 1958, 266). Thus, at the junctions where the Banyun-Bak and Biafada-Sapi networks intersected with Mande networks, there was a "cloth" mansa ruling Casa and a "kola" mansa ruling Badour (formerly Degola), their titles testifying to the most important commodities exchanged by the trade diasporas.

North of Bichangor lay the Banyun states of Jase, Jagra, and Foni. Jase was located along the east bank of the Songrougrou River, extending some distance

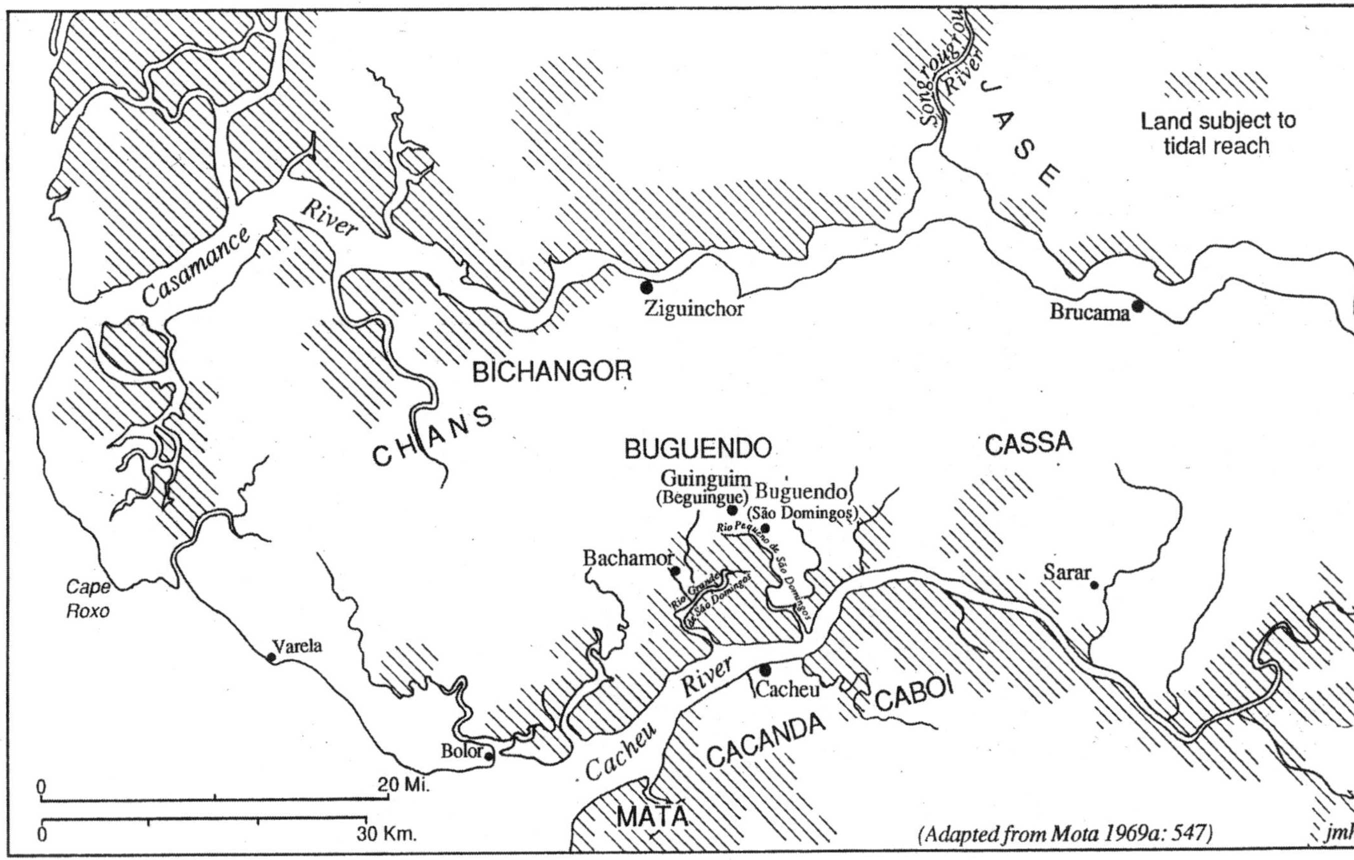

Map 2.5 The Cacheu and Casamance Rivers

along the north bank of the Casamance River. Jase bordered Jagra along Vintang Creek. Foni territory extended from Vintang Creek west along the lower Gambia River past Brefet Creek (Map 2.3). Trade between Bichangor and Foni was conveyed along the Bignona and Diouloulou Creeks and by overland portages to Brefet Creek, where the Foni ruler lived. Banyun trade routes connected Niominka riverine traders in Brefet Creek, Vintang Creek, and other tributaries of the Gambia River.

Niominka seafaring groups living on the islands in the Sine-Saloum estuary (Map 2.4 insert) and along the Petite Côte linked the Banyun-Bak commercial network with caravan routes connecting the Petite Côte with the upper and middle reaches of the Senegal River. A considerable portion of the kola and malaguetta pepper carried across the Sahara may have passed along these routes. Cape Verde marked the northern terminus of Niominka seafaring, for the force of the Canary Current and northeasterly winds prevailing during most of the year precluded navigation along the Grande Côte to the Senegal River. Together with other Serer-speaking groups, Niominka exploited the long dry season of the savanna zone to make salt by solar evaporation, which was traded in baskets made from woven palm fronds, and they prepare dried fish and oysters for storage in earthenware containers (Wright 1997, 56–58; Gamble and Hair 1999, pl. 1 after p. 312). Besides locally produced salt, dried fish, and dried mollusks, Niominka and Serer middlemen traded kola, malaguetta pepper, and other commodities obtained from the Banyun-Bak commercial network. Much of Niominka trade was conducted with Mandinka states along the Gambia River, extending from Niumi at the river mouth to Wuli and Cantora at the head of navigation.

Lançados, Tangomaos, Luso-Africans, and Grumetes

When Portuguese arrived in western Africa, they were constrained to accommodate to the landlord-stranger reciprocities that had evolved over centuries regarding traders, hunters, migrants, and other travelers. Portuguese had to practice different modes of barter commerce; settle ashore and travel only where their hosts gave permission; pay tolls, taxes, and gifts; and submit disputes to African judicial processes, or *palavers* (from the Portuguese *palavra,* meaning word or speech—a loanword adopted by numerous West African groups). Many of the goods that Portuguese and other Europeans carried to western Africa (like those transported across the Sahara) were luxuries, such as the horses, wines, spirits, and textiles that only elites and their retinues could afford. Other European imports included iron bars and copper rods, which African smiths fashioned into tools and weapons according to their clients' preferences, and iron cooking pots, which, along with copper and brass basins, were used for salt making. In return, Portuguese obtained slaves, gold, ivory, malaguetta pepper, beeswax, animal pelts, and other tropical products, as well as millet, rice, livestock, and other provisions (Brooks 1993b, chap. 7).

The lançados, the Portuguese men who lived in African communities, were aptly named, for the term *lançado* came from the Portuguese *se-lançar* (throw oneself), which may be freely translated as "casting one's lot" among African societies. Following long-standing landlord-stranger practices, community leaders guaranteed the lançados' personal safety and security of possessions, assisted them in commercial exchanges, and otherwise promoted mutual interests. Landlords refused to rent lançados more land than needed for dwellings and stores; this restriction was in accord with western African practices, whereby societies allocated rights to land *use*, not ownership. Denial of land for cultivation rendered lançados dependent on the landlords for food supplies, a factor of no small consequence in times of disagreement and dispute. Lançados and European slavers who subsequently resided in western Africa were disadvantaged vis-à-vis African competitors by expenses incurred in maintaining slaves awaiting shipment; African traders put slaves to work cultivating food for their own subsistence and engaging in weaving and other crafts (Rodney 1970, 204; Curtin 1975, 170; Wright 1976, 181; Brooks 1993b, 137).

By the close of the fifteenth century, some lançados came to be known as *tangomaos,* which in Portuguese and Luso-African usage connoted renegades or outcasts, as in individuals who had forsaken European ways. Tangomaos manifestly found it to their advantage to integrate their lives with Africans even more closely than did lançados, for they wore African garments and protective amulets, underwent circumcision and scarification, participated in African rituals such as divination, and otherwise adopted African lifeways. Tangomaos were principally (if not exclusively) associated with Biafada-Sapi traders. The origin of their designation would seem to be derived from *tangomaas,* the Temne/Sapi name for the priestly lineage in charge of the shrines of the Simo society that controlled the highly remunerative Serra Leoa kola trade. It appears that lançados were inducted into the Simo power association for reasons of mutual advantage, including the shared use of European sailing craft that could transport large amounts of kola, iron, and other cargoes. Some accounts use the words *lançado* and *tangomao* interchangeably, reflecting the fact that both groups were integrated into African communities, relied on their hosts for security of persons and property, and, during frequent periods of illness, depended on nursing by African wives and treatments by African medical practitioners (Brásio 1968, 4:575–76; Hair 1967b, 54; Silva 1970; Carreira 1972, 47–62; Rema 1982, 69–73; Brooks 1993b, 191–92). Indubitably, many social and cultural influences combined in the making of the Luso-African heritage.

One of the most important privileges accorded resident strangers, European as well as African, was that of consorting with local women—usually women who were related to or dependents of influential persons in the communities who sought to derive additional advantages from affiliations with strangers. Ignorant as they were of African ways, lançados found women invaluable companions as interpreters of languages and cultures and as collaborators in commercial exchanges. African women took advantage of these circumstances for their own benefit no less than that of their male relatives, with the consequence that they came to exercise a crucial role as commercial intermediaries and culture brokers between African societies and lançados, a role that was subsequently exploited by their Luso-African children.

Luso-Africans represented a new and unprecedented element in western African societies (Boulègue 1972 and 1989; Brooks 1980a and 1993b; Mark 1995, 1996, and 1999; Wright 1997, 87–91; Horta 2000). In social and cultural terms, Luso-Africans were much more African than Portuguese, hence, the short prefix *Luso* (and *Eur* in the word *Eurafrican*) serves to communicate the proportionately much smaller European cultural heritage of individuals raised by African or Luso-African mothers in African milieus. Living in African cultures and possessing some knowledge of European ways (more or less, depending on circumstances), Luso-Africans had unique potential to function as commercial and cultural intermediaries. Nonetheless, their opportunities and range of possibilities were largely determined by their mothers' societies—the extent to which they inherited their mothers' social ranking, rights to land use, and other prerogatives. In regard to such matters, however, there were significant differences between stratified and acephalous societies.

Stratified societies with patrilineal or bilateral descent systems (for example, the Mandinka, Wolof, and Serer states of Senegambia) systematically excluded Portuguese and Luso-Africans from access to marriage partners of free status who might provide them or their descendants with claims to leadership positions. Luso-Africans were not allocated land to cultivate, and they were dependent on landlords for their food and water. Of surpassing importance, Luso-African children were denied admission to the "bush schools" controlled by the power associations that educated youths and supervised the circumcisions and clitoridectomies that bestowed adult status. Consequently, Luso-Africans were excluded from membership in age grades, and they were disdained as marriage partners by elites and members of nyamakalaw groups. Numerous Europeans derisively recorded Luso-Africans' passionate assertions that they were "whites," "Portuguese," and "Christians." These were the litanies of social outcasts—persons who could not claim to be Africans as defined by kinship, membership in power associations, participation in community activities, rights to land use, and other attributes of free persons. Luso-Africans living in stratified societies had no option other than to engage in trade, knowing that whatever wealth or possessions they might acquire could not be inherited by their children—children whose mothers were fellow Luso-Africans or slaves—but would be arrogated by rulers and other elites.

Circumstances were considerably different in acephalous African societies south of the Gambia River. Elders and community leaders among the Banyun, Papel, Biafada, and other societies permitted lançados to marry members of their families. Access to European goods enabled African women to expand their commercial activities from local markets to regional places of trade. When lançados became incapacitated by illnesses, died, or returned to Europe or Cabo Verde, wives were not dispossessed and could continue to trade. In some societies, women parlayed commercial success into leadership roles, some even founding their own trading settlements. In addition, Luso-African children generally shared the same upbringing and opportunities as other children—attending bush schools, experiencing rites of passage, and becoming members of the Simo, Poro, Sande, and Bundu power associations. On becoming adults, Luso-Africans might participate in their parents' commercial undertakings, using to advantage their kinship affiliations and memberships in power associations, or they might follow the same lifeways as their African peers, intermarry with them, and "disappear" into their societies.

Indispensable to the prosecution of Portuguese and Luso-African commerce were the grumetes hired for their skills as sailors and trade intermediaries and to assist with such ancillary tasks as building and repairing boats (Nardin 1966). *Grumete* is the Portuguese variant of a word in medieval European languages designating a cabin boy or apprentice seaman. African seafarers were prized for their intimate knowledge of winds, tides, currents, reefs, bars at river mouths, and the labyrinths of interconnecting rivers, marigots, and mangrove swamps. Grumetes' linguistic abilities, kinship affiliations, and memberships in power associations made them invaluable in prosecuting commerce. They were recruited from many groups, notably, the Lébou, Niominka, Papel, and Biafada. They served varying lengths of time and were paid in trade goods. Some were the sons of rulers and elites, sent to work for Portuguese or Luso-Africans as apprentices in order to learn to navigate European-type vessels and gain commercial experience. Other grumetes were domestic slaves hired out by their owners.

André Alvares de Almada, a Cabo Verdean who traded in western Africa during the 1560s and 1570s, testified to the contributions made by grumetes: "These blacks, especially the Banyun, are very quick to learn. Both men and women work for our people, and they travel with them to the other rivers as *grumetes* (native assistants), to earn money, as confidently as if they had been born and brought up among us in full security (of life and liberty)" (Hair 1984a, 88). By contrast, Almada used the word *tangomao* in describing Biafada women affiliated with lançados: "Among these blacks there are many who can speak our Portuguese language. They dress as we do, as do many black women of the advanced kind, known as *tangomas,* because they serve the [lançados] who go to these parts. These blacks, men and women, go with the [lançados] from one river to another, and to Santiago Island and other places. But our people do not take them without first obtaining permission from their fathers or their uncles, their fathers' brothers (Hair 1984a, 107). Almada was unique in employing the term *tangomaos* for women as well as men.

Grumetes resided at or near the lançados' and Luso-Africans' dwellings in African communities and at the factories, forts, and other places of trade that developed over the centuries. Little information is available concerning their lives. Were grumetes at places of trade from the same ethnic groups, or were they a mixed lot? Did their settlements comprise transient males who lived together as bachelors, or did they bring wives or marry local women? Did grumetes become more or less permanent residents in trading communities, or did they engage in regular patterns of labor migration, traveling back and forth to their home villages? Did many grumetes capitalize on their experiences to become traders in their own right? To what extent did grumetes or their children marry with Luso-Africans? Did Luso-Africans who became grumetes become incorporated into the African societies of fellow grumetes, or were they excluded?

Grumetes contributed significantly to a number of "Luso-African" social and cultural attributes. Perhaps most important was the development and spread of Crioulo, the language combining elements of Portuguese, West Atlantic, and Mande languages that rapidly became established as a lingua franca for coastwise and riverine traders in Senegambia and along the Upper Guinea Coast and served as the principal language of the inhabitants of the Cabo Verde archipelago (W. Wilson 1962; Scantamburlo 1999, 19–32). Grumetes, most likely Niominka with experience aboard Portuguese caravels and small craft, developed the pirogue, a composite craft derived from both African and Portuguese maritime traditions that transformed Senegambian seafaring.

Just as lançados and tangomaos living among African societies adapted to their ways, grumetes shared some of the attributes of the Portuguese and Luso-Africans who employed them. They commonly wore European-style shirts and trousers. They employed many Portuguese and Luso-African skills and practices, including building and repairing ships as well as constructing and furnishing dwellings, and adopted their food preferences and modes of preparation—all of which they helped to diffuse widely across western Africa.

Transmutations of Commercial Networks

Lançados and their descendants became increasingly associated in commerce and kinship affiliations with groups affiliated with the Banyun-Bak and Biafada-Sapi trade networks. During the fifteenth century, the Banyun of Buguendo permitted lançados to trade and settle at the head of the two marigots along the north bank of the Cacheu River. Such was the importance of São Domingos, as Buguendo's entrepôt was named in honor of the founder of the Dominican Order, that lançados titled the lower Cacheu River the Rio de São Domingos; the river upstream past the two tributaries leading to Buguendo (the Rio Grande de São Domingos and the Rio Pequeno de São Domingos) was accorded a different name, Rio de Farim, referring to the Mandinka trading community at the head of navigation some 155 kilometers upriver. Biafada likewise allowed lançados to settle at Guinala and several other communities along the Grande River.

Reside ashore they might, but for many years, lançados were not permitted by the Banyun or Biafada to venture inland. Similarly, Mandinka living at the heads of navigation of the Cacheu and Geba Rivers welcomed visitors during the trading season but denied them access to caravan routes. This was also the practice with Banyun and Mandinka along the Gambia River, with Niominka, Serer, and Wolof in Senegambia, and with groups belonging to the Biafada-Sapi trade network.

Living and working within these restrictions just as their husbands did, the wives of the lançados and Luso-Africans transformed previous commercial patterns. Little is known concerning women's participation in commerce prior to the arrival of the Portuguese. We do know, however, that women were involved in marketing activities—selling foods, condiments, medicines, pottery, and other products they had made. Seemingly, women in the stratified societies north of the Gambia River were restricted to their own communities, but those in the matrilineal acephalous societies south of the Gambia River participated in markets held in neighboring villages on different days, including the markets of other ethnic groups. It was women in acephalous societies who, from the outset, took advantage of opportunities that came with the arrival of the lançados.

Portuguese sources attest that Biafada and Banyun women associated with lançados became extensively involved in regional trade. As quoted previously, André Alvares de Almada observed that Biafada women "of the advanced kind, known as *tangomas*" dressed in Portuguese fashion and accompanied lançados from one river to another, to São Tiago Island, and to other places, adding that the lançados first obtained the permission of the women's fathers or paternal uncles (Hair 1984a, 107). Fr. Manuel Alvares was informed that Banyun women traveled from market to market earning their livelihoods (Hair 1990, pt. 1, chap. 7: 3). Banyun territory was the commercial arena of some of the prominent women entrepreneurs that will be mentioned in the chapters that follow.

Along the Grande River, lançados lodged with Biafada landlords in large compounds. The weekly market in Guinala reputedly attracted more than twelve thousand people (Hair 1984a, 110). André Donelha, a Cabo Verdean who traded in western Africa during the 1570s and 1580s, characterized the Grande River as the best slaving district in Guinea, furnishing "nearly 3,000 captives annually, plus gold, wax, ivory, and sometimes amber and other goods" (Mota and Hair 1977, 174–75). Donelha's estimate of slave exports was surely inflated, but his opinion of the commercial importance of the Grande River was endorsed by Francisco de Andrade, the sargento-mor (sergeant-major) of Cabo Verde, in his report to King Philip II in January 1582. Andrade urged construction of a fort to offer protection against French raiders who had pillaged trading vessels in the river during the previous two years, to secure traders' property and persons against "robberies and insults" by local Africans, and to safeguard a proposed church and its priests (Brásio 1964, 3:105). Following a visit by the governor of Cabo Verde in 1574, the ruler of Guinala permitted the erection of a large cross, after which the anchorage was known as Porto da Cruz or Porto da Santa Cruz. A church was built in the 1580s (Mota and Hair 1977, 350–55).

According to Almada and Donelha, except for the Nunez River where slaves, ivory, gold, and cakes of indigo dye were obtained, Cabo Verdean vessels bypassed the coast between the Nunez River and the Iles de Los, leaving commerce in the Cacine, Compony, and lesser rivers to Biafada-Sapi traders and tangomaos using small craft. Two brothers from São Tomé, Bento and Jordão Correira da Silva, were settled along the Pongo River, apart from the Cabo Verdean trade network. According to Almada, their families and retainers, together with those of relatives, friends, and descendants, constituted a community of nearly five hundred persons ruling over some three thousand Africans (Hair 1984a, 132).

Almada's description of landlord-stranger reciprocities along the Pongo River delineated long-standing accommodations among Sapi elites that were applied to lançados:

> The custom of these blacks is that when people come to their houses, either to stay or to visit, the first thing they do on their arrival to make them comfortable, before discussing the reasons for their coming, is to take them into a hut and give them hot water in which to wash themselves. After washing and changing their dress, the visitors come to the apartment where the master of the house is. They sit down and after the normal forms of polite greeting employed here state the reason for the visit. If the visitor has to spend several days in the place, the master of the house orders all his wives to appear, from whom he demands that the guest should choose the one who seems to him the best, and the wife who is selected is obliged to serve him all the time he stays there, in all manner of service, so that the guest will have no excuse to take any of the other wives, and for this reason he is given this particular one of his choice. And if it comes about that he takes any of the others, by their laws he is obliged to forfeit the goods he has brought. After this, no matter where he goes, each time he returns to the house this woman is under the same obligation as before to serve him. (In return) the obligation of the guest to the woman supplied him, to keep her content, is to give her clothes, that is, a length of cotton cloth, or some wraps, and a span of white India cloth or cotton cloth for a sash. The children the Sapes get by the wives they give to their guests are considered children of the master of the house, like the other children, but if one happens to be begotten by a white, he gives it to the father who takes it away. (Hair 1984a, 133–34)

Possibly, Almada overgeneralized, and "wives" may have included members of a host's extended kinship affiliations and domestic slaves. Such was implicit in the accounts of Fr. Manuel Alvares and Francisco de Lemos Coelho, which will be quoted later in this chapter.

Portuguese navigators described "Serra Leoa" as the coast extending from the Iles de Los in the north to Cape Mount in the south. The Iles de Los were havens for mariners and entrepôts for trade. The two principal islands provided safe anchorage for seamen during storms, and there was excellent springwater on several of the islands and abundant fish in the surrounding waters (Map 2.1 insert). The Portuguese name for the small archipelago derived from the Baga practice of bringing wooden "idols" to the rice fields they cultivated on the islands during the rainy season to ensure good harvests (Brooks 1993b, 278–79; Mouser 1996, 77–82).

The Kolente River south of the Iles de Los was a major place of trade for kola, and tangomaos co-opted by the Simo power association participated in a highly remunerative coastwise trade using sail-driven vessels to transport kola, iron, and other commodities to the Grande, Geba, and Gambia Rivers. Mande caravans had previously brought gold, cotton textiles, and iron to the Kolente River to barter for kola, salt, and malaguetta pepper, and with the inauguration of Portuguese trade, Mande brought slaves and iron bars in growing quantities. As iron smelting in Senegambia (but not iron working) was progressively curtailed during the c. 1100–c. 1500 dry period, Mande smiths expanded iron production in the virgin woodlands of the Futa Jallon massif. Some of the iron was transported to markets overland, and some was moved in dugouts and sailing vessels via the Biafada-Sapi-tangomao network. The ongoing exploitation of Futa Jallon's timber resources for charcoal making opened the wilderness for Mande cultivators and Fula herders with ndama cattle. Although Fula migrations southward into Futa Jallon were probably insignificant during the c. 1500–c. 1630 wet period, Fula cattle drives into the massif increased during the droughts that desiccated northern pastures in the c. 1630–c. 1860 dry period that followed (Mota 1969a; Brooks 1993b, 174, 279–80).

Mariners engaged in coastwise commerce in Serra Leoa at the time of kola harvest or during other trading visits were offered concubines for the duration of their stay, as was customary among male elites when subordinate rulers, friends, and relatives visited (Hair 1990, pt. 2, chap. 8: 5). Fr. Manuel Alvares, who spent a decade evangelizing African groups neighboring the Sierra Leone estuary while exhorting lançados to behave like Christians, fulminated against the "abominable practice of *cabondos,* women of a nefarious kind"—condemning women for what both he and Almada, in the passage cited earlier, clearly identified as a male-controlled practice that entailed obligations as well as privileges.

> [A lançado] goes to one of their villages to deal in cola, rice, etc. He selects his host, who parades in front of the trader his whole household of women/wives and tells him to chose one. If he says that he does not want a woman, no more happens and this puts a stop to the thing. But what man does, and

> shall we praise him if he does? If he wants a woman, he is given one, for all purposes; and they are content to accept this, out of self-interest. For apart from the normal expenses, so long as the trade goes on with the woman's parents and relatives, and until he leaves, the poor "son-in-law" pays up because he clothes the "father-in-law" and pays very steeply for these devilish arrangements. If it happens that after saying he does not want a woman the guest takes one from a neighbour, they attack and rob him. And if after taking one he goes off with another of those he was shown, his own woman reports him. All the children that wives of these panders have by those men to whom their husbands give them are accepted by the husbands as their own, without any fuss. Since profit is made by being a pander, men prize the role, to the extent that they will go long journeys and endure great hardships (? to offer their wives). Such fathers do girls here have, etc. (Hair 1990, pt. 2, chap. 4: 4)

The estuary of the Sierra Leone River is the finest harbor in western Africa, and Temne landlords encouraged lançado commerce involving the same commodities as in the Kolente River. Supernatural sanctions ensured fulfillment of agreements and debt collection by means comparable to the *hatichira* ceremony associated with the Banyun commercial network. Father Alvares explained the powers of the "idol Obei":

> [Obei] is a bundle of twigs called *malilas* here, fastened together with *matampa.* The bundle is placed on some little forked sticks, with *macone* bark underneath, and a firebrand soaked in oil is placed on the ground. This idol is employed to collect debts due to creditors, and masters use it to recover slaves who have fled from them. The person who is owed a debt, or whose slave is in someone else's possession, comes to the priest in charge of the rite, and explains the case to him. He replies: "Very well, I will communicate it to the devils. Lift the brand and put it underneath." If the brand goes out, the *bexerin* says: "You will recover your black (slave) or your debt, since the devil favours you." If the bundle falls apart through the cord snapping, they consider the matter entirely resolved: either the debt will be paid or the debtor will die. Should the debtor fall ill, or an accident happen to him, he instantly rushes to pay. If he scorns the rite, and afterwards dies, they consider that his death is entirely due to this; and no more is said about the debt, which is not sought from the heir. They say that what is given to the devil cannot be recovered without great peril, and they act accordingly. This rite is called *cenar.* (Hair 1990, pt. 2, chap. 5: 12)

Some of the poorest Cabo Verdeans traded in the Sherbro River, where they could make considerable profits with little capital. Portuguese and other European shipmasters generally bypassed the Sherbro area, daunted by the shoal waters and dangerous reefs off Cape Ann and by the hostility of Bullom determined to protect their middleman role in gold trade with Mande groups in the interior. Instead, European vessels sailed to Cape Mount to engage in the highly remunerative pepper trade along the Malaguetta Coast (Hair 1984a, 143, 147; Brooks 1993b, 280–81).

An abiding concern of lançados and their Luso-African descendants was that landlords would confiscate the possessions of deceased traders. This "evil custom," as the Cabo Verdean André Alvares de Almada termed it, was practiced everywhere but along the Cacheu River. "In all other places, if our people do not take refuge at sea when they are ill, so as to die aboard their ships, and instead die on the land, the kings of the place inherit all their property" (Hair 1984a, 117). This policy of landlords would be of crucial importance in the lives of Luso-Africans in many places of western Africa for generations to come, for it precluded their children from inheriting their property. This liability, together with preemptory demands for gifts by predatory elites, dissipated Luso-Africans' earnings and made them dependent on visiting traders for goods advanced on credit. Few were able to overcome these handicaps and function as independent traders, and fewer still contrived to pass on wealth and possessions to their descendants. Denied access to cultivable land, security of possessions, and rights of inheritance, Portuguese and Luso-Africans were marginalized, unable either to integrate fully into African communities or to follow European social and cultural practices.

Cabo Verdean–Lançado Networks

Beginning with the earliest settlements in the 1460s, the Cabo Verde archipelago served as the advance base for Portuguese and lançado trade with Senegambia and the Upper Guinea Coast (Map 1.6). Two of the largest islands, São Tiago and Fogo, received sufficient rainfall to support plantation agriculture; consequently, captives were brought in growing numbers from western Africa to cultivate sugar, cotton, indigo, tobacco, and other crops and to herd livestock on these and other islands where mountainous terrain or sparse rainfall precluded cultivation. The arid islands of Sal, Boa Vista, and Maio could supply unlimited quantities of salt for trade with western Africa and with vessels bound for numerous Atlantic ports. The settlement of Ribeira Grande on São

Tiago became the principal port for trade with western Africa and the reexport of slaves to the Americas (Duncan 1972, 174–94; Torrão 1995).

Cabo Verde–based Portuguese and, increasingly, Cabo Verde–born Luso-Africans carried on a larger and larger proportion of Portuguese commerce with western Africa, which they called the "Rios de Guiné do Cabo Verde" in appreciation of the rivers that gave access to the commerce of the vast hinterland. Children born in the archipelago acquired immunities and resistance to malaria, dysenteries, and other diseases endemic in western Africa. No less advantageous, they learned Crioulo, the language of the islands and the lingua franca that expedited the commerce of Senegambia and the Upper Guinea Coast. Cabo Verdeans likewise acquired invaluable knowledge of numerous western Africa languages, social institutions, and cultural practices from parents and relatives and also from captives brought to the archipelago for use in the islands and for resale and shipment to the Americas. Many men born in Cabo Verde visited western Africa for extended periods as traders, seamen, soldiers, government officials, and priests, and those returning to the archipelago often brought families and dependents with them. The evolution of Luso-African social and cultural attributes derived from the ongoing, two-way flow of people between western Africa and the Cabo Verde archipelago (Brooks 1993b, chap. 8).

By the 1520s and perhaps decades earlier, Portuguese and Cabo Verdean mariners using sail-driven craft began to transform preexisting commercial networks. Vessels from the island of São Tiago transported salt, cotton cloth, and other commodities to the Kolente River and other markets in Serra Leoa, anticipating the kola harvest that began in December. The changes in wind patterns and ocean currents during the rainy season that started in April enabled seamen to sail north to markets in Senegambia and the Guinea-Bissau region to barter cargoes for slaves, before returning to the Cabo Verde archipelago. Writing of his experiences in the 1560s and 1570s, Almada, a São Tiago–born Luso-African, characterized the Cacheu and the Grande as the two leading rivers for commerce in western Africa (Hair 1984a, 106). These were, respectively, the chief entrepôts of the Banyun-Bak and Biafada-Sapi networks, which had incorporated numerous lançados and Luso-Africans by that time.

The most important trading centers along the Petite Côte of Senegambia were Rufisque, Portudal, and Joal (Map 2.4). Rufisque (from the Portuguese *Rio Fresco,* meaning freshwater stream) was the principal port of the Wolof state of Cayor. Portudal, or Porto de Ale (port of Ale, the name of a former ruler [Hair 1990, pt. 1, chap. 4: 1; cf. Boulègue 1989, 34 n. 12]), was the chief place of trade of the Serer state of Baol. Joal was the coastal entrepôt for the Serer state of Siin, which also had trading outlets via the Sine and Saloum Rivers. Ponta do Sereno (calm roadstead), located along the coast between Portudal and Joal, marked the frontier between Baol and Siin. Niominka controlled the estuary of the Sine and Saloum Rivers to the exclusion of rivals. The state of Saluum encompassed a large territory that bordered Siin to the west and extended a considerable distance along the north bank of the Gambia River. Lançados residing along the Petite Côte were under the control of *alcaides* (governors), who supervised trade and collected substantial tolls from vessels and tribute for rulers (Brooks 1993b, 204–8).

On arriving from Europe, vessels generally anchored in the roadstead between Gorée Island and the Cape Verde peninsula (in the outer and inner harbors of modern-day Dakar). Anchorage payments were due to the alcaide appointed by the ruler of Cayor. No trade was permitted, but vessels could obtain provisions and water, and the small cove on Gorée was used to assemble small craft brought from Europe and to careen vessels for repair. Chaloupes, yachts, and pinnaces were used to trade at Portudal, Joal, and other places along the Petite Côte with shallow anchorages. The rulers of Cayor, Baol, and Siin were notorious for "inheriting" the property of deceased traders. The situation in Saluum was an exception, and in Almada's time, Saluum was characterized by lançados as the "safest country on this coast." Successive rulers so persistently cautioned against harming lançados that their subjects called them (possibly derisively) "Father of the Whites" (Mota and Hair 1977, 128–31; Hair 1984a, 31).

Lançados and Luso-Africans who settled along the Petite Côte were the subject of numerous allegations of apostatizing from Christianity. Allegedly, many New Christians (*cristãos novos*)—individuals descended from Jewish families forced to convert to Christianity—left Portugal to seek their fortunes in Cabo Verde and western Africa. There was no respite from persecution: New Christians were frequently denounced and made scapegoats for the failures of government officials, as well as being condemned for reverting to Jewish practices. Persecution intensified with the arrival of Dutch competitors at the close of the sixteenth century and allegations of commercial ties between New Christians and Jews residing in Holland (Boulègue 1989, 54–57; Brooks 1993b, 159, 178–79, 185–87).

From the mid-sixteenth century forward, lançado vessels conveying kola acquired from the Biafada-Sapi trade network and Cabo Verdean vessels loaded with wine, spirits, and a variety of European merchandise carried on an expanding trade with Mandinka-ruled states along the Gambia River, in competition with the long-established Banyun trade network (Brooks 1993b, 244–50). André Donelha, a Luso-African based on São Tiago, recorded in considerable detail his experiences in trading along the Gambia River during the 1570s and

1580s. He described Kassang (Caçao), the entrepôt for the Mandinka state of Niani on the north bank, as the most important place of trade and a center for skilled artisans. Donelha's account confused rather than clarified the tangled and complex relationships between lançados, tangomaos, grumetes, and slaves, as well as the difficulties in trying to establish parentage and kinship relationships.

Donelha mentioned that "many well-known *tangomaos*" were residing at Kassang, none of whom he named. He described trading with Gaspar Vaz, a Mandinka youth who had formerly been a slave on São Tiago, owned by a tailor named Francisco Vaz. Donelha did not explain how Gaspar Vaz was freed, but the young man's success as a interpreter and broker derived from the fact that he was the nephew and heir of Kassang's *satigi* (governor). Vaz wore Muslim amulets around his neck and a rosary concealed under his Mandinka garments (Mota and Hair 1977, 146–49, 300–301 n. 255). As indicated in the chapters that follow, numerous Luso-Africans bore the surname Vaz, but information concerning kinship links is sparse.

Cabo Verdean vessels transported large quantities of kola and iron bars from Serra Leoa to the Petite Côte to barter for captives, panos, sewn garments, and beeswax. The latter was a commodity that had previously been little traded among African groups, but in response to a growing demand from European candle makers, the inhabitants of woodlands in Senegambia and the Guinea-Bissau region accelerated their collection of honeycombs from hives placed in trees to attract wild bee swarms. The beeswax was traded, and the honey was made into mead, which was consumed in great quantities at festivals. Captives purchased along the Petite Côte were transported to Cacheu, whence, during the time of the joint Spanish-Portuguese monarchy (1580–1640), Spanish vessels engaged in a burgeoning slave trade with the Americas. The panos and sewn garments were in great demand in markets in the Guinea-Bissau region and along the Upper Guinea Coast.

In fact, the demand for panos was so strong among African elites that Cabo Verdean entrepreneurs expressly sought Wolof, Mandinka, and Banyun weavers, for their societies were most renowned for the quality of their textiles. From the mid-sixteenth century on, plantation households on São Tiago and Fogo included slaves skilled in cultivating, harvesting, cleaning, carding, dyeing, spinning, and weaving cotton. Textiles manufactured in Cabo Verde were woven on African-type looms, producing narrow bands of cloth twelve to fifteen centimeters wide that were sewn together lengthwise to produce panos about two meters long and one meter wide. Most cotton thread to make panos was dyed blue or black by using indigo grown in Cabo Verde, but some was red from dyes made from orchil collected in the archipelago. Orchil is a dye-producing lichen that grows on cloud-moistened peaks, particularly those on São Tiago, Fogo, and Brava; depending on processing, orchil yields blue, violet, purple, and scarlet dyes (Duncan 1972, 19–21, 191–92). Orchil remained a royal monopoly through the nineteenth century, and the list of the names of those who held the privilege of exporting it to Portugal constitutes a virtually infallible guide to identifying persons of wealth and influence in the archipelago at a given time.

Weavers in Cabo Verde reproduced traditional western African patterns, introduced Portuguese motifs (such as the square blunt cross that was the emblem of the Order of Christ), and created new designs. Some of the most celebrated and expensive panos were produced by interweaving cotton thread with silk and worsted wool yarns imported from Europe (Carreira 1968). During the c. 1630–c. 1860 dry period, when Senegambia was afflicted by sporadic droughts, cloth production there greatly declined, enabling Cabo Verdean panos to supplant Senegambian panos as the principal textiles traded in coastwise commerce.

Panos manufactured in Cabo Verde were greatly esteemed by African rulers and elites, and for centuries, they commanded premium prices in competition with cloth from Europe and India. Cabo Verdean panos set the standard for ceremonial occasions, bridewealth exchanges, and funeral shrouds—status markers for the dead and for the living. Africans' insistence that panos be included in the bartering assortment of major exchanges, particularly for captives, was a factor of inestimable importance in the survival of Cabo Verdean and Luso-African traders in western Africa. Panos were virtually the only manufacture they could sell advantageously in competition with European traders, who possessed vastly greater resources and varieties of commodities. Indeed, Europeans found they had to acquire Cabo Verdean panos in order to meet the African traders' demands that some be included in their assortments of trade goods. Panos long served as currency in both the archipelago and western Africa, and they were used by the impecunious government to pay the salaries of officers and soldiers stationed in Guinea (Carreira 1968; Duncan 1972, 193, 219–20; Moraes 1973, 72; Meintel 1984, 43–44).

Serra Leoa and the Mani-Sumba Conquests

Commerce in Serra Leoa was transformed during the second half of the sixteenth century by the Mani-Sumba invasions (Map 2.6). Mobilized by leaders of the Poro power association, Mani-Sumba raiders ruthlessly pillaged West Atlantic–

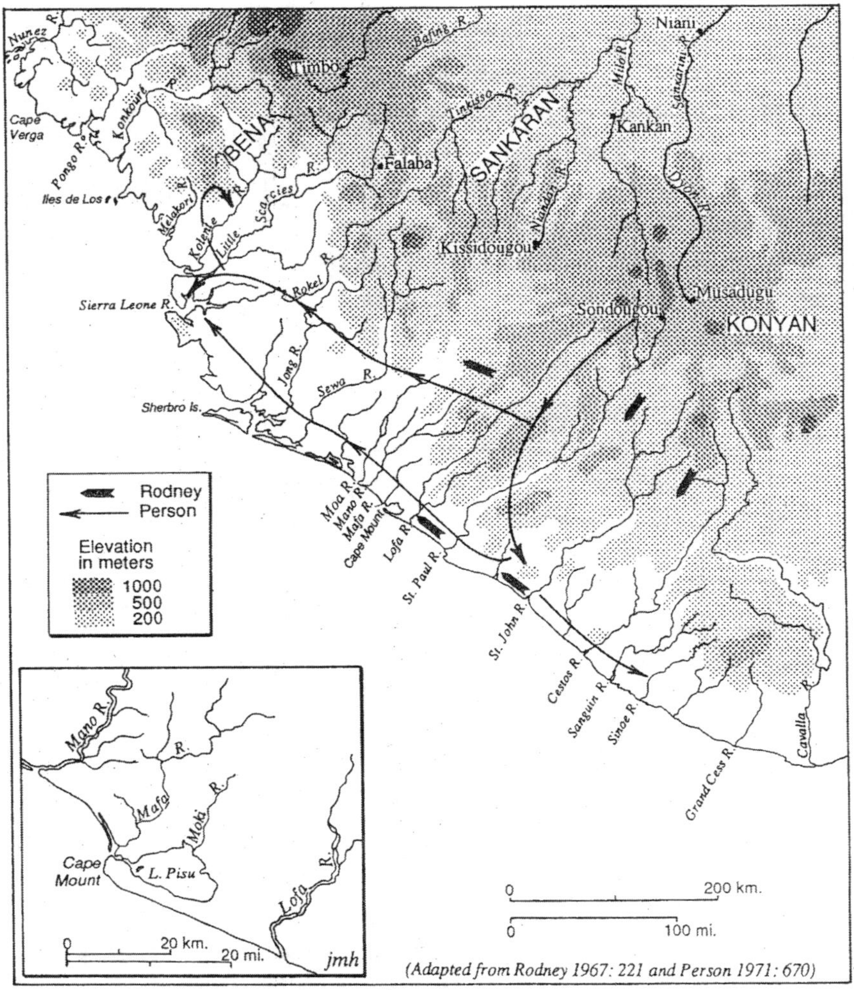

Map 2.6 Mani and Mani-Sumba conquests

speaking groups as far north as Cape Verga before consolidating their control over the littoral from the Kalum peninsula southward. Lançados were not spared—notably, João Afonso, reputed to be the richest (and most arrogant) of all, whose establishment along the Kolente River was destroyed (Hair 1990, pt. 2, chap. 9: 2–5). Portuguese, Cabo Verdean, and Luso-African vessels shadowed the marauding groups of Mani-Sumba, purchasing numerous captives. Following their conquests, the Poro leaders of the Mani-Sumba founded states incorporating conquered Bullom/Sherbro, Temne, and Baga groups (Map 2.7). The ruler

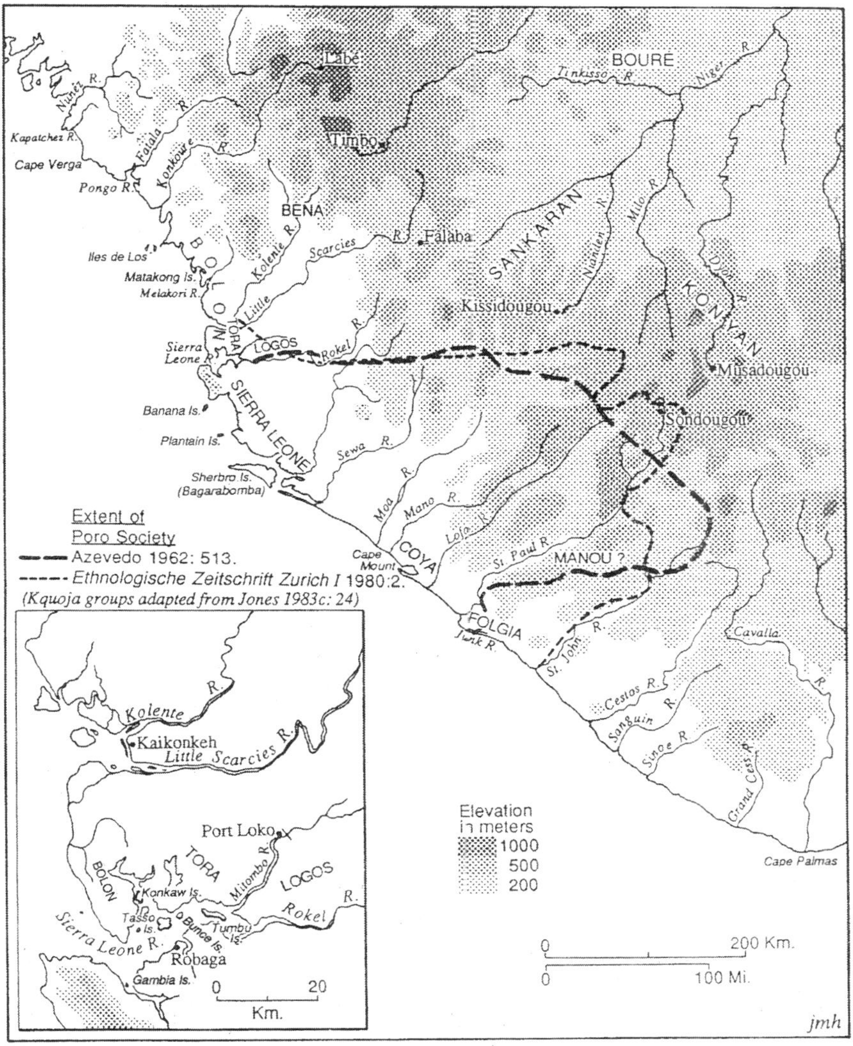

Map 2.7 The era of Mani-Sumba overlords

of the Coya/Kquoja state at Cape Mount was overlord of four states along the Serra Leoa littoral that controlled seaboard and riverine commerce as far north as the Iles de Los until the eighteenth century. During the sixteenth and seventeenth centuries, Port Loko on the Mitombo tributary of the Sierra Leone estuary was a major place of trade for lançados and Luso-Africans (Map 2.7 insert).

One of the integrative elements of the Mani-Sumba state system was a "university" maintained by the Poro society, to which youths were sent. Fr. Alvares recorded what little he learned about this university after protracted inquiries:

> The "University" is . . . beyond Cape Mount. The pupils spend four years on their training; during this time they do not carry arms or inflict wounds. All is peaceful; as the teaching is directed towards keeping the peace, so it suits them to have it thus. These false religions carry the sign which distinguishes them from others on their backs, which they have scored with certain marks resembling large warts. Anyone who touches them on this place incurs the penalty ordained by their laws, to avoid which there is no connection or favour more effective than money. And so they say that the *poro* [is?] nobody—the wick has no pedigree. It keeps everything here peaceful and free from common murders and affrays. The professed (members) have their own private idol. And since this group keeps itself to itself, their superstitious acts are very secret, that is, their deliberations, their burials, and their wakes or private obsequies of the dead which those who profess other forms of superstition cannot attend. (Hair 1990, single chap. B: 1)

The Mani-Sumba states declined and fragmented during the eighteenth century, but there is evidence that a Poro university continued to function into the nineteenth century (Bennett and Brooks 1965, 273–74).

The shattering of Bullom/Sherbro societies during the Mani-Sumba conquests enabled Mande traders to extend their caravan routes to the littoral, where they engaged in direct trade with Europeans and Luso-Africans, promoted the diffusion of Mande social and cultural patterns among coastal groups, and introduced the practice of Islam (Brooks 1993b, 286–303). One change of commercial patterns introduced during the Mani-Sumba conquests was the practice known as *Quelala.*

> [Quelala] has its own particular idol and is peculiar to the Manes and Boulons. Anyone touching the nose of a man belonging to the sect incurs a fine by the rules. Some of the true *lançados* sometimes treat these people abusively, in order to obtain debts from parties because they serve as executors of debts. So it happened with one Simão Vaz, a native of Santarem, who said to Tora that if he did not make N. pay what he owed him, it/he was not *Quelala.* The king did his best to see that his guest was satisfied; the latter then contributed not only to rewarding it (? *Quelala*) but also to the penalty for the affront. (Hair 1990, single chap. B: 2)

Quelala clearly offered lançados and Luso-Africans a means of collecting debts and enforcing obligations comparable to the Banyun hatichira—which may likewise have derived from Mande origins.

Tangomaos "disappeared" from records during the seventeenth century, presumably as a consequence of the Mani-Sumba conquests of West Atlantic groups that transformed the Serra Leoa littoral. Poro supplanted Simo, and the Mande-dominated Mani-Sumba states imposed restrictions on lançados and Luso-Africans like those imposed in the stratified states in Senegambia. Possibly, the treatment of visitors and resident traders only gradually changed in Temne, Bullom, and other communities where Luso-Africans had traded and established kinship affiliations over a number of generations. Meanwhile, growing numbers of Mande and Fula traders coming from the interior spread Islam among coastal groups, and the accelerating growth of the Atlantic slave trade affected all the peoples of Serra Leoa.

Chapter 3
Portuguese, Luso-Africans, and European Competitors

> Let us proffer some advice (on how to behave in Guinea). Always act with courtesy, otherwise all will be lost.
>
> —Alvares c. 1615 (Hair 1990, chap. 9: 4)

> Whensover the [Luso-African] husband, father, or maister of the familie dies, if hee be of any worth, the King seizeth upon what hee hath, without respect, either to wife, children, or servant, . . . whereby we finde in some those few places we trade with them, poore distressed children left, who as it were exposed to the charitie of the country.
>
> —Jobson 1623 (Gamble and Hair 1999, 98)

Portugal's commerce with western Africa, along with its global trade network, became vulnerable to European rivals after the young and impetuous King Don Sebastian undertook a disastrous "crusade" in Morocco. The king died in the catastrophic battle of Al-Ksar-al-Kebir, as did thousands in his army, and the victorious Moroccans exacted exorbitant ransoms for survivors. Don Sebastian died childless, enabling Philip II of Spain to claim the throne and subordinate Portugal in a joint monarchy that lasted from 1580 to 1640. During Portugal's "captivity" by Spain, Spain's enemies became Portugal's enemies as well. French, English, and Dutch military forces and merchant adventurers mounted a sustained assault on Portugal's maritime networks and places of trade in western Africa and elsewhere around the globe. Senegambia was closest to Europe, and from the 1580s forward, Portuguese, Cabo Verdeans, Luso-Africans, and Spanish trading along the Petite Côte were increasingly challenged by French, Dutch, and English vessels that brought iron bars, spirits, European cloth, hardware, and a variety of other manufactures to barter for dried and salted cowhides, wax, and gold. But with the exception of a few buccaneers, English vessels did not transport cargoes of slaves to the Americas until the capture of Spanish plantation colonies during the early decades of the seventeenth century.

Cacheu: A Luso-African Entrepôt at the Nexus of the Biafada-Sapi and Banyun-Bak Trade Networks

Until the 1580s, lançado commerce along the Cacheu River was concentrated on the Banyun traders of Buguendo via the Rio Grande de São Domingos and the Rio Pequeno de São Domingos (Map 2.5). Beginning at an unrecorded time, perhaps during the 1530s or 1540s, lançados were permitted to settle among the Papel of Cacanda. In the mid-1560s and possibly earlier as well, the principal Cacanda community was more than a kilometer inland from a wharf constructed along the river, where, it seems, mariners lived aboard their vessels rather than ashore (Unwin 1960, 85; Hair 1970a, 6). Diola were also involved in changing circumstances. Almada reported that acephalous Diola living between the Gambia and Cacheu Rivers refused to sell members of their own groups into the slave trade and had learned to defend themselves from Mandinka slave raiders in war craft coming from the Gambia River. Due to population increases, some Diola had crossed the Cacheu River to occupy the forest of Putam, where they had recently begun to trade slaves and cows with Papel and lançados (Hair 1984a, 61–64).

The development of commerce linking the Biafada-Sapi and Banyun-Bak trade networks by the use of sailing vessels explains why, around 1550, Cabo Verdeans rescued several shiploads of Sapi (that is, Temne and Bullom) who were endangered by the Mani-Sumba force invading northward along the coast of Serra Leoa and transported them to Cacanda. Such compassion stands in sharp contrast to the fate of other Sapi victims of the Mani, whom Cabo Verdeans opportunistically carried as captives to Cabo Verde or sold into transatlantic slavery. The Papel of Cacanda, for their part, hospitably allowed the refugees to settle in separate villages in their territory. One may confidently surmise that the Sapi who were rescued came from the Kolente River and other centers of kola and iron trade and that Sapi mariners and compradors served on Cabo Verdean vessels trading with Serra Leoa after they were settled with their families in

Cacanda. Many of the Sapi refugees became Christian converts, and some of their children were taken to São Tiago for education (Hair 1978b, 36–37). At least two such individuals who settled in São Tiago subsequently fled the island during the famine year of 1583, opportunistically joining relatives in Cacanda and Serra Leoa (Mota and Hair 1977, 108–11). By the 1590s, the ruler of the Sapi community at Cacanda was a Christian called Ventura de Siqueira who had learned to read and write while growing up on São Tiago, where he had been sent by his father. Almada noted that all the members of the community were Christians, that the babies born there were baptized, and that nightly instruction in Christian doctrine was also attended by "the more advanced blacks of the country, although they are not Christians" (Hair 1984a, 81; 1997b, 5–6).

From the mid-sixteenth century onward, French and English commerce raiders increasingly threatened Portuguese, Cabo Verdean, lançado, and African mariners and traders. The Cacheu River was early targeted for plunder by English and French mariners who had learned about western African commercial patterns from renegade Portuguese. The first and only European attempt to pillage Cacheu came at the end of November 1567, with the arrival of a flotilla commanded by the English buccaneer John Hawkins, who had previously raided the inhabitants of the Cape Verde peninsula. On November 29, Hawkins's men crossed the dangerous bar at the mouth of the river in small craft and captured a half dozen trading vessels laden with a variety of merchandise but no slaves. Afterward, they launched a 240-man attack against the Papel community located more than a kilometer inland. When the English began looting and burning dwellings, they encountered stiff resistance from hundreds of Papel, joined by dozens of lançados and seamen. The English were fortunate to escape to their vessels with losses of only a few men killed and a number wounded (Williamson 1927, 127, 152–55; Unwin 1960, 84–90; Hair 1970a, 5–10, 1970b, 209–10, and 2000a, 38–54; Blake 1977, 218).

During the 1560s and 1570s, trade across the Cacheu River at São Domingos became less profitable due to warfare between the Banyun of Buguendo and the Mande-ruled Casa state extending to the east between the Cacheu and Casamance Rivers (Mota and Hair 1977, 166–67). Mansa Tamba's reign during the 1570s and 1580s marked the apogee of the Casa state. Tamba was astute in his dealings with lançados, and during the 1580s, he persuaded some to abandon São Domingos for Sarar, a river port on a creek some twenty kilometers upriver that Casa had captured from Buguendo. Meanwhile, lançados associated with the Biafada-Sapi network began to bypass the Banyun network linking the lower reaches of the Cacheu and Gambia Rivers by carrying kola in their vessels from the Biafada state of Guinala along the Grande River to Mandinka traders along the upper Gambia River.

Following Mansa Tamba's death (c. 1582–84), the Banyun of Buguendo and Bichangor regained their former territories along the Cacheu and Casamance Rivers. When Sarar was recaptured by Banyun, some lançados returned to São Domingos; others accepted the hospitality of the Papel of Cacanda. Probably in response to Papel competition, Banyun gradually opened their overland and riverine trade routes and markets to lançados and permitted them to settle in Banyun communities. For some years, however, lançados could only enter Bichangor territory via Buguendo. When Banyun permitted trading vessels to enter the Casamance River is not recorded, but it seems it was not before 1605 (Hair 1989, bk. 4, chap. 9: 3; 1976c, 58). Cacheu had long since supplanted São Domingos as the principal entrepôt along the Cacheu River.

For many years, apparently, the Papel of Cacanda pursued a strategy of attracting lançados and Cabo Verdean trading vessels away from the Banyun of Buguendo. This was evidenced, for example, by the welcome accorded Gov. António Velho Tinoco of Cabo Verde, who visited the Cacheu River in 1574. Governor Tinoco was cordially received by the ruler of Cacanda, who spoke Portuguese. Later, he favorably compared Papel with the people of the Petite Côte, describing them as "more kindly" and "more easy-going, and more willing to have contacts with Portuguese, of whom there are many [in Cacanda]" (Mota and Hair 1977, app. 1: 346–49). Almada singled out the Cacheu River as the only locality in western Africa where rulers did not confiscate the property of deceased lançados (Hair 1984a, 117).

During this period, Papel may have supplanted Banyun as middlemen controlling the trade between the Cacheu and the Mansoa and Geba Rivers. With Buguendo distracted by its long conflict with Casa, this would have been an opportune time for Papel to curtail Banyun commercial privileges in their territories. That seems to have been the case, for Portuguese sources dating from the seventeenth century onward made no mention of Banyun traders being active south of the Cacheu River. Apparently, Papel-lançado relations were mutually satisfactory for some years and then deteriorated. Portuguese sources related that lançados were increasingly concerned about the safety of their persons and property, but they did not record any Papel grievances other than the trampling of their rice fields (Hair 1990, chap. 4: 6).

At the close of the 1580s, landlord-stranger relations escalated to a crisis, provoked by an ill-conceived scheme on the part of lançados and associated Cabo Verdeans. Sometime in 1588 or 1589, in a rash attempt to gain the upper hand, lançados devised a stratagem: their spokesman, the Cabo Verdean trader Manuel Lopes Cardoso, persuaded Chapala, the Diola (Felupe) ruler of Mata de Putam (forest of Putam) and overlord of the Papel of Cacanda, to allow the building of a stronghold along the Cacheu River to defend against European commerce raiders. Diola and Papel had reason to be concerned about protection, for French raiders were active along the coast of western Africa during the 1580s, and the principal Cacanda settlement had been pillaged by John Hawkins's raiding party two decades earlier. The same stratagem was also used contemporaneously by lançados living among the Biafada of Guinala along the Grande River, and both unsuccessful initiatives were probably encouraged by the more militant policies of the Spanish-dominated joint monarchy inaugurated in 1580.

To the surprise and outrage of Diola and Papel, once a strong stockade was constructed and cannons were mounted, lançados moved inside with their grumetes and possessions and defied their landlords. The African response to the lançados' duplicity was an ill-advised and unsuccessful attack in 1590. Forewarned by two of the "more civilized" black women, presumably Sapi refugees, the lançados and their retinues inflicted heavy losses on their besiegers during a three-day battle in 1590. The lançados celebrated their success by consecrating the settlement's church to Our Lady of Victory (Nossa Senhora do Vencimento), a name derived from an image of the Virgin copied from one in the church of Carmel in Lisbon that was brandished by the defenders during the conflict. Africans subsequently initiated safer and more sensible means of coercion. By cutting off water and food and boycotting trade, they compelled the opening of the stronghold, exacted payments in retribution, and otherwise reestablished their prerogatives as landlords (Hair 1984a, 76–77, and 1990, pt. 1, chap. 4: 1, 4–8; Mota and Hair 1977, 314–17 n. 29).

Luso-Africans and Cabo Verdeans prospered from the expanding Atlantic slave trade during the era of the joint monarchy. So did their landlords, who increased the payments demanded of residents and trading vessels. Cacheu's growth as an entrepôt derived from the fact that the Cacheu River was the nexus of four commercial networks: Biafada-Sapi, Banyun-Bak, Mande, and Cabo Verdean–lançado. The settlement was sited twenty kilometers upriver on the south bank where the river is approximately two kilometers wide, midway between the Rio Grande de São Domingos and the Rio Pequeno de São Domingos, which rivers connected the territory of the Banyun state of Buguendo on the north bank (Map 2.5). The commercial potential of the Cacheu River was diminished by dangerous and unpredictable tidal currents at the river's mouth, where the narrow channel was flanked by numerous large and small sandbanks and rock shoals that prevented the entry of vessels drawing more than three meters of water (Rouzaud 1884, 349–50, 352–53). With the advent of larger European vessels, Bissau supplanted Cacheu as the principal port for the Guinea-Bissau region, but Cacheu was the chief entrepôt in western Africa for a century or more, and it remained an important market until the nineteenth century.

Potable water, as elsewhere in western Africa, was a crucial focus of landlord-stranger relations. Except during the rainy season when water might be collected in cisterns, Cacheu's population depended on the spring-fed Bouganbor streamlet that entered the river hundreds of meters downstream from the stockade, and this source was controlled exclusively by Africans (Rodney 1965, 318; 1970, 135–36). The Diola ruler of Mata de Putam, which extended to the southwest of Cacheu, collected tribute as the principal landlord, in addition to anchorage dues from trading vessels visiting Cacheu (Hair 1985, chap. 3: 9). Lesser dues were owed the Papel ruler of Mompatas, which extended upstream from Mata de Putam. The widely traveled Portuguese Jesuit missionary Fr. Balthasar Barreira, who visited Cacheu in 1608, reported that, following the conflict in 1589–90, landlords initiated new palavers and fines as a means to punish the lançados. The ruler of Mata de Putam visited the settlement at his pleasure, claiming hospitality for himself and a large retinue—demands that could not be denied. Father Barreira asserted that the more the ruler received, the more he demanded; in fact, he took such liberties that "'one would have imagined that the Portuguese were his slaves'" (Rodney 1970, 93; cf. Hair 1990, pt. 1, chap. 5: 5–6).

Such exactions did not inhibit the growth of the lançado and Luso-African community. By the 1590s, Cacheu reportedly had seven to eight hundred Christians, including Cabo Verdeans and the Sapi refugees and their descendants. The latter group lived in a separate community with their own ruler, Ventura de Sequeira, the son of a Sapi ruler who had received instruction while living on São Tiago. When he pressed his followers to adhere more closely to the Christian practices he had learned in Cabo Verde, they rejected his leadership. He subsequently became one of the rulers along the Sierra Leone estuary, where he and his family and followers contributed to the implantation of Luso-African practices (Hair 1984a, 81; Mota and Hair 1977, 12–15, 108–111 and n. 161; Hair 1998b, 116).

Missionary priests made a significant contribution to the development of Cacheu, drawing together the several communities (Rema 1982, 75–82). By 1596, the Papel ruler of Caió, opposite Jeta Island, requested baptism and the construction of a church, and the priest residing at Cacheu asked for instructions concerning marriages between lançados and the daughters of rulers (Brásio 1964, 390–94). By 1608, Cacheu boasted two churches, and the Papel ruler was a baptized Christian (Hair 1989, document 31, p. 7). Cacheu was accorded special recognition in 1605 when it was granted a municipal charter by Philip II, an honor the inhabitants refused (Brásio 1968, 88–89; Rodney 1970, 76). Among the royal directives that could not be refused were the kings' appointments from 1614 of *capitães-mores* (commandants), who also served as *feitors* (royal factors), supervising commerce (Carreira 1984, 40). Whether by oversight or otherwise, Cacheu and other places of trade in western Africa were spared the royal *carta* (charter) of October 20, 1620, which ordered female criminals be sent to Cabo Verde instead of Brazil for the purpose of extinguishing the "mulatto race" insofar as possible (Barcellos 1899–1913, 1:210).

Missionaries also played an important role in fostering friendly relations between lançados and the Banyun of Bichangor. The development of a lançado settlement at Ziguinchor, the principal market and crossing-point on the Casamance River, was associated with Fr. João Delgado, a Jesuit priest who died there in July 1609 a few months after his arrival via Cacheu. Father Delgado's reputation for holiness was enhanced by a reputed miracle attributed to prayer at his grave (Hair 1990, pt. 1, chap. 6: 2–3, and 1989, chap. 41: 23–24; Brásio 1968, 396, 458–59; Thilmans and Moraes 1972, 12, 39 n. 52). Father Alvares, one of Delgado's colleagues, was informed that Banyun women were "keen traders" who traveled from market to market making their livelihoods. Lançados associated with the women were said to be scrupulous regarding their behavior toward the women's male relatives, but Alvares excoriated the lançados for their corrupt morals and failure to consecrate Christian marriages, "to the damnation of their own souls" (Hair 1990, pt. 1, chap. 7: 3–4). Whether the women were concerned about entering Christian unions is unknown.

In 1621, Ziguinchor was reported to have fifteen dwellings of Portuguese traders, a church and a priest, and many local Christians (Brásio 1968, 458 n. 10, 665). In the following years, Ziguinchor (a name derived from the local Iziguichos, a Banyun group [Mota 1950, 117; Roche 1976, 68]) was the principal entrepôt for Banyun and Luso-African commerce along the Casamance River and its tributaries. It is not recorded when and under what circumstances lançados were permitted to trade in river craft along the Casamance and Songrougrou Rivers, nor do we know when they were allowed to traverse the overland portage between the Songrougrou River to Vintang Creek, a tributary of the Gambia River. Banyun elites sold numerous captives, and large quantities of millet and rice grown in Bichangor and Buguendo fed Cacheu's inhabitants and provisioned trading vessels (Hair 1990, pt. 1, chap. 5: 4, chap. 6: 3). The Diola groups living along the lower reaches of the Casamance River were a persistent threat to the crews of trading vessels. Father Alvares characterized the "Falupos" and "Arriatas" as the "mortal enemies of all kinds of white men. If our ships touch their shores they plunder the goods and make the white crew their prisoners, and they sell them in those places where they normally trade for cows, goats, dogs, iron-bars and various cloths. The only thing these braves will have nothing to do with, is wine from Portugal, which they believe is the blood of their own people and hence will not drink" (Hair 1990, pt. 1, chap. 3: 11–12).

African trading craft and lançado and Cabo Verdean vessels linked Cacheu with markets along the length of western Africa, transporting kola, indigo dye, ivory, and iron bars from Serra Leoa, slaves and beeswax from the Gambia River, and slaves and cotton textiles from the Petite Côte of Senegal. In 1608, Father Barreira noted that the annual "kola fleets" dispatched from Cacheu to Serra Leoa comprised seven or more vessels each year (Hair 1976b, 51). Indigo brought to Cacheu from the Nunez River was bartered for foodstuffs needed by the trading community, with pieces of indigo cakes serving as currency for small transactions (Hair 1974b, 50). To prevent Cacheu from becoming a rival place of manufacture for textiles, when the governor of Cabo Verde learned in 1614 that several Christian women skilled in weaving panos had left Cabo Verde for Cacheu during the preceding famine years, he ordered the commander of Cacheu to return the women to São Tiago without delay (Carreira 1968, 37–38). Cacheu's inhabitants purchased beeswax and other commodities from the residents of the Cacheu River and its tributaries, but the principal commerce was the exchange of kola for slaves with Mande traders visiting Farim 135 kilometers upriver from Cacheu at the head of navigation for sailing vessels. Mande called the trading community Tubabodaga (white man's village), while lançados named it Farim for their landlord, the *farim* (governor) of Birassu, ruler of one of the states of the Kaabu Empire that controlled the territory between the upper Cacheu and upper Casamance Rivers. Lançados, Luso-Africans, and grumetes resided at Farim only during the dry or trading season extending from November to April. The temperatures and humidity at Farim were significantly lower than downstream, making residence there more comfortable and considerably healthier for humans and domestic animals alike. From Farim, small craft might continue two tides upriver to Jandegu, trading for beeswax at villages along the way. A caravan route linked Jandegu with Geba on the Geba River, Kolda at the head of navigation for dugout craft on the Casamance River, and the Mandinka state of Jimara along the upper Gambia River. Paralleling this route to the east, another Mande caravan route linked the upper Geba and upper Gambia Rivers (Hair 1985, chap. 4: 5–9; Peres 1953, 37–38; Bertrand-Bocandé 1849, 277–78, 281). Contributing to Cacheu's prosperity was the disruption of the Biafada-Sapi network caused by the competition of Cabo Verdean and Luso-African sailing vessels and by the depredations of Bijago raiders.

The export of slaves from Cacheu was an integral part of the Cabo Verdean commercial network linked to western Africa that was concealed and obfuscated by the Cabo Verdean authors André Alvares de Almada and André Donelha and by compilers of trade reports and other official documents. Due to the enterprise of Dutch traders who systematically collected commercial intelligence, the nature and extent of Cabo Verdean commerce became known to rivals. Dierick Ruiters's 1623 compendium delineated Cabo Verdean and Luso-African trade linkages between markets in western Africa.

> The trade we call "coastal" is mostly undertaken, in small ships, pinnances and launches, by Portuguese who live on Santiago Island. First they load these with salt, which they conveniently obtain for nothing on the islands of Maio and Sal, and they sail to Serra-Lioa with the salt and trade it for gold, ivory and kola. Then from Serra-Lioa they sail again to Joala and Porto d'Ale [along the Petite Côte], where they trade a portion of the kola for cotton cloths. They also sometimes trade ivory obtained in Serra-Lioa for Cape Verde cloths (so called because they are made at Cape Verde [that is, by weavers living along the Petite Côte]). From there they sail again east to Cacheo where they trade the rest of their kola and their remaining goods for slaves. They acquire fifty to sixty slaves in exchange for the goods they have obtained by trade along the coast, and each slave is worth to them 150 *reals,* or pieces-of-eight. So they make 9,000–10,000 *reals* out of nothing, in a manner of speaking. (Hair 1974b, 51–52)

It is hardly surprising that Cabo Verdean mariners and associated lançados and tangomaos were reticent concerning their commercial activities!

Ruiters's intelligence gathering was not infallible: he did not, for example, mention the shipment of panos, *aguardente* (sugarcane brandy), or tobacco from Cabo Verde to Serra Leoa. Regarding panos, in 1606, Father Barreira characterized cotton fiber and cotton textiles as the principal products carried from São Tiago to western Africa to barter for slaves and other commodities (Hair 1976c, 54–55). By sustaining their monopoly trade in panos and kola, Cabo Verdeans and Luso-Africans would maintain these linkages and exchanges during the centuries that followed.

By the second decade of the seventeenth century, Cacheu's population was estimated at fifteen hundred inhabitants, including grumetes and slaves. Some five hundred were designated *brancos* (whites), comprising Portuguese, Cabo Verdeans, a few Spanish traders, and, it would appear, many Luso-Africans accorded "white" status. The community had two neighborhoods, termed—with, one supposes, exaggeration and ironic humor—Villa Fria (cool town) and Villa Quente (hot town). The privileged white inhabitants of Villa Fria, fronting the river, presumably had first enjoyment of afternoon and evening onshore breezes sweeping up the estuary; those living in the grumete and Papel compounds located upriver behind them in Villa Quente were less fortunate. The most affluent traders enjoyed such an extravagant lifestyle that Cacheu was renowned as "Little Babylon" (Hair 1990, pt. 1, chap. 4: 1–5, 1985, chap. 3: 10–11).

A report on the evangelization of western Africa compiled in 1621 described Cacheu as having seventy to eighty dwellings belonging to lançados and Luso-Africans (Brásio 1968, 665). During the long dry season, residents were preoccupied with the risk of fire: because desiccated thatched dwellings were especially susceptible to conflagration, roofs were removed during the dry season and replaced with sailcloth, and merchandise was stored in *cumbetes,* storehouses with earthen roofs. In times of dispute and conflict, Papel threatened to set fire to traders' compounds, a menace that compelled negotiation and a resolution of differences. A chronic problem for Cacheu's residents was that of runaway slaves who took refuge in African communities; subordinate to African landlords, the stranger community at Cacheu had few means of recourse in such contentious matters. When disputes arose, they negotiated as skillfully as they could to restore peaceful conditions for commerce, maintain the status quo, and keep tribute payments as low as possible (Brásio 1968, 615; Rodney 1970, 136; Carreira 1984, 44–47; Hair 1985, chap. 3: 11–12, and 1990, pt. 1, chap. 5: 6).

Francisco Pirez de Carvalho, a Portuguese who lived in Cacheu for fourteen years during the 1620s and 1630s, described the settlement's fort as being palisaded along the riverside and surrounded by a ditch filled with water at high tides. Cacheu during this period was represented in a Dutch etching by Pierre de Hondt (Brásio 1964, facing p. 416). The fort failed in its purpose in November 1623, when two Dutch yachts attacked Cacheu and captured one vessel, sunk another, burned two others, and fired forty to fifty cannon shots into the settlement—but due to the small number of sailors manning their vessels, the Dutch did not attempt a landing (Moraes 1995, 238). Cacheu's defenses served to protect against European raiders, not to dominate or coerce Papel landlords. As Carvalho acknowledged, the local Africans were bellicose, versatile, and protective of their interests, and good relations were maintained only by customary payments. The ruler of Mata de Putam assessed each trading vessel a cask of wine, a barrel of bread, four braided strings of garlic and onions, two boxes of marmalade, and a quantity of wine for his alcaide. A subordinate ruler exacted a half cask of wine and some of the other commodities paid to the ruler of Mata. Smaller vessels owed half casks of wine or large sacks of cotton fiber, plus various other items (Thilmans and Moraes 1970, 349).

Guinala: Biafada-Lançado Conflict and Collaboration

While lançados attempted to subdue landlords at Cacheu, Biafada landlords at Guinala were similarly challenged. During the 1570s, lançados learned to negotiate the Geba River's treacherous tidal floods and to navigate the upper river in caravels, thereby initiating commerce with Mande traders in Badour/Degola—a commerce that had previously been monopolized by Biafada middlemen (Map 2.2). Subsequently, landlord-stranger relations along the Grande River deteriorated, with the principal dispute arising when Biafada landlords—like others in western Africa—confiscated the property of deceased lançados. In an attempt to stop this practice and improve their circumstances, the lançados persuaded the Biafada of Guinala to allow the construction of a stronghold similar to that built at Cacheu in 1589 and perhaps for the same alleged reason: to protect against French (and Bijago?) commerce raiders.

The richest lançado living in Guinala during the 1570s was Diogo Henriques de Sousa, the licensed contractor for Cabo Verdean trade. His possessions, including twenty-two vessels, were inherited by his *filho da terra* (son of the country, i.e., western Africa), Mateus Fernandes. Mateus Fernandes became the leading trader in Serra Leoa, monopolizing the trade in salt transported from Cabo Verde. Another successful trader was Sebastião Fernandes, who lived at Biguba around the turn of the century; there, he constructed numerous vessels and departed a rich man, later to return to western Africa and die at Cacheu (Hair 1985, chap. 8: 5–6, 10; Mota and Hair 1977, 304–5 nn. 265, 266).

The date when the stronghold at Porto da Cruz was completed was not recorded in Portuguese sources. Possibly, Carmelite missionaries helped negotiate permission to begin construction; several friars stayed at Guinala for four or five months in 1584 and favorably impressed the Biafada (Hair 1984a, 112). Once the palisaded stronghold was complete, the lançados armed it with cannons (Mota and Hair 1977, 174–75). In contrast to the frontal attacks attempted by the Papel at Cacheu, which resulted in many casualties, the Biafada response was to withdraw protections formerly provided according to landlord-stranger reciprocities and to increase the tolls for lançados engaging in commerce (Hair 1984a, 113). Eventually, the lançados withdrew from the stronghold at Porto da Cruz and reestablished their former landlord-stranger relations with Biafada rulers and elites.

That the Biafada were so forgiving of the lançados' duplicity might be explained by political as well as economic considerations, for the Biafada evidently used lançados and priests as counterweights to Mandinka traders and marabouts, concerned that the existing Mandinka suzerainty might be supplanted by direct control. During the 1590s, the Biafada ruler permitted the residence of a royal factor, Nun Frances da Costa, a New Christian who was denounced to the Inquisition in 1597, allegedly for recklessly asserting that he cared more for the fingernail of his African wife than "all the confessions and masses" (Moraes 1972, 38). Increasingly, Biafada and lançados had compelling reasons to cooperate in defense against Bijago raiders, who caused both groups to abandon the lower reaches of the Grande River (Rodney 1970, 92). It may have been the growing Bijago domination of the waters off the mouth of the Grande River that promoted the collaboration of lançados and Biafada mariners transporting kola in caravels to the upper Geba River. Formerly, Biafada had monopolized the trade, using huge dugouts that could carry more than one hundred people or large cargoes of commodities. Yet dugout craft, however large, were no match for sail-driven caravels. The chief commodity that Biafada traded along the upper Geba River was kola, which was bartered for captives and black and white cotton cloth (Hair 1984a, 93). The principal market in Badour/Degola was almost certainly the site later known as Geba, located at the head of the tidal reach and of navigation for large sailing craft. During the dry season, the Geba River shrinks to less than two hundred meters in width, with less than five meters of depth in midchannel. Dugout craft could continue upstream as far as Bafatá (divided river), the confluence of the tributary Colufe River (Bertrand-Bocandé 1849, 289). Geba had a more salubrious climate than the estuary due to its higher elevation, its lesser rainfall and lower humidity, and the absence of mosquito-infested mangrove swamps—attributes appreciated by both lançados and Mandinka traders.

Caravan routes linked Geba with markets along the Gambia River. While trading at Kassang on the upper Gambia in 1585, Donelha was informed by Mandinka marabouts that kola trade from the upper Geba had greatly increased in recent years in comparison with kola transported up the Gambia River because "it is nearer and less dangerous" (Mota and Hair 1977, 162–63). The period that followed was associated with the development of the Kaabu Empire, whose constituent states commanded trade between the Geba and Gambia Rivers (Map 2.3). Carvalho, who resided for many years at Cacheu prior to compiling his *roteiro* (sailing directions) in 1635, reported that large quantities of kola obtained in the Kolente River were shipped to the Geba River, the round-trip voyages beginning in Serra Leoa (Hair 1974b, 50–51). Carvalho did not identify the mariners, but Biafada traders would have been involved. Prior to that time, they had dominated the commerce of the upper Geba in dugout craft, and their cooperation was essential to lançados, for they could blockade the narrow river channel whenever they wished—as, in fact, they did whenever it served their purposes until the imposition of Portuguese rule at the close of the nineteenth century.

Papel-Lançado Collaboration at Bissau

Papel living on Ilha de Bissau were alert to the opportunities afforded by the growing lançado commerce along the Geba River, and they made friendly overtures to Cabo Verdean traders. In 1570, Almada was so hospitably received by the leader of Bissau (presumably, the ruler of Intim, the most senior of four rulers) that he characterized him as "a great friend of ours" whose people gave refuge to Cabo Verdean vessels fleeing French and English vessels (Hair 1984a, 92). Inasmuch as the leader of Intim was invested in office by the Biafada ruler of Guinala, one can only speculate about the extent to which the rulers of Guinala may have sanctioned or discouraged Bissau's expanding role in Geba River commerce. It is evident, however, that trade at Geba and Bissau increased even as that at Guinala declined.

The date of the first lançado settlement at Bissau was not recorded. Possibly, some lançados were settled there at the time of Almada's visit; when Father Barreira arrived in 1605, he found men who had not gone to confession for many years for lack of a priest. Lançados had their own dwellings and carried on extensive trade. Barreira characterized lançado-Papel relations as excellent, and he praised the ruler as "a great friend of the Portuguese" (Brásio 1968, 52–53; Hair 1976c, 60). Father Alvares, who visited Bissau in March 1607, echoed Barreira in describing the ruler Fernão, adding that Bissau's rulers invested those of Pecixe Island with a bow and cap (Map 2.4). Pecixe Island's strategic position enabled its rulers to trade to advantage with Portuguese and French vessels (Hair 1990, pt. 1, chap. 8: 6, and chap. 11: 1, 4). A Dutch report in 1630 characterized the inhabitants of Bissau as "friends of the Portuguese," adding that some Papel dressed in Portuguese fashion. In addition, Bissau had a small church and a resident priest (Thilmans and Moraes 1970, 363 n. 23).

Biafada and Mandinka traders along the Geba River and the Papel of Bissau greatly benefited from the precipitous decline of Grande River trade as Bijago raiders increasingly disrupted Biafada and lançado commerce and harried Biafada communities along the river. During the early years of the seventeenth century, the Bijago ceased interisland strife and collaborated in joint campaigns against mainland groups, coordinating fleets of craft from different islands in their depredations. Bijago craft raided as far north as the Cacheu River, causing victimized groups to develop labyrinth-style dwellings as a means of defense against surprise attacks (Rodney 1970, 104; Mota 1974a, 260–62, map facing p. 262; Hair 1989, document 24).

Biafada and lançados passing through the Bolama channel and trading along the Grande River were pillaged by Bijago raiders. The lançado community at Biguba, at the head of navigation, was pillaged in 1603. Padre Manuel Alvares, who spent a month at Guinala in 1607 en route to the Sierra Leone estuary, reported that Bijago had put numerous villages to fire and sword, decimating Biafada populations. The church at Guinala was destroyed by a raid in 1609 or 1610 (Hair 1990, chap. 8: 2, chap. 9: 1, and chap. 13: 5; Mota 1950, 169–70, and 1974a, 262). Thereafter, fewer Cabo Verdean vessels frequented the river, and many lançados departed.

Made desperate by the Bijago menace, Biafada rulers were coopted by lançados and Jesuit priests in a scheme to obtain military assistance from King Philip II. Fathers Barreira and Alvares assured Biafada that, besides ensuring salvation, their conversion to Christianity would greatly enhance their chances of obtaining aid from Portugal (Bane 1956, 74–75; Mota 1974a, 260–62; Hair 1989, document 28). Sebastião Fernandez Caçao, one of the leading traders in the Geba and Grande Rivers, pledged to arm as many as ten thousand Africans at his own expense; together with the forces of three Biafada rulers, they could defeat the Bijago and make their territories royal possessions (Hair 1987a, 182–83). Nothing came of these grandiose plans; meanwhile, the militant Father Barreira had redirected his efforts to persuading the king of Portugal to conquer Serra Leoa.

Subsequently, Bijago raids were countered by lançados, and Guinala recovered some of its former prosperity as the intermediary for Mande trade along the Corubal River. The market at Xitoli ("Curubale"), the head of navigation for sailing craft, was attended by numerous Mandinka traders and was held daily. Great quantities of dyestuffs were traded, the quality considered to be "six times" that of dyes obtained in the Nunez River (Hair 1985, chap. 8: 13). A 1621 report on the Cabo Verde diocese described Porto da Cruz at Guinala as having some ten residences of "Portuguese traders" and a priest at the Igreja de Nossa Senhora who ministered to numerous African Christians (Brásio 1968, 665; Mota and Hair 1977, 176–77). The Cacheu-based lançado Carvalho related that during the 1620s and early 1630s the Biafada and lançados living along the Grande River continued to trade for kola along the coast to the south, attesting to the resiliency of the Biafada–Sapi–Luso-African trade network competing with Cacheu-based vessels transporting kola directly from Serra Leoa. However, the formerly great market at Guinala now attracted few traders, and the only vessels that visited were associated with Serra Leoa commerce, which centered on trade in kola (Thilmans and Moraes 1970, 351). Except in regard to the Nunez River, where Cacheu-based vessels obtained slaves, ivory, and indigo dye, Carvalho recorded only negligible information concerning the coast and rivers south of the Grande River—indirect evidence that Biafada and associated lançados monopolized trade.

Guinala remained the principal place of lançado commerce until 1636, when a dispute with the Biafada ruler caused Captain Cristovão de Melo and other traders to move upriver to the head of navigation to develop an extensive trade with the Biafada of Biguba and Bolala. Coelho did not explain the dispute, but with the Bijago threat diminished, the Biafada ruler may have reasserted landlord prerogatives. Bolala had considerable trade in ivory and "very good" slaves obtained from Landuma ("Cocolis") and Nalu in exchange for iron, cloth (including panos from Cabo Verde and fabrics from India), wine, brandy, beads, and cowries used as small change. Captain Cristovão de Melo constructed fortress dwellings protected by cannons, and he sponsored a church served by a priest sent by the bishop of Cabo Verde. When his residence and the church were destroyed in a Bijago raid, Melo took revenge on the inhabitants of Ilha de Rubane ("Ilha do Esteiro") who launched the raid (Hair 1985, chap. 7: 3–4, and chap. 8: 8–9, 11–13).

African Landlords and Competing European Strangers along the Petite Côte

The influx of European rivals was welcomed by African rulers and traders, who gained from their competition. Nowhere was this more evident than along the Petite Côte, where the circumstances were transformed by the disintegration of the Jolof Empire. Led by Cayor, the coastal states of Cayor, Walo, Baol, Siin, and Saloum broke away from the control of the *burba* (ruler), probably in the late

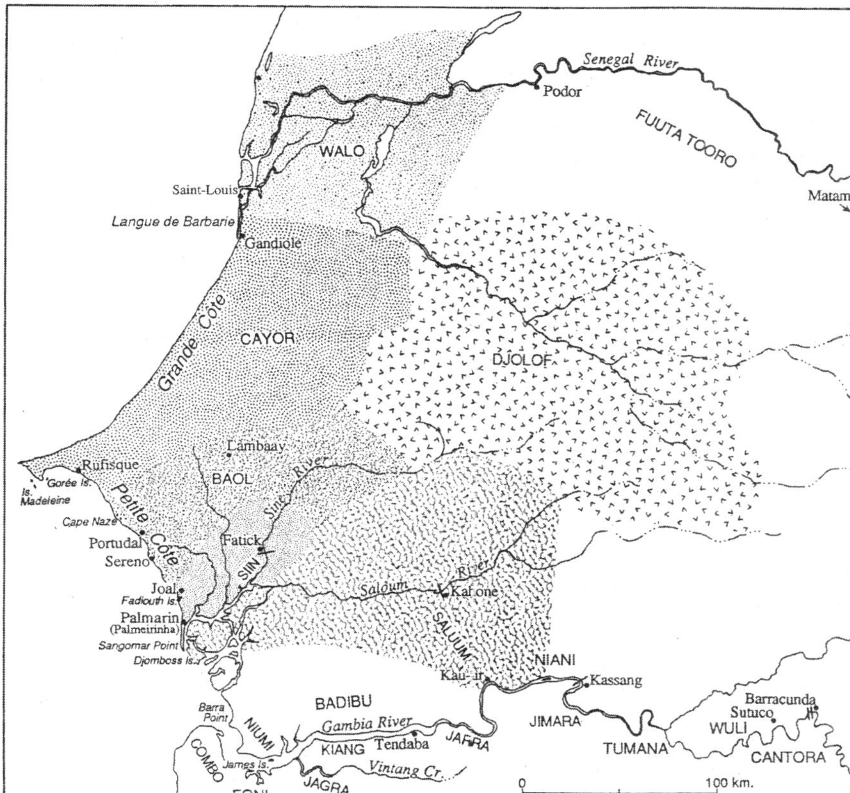

(Adapted from Lombard 1970: 239 and Boulègue 1977: 175, 1987: 126)

Map 3.1 Senegambia in the seventeenth century

1540s (Boulègue 1987, 165–73). As Maps 1.2 and 3.1 illustrate, only Cayor's territory extended north of the tsetse fly line during the c. 1500–c. 1630 wet period, when the horse herds of the Jolof Empire were decimated. Each of the former states of the empire, Djolof excepted, subsequently maintained corridors to the sea as links with the Banyun-Bak trade network, resident lançados, and visiting Cabo Verdean and European vessels.

Taking advantage of competition, alcaides (from the Arabic word for governors) along the Petite Côte greatly increased tolls and exacted exorbitant fees for a variety of services: there was a proliferation of "captains" responsible for procuring fresh water, firewood, fresh fish, and livestock and overseeing the sale of hides. Alcaides acted as receivers of the tolls shipmasters paid to obtain water and provisions (Brooks 1993b, 205, 218). Alvares was informed that the Wolof ruler of Cayor living at Ancalhor used a slave as an alcaide to supervise the watering place at Cape Verde, "as is commonly the case" at the other ports along the Petite Côte (Hair 1990, pt. 1, chap. 1: 4–5). However, in 1615, the alcaide at Cape Verde—a Luso-African named Gaspar Gonçalvo who could communicate in several European languages—asserted that he was a Christian and had four wives and six children (Moraes 1993, 168–69).

Tenacious and resourceful, lançados and Luso-Africans living along the Petite Côte welcomed trade with European vessels but used every means at their disposal to prevent European rivals from supplanting them as middlemen or gaining access to sources of kola and panos. An English trader who visited the Petite Côte in the 1590s reported that resident Portuguese and Spanish at Joal killed forty Englishmen and confiscated their goods, and he accused the Portuguese interpreter who accompanied his expedition of plotting its destruction. Previously, a French vessel attempting to trade in the Gambia River had been captured by two Portuguese vessels (Rainolds 1591/1904, 90–99; Boulègue and Marquet 1971).

Ruiters, whose account of the Petite Côte was dated by Moraes to approximately 1602, wrote that the ruler of Cayor rarely visited the coast and that the "Portuguese" living at Rufisque, Joal, and Portudal were compelled to visit him frequently and in person, bringing two to three hundred bars of iron and many other presents in order to keep his favor. Luso-Africans living at Joal possessed camels used along the interior routes (Moraes 1993, 70–71, 73). Ruiters described women's hair combed into towerlike "imperial crowns" that were narrow and pointed at the top; these may have served as prototypes for the tall, cone-shaped turbans created from handkerchiefs that distinguished the *signares* in later years (Thilmans and Rossie 1969, 117–18; Moraes 1993, 72 and n. 14).

An influx of Dutch and French vessels and resident traders significantly reduced Luso-African commerce along the Petite Côte during the following years. Pieter Van den Broecke, a Dutch trader who was based at Portudal for six months in 1606, engaged in what he characterized as the "house" trade—that is, he lived ashore with a black woman in a dwelling rented for two iron bars a month (Thilmans and Moraes 1977, 478–81; La Fleur 2000, 28). Van den Broecke said nothing more concerning the woman, but it is likely that she was a Luso-African; it is possible she was the person renting the dwelling, and she may well have assisted him as an interpreter and informant—a precursor of the signares who subsequently were so influential along the Petite Côte.

Van den Broecke related that, due to famine conditions caused by locusts, parents sold their children and offered virgin daughters "for handfuls of rice." He himself purchased a beautiful ten-year-old girl from her mother for the equivalent of 130 pounds of rice. Portuguese living at Portudal and Joal, most of whom were banished from Portugal, purchased slaves who were taken to Cacheu and São Domingos for shipment to the West Indies. Van den Broecke was informed that after acquiring fortunes in the slave trade, such Portuguese were able to obtain pardons and return to their homeland. When he visited Joal in March 1606, Van den Broecke lodged not with a Portuguese but with a Luso-African, "Anthoni de Moor" (Thilmans and Moraes 1977, 482, 488–90; La Fleur 2000, 30, 39, 41).

On a second visit to Portudal in February 1608 en route to Angola, Van den Broecke encountered Hans de Haese, a trader from Holland who had contracted to live on the Petite Côte for three years. Together, they visited the dwelling of a Portuguese named Symon Rodrigos, whom Van den Broecke characterized as a very capable merchant who had previously lived in Amsterdam. Thilmans and Moraes and La Fleur identified both men as having a Jewish heritage (Thilmans and Moraes 1977, 490–91; La Fleur 2000, 47). Haese was still trading at Portudal when Van den Broecke revisited in November 1609. Van de Broecke stated that some thirty "Portuguese and mestizos" resided at Portudal (La Fleur 2000, 71). Dutch competition in western Africa fostered claims of commercial ties between New Christians and Jews residing in Holland. For example, an anonymous 1612 memorandum cited fifteen alleged *judeus ou judaizantes* (Jews or observers of Jewish rituals) who were dealing with French and English traders between Cape Verde and the Cacheu River. Most of the men were from Holland (Carreira 1984, 125–26).

French mariners careened their vessels and assembled launches and sloops at Cape Verde, exerting such influence by their presence that many Wolof came to speak French "as if it were their native language." Father Alvares, whose knowledge of the Petite Côte derived from accounts of numerous individuals who visited the Sierra Leone estuary, stated that French and Dutch "pirates" mercilessly pillaged vessels from Cacheu that ventured to the Petite Côte. Their only refuge was the inlet at the village of Joal, the entrepôt for the Serer state of Siin. Protected by friendly Serer, a Luso-African settlement comprised some twelve to fifteen dwellings (Hair 1990, pt. 1, chap. 1: 4–5, 11–12).

Father Alvares railed against lançados and tangomaos for their collusion with Dutch and French "pirates":

> These names properly apply only to those who, not content with cooperating with the idolatrous heathen in the practices and sacrifices of their false religion, erect huts and build pedestals for their infernal idols. The *lançados* are truly "run-aways," and not only from the lord's grace, a precious jewel their

> souls are as far from as they are close to divine justice. These are truly *tangos maos,* for at the repast of guilt they not only snatch the dish but fill themselves like starving dogs, yet they remain famished for the Word of God. . . . By the bad example of their lives they discredit the purity of the Gospel faith in the eyes of the heathen. . . . They are evil itself, they are idolaters, perjurers, defiers of God, homicides, libertines, thieves who steal reputation, credit and good name from innocents as well as property, and also traitors—for they run away in order to help pirates, leading their ships to those places where our vessels are in the habit of anchoring and trading. They are people without understanding of right and wrong, without respect for anything other than their own appetites, and are the very spawn of hell. (Hair 1990, chapter 4: 4–5)

Alvares noted how women and bards along the Petite Côte collaborated with Luso-Africans to mutual advantage. He characterized Wolof women as better groomed and more stylishly and expensively dressed than other women due to their association with Luso-African traders. He also said that forewarnings from the women often enabled traders to "escape great misfortunes" (Hair 1990, pt. 1, chap. 1: 7–8).

Traders unable to collect debts from Wolof elites sometimes contracted Wolof bards to employ their skills as praise-singers in an unusual manner: "The whites speak to one of the [bards] and explain the position, and at the same time give him a fee for the job. What he does is this. He goes as a singer to the house where the king who is in debt lives, and he talks about the debt loudly and with many grimaces and gestures, and in a disparaging aside, he says, 'No honour to you for not paying your debt!' The wretched king finds himself so importuned that sometimes these [bards] end up by going back to the creditor with the money in their hand" (Hair 1990, pt. 1, chap. 1: 10–11).

Luso-Africans contrived to maintain trade along the Petite Côte, by whatever means necessary. Nicolas van Wassenaer, who visited the Petite Côte in June 1624, was informed that so-called Portuguese had poisoned a French shipmaster (Moraes 1995, 242). Allegations about the use of poison had widespread credibility in western Africa among both Africans and Europeans due to the sometimes frightening rapidity of deaths caused by malaria and other diseases. Rumors that Luso-Africans used poison against rivals, whether true or not, long served as potent deterrents to traders thinking of intruding into their commercial spheres.

It would seem that Dutch traders restricted their activities to the Petite Côte and did not attempt to trade along the Gambia River. Van Wassenaer related that "Portuguese" living along the Petite Côte were intermediaries, purchasing barks from Dutch and other Europeans to ascend the Gambia and return with large quantities of hides, ivory, and beeswax (Moraes 1995, 241). Van Wassenaer was one of few visitors to the Petite Côte to express disdain for the local women, as well as his fellow Europeans who consorted with them: "The women take little heed concerning their virtue, besides which they are dirty by nature, because they smell bad due to the palm oil which they pour on their hair, which in hot weather drips the length of the body. Men of all nations are not in the least dissuaded from sinning with them, as a consequence of which one sees running about children of all sorts, French, English, Dutch, and others, many of them. Out there is no order, all is confusion" (Moraes 1995, 241; cf. Pieter De Marees in Purchas 1613/1905, 5:251).

Van Wassenaer did not give the names of the children or their parents. And he and other short-term visitors provided little or no information concerning women's social status in the stratified societies along the Petite Côte—whether the women described were elites and freeborn individuals, members of endogamous occupational groups (smiths, leather workers, or bards), or slaves (domestic or transit). There were strong sanctions against fornication with women of free status. Among Wolof, a girl's lapse from chastity prior to her marriage was considered an embarrassment to the family and grounds for immediate divorce if discovered after she wed. Following her marriage, a Wolof woman guarded her reputation by maintaining chaste behavior and by demanding the same of her husband as well. The Lébou community on Cape Verde enforced fierce sanctions regarding casual affairs: illegitimate babies fathered by Europeans or Eurafricans were killed, and their mothers were enslaved (Ames 1956; Gamble 1967, 65–68; Brooks 1976, 34–38). One may suppose that it was chiefly slave women who consorted with transient Europeans—their behavior condoned or encouraged by masters seeking privileged access to visiting traders.

Along the Petite Côte, Wolof and Serer landlords compelled Luso-Africans to accommodate to European traders, but Luso-Africans connived with Niominka allies to exclude Dutch, French, and English rivals from Gambia River trade by a combination of attacks on vessels, intimidation, and treachery. Trading on the Petite Côte in 1606, Van den Broecke matter of factly stated that "the Portuguese control the Gambia River and have many places where they trade alone" (La Fleur 2000, 41).

In 1618, the crew of the English vessel *Catherine,* anchored at Kassang in the Mandinka state of Niani, "was betrayde, and every man left in her, his throat cut, by a few poore dejected *Portingals* and *Molatos.*" The alleged perpetrator of the massacre, Hector Nunez, seized the vessel, but the people of Kassang expelled

Nunez and the men associated with him and rendered assistance to members of the crew who were absent from the ship (Gamble and Hair 1999, 17–18). George Thompson, the *Catherine*'s supercargo, had meanwhile made a reconnaissance upriver, where Luso-Africans traded but were not allowed to settle. Thompson was treated so well by Mandinka rulers and traders that the investors in the "Ginney and Binney Company" (that is, the Guinea and Benin Company) resolved to continue in Gambian trade. An expedition dispatched in 1620 entered the Saloum River and seized part of the cargo of a small bark of which Hector Nunez was part owner (Gamble and Hair 1999, 18–19, 185–86). Buoyed by chimerical prospects of gold trading, the English entrepreneurs lost large sums and ceased to outfit voyages. In 1631, the investors reorganized as the Company of Merchants Trading to Guinea (Gray 1940, 20–28; Porter 1968, 58–62). English traders did not become residents along the Gambia River until the 1660s, when another company, the Royal Adventurers, established an entrepôt on James Island.

Richard Jobson, who chronicled the vicissitudes of the Ginney and Binney Company, was enthralled by the value of kola: "Ten is a present for a King. . . . Fifty, of these nuts . . . would buy a wife, and many times as a wonderfull great present, I have had sixe of them sent me." The inquisitive Jobson endeavored to learn the source of kola, but "Portingall" informants would say only that they came from "the golden countrey" and were obtained in trade in a "great baye" beyond Cacheu (Gamble and Hair 1999, 169–70). Luso-African traders had no intention of sharing valuable commercial intelligence with potential rivals.

Jobson was a shrewd observer and wrote down what he learned concerning Luso-Africans along the Gambia River. He characterized them as "dwelling, or rather lurking" among Mandinka:

> They call themselves, *Portingales,* and some few of them seeme the same; others of them are *Molatoes,* betweene blacke and white, but the most part as blacke, as the naturall inhabitants: they are scattered, some two or three dwellers in a place, and are all married, or rather keepe with them the countrey blackewomen, of whom they beget children, howbeit they have amongest them, neither Church, nor Frier, nor any other religious order. . . . They doe generally imploy themselves in buying such commodities the countrey affords, wherein especially they covet the country people, who are sold unto them, when they commit offences. . . . The conditions they live subject unto, under the blacke Kings, makes it appeare, they have litle comfort in any Christian countrey, or else themselves are very carelesse what becometh of their posteritie; for whensover the husband, father, or maister of the familie

> dies, if hee be of any worth, the King seizeth upon what hee hath, without respect, either to wife, children, or servant, except they have warning to provide before, or are capable of themselves, to looke out for the future time; whereby we finde in some those few places we trade with them, poore distressed children left, who as it were exposed to the charitie of the country, become in a matter naturalized, and as they grow up, apply themselves to buy and sell one thing for another as the whole country doth, still reserving carefully, the use of the *Portingall* tongue, and with a kinde of an affectionate zeale, the name of Christians, taking it in a great disdaine, be they never so blacke, to be called a *Negro*. (Gamble and Hair 1999, 134–35, 196)

As described by Jobson, the circumstances of the wives and children of deceased Luso-African traders were tenuous indeed. Born of slave mothers, the children reflected the kinless status of slaves and Luso-Africans. The orphaned children of free persons would have been cared for by relatives and supported by members of their age grades.

Jobson related that Luso-Africans did not trade upriver beyond Setuco, which he described as the largest town he had visited along the Gambia River and a place where Luso-Africans acquired much gold. The community was governed by a marabout and had many marabouts residing there. By happenstance, Jobson was present for the funeral of the chief marabout, noting, "Much Gold is buried with them, or before by themselves in a private place, for their use in another World" (Gamble and Hair 1999, 134–35, 196).

Jobson contrasted the abstinence of Gambian Muslims with the reckless consumption of European spirits by Mandinka elites: "[Regarding] *aqua vitae* for which they sell all things they have, and the Kings and all will drinke, untill they be starke drunke and fall fast asleepe, so that to describe the life of the Kings truly, is, that they doe eate, drinke and sleep, and keepe company with their women, and in this manner consume their time, untill Time consumes them" (Gamble and Hair 1999, 120). Other sources similarly alluded to Gambian elites' addiction to alcohol, which promoted a lucrative trade in brandy and wine from Portugal and grog, the sugarcane brandy produced in Cabo Verde.

In 1629, the king of Spain dispatched a flotilla to disrupt Dutch trade and apprehend New Christians living in western Africa. Portuguese and Spanish authorities were obsessed with reports of collaboration between Iberian Jews staying in Holland and New Christians living in Cabo Verde, along the Petite Côte, and at Cacheu. The Portuguese expedition destroyed a Dutch fortification erected on the island of Gorée the previous year, demolished a synagogue at Rufisque, and apprehended several Jews living there and at Cacheu. The existence of a synagogue suggests that there were at least ten Jewish males above thirteen years of age to attend the synagogue and hold services (Boulègue 1989, 29).

An individual's decision to reclaim his or her Jewish heritage was not taken lightly. Most New Christians who took refuge in Holland had no knowledge of Hebrew, and the males were uncircumcised; the prospect of undergoing circumcision was doubtless daunting for grown men. Contemporaries in Holland characterized New Christian refugees from Iberia as "Roman Catholics without faith and Jews without knowledge, but wishing to be Jews" (Dubiez n.d., 1). By the last quarter of the seventeenth century, there were some twenty-three hundred Sephardic Jews living in Amsterdam. The considerable wealth they derived from European and Atlantic commerce is manifested by the Esnoga, the elegant synagogue completed in 1675 that still serves the Sephardic community (Belinfante 1991, 31).

The Portuguese expedition in 1629 was of transitory consequence in all respects, for the Dutch reoccupied Gorée the following year, and except for brief occupations by the Portuguese (in 1645), the French (in 1659), and the English (in 1664), they retained possession of the island until 1677. Lapsed New Christians continued to practice Judaism at several ports along the Petite Côte and trade with Dutch and other European vessels. However, apart from observing Saturday as the Sabbath, Jews on the Petite Côte lived much as other lançados—marrying African women according to local custom, raising families, and acquiring entourages of slaves and grumetes (Moraes 1969, 989–96, 1972, 40, and 1995, 321; Teixeira 1950, 92–93).

The vagaries of official repression and tolerance and the New Christians' personal influence were exemplified by the careers of Alvaro Gonçalves Francês and his son, Jorge Gonçalves Francês, a Luso-African born at Cacheu. The elder Francês was apprehended at Cacheu in 1634. Imprisoned at São Tiago, he escaped to Joal, his principal place of business. Recaptured, he was set free by royal pardon. His Luso-African son, Captain Francês, earned a considerable reputation as a Portuguese patriot. He joined the revolt against Spain that began in December 1640 and fought against Spanish vessels along the Petite Côte, in the Gambia River, and at Bissau. For a time, he was acting commander of Cacheu, a responsibility also exercised by other New Christians (Barcellos 1899–1913, 1:239–40; Esteves 1988, 59–60; Moraes 1995, 300–310, 340–44).

The Petite Côte became an arena of religious competition in November 1634 with the arrival of Capuchin missionaries aboard French trading vessels dispatched by merchants in the Normandy ports of Rouen and Dieppe who had obtained exclusive trading privileges from Cardinal Richelieu. The dual challenge outraged Portuguese clergy no less than Portuguese with mercantile interests, not least of all the bishop of Cabo Verde, for the Capuchins were intruding into his diocese—claiming to be the first priests in eight years to minister to Christians along the Petite Côte. Portuguese protests to the Vatican ultimately led to the withdrawal of the French priests in 1638 and 1639 (Moraes 1995, 274–99).

Fathers Alexis de Sainct-Lô and Bernardin de Renouard of the first Capuchin mission, which lasted six months, recorded the names of persons they baptized at Joal (51), Rufisque (28), Portudal (6), and Seraine (5), together with the names of their godfathers and godmothers. At Joal in January 1635, 44 baptismal names were recorded together with the surnames and given names of the godparents, some of whom sponsored several individuals (Moraes 1995, 283–84). Sainct-Lô reported that when Joal was attacked by the ruler of Baol, the Luso-Africans joined Siin's forces to repel the assault (Sainct-Lô 1637, 117–18, cited in Boulègue 1989, 63). As time passed, Luso-Africans with entourages of armed grumetes acquired a wider influence in western Africa.

At Seraine—which was located along the coastline between Portudal and Joal, the frontier between Baol and Siin and probably not controlled by either state—a separate village of Christian cultivators was headed by a man known as Padre Bernard. The village's inhabitants included some Luso-Africans, but most residents were former slaves of a Luso-African who had granted them freedom at his death (Sainct-Lô 1637, 103–11, cited in Curtin 1975, 96). When Father Sainct-Lô officiated at a funeral, he was surprised to observe that the dead woman's cooking pot was placed next to her grave. During the following year, relatives were to bring couscous and palm wine or brandy so that the deceased would not lack nourishment in the next world—a practice congruent with both African beliefs and those of Catholics in Europe observing All Souls' Day (Sainct-Lô 1637, 110–11, cited in Boulègue 1989, 53; Curtin 1975, 96; cf. La Fleur 2000, 39).

At Rufisque, the Capuchins encountered two Jewish families who were extremely rich. One of the traders was Hierosme Gomme (Gomez?), who had lived in France as a practicing Christian for many years (Sainct-Lô 1637, 89, cited in Boulègue 1989, 55). There were "three or four" Jews at Portudal, led by a Portuguese named Peregrin who had taken refuge in Flanders and who allegedly had converted several Christians to Judaism. Fulano Peregrino (Peregrin/Peregrine), previously reported to be trading on the Petite Côte in 1622, was the pseudonym of Manuel Henriques, described as the sage of the Jews living along the coast. Presumably, he was the "Manoell Henriques" living at Geba in March 1641 who was denounced as a Jew in 1644 (Sainct-Lô 1637, 104, 107, cited in Moraes 1995, 305 n. 614; Barcellos 1899–1913, 1:222). One of the Jews Sainct-Lô encountered was the interpreter for the ruler of Baol—obviously, someone well placed to advance the interests of coreligionists (Sainct-Lô 1637, 143, cited in Boulègue 1989, 56).

At Bezeguiche (Cape-Gaspard, site of modern-day Dakar), Father Sainct-Lô found a single Christian family, that of the *alkaire,* a royal slave who had been captured as a child and taken to Cabo Verde (Sainct-Lô 1637, 14–15, cited in Curtin 1975, 96). He had a son who had lived for five or six years in France and served in the royal army (Sainct-Lô 1637, 56–62, cited in Boulègue 1989, 31, 35 n. 29). Of particular interest in Sainct-Lô's account was the mention of "a Portuguese lady called Signora Philippa" and a sister-in-law "Signora Pacha" (Patrícia?), who, along with other Catholics at Rufisque, accorded the Capuchins an effusive welcome. The two priests converted part of Signora Philippa's dwelling into a chapel, where they examined persons seeking baptism. According to Father Sainct-Lô, the adults "replied pertinently enough, for they had been instructed by the Portuguese who live along this coast" (Sainct-Lô 1637, quoted in Hargreaves 1969, 29). Some Luso-Africans manifestly benefited from their association with French traders along the Petite Côte. A Rouen trader reported that in 1639, Diogo Vaz of Rufisque paid twenty-five thousand livres for a Spanish caravel captured by a Norman vessel (François Cauche 1651, 6, cited in Boulègue 1989, 65; Moraes 1995, 330–32).

Credit for the extirpation of Judaism along the Petite Côte was subsequently claimed by Spanish Capuchins, whose 1646–47 mission was condemned by enraged Portuguese authorities. The Spanish priests were accused of being spies due to the continuing state of war between the two nations following the breakup of the Spanish-Portuguese union on December 1, 1640; a peace treaty was not signed until February 1668. During tours of the Petite Côte, the Capuchins ministered to a hundred Christians at Joal, a community comprising some forty dwellings and a thatched church in good repair. At Portudal, they found two hundred Christian slaves and their trader-masters, as well as a Dutch "heretic" who allowed them to use his warehouse to offer masses. Three "white" traders were dwelling at Rufisque, along with Luso-African traders and some three hundred other Christians—presumably slaves—whom they characterized as greatly deficient in religious knowledge and bereft of anyone to instruct them (Moraes 1995, 351–52; cf. Boulègue 1989, 28–29). The traders at Rufisque were prospering, living in peaceful and secure conditions compared to the circumstances at other ports along the Petite Côte.

The conversion of Jews at Rufisque stemmed from an allegedly fortuitous meeting with a rich and popular Jewish trader, who, after several days of proselytizing, was (improbably) convinced of his errors and accepted baptism together with his wife, children, relatives, and slaves—twenty-two in total. A French shipmaster acted as godfather at the ceremony—and the newly baptized Christian doubtless engaged in trade with this individual, having assessed the potential value of commercial links with Norman merchants (Moraes 1995, 354, 305 n. 614). The Spanish Capuchins were unsuccessful in their overtures to Wolof and Serer rulers along the Petite Côte, who disdained their advances. After a year and a half in western Africa, all but two Capuchins departed for the West Indies. The two Spanish priests remaining in western Africa were arrested as spies by the commandant of Cacheu and dispatched to Lisbon as prisoners (Moraes 1995, 351–54).

Francisco de Lemos Coelho, a Cabo Verdean whose experiences in western Africa probably began around 1640 and ended around 1663, related what he knew about Jews living along the Petite Côte in former times. Many lived at Rufisque, where they had very large premises: "They had been born in Portugal and came here to declare themselves (Jews), because the kings of the land protected them and they could not be punished (for practicing their religion)." Coelho added that Jews paid more tribute to rulers than others but did so "in order to practice in freedom their own religion and law." Other Jews lived at Portudal, but no self-acknowledged Jews lived in Joal (Hair 1985, intro.: ii–iii, and chap. 1: 5, 8–10). References to New Christians reverting to Judaism ceased during the decades that followed, their descendants reportedly converting to Christianity (Hair 1985, chap. 1: 5, 8–10). Jean Boulègue identified two reasons for the gradual disappearance of Jews in western Africa: the development of Cacheu as the principal Luso-African center with resident priests and the strictures of Mosaic law stipulating that Jews must be born of Jewish mothers (Boulègue 1989, 57).

Serra Leoa Trade, 1600s–1630s

During the first decades of the seventeenth century, lançados and Luso-Africans living in Serra Leoa were increasingly challenged by European competitors. Nonetheless, Luso-Africans, backed by redoubtable Jesuit priests, contrived by a variety of means to retain their ascendancy as middlemen along the estuary, and they continued to monopolize coastwise kola trade. There were political changes, as the ascendancy of Coya over the other Mani-Sumba states declined during the first half of the seventeenth century. The death of the warlords who founded the states, the progressive integration of Mani-Sumba with conquered groups in Serra Leoa, and rivalries caused by Luso-African, Dutch, and English competition contributed to these changes (Brooks 1993b, 308–9).

Dierick Ruiters, whose reporting on Serra Leoa probably dated to the same era (c. 1602) as his reports on the Petite Côte (Moraes 1993, 73), related that the Luso-African Mateus Fernandes was the most important trader in the Sierra Leone estuary at the beginning of the century. Fernandes was the son of Diogo Henriques de Sousa, a prominent trader at Guinala during the 1570s and 1580s and a great-uncle of Francisco de Lemos Coelho (Hair 1985, chap. 8: 6). Ruiters found that the "leading Portuguese" (that is, Cabo Verdeans) trading there were all associated with him in commerce, and two of the most important were married to his sisters. Fernandes's mother and wife or wives were almost certainly well connected among Mani-Sumba elites.

Luso-Africans carried on a remunerative middleman commerce along the coast and rivers south of the Sierra Leone estuary. Ruiters commented, "They have their own boats, so that when occasionally ships arrive and trade goods with them, they can take the goods to St. Ann's Bay and exchange them for gold and ivory. On the goods that they buy from the English, the French and our own nation when we come in our ships, they make over 100% profit" (Hair 1975b, 62). Ruiters's account indicated that Luso-African middlemen were unable to accumulate savings in order to trade with Africans before the arrival of European vessels: they required goods on credit before organizing a trading expedition. Here, as elsewhere in western Africa, the demands of African wives and relatives and the practice of landlords confiscating the property of deceased traders combined to restrict Luso-Africans to the role of compradors, rather than merchants in their own right.

Ruiters proposed that Dutch traders employ the services of a Luso-African named Francisco Mendes as a pilot and agent. All that was needed was a small, shallow-draft sailing craft laden with salt from the island of Maio in the Cabo Verde archipelago and an assortment of European goods, which he itemized (Hair 1975b, 59–63). It is not known whether any Dutch entrepreneurs attempted Ruiters's scheme, but Dutch competition in Serra Leoa significantly increased during the years that followed.

In 1606, the lançado Bartolomeu André, living in the Sierra Leone estuary, prevailed on the Coya ruler to kill the Dutch traders residing at Cape Mount.

However, he did so to no avail, for in the following years, Dutch and French traders came to dominate Coya's trade (Hair 1976b, 45, 56 n. 8; Adam Jones 1983c, 29). As happened along the Petite Côte, Dutch and French vessels attacked Portuguese and Luso-African ships trading in Serra Leoa — more than twenty in 1607, according to Father Barreira. Dutch and French traders who visited the Sierra Leone estuary were protected from lançados' reprisals by the ruler of the Sierra Leone state (Hair 1976a, 65–66, 70 n. 13). English visitors in August and September 1607 learned that André sailed a bark between São Tiago and the estuary, transporting salt, panos, and European cloth. He possessed several dwellings where ivory and gold — and slaves, undoubtedly — were stored between his voyages. André's influence was such that when his vessel arrived, local Africans would not trade with anyone else (Hair 1981d, 32).

Luso-Africans trading with the Mani-Sumba states along the Sierra Leone estuary were energetically seconded by the enterprise of the Jesuit mission established there from 1605 to 1616. The priests tried to persuade Mani-Sumba rulers to trade exclusively with Portuguese and Cabo Verdean vessels. And in 1607, the intrepid Barreira launched a mission to Futa Jallon in the expectation of baptizing Mansa Canda, the ruler of Bena, which was an important source of trade located along the upper Kolente River. While a youth, Mansa Canda had been employed by Simão Caldeira, a trader from São Tiago. He had adopted many "Portuguese" attributes and practices, including sometimes wearing European garments, and one of his sons was a converted Christian. Several lançados were living in his village, among them the Cabo Verdean António Fernandes, who served as a scribe and wrote the letter inviting Father Barreira to Bena (Hair 1990, single chap. (Barreira); Brooks 1993b, 309–12).

After weeks of preaching, teaching, and engaging in discussions with Barreira, Mansa Canda refused conversion. In addition to the opposition of Muslims and concerns regarding the disapproval of his overlord, Farim Concho, Mansa Canda was confounded by Barreira's demands. The priest insisted that prior to baptism, the ruler had to burn his amulets and his shirts covered with amulets, as well as his "idols." Regarding the latter, Mansa Canda expostulated, "How can I burn my father and my sons and my wives who are with God?" To this, Barreira unsympathetically replied, "Your father and all the others you name are in the company of demons!" (Hair 1990, single chap. (Barreira): 3–4). Both Barreira and Father Alvares believed in demons and were convinced of Satan's active opposition to the Jesuit mission, with African "witches" acting as Satan's agents (Hair 1998, 138–40).

Prior to António Fernandes's departure from Bena with Barreira, Mansa

Canda reputedly contrived to have him poisoned and slowly tormented to an agonizing death by evil spirits. Fernandes eventually succumbed at Cacheu after being expulsed by traders at Portudal who could not tolerate his afflictions (Hair 1990, pt. 2, chap. 25: 7–8). Accounts of António Fernandes's fate were representative of the many cautionary tales that had long circulated among Luso-Africans and visiting traders, reminding them that they lived in Africa at the sufferance of their landlords' psychological powers as well as their physical constraints.

Father Barreira's mission to Serra Leoa coincided with the Spanish-dominated joint monarchy's decision to take possession of the Sierra Leone peninsula in order to expel European rivals. In March 1606, Philip III awarded a Portuguese courtier, Pedro Alvares Pereira, the captaincy of Serra Leoa on the condition that he found settlements, construct forts, and fulfill other obligations within a specified number of years. The attempt to implement the proposed conquest was delayed for almost a decade when Pereira became embroiled in court politics, which resulted in his imprisonment and significant financial losses (Hair 1987a, 176–77, 188–91, 195).

The success of the Jesuit mission was undermined by the despicable behavior of lançados and visiting traders. Around 1611, Fr. Manuel Alvares reported that Serra Leoa was commonly regarded as "an asylum for ill-doers" from Cabo Verde, and he was constantly challenged to find ways to ameliorate their behavior (Hair 1989, no. 46, 6). Alvares excoriated lançados and tangomaos as "a great scandal to our holy faith," noting that "they are a worldly rabble, and with their licence and loose habits, are only interested in profits. They lack concern for the great cause of bringing a multitude of souls to Christ" (Hair 1990, pt. 2, chap. 1: 2). The depravity of these reprobates greatly hindered the proselytizing of local Africans, for, as Alvares lamented, "their false ideas are strengthened by what they see of the bad Christianity of our people out here, the licence of their very corrupt lives; the bad example they set in not keeping feastdays and vigils, and in eating meat on these days with great abandonment; and their sensual behaviour; and from this, they conclude, 'Our way is a better way'" (Hair 1990, pt. 2, chap. 5: 3–4).

Unfortunately for the Jesuits and their converts, a promised cornucopia of commercial and spiritual blessings did not materialize. Portuguese and Cabo Verdean traders were incapable of meeting the expectations of the Mani-Sumba elites in competition with growing numbers of English, French, and Dutch vessels (Hair 1981b, 129, 131, 136–40, 1987a, 198–201, and 1990, pt. 2, chap. 2: 7–8; Brooks 1993b, 308–19). It was kola trade that sustained Luso-Africans' commerce in Serra Leoa, as Father Alvares explained: "They respect the Portuguese [that is, the Luso-African traders] more than foreigners of any other (European) nation, because of the benefits of their commerce, and especially because the Portuguese come annually to trade in their commonest product, one which only they know how to produce, cola. This trade always brings them more than does the trade with other foreigners, who only take from them ivory and rice" (Hair 1990, pt. 2, chap. 2: 7).

Francisco Pirez de Carvalho, who resided at Cacheu for fourteen years, stated that large quantities of kola from the Kolente River were shipped to the Geba River, bypassing Cacheu; it is noteworthy that the round-trip voyages began in Serra Leoa. In deference to royal officials, Carvalho remarked, "It would be a very great convenience if this kola came to Cacheo settlement, for if the ships came here it would make more business and more wealth. Instead, from Serra Leoa they go to Rio Jeba, then (back) to Serra Leoa, without recognizing the authority of, or obeying, Your Majesty's administrators" (Hair 1974b, 50).

By 1613, Pedro Alvares Pereira had regained the favor of King Philip, and during the next two years, he dispatched a number of individuals to the Sierra Leone estuary, including a cousin to serve as governor and two Augustianian friars. By this time, the disenchanted Mani-Sapi rulers and elites had no intention of dealing exclusively with Portuguese or traders from any European nation. By the end of 1616 or early 1617, all the people dispatched by Pereira had left Sierra Leone, including the friars. Meanwhile, the death of Fr. Manuel Alvares sometime in 1616 terminated the Jesuit initiative; no priests were assigned to Serra Leoa to replace him, although the official withdrawal of the Jesuits did not occur until midcentury, when Capuchins were assigned the mission field. During the intervening decades, there were no resident priests to serve Christians and evangelize converts (Barcellos 1899–1913, 1:208; Hair 1981b, 129, 131, 136–40, and 1978a, 198–201).

The legacy of the Jesuit mission in terms of Luso-African social and cultural patterns is moot. It is significant that the priests' extensive correspondence concerning pastoral activities did not reveal whether Luso-Africans and Africans were instructed in reading, writing, and record keeping. That there may have been some educational initiatives was suggested in the "Remembrances" of William Finch, an English merchant who visited the Sierra Leone estuary in August and September 1607. Finch visited the Jesuits' chapel, "wherein are written in a table, such dayes as they are to observe holy." He also recorded that the ruler and some of his entourage were "decently cloathed in Jackets and Breeches, and some with hats (Purchas 1613/1905,4:2).

Finch was a member of an English expedition of two vessels bound to the

East Indies that spent thirty-eight days in the Sierra Leone estuary to treat an outbreak of scurvy with lemon water and fresh provisions. Finch and William Keeling, the expedition's commander, issued favorable reports concerning Lucas Fernandes, who served as interpreter and commercial agent for Farim Buré, the local ruler. Possibly a descendant of the Sapi refugees or of captives taken to Cabo Verde in the mid-sixteenth century, Fernandes had become a Christian while living in São Tiago. He was probably literate and was described as "a man of marvaillous redie witt and speakes in eloquent Portugues." Fernandes's sister was one of the wives of Farim Buré and likely was very helpful to the Jesuit Barreira in convincing her husband to accept baptism and become a Christian (Hair 1978b, 21, 29, 32).

From the 1610s forward, the magnificent harbor of the Sierra Leone estuary attracted vessels of all nations plying Atlantic routes. It was a refuge from storms where ships' crews careened and repaired their vessels. The nearby forests supplied all the necessities for ship construction, including planking, masts, cordage, caulking, and a tarlike substance (Hair 1990, pt. 2, chap. 1: 6–7, 18). Seamen from many countries carved their names on the rocks and trees at the renowned watering place on the south shore. Crews from the vessels stocked their holds with bananas, lemons, oranges, limes, and other provisions, and they captured shoals of fish with seines. The citrus fruits were especially valuable for the prevention and treatment of scurvy, a deficiency disease afflicting seafarers who were deprived of fresh provisions during long voyages.

During the decades of warfare between the European states, Luso-Africans trading with local Temne were endangered by warships and commerce raiders frequenting the Sierra Leone estuary to restock water and provisions. In the circumstances, it seems that Luso-Africans avoided the watering place and secluded themselves along the upper reaches of the estuary. It is noteworthy that accounts by Dutch visitors to the estuary in 1617 and 1625, seeking only water and food supplies, made no mention of Luso-Africans, but the crew of a French trading vessel loading dyewoods was massacred, allegedly because they acted against the wishes of the local ruler.

Samuel Brun, a Swiss surgeon traveling on a Dutch vessel, spent several days in the estuary in October (?) 1617 while the crew loaded the vessel with fresh fruit. Brun characterized the local Africans as "good" and thankful for even the smallest things. "Yet," he added, "they are not entirely to be trusted. For they are often attacked and injured by the thievish French under the guise of trade." Brun made no mention of Luso-Africans or anyone serving as interpreters or intermediaries (Jones and Hair 1977, 54 n. 2, 61–62).

In November 1619, three French warships commanded by General Beaulieu spent three weeks in the estuary making repairs and reprovisioning. During their stay, the local ruler sent two emissaries to the general to inform him that "Portuguese" upriver had massacred the captain and crew of a French vessel from Saint Malo that was engaged in cutting dyewood. The ruler offered guides—but no warriors—to help the French take revenge. An expedition of three armed craft dispatched upriver was stymied by the progressively shallow waters and submerged rocks along the upper estuary; it retreated without encountering any Luso-Africans (Hair 1974a).

In 1625, the year after capturing Bahia, a Dutch flotilla of three vessels transporting some six hundred soldiers spent several months in the Sierra Leone estuary to improve the health of scurvy-ravaged soldiers and seamen before sailing to the Gold Coast, where they would make an unsuccessful attempt to capture the Portuguese fort at Elmina. The interpreter for the elderly Farim Buré ("Frambore") was an African known as Harry ("Herry") who lived for many years in England, visited on other occasions, and spoke several European languages. While in England, Harry had become a Christian, but he reverted to local cultural practices after he returned home and married (Adam Jones 1986, 50–52). Remarkably, the anonymous Dutch writer made no reference whatever to Luso-Africans or to any Dutch or English residing in the estuary in the course of discussing his visits to Farim Buré's village, hunting parties, and other activities ashore during several months' time. A likely explanation is that the arrival of the Dutch fleet caused Luso-Africans to seclude themselves for the duration of the visit; nonetheless, it is surprising that the Dutch did not inquire about or search for "Portuguese" enemies during their stay.

A decade later, there were Luso-African, Dutch, and English traders living in the Sierra Leone estuary. Francisco Pirez de Carvalho related that the Dutch and English established at Port Loko built houses "like those in their own countries" and each year loaded ten to twelve vessels with timber, ivory, wax, gold, and many lesser commodities (Hair 1974b, 50–51). According to Dutch accounts, there was sporadic conflict: "Portuguese" in the Sierra Leone estuary seized a vessel in 1635 and pillaged and burned a trading establishment the following year (Moraes 1995, 325, 328). Such actions doubtless caused European traders to collaborate for mutual interest. A German named Hemmersam, employed by the Dutch West India Company, reported that he was as hospitably received by an English trader in 1639 as by Gidion Moris, the Dutch trader. The African elites that Hemmersam encountered spoke Portuguese, but he did not mention meeting any Luso-Africans or note anything concerning them (Adam Jones 1983b, 100–102).

The 1630s marked a watershed in western African commerce. The slave trade greatly increased during the following decades, along with growing competition between Dutch, English, and French trading companies that contended for exclusive trading spheres and established resident traders, or "factors," in "factories" along the coasts and rivers of western Africa. Challenged as never before, Luso-Africans tenaciously clung to their commercial networks—at times beleaguered by European competition, at times benefiting from European wars that damaged their rivals or drove them from western Africa.

European factors bound for western Africa during the seventeenth century would have been fortunate indeed to make the acquaintance of Francisco de Lemos Coelho. In the "Prologue to the Reader" of his long-unpublished manuscript, Coelho encapsulated the lessons he drew from his experiences trading in western Africa from the 1640s to the 1660s:

> In composing this brief and summary account, which leaves the door open to learned men (for fuller descriptions), I was also moved by the desire to inform and warn any who may decide to come and live in certain of the ports of the many kingdoms that, if they arrive without resources, then in order to acquire these they must spend a good number of years here, the number depending on their industry and their good fortune. For those who cannot bring capital, the best of the resources they can bring is good behaviour. They should be very tractable, benevolent and well disposed; they should realize that they are guests and visitors, and that they are in alien lands, which the blacks do not allow them to have dominion over, or over their religion. Although the blacks are barbarous, a fault they have through their lack of the light of the Faith, they are very clever in their dealings, very grateful for benefits to them, and very vindictive over injuries received. Hence, in the first place, (visitors) should be very liberal, and if they have nothing to give them which would make them happy, and they are satisfied with small gifts, they should use kind words when in their company, and not shock them with (harsh) words, and when they are importunate they should be very patient and tolerant towards them. They should not seduce their women, which is the greatest crime that visitors can commit, in many parts costing them their lives and in other parts their possessions. They should treat well the black they take for their host, since he is always one of the nobles of the land. They should not deny the king and his officers anything they possess, for since these blacks are in a position to demand anything or take it from visitors at will, it is not tactful to let matters go so far. Attend and accompany the blacks in their mournings

> and festivities, for in this way, wherever the (visiting Portuguese) live, they will (be allowed to) stay there, in affection and tranquility; they will profit from the resources of the land, will do business more conveniently, and will sleep more soundly. (Hair 1985, 1–2)

Unlike many impecunious Cabo Verdeans, factors employed by European trading companies received salaries and were provided accommodations, provisions, and other amenities, depending, to be sure, on often unpredictable circumstances. Once established in western Africa, many factors became obsessed with enriching themselves as quickly as possible so as to return to Europe before their constitutions were undermined by chronic illness. To this end, they flouted company regulations forbidding private trade. In their pursuit of illicit wealth, many factors contracted marriage alliances with *nharas,* Luso-African women who played increasingly influential roles in western African commerce during the seventeenth and eighteenth centuries.

Chapter 4
Western Africa and the Onset of an Era of Droughts, Famines, and Global Economic Transformations

> The fundamental characteristic of this era is the universal insecurity caused by warfare. Like Japanese historians, we can, without exaggeration, term this period "the age of countries at war" or the age of turmoil.
>
> —Cissoko 1969, 4

The dry period that began around 1630 and continued for two centuries coincided, both fortuitously and tragically for the peoples of western Africa, with a rapidly growing European demand for slave laborers on American plantations. During the c. 1630–c. 1860 dry period, diminished rainfall, combined with overgrazing and improvident cultivation practices, contributed to environmental degradation and social dislocation in the Sahel, savanna, and savanna-woodland zones. Sporadic but widespread droughts causing famine conditions added to human misery and contributed to inter- and intragroup conflicts that supplied captives in growing numbers for the Atlantic slave trade. Meanwhile, political, economic, and military developments in Europe transformed circumstances increasingly to the disadvantage of Portugal vis-à-vis France, England, and Holland.

The consequences of renewed desiccation in western Africa beginning around 1630 were compounded by population increases that had occurred during the favorable circumstances of the c. 1500–c. 1630 wet period. Rainfall during the c. 1630–c. 1860 dry period was unpredictable, as were devastating locust swarms. Periods of severe drought and famine conditions were interspersed with years of relatively abundant rainfall. Drought and locusts caused a severe famine in Senegambia and the Guinea-Bissau region in 1639 and into the 1640s, and renewed drought conditions began in the 1670s. During the 1680s, people sold themselves into slavery to avoid death by famine. There were droughts in each decade from the 1710s to the 1750s and in the 1770s and 1780s, and famines were frequent between 1790 and 1840. The human misery and social dislocation resulting from such conditions contributed to the phenomenal growth of the Atlantic slave trade during this era (Nicholson 1979, 44–47; Curtin 1975, *Supplementary Evidence,* 3–5; Becker 1985; Moraes 1995, 334–38).

The ongoing desiccation of western Africa compelled the southward migration of Fula herders, who became increasingly interspersed among groups of cultivators in many areas. The southward movement of the tsetse fly, possibly by several hundred kilometers in some areas, promoted the expansion of cavalry warfare, just as happened during the c. 1100–c. 1500 dry period (compare the projected isohyets on Map 1.2). During the first part of the c. 1630–c. 1860 dry period, Mandekalu horse warriors maintained their ascendancy, but as time passed, Fula cavalry increasingly dominated the savanna and savanna-woodland zones as Fula military leaders and Torodbe marabouts combined forces.

There were significant changes in landlord-stranger relations as well. European strangers had formerly traded at the sufferance of landlords, but in the seventeenth century, Europeans and Eurafricans acquired a growing number of allies in African societies who shared mutual interests with respect to prosecuting the slave trade. African traders and warrior elites depended on Luso-Africans and other Eurafrican intermediaries to obtain consumer goods and weapons for themselves and for distribution among their subordinates and dependents. More and more, rulers of stratified states relied on warriors of slave origins; termed *nyanchos* in the Kaabu Empire and *tyeddos* in Senegambia, these groups became more predatory over time. Some rulers and their warrior entourages became so addicted to spirits, tobacco, and other luxuries that they raided and enslaved members of their own societies as the most convenient means of satisfying their cravings. Besides warfare, slave raiding, man stealing, and the kidnapping of children, the growing European demand for slaves contributed to the corruption of judicial processes, which meant that innocent people as well as convicted criminals and other undesirables were sold into transatlantic slavery.

Augmenting European Slaving Voyages

Dutch, French, and English competition in western African trade, which began in the first half of the sixteenth century with sporadic trading voyages and raids by privateers, intensified greatly during the period when Portugal was under Spanish rule (1580–1640). Portugal's military and naval weakness was compounded by the inability of Portuguese merchants to compete with European rivals possessing a greater variety of trade goods for sale at cheaper prices. By the mid-seventeenth century, France controlled the commerce of the Senegal River, England dominated trade in the Gambia River, and English traders based in the Sierra Leone estuary were extending their commerce northward. Luso-Africans contended to maintain their ascendancy in the region that reached from the Gambia River southward to the kola-producing areas in Serra Leoa.

During the seventeenth and eighteenth centuries, France, England, and Holland aggrandized more and more of the world's commerce, including that of western Africa, while Portugal experienced almost uninterrupted economic decline. A small and lightly populated country with archaic political institutions and economic practices, Portugal was incapable of meeting the challenges of the rising mercantile and industrial nations of northern Europe whose seafarers raided Portugal's global commercial networks and seized entrepôts and colonies. Holland, France, and England entrusted such initiatives to monopolistic joint-stock companies, which sought to supplant Portuguese and Spanish traders and settlers wherever they could.

Like the Portuguese monarchs before them, the rulers of Holland, France, and England vainly attempted to enforce mercantilist practices through means of chartered companies granted "exclusive" commercial privileges for enormous areas of poorly mapped out territories. In this effort, they ignored the competing claims of foreign charters, as well as interlopers of every nation. In 1621, the Dutch West India Company was accorded the monopoly of Dutch commerce from Newfoundland to the Straits of Magellan, from the Canary Islands to the Cape of Good Hope, and from the west coast of America to the eastern tip of New Guinea. In 1628, Dutch provinces were allocated spheres of commerce: the Gambia River went to the Chamber of Stadt and Lande, and Serra Leoa went to Maas. In like manner, the English Company of Merchants Trading to Guinea, chartered in 1630, was granted exclusive trading rights from Cape Blanco to the Cape of Good Hope for a thousand years; this enterprise was succeeded only thirty years later by the Company of Royal Adventurers, which, in turn, was followed in 1672 by the Royal African Company. The latter firm was accorded a thousand-year trade monopoly, which survived with modifications until 1752, when supervision of British trade was undertaken by the Committee of Merchants Trading to Africa. Thereafter, African trade was open to all merchants, with the upkeep of forts and factories and the expense of garrisons subsidized by the government—

an arrangement that continued until 1821. French trading companies received comparable privileges to those of English merchants until the French Revolution (Rodney 1970, 127, 163; Kup 1961, 42–43, 78; Curtin 1975, 103–5).

Besides competition between the companies of rival nations and losses from warfare and privateering during European wars, chartered companies were plagued by interlopers—private traders who violated monopolies. The companies were liable for the costly overheads of forts, garrisons, factories, traders, and other employees, but interloping vessels of whatever nation had no such expenses and could trade at greater profit. Moreover, interlopers seized opportunities to subvert company employees and induce such individuals to trade with them for personal advantage. Most damaging to chartered companies, interlopers ruptured landlord-stranger relationships by cheating African traders, kidnapping free persons, and engaging in other irresponsible practices that halted trade, provoked conflicts, or otherwise caused the companies to suffer losses while interlopers fled the consequences of their actions.

As Holland, France, and England acquired plantation colonies in the Americas, they contended for the most valuable slaving markets in western Africa. Astute landlords along the coasts and rivers of western Africa welcomed the rival strangers, exploiting European competition to increase prices, taxes, and tolls. As the demand for slaves increased during the seventeenth and eighteenth centuries, African middlemen were able to alter the terms of barter exchanges increasingly to their advantage. Traders organizing caravans in the interior of western Africa, in places as far distant as markets along the upper Niger River and its tributaries, had to assess factors of distance, tolls, kinship networks, and areas of current and potential conflicts along with information concerning the prices, quality, and variety of goods available in markets where different Europeans traded (Davies 1957, 236–38; Curtin 1975, 340).

If African elites and traders gained significant advantages from the augmented European competition and the burgeoning demand for slaves, the consequences for their societies grew more and more pernicious. Afflicted by deteriorating climatic, economic, and political circumstances, the peoples of western Africa were subjected to chronic warfare, unprovoked raiding by predatory warrior groups, and pervasive corruption of political and social institutions and lifeways. Some rulers and elites in western Africa became so addicted to foreign luxuries (especially brandy, rum, and other spirits) that they initiated unprovoked wars on neighboring groups, and in flagrant cases, they sold their own people into slavery. Certain military elites enjoyed extravagant lifestyles from slave raiding, notoriously, the rulers of the Kaabu Empire and the nyancho warriors. Acting out of self-interest, some acephalous societies—especially the Diola and Balanta in the Guinea-Bissau region and the Baga of Serra Leoa—refused to enslave or sell members of their societies and excluded slave traders from their territories, whether Mandinka, Luso-Africans, or Europeans.

European shipmasters involved in coastwise and riverine commerce scheduled voyages to intersect with African caravans, their vessels departing European ports in the late fall or early winter. Ships' passages were facilitated by the prevailing northeasterly winds and southward-flowing Canary Current. African traders meanwhile awaited the onset of the dry season, when trade goods would not be damaged by rain, streams were fordable, and rivers could be safely crossed. The dry season was also the healthiest time for Europeans because (unknown to them) once pools of rainwater dried, there were fewer mosquitoes and hence a diminished risk of contracting malaria. Vessels laden with supplies for European forts and factories were irregularly dispatched, sometimes arriving during the rainy season.

One consequence of the internationalization of western African trade was the use of iron "bars" to reckon prices. These pieces were actually made from strips of the flat wrought iron that was common along the lower Rhine River and were initially brought to western Africa on Dutch vessels. Africans, having no use for European metal or paper currencies, valued a given commodity as worth so many bars—a figure that fluctuated with supply and demand (Wright 1997, 120; Fyfe 2000, 35 n. 32). By the latter part of the sixteenth century, western African commerce was facilitated by the use of bars as a notional currency: ivory tusks, slaves, quantities of wax, and other goods were valued as worth so many iron bars according to weight, quantity, and other criteria. This expedient derived from the iron bars forged by Mande smiths. They were approximately twenty-three centimeters long, two fingers thick at one end, and three fingers thick at the other, and they served both as a convenient means of transporting iron for manufacture into implements and weapons and as a circulating currency. Portuguese and competing European traders increasingly catered to demand by shipping large amounts of iron to western Africa in narrow, flattened bars, approximately four to six meters in length and weighing about twelve to fourteen kilograms apiece. These bars could be cut by African smiths to form "country bars" twenty to thirty centimeters long, each weighing about seven hundred grams, which closely approximated African bars (Rodney 1970, 194; Curtin 1975, 240–41). Trade in European—and African—forged iron led to the standardization of iron bars and their value. Philip Curtin explained:

> By the 1660s, the bar was fully established as a piece of flat wrought iron about 3 meters long, 5 cm wide, and 9 mm thick, weighing about 13 kgs. It

> was often notched for convenient subdivision into smaller pieces, each about 20 cm long and the proper shape and weight for making a hoe blade. . . . Every commodity entering international trade had a price in bars of iron [that was] unchanging. They were not, in fact, price quotations so much as a system of equivalents for translating the value of other imported commodities into a certain quantity of iron. (Curtin 1975, 241)

Tenacious and resourceful, Luso-Africans welcomed trade with European vessels, but they used every means at their disposal to prevent European rivals from becoming established ashore, supplanting them as middlemen in trade, or gaining access to sources of kola and panos. Luso-Africans exploited to the fullest their advantages as residents of western Africa, including kinship networks among acephalous groups; command of the Crioulo and Mandinka languages, which European newcomers had to learn; and greater immunities to various diseases. Wherever they could, Luso-Africans appropriated the role of translators and intermediaries, and in these capacities Luso-African women also achieved notable success.

The Braganza Dynasty and Three Decades of War with Spain

The Spanish-Portuguese union was ruptured on December 1, 1640, by a Portuguese revolt that took advantage of Spain's involvement in a prolonged struggle with a Catalonian irredentist movement and war with France, during which France opportunistically provided assistance both to the Portuguese and to the Catalans (Lang 1979, 99; Blackburn 1997, 196). Hostilities between Portugal and Spain continued until 1668, while the rival maritime powers of Europe contended for control of global sea-lanes and markets. Spain's rulers sought to damage Portugal's economy in every way possible, depriving Portuguese merchants of Spanish capital and commodities and excluding them from participation in the highly remunerative slave trade with Spanish colonies in the Americas. Meanwhile, Spanish vessels continued to frequent Cacheu and other Luso-African entrepôts in western Africa, where they were welcomed by the resident Portuguese, Spanish, and Luso-Africans alike (Rodney 1970, 128, 136–37).

Portugal's economic and military weakness vis-à-vis Spain and the continuing hostilities between the two countries, including wars during the 1640s, 1650s, and 1660s, time and again compelled Portugal's rulers to seek assistance from England—a weakness and dependence that England exploited to its own advantage. In return for helping Portugal by recognizing the Braganza dynasty, forming an alliance against Spain, and rendering military assistance, England negotiated lucrative commercial concessions. The treaties crafted in 1642, 1654, and 1656—the last imposed by an English squadron dispatched to Lisbon to compel ratification—and the capstone Methuen Treaty of 1703 exacted commercial privileges for English traders in Portuguese colonies and entrepôts, including participation in slave trading. A secret clause in the 1654 treaty stipulated that English goods could not be taxed more than 23 percent ad valorem, a rate even lower than that assessed Portuguese merchants—a concession that worsened a chronic balance-of-payment problem. The Methuen treaty, negotiated by the English ambassador in December 1703 on the eve of Spain's invasion of Portugal during the War of the Spanish Succession (1702–13), extorted the duty-free admission of English textiles into Portugal in return for the unequal concession that Portuguese wines be admitted into England at a greatly reduced tariff. As a consequence, English merchants gained a dominant role in Portugal's commerce at the expense of Portuguese commercial and manufacturing interests, both existing and potential (Sideri 1970, 19–20; Hanson 1983, 498–99).

The Conselho Ultramarino (Overseas Council), founded in 1642, was bereft of the requisite funds and personnel to address Portugal's far-flung commercial and colonial involvements. Portugal's trade with western Africa comprised only a small and relatively unimportant portion of its overseas commerce, and when members of the Conselho Ultramarino or other government officials considered western Africa, it was primarily with respect to its potential for supplying slaves for the exploitation of Brazil's plantations and mines (Bardwell 1974, chap. 5). In the circumstances, successive capitães-mores dispatched to Cacheu to oversee Portuguese interests in western Africa were allocated grossly insufficient resources to achieve their mandates. Conditions did not improve until Portugal and Spain made peace in 1668, and Portugal afterward contrived to avoid involvement in the spate of European wars involving Holland, England, and France in the 1660s and 1670s that significantly weakened these rivals in western African commerce.

Cacheu: Landlord Intransigence versus Portuguese Initiatives, 1640s–1660s

When Portugal gained its independence from Spain in 1640—and for decades thereafter—slave trading at Cacheu and other entrepôts in the Guinea-Bissau region was dominated by Spanish traders whose vessels crossed the Atlantic without paying customs duties to the Portuguese treasury. Due to the continuing state of war between the two countries, João IV decreed on December 20, 1640, that Spanish vessels would be excluded from trade in the Cabo Verde archipelago and western Africa unless they deposited securities in Portugal—a decree that proved unenforceable (Rodney 1970, 128; Esteves 1988, 4–11).

News of the Portuguese revolt in Lisbon and the accession of the new monarch, João IV, reached the island of São Tiago on January 25, 1641, and was delivered to Cacheu on February 18, 1641, by two caravels carrying Cabo Verde's *ouvidor geral* (chief magistrate) and *provedor da fazenda* (superintendent of the public treasury), who managed to seize some of the Spanish traders and confiscate their slaves and other possessions. The inhabitants of Cacheu and other trading communities celebrated Portugal's independence, with the leading residents signing proclamations attesting their loyalty to the new king (Faro 1958, 491–93).

The aclamação for Cacheu and São Domingo was drafted on February 18 and 19, with the following names registered by the clerk, João de São Migell Salgado: Luis de Magalhãies (the capitão-mor), Jerónimo de Souza Santiago, João d'Almeida, João Roiz da Costa, Fernão Lopes de Misquita, Manoel da Costa, Tomás Roiz Baraza, Dioguo Baraza Francês, Salvador Roiz Pinheiro, the padre Thomé Afonço, Juzé Vieira de Lisboa, Juzé Roiz Pinheiro, João Gomes figueira, Simão Roiz Preto, João de Aguiar, Anrique Dias de Carvalho, Luis Botelho, Domingos Fernandez, Bertholomeu Gilherme, and Mário da Costa (Faro 1958, 499–500). Padre João de Almeida was Cacheu's *vigário* (parish priest) and *visitador geral* (inspector general) for Guinea (Rema 1982, 115–17). The individual listed as "Simão Roiz [Rodriguez] *Preto*" was most likely a *pardo,* or Luso-African, possibly a son of Symon Rodrigos, a Marrano who had left Iberia for Amsterdam and was trading at Portudal in 1609 (Thilmans and Moraes 1977, 491). One may suppose that, for the purpose of impressing João IV and his ministers, no one of consequence who was present at the signing of the aclamação failed to record his name. No one was identified as being Spanish or Luso-African, and there were no female signatories; the same is the case regarding the lists of names that follow.

The names recorded on the proclamation at Bissau signed on February 27 were Manoel Fernandes Gil, Francisco Nunes d'Andrade, João Carvalho, Marçal Cardozo, Manoel Ramos, Gaspar Dias Demisquita, Francisco Dias Cardozo, Francisco Godhino, and Baltazar Martins (Faro 1958, 503). And on March 10, the following names were recorded on the proclamation at Geba: Manoell Anriques, Manoell Roiz Salgado, Dioguo Demisquita, Manoell de Matos, Vicente

Roiz, Baltezar Dias, Pero Roiz, Miguel Ribeiro, Francisco de Andrade, Paulo Roiz, Simão Roiz Idanha, Juzé Roiz, and António Roiz Salgado (Faro 1958, 505). The names listed at Guinala on April 24 were Vicente Ferreira, Manoel Fernandez Gil, Vicente Fereira, Francisco Soares, António Janes, Manoell Soares, Dioguo Soares, Lionardo Lopes, Manoell Soares, Migell da Veigua, Francisco Fernandez da Costa, Bernardo Gomes, Pero Nunes, Graviell Mendes, Nocolao Afonço, Jorge Mendes, and Fernão Gualego (Faro 1958, 507).

Less than a year later, on December 5, 1641, when the inhabitants of Cacheu sent a petition to João IV concerning a disastrous decline in commerce due to the embargo of Spanish slavers and the consequences of three years of famine in the region, the names subscribed included a half dozen listed on the February aclamação, plus fourteen new names—presumably men absent from Cacheu in February or recently arrived from Cabo Verde or Europe: Lizardo Manoel Henriques, Francisco Alvarez de Britto, Bertolameu Roiz Machado, Salvador Roiz Pinto, Rui de Souza, Gaspar Dias Damesquita, Rodrigo Peres, Gonçalo Costa, Gil Gonçalvez, Jerónimo Nunes Peres, Jorge do Frances, Phelipe Camacho, Manuel Luis Focivell, and Manoell Gonçalves (Faro 1958, 512–15).

The December 1641 petition was a sham, for the capitão-mor of Cacheu, Luis de Magalhães (1641?–1644), had been unable to enforce the ban on Spanish vessels against the opposition by African, Luso-African, Portuguese, and Spanish traders. Infuriated by the embargo, Papel threatened to kill the Portuguese inhabitants, and Magalhães was compelled to accede to their demands for free trade and to increase customs payments to Papel rulers. There were more Spanish traders than Portuguese traders at Cacheu, and other Spanish traders lived in African communities along the Cacheu River and elsewhere in the Guinea-Bissau region (Faro 1958, 510; Rodney 1965, 318, and 1970, 128–30, 133; Esteves 1988, 4–11).

Cacheu's prospective importance as a source of slaves for Brazil was accorded priority consideration by the Conselho Ultramarino when it was created by royal decree on July 14, 1642. The council was given the responsibility of overseeing colonial affairs, including dispatching fleets and recommending candidates for most of the important overseas civil, military, and ecclesiastical assignments (Bardwell 1974, 95–96). Two days after the council convened, Gonçalo de Gamboa de Aiala, a veteran of sixteen years of service in India and three in Brazil, was selected for a three-year term as capitão-mor of Cacheu. He was instructed to establish a fortified settlement to defend against a Spanish attack, possibly in alliance with local Papel. Aiala was promised building materials, munitions, masons, carpenters, sixty soldiers, and funds derived from possessions seized from Spanish traders that were deposited at Ribeira Grande in São Tiago, plus moneys allocated for the construction of the cathedral at Ribeira Grande, and the inhabitants of Cacheu were enjoined to contribute the services of their slaves to construct fortifications.

In addition to his responsibility for the trading communities of Cacheu, Farim, Bolor, and Ziguinchor in the Cacheu-Casamance-Gambia network, Aiala was to oversee trade at Bissau, Geba, along the Grande River, and elsewhere in western Africa—the very enumeration of which makes evident the impossibility of his fulfilling the council's mandate (Barcellos 1899–1913, 2:4; Rodney 1970, 129–30). After these decisions were expeditiously resolved by the Conselho Ultramarino, a two-year delay in implementation ensued, during which royal officials struggled to collect the requisite personnel and resources while contending with the economic, military, diplomatic, and other challenges confronting the new government. Aiala's expedition did not sail until the end of 1644, following a spate of frontier warfare with Spain.

Meanwhile, members of the Conselho Ultramarino addressed a number of policy issues and agonized over false rumors of Spanish expeditions mobilizing to capture Cacheu. Promoting slave exports from Cacheu to Brazil's sugar plantations was a priority concern. Previously, Brazil had been supplied with captives from the Gold Coast, Kongo, and especially Angola. But the Dutch had captured São Jorge da Mina, the chief fort on the Gold Coast, in 1637, and in August 1641 they captured Luanda and Benguela (Barcellos 1899–1913, 2:3–4; Rodney 1970, 136; Esteves 1988, 11–18; Blackburn 1997, 195). In the circumstances, western Africa's potential as a source of slaves was accorded inflated importance by the Conselho Ultramarino, whose members were informed in 1643 that Spanish vessels had exported an average of three thousand captives annually in the years prior to the dissolution of the joint monarchy, not including slaves sold to vessels of other European nations (Rodney 1970, 98). These estimates, derived from André Donelha, were probably valid for only the best years shortly before 1600 and 1622 (Curtin 1969, 109–10). Inflated estimates such as these influenced policy makers when Cacheu trading companies were founded in 1676 and 1690.

Even if traders at Cacheu and other entrepôts in western Africa could supply greater numbers of captives, the Portuguese slave trade confronted the formidable deterrent of Atlantic passages made dangerous by the almost continuous European warfare in the decades following Portugal's independence, with shipping menaced by Spanish, Dutch, and French warships and privateers. Few Portuguese shipmasters dared traverse the Atlantic from western Africa to Brazil.

Consequently, the slaves collected by Portuguese, Cabo Verdean, and Luso-African traders at Cacheu, Bissau, and other entrepôts were sold to Spanish, Dutch, English, and French vessels for transportation across the Atlantic.

To encourage participation in the Atlantic slave trade, a royal decree of October 7, 1642, opened western African trade to all Portuguese citizens and abrogated the commercial privileges accorded the inhabitants of the Cabo Verde archipelago by King Afonso V in 1466. Another royal ordinance in December 1644 rescinded the long-standing regulation—honored in the breach for many years—that required vessels trading with western Africa to stop at São Tiago to pay royal duties on captives and other commodities. Thereafter, duties could be paid at Cacheu, enabling Portuguese vessels to sail to Brazil without routing voyages via the Cabo Verde archipelago. This decision was detrimental to Cabo Verdean mercantile interests and to the funding of the royal administration of the archipelago, and it provided few benefits to Cacheu, where Spanish slavers continued to dominate trade. In the circumstances, the governor of Cabo Verde, João Serrão da Cunha (1640–45), accused Capitão-Mor Magalhães of complicity with resident Spanish traders and visiting English vessels and dispatched him to Portugal under arrest for treason (Rodney 1970, 123–24, 129; Esteves 1988, 14, 21–27).

Prior to his long-delayed departure for Cacheu in October 1644, Aiala requested royal orders commanding traders living at Geba and along the Gambia River to move to Cacheu as a means to strengthen the settlement and break commercial links with "foreigners and Jews" that were prejudicial to the collection of royal customs duties. The inhabitants of Cacheu from whom assistance was specifically required were Cristóvão de Melo Coelho, Fernão Lopes de Mesquita, Tomaz Rodriguez Barrasa, Tristão de Sotomayor, Salvador Rodriguez Pereira, and Ioão Luiz da Cunha; at Geba, Capitão Nunes d'Andrade was likewise obligated (Esteves 1988, 23–24, 80–81).

During his residence at Cacheu from 1644 to 1649, Aiala achieved few of the objectives he undertook to accomplish. He was constrained to continue Magalhães's policy of appeasing African rulers with higher customs payments. Indeed, due to the exclusion of Spanish vessels and the consequent loss of customs duties, Aiala was obliged to commit the Conselho Ultramarino to a substantial increase in annual payments made to the rulers of Mata and Mompatas: 7.5 pipes of wine, 40 quintals of cotton, and 187 cruzados, besides the customs the rulers levied on vessels (Rodney 1970, 129–30, 135–36).

Whether because of Africans' intransigence or because of a spiteful disagreement with a brother officer, as Francisco de Lemos Coelho alleged, Gamboa de

Aiala did not move the settlement to a reef of rocks called the Calaca, commanding the riverside where the Bourganbor streamlet flows into the Cacheu River (Hair 1985, chap. 3: 14–15). The first explanation seems more likely, for of the sixty soldiers that accompanied Gamboa de Aiala from Portugal, only twenty were alive six months later—a dwindling force that could not have defeated local Africans (Esteves 1988, 42). In addition to the issue of controlling the supply of potable water, the shallows where the Calaca reef extends into the Cacheu River had to be taken into consideration; the site was suitable for beaching small craft but not for mooring seafaring vessels. The original stockade and subsequent fortifications were sited where the river was sufficiently deep for anchoring vessels close to protecting cannons. As an alternative, Aiala proposed moving the garrison and settlement from Cacheu to the Diola (Bayot) community of Bolor ("Bulol") on the north bank near the mouth of the Cacheu River, but he was denied permission by his superiors in Lisbon (Hair 1985, chap. 3: 7). Bolor's inhabitants controlled the entrance of the Ename and Bolor marigots, which comprised the southern entrance of the Banyun marigot and portage routes connecting the Casamance River, and Bolor was a place of extensive trade in rice grown by Diola groups in the region (Labat 1728, 5:237–38; Rodney 1970, 136).

Aiala initiated a policy of leasing access to the Casamance River to only one trader, with the rent designated to support Cacheu's garrison (Hair 1985, chap. 3: 2). But he was unable to persuade Portuguese and Luso-African traders to abandon their establishments north and south of the Cacheu River and settle along the Cacheu under his supervision. In a dispatch dated October 6, 1646, he charged that the discontented residents would surrender Cacheu to Spain at the first opportunity. To prevent them from doing so, he appealed for reinforcements consisting of two frigates and fifty to sixty soldiers, the frigates to be used to blockade the Gambia River (Teixeira 1950, 96; Rodney 1970, 130–31).

Aiala's most notable accomplishment was to persuade traders at Geba on the Geba River to move to Farim at the head of navigation on the Cacheu River and make it the chief entrepôt for trade with the Kaabu Empire and markets along the upper Gambia River. Previously, commerce at Farim was restricted to one person who leased a trade monopoly, whereas Geba was the principal port for kola vessels and was a large Portuguese and Luso-African trading community. Farim subsequently prospered, and Aiala and his successor capitães-mores were able to monitor its commerce. Meanwhile, the individual granted a monopoly of Geba's commerce had little success, with his one vessel trading kola, iron, and other goods in competition with resident Luso-Africans (Hair 1985, chap. 6: 4–5; Rodney 1970, 131). Aiala seemingly had little or no control or influence over traders south of the Geba River; in 1645, the governor of Cabo Verde reported that an English and a French vessel had purchased slaves along the Grande River (Mauro 1959, 200).

Mande traders visiting Farim purchased huge quantities of kola. In contrast to the seven or more vessels dispatched from Cacheu to Serra Leoa at the time of Father Barreira's visit in 1608, Coelho reported that during the 1640s and 1650s, he observed ten to twelve vessels or even as many as eighteen transporting kola to Farim. The vessels carried four to five thousand barrels, each containing some thirty-three hundred kola. Besides kola, Coelho noted, large quantities of *patacas* (silver coins), iron, and beads were bartered at Farim for captives. Coelho characterized the traders at Farim as Muslim Soninke, adding that Soninke had converted all Mandinka to Islam. From Farim, small craft might continue two tides upriver to Jandegu, trading for beeswax at villages along the way. A caravan route linked Jandegu with Geba on the Geba River (Hair 1985, chap. 4: 6–9).

Coelho stated that Cacheu's capitão-mor appointed a *cabo* (headman), who was responsible for settling disputes among traders at Farim and dealing with Mande rulers and traders. A cabo invariably parlayed his authority to become one of the wealthiest traders. Farim's trading community was served by a priest dispatched from Cabo Verde.

> If [the priest] gets on well with the inhabitants he can acquire a substantial income, for they provide him with everything. Each year, if he is well thought of, they make him a gift, which they call the *bolo* (the total sum in the kitty), which in my time was as much as ten or twelve *negros de fato* [trade slaves]. In the town is a church dedicated to Our Lady of the Conception. The houses of the residents are like those at Cacheo. The settlement is fortified on the landward side with an enclosure or *tabanca,* like that at Cacheo, with two gates, which when there are wars are closed at night. At one gate is a little platform, on which, in my day, was sited a cannon; since then the settlement has undergone many changes, but I understand that today it is in the same state (?in respect of defences). (Hair 1985, chap. 4: 6)

One may suppose that the cannon and tabanca were more for display than defense: it was the farim of Birassu who ensured the safety of strangers and peaceful circumstances for their commerce.

Coelho described how residents of Cacheu dispatched vessels to the Nunez River to purchase cakes of indigo dye for sale at Cacheu and Banyun markets:

> In one year I saw more than 100,000 items (balls) of dyestuff traveling from this port, and all were made use of at Cacheo and the ports of the Banhus. On Rio de Nuno the cost to the owners of the ships which go from Cacheo to obtain them, by buying them from the whites of the river who in turn buy them from the blacks, is one slave for 500 balls. But at Cacheo it is usual to offer only 120 balls for a slave, or when they are in good supply, 160. From these figures it can be seen what the profits of Guinea are. For trading in this river it is necessary to have cloth and more cloth, and the better the cloth the better the trade; also wine, Indian cloth, cowries, iron and foreign goods—these latter used to be taken there before it had a foreign trading post. (Hair 1985, chap. 9: 9)

The last reference was to a Royal African Company factory that had been established by the Royal Adventurers during the 1660s and reoccupied by the Royal African Company during the 1670s (Kup 1961, 98). Coelho did not mention it, but presumably, some of the cloth used to purchase dyestuffs was obtained from Mande traders at Farim. Some of the Cacheu vessels "wintered" in the Pongo River (Hair 1985, chap. 9: 10).

Aiala relentlessly strove to assert Portugal's sovereignty and to strengthen his tenuous authority. In January 1647, when three Spanish Capuchin friars arrived at Cacheu as members of a mission dispatched to western Africa under the pope's auspices, he treated them as spies and deported them to São Tiago, whence they were sent to Lisbon (Hair 1985, chap. 9: 42–45; Anguiano 1950/1957, xxvi). Aiala's endeavors notwithstanding, Spanish traders continued to monopolize the slave trade. In a dispatch dated February 25, 1647, Aiala accused the traders at Cacheu and elsewhere along the Upper Guinea Coast of disloyalty and of preferring Spain to Portugal. Aiala's warning and a communication from Cacheu's vigário, João de Almeida, that French, English, and Dutch traders were dominating western Africa's trade caused the members of the Conselho Ultramarino to caution João IV that with Luanda's trade controlled by the Dutch, the loss of Cacheu would cut off the supply of slaves needed in Brazil (Teixeira 1950, 96).

João IV was persuaded to issue a decree on June 1, 1647, permitting Cacheu's inhabitants to sell slaves to vessels bound for the Spanish West Indies if the shipmasters deposited financial securities in Portugal or São Tiago (Teixeira 1950, 95–96; Bardwell 1974, 139; Barcellos 1899–1913, 2:12–13). This decree loosening trade restrictions with Spanish possessions might be explained by the fact that few Portuguese shipmasters dared to cross the Atlantic to Brazil or anywhere else in the Americas due to the continuing state of war with Spain and for fear of attack by vessels of other European countries. Dutch mariners harried the annual Brazilian sugar fleet, and in 1647 and 1648, they captured some 220 Portuguese vessels (Livermore 1969, 182). In June 1648, when Holland made peace with Spain, Portuguese mariners and merchants must have despaired of ever seeing better times.

Meanwhile, Aiala's tense relations with resident traders had escalated to a crisis. In a June 29, 1647, dispatch, he denounced Fernão Lopes de Mesquita, João Lopes da Costa, Tomás Rodrigues da Costa, Diogo Barraza Francês, and Salvador Rodrigues Pinheiro for treason. These men and five other traders—Manuel de Matos, Rodrigo Peres, Simão Lopes de Cunha, Manuel Rodrigues Salgado, and Francisco Fernandes da Costa—countered with a complaint dated the same day, charging Aiala with interference in their commerce. They asserted that members of the trading community were loyal to the king of Portugal—notwithstanding the fact that the resident traders included almost eighty Spaniards and no more than five or six Portuguese (Esteves 1988, 43–44).

Francisco Fernandes da Costa reputedly was a brother of the "very powerful" Manuel da Costa. According to rumors current in December 1647, the latter had been appointed capitão-mor of Cacheu by the king of Spain, who allegedly was outfitting four or five warships to capture Cacheu. Reportedly, too, a number of Portuguese with trading experience in western Africa were associated with the venture (Esteves 1988, 46, 119). The Portuguese government was sufficiently alarmed by the false rumors to dispatch the frigate *S. Teodósio* and another vessel on February 20, 1648, with reinforcements and supplies for Cacheu's garrison. The expedition sailed via São Tiago and reached Cacheu on May 10.

The *S. Teodósio*'s captain improbably claimed to have prevented "five powerful New Christians" from professing allegiance to Spain (Esteves 1988, 46–47, 120–22). Diogo Barrassa, Thomas Barrassa, Fernão Lopes de Mesquita, Manuel Fragoso Sotto Maior, and João Rodrigues da Costa, all of whom had business dealings with Spanish traders, were taken prisoner and transported to São Tiago, as was the Cacheu resident António da Cunha, who was apprehended for piloting two Seville vessels into the Gambia River (Barcellos 1899–1913, 2:12–13). Not long after the *S. Teodósio* and the accompanying vessel arrived in Cacheu, the sailors and soldiers began to sicken and die, which inevitably restored the balance of power in favor of resident traders, with their retinues of armed grumetes and family ties with the leaders of the Papel communities A year later, on June 29, 1649, João IV pardoned the accused traders (Esteves 1988, 42–43, 121–22).

In April 1649, a new royal measure levied a 5 percent tax on coastwise trade in indigo dye, kola, and iron, the proceeds intended for the support of Cacheu's garrison and two coastal patrol vessels (Esteves 1988, 42, 123). It is, however, unlikely that many taxes were collected by Gamboa de Aiala or his successors or that the funds were used as intended. Gamboa de Aiala was rewarded for his loyal service with the governorship of Cabo Verde and Guinea, only to die in 1650 during his first year in office (Rodney 1970, 131). Meanwhile, the vigáro Gaspar Vogado was appointed acting capitão-mor of Cacheu and charged with the responsibility of strengthening the *praça's* (stronghold's) fortifications against a Spanish expedition that was rumored to be in the offing. Vogado had been the superintendent of fortifications in Cabo Verde for a number of years. He possessed considerable wealth and had used his personal funds and slaves to construct a fort and two churches, besides making generous contributions of provisions and munitions to the government. How Vogado came by his riches is not recorded, but as *visitão-geral dos rios da Guiné* (inspector general of the rivers of Guinea), he might have behaved as others before and after him, engaging in slave trading and soliciting generous donations from traders grateful for priestly services and dispensations (Barcellos 1899–1913, 2:10; Bardwell 1974, 136–38; Esteves 1988, 49). Coelho disparaged the fortifications that Vogado constructed at Cacheu as "more like pens for cattle than walls intended for the defence of men" (Hair 1985, chap. 3: 15).

With rumors continuing to circulate in Lisbon about Spanish plans to attack Cacheu, a new capitão-mor, João Carreira fidalgo (1650–54), was dispatched to the area. He was given two caravels loaded with fifty men, cannons, and other armaments to construct a new fort that would command Cacheu's water supply, the spring-fed Bourganbor streamlet. However, local Africans refused to grant the land, supply building materials, or provide labor, and the project was abandoned. Carreira's term as capitão-mor was marked by peculation on such a scale that he was arrested at São Tiago en route to Lisbon in 1654. Some forty thousand cruzados were found in his baggage, of which twenty-four thousand allegedly were given by five Spanish shipmasters in return for exemptions on the sale of liquor, tools, guns, and other contraband (Bardwell 1974, 139–40).

An expedition outfitted in Rio de Janeiro recaptured Luanda, Benguela, and the island of São Tomé in August 1648—successes that had the consequence of diminishing Cacheu's importance as a potential source of slaves for Brazil (Blackburn 1997, 200). The opportunistic founding of the monopolistic Companhia Geral do Comércio do Brasil (which operated from 1649 to 1720) exemplified the unprincipled treatment meted out to New Christians: the capital financing the new company was chiefly raised among New Christian merchants in return for promises that their properties would be exempted from confiscation by the Holy Office (Winius 1981, 128–31; Hanson 1983, 497).

A substantial decline in Cacheu's trade in subsequent years was indicated by a report by Cabo Verde's *ouvidor* (magistrate) in April 1656 that Cacheu had only six white inhabitants, all of whom allegedly were Jewish (Teixeira 1950, 89). In January 1654, with the capture of Recife, the Dutch were expelled from Brazil, but competition for Brazil's wealth led to renewed Portuguese-Dutch warfare from 1657 to 1661 (Langer 1958, 439, 453; Boxer 1969, 112–13).

Successive capitães-mores of Cacheu accommodated to the realities of their circumstances, though they rarely acknowledged this in dispatches. African control of Cacheu's potable water supply, refuge given to runaway slaves, trade stoppages, threats to set fire to the settlement, and other sanctions time and again cautioned Portuguese and Luso-Africans about the precariousness of their situation. Self-interest coincided with accommodation; for contrary to military regulations, capitães-mores and subordinate officers profited from commerce, whether by private trade, peculation, or both (Rodney 1965, 316–17; 1970, 129–30, 135–37). In sporadic instances when Portuguese commanders resorted to military force, the effort generally proved counterproductive. The combative capitão-mor Manuel Dias Quatrim (1657–62) dispatched a force to burn several Diola villages at Bolor in retaliation for the plundering of trading craft. More than twenty soldiers were killed, the sole survivor being a Luso-African inhabitant of Cacheu who was badly wounded. Hostilities continued for the remainder of the decade, with Diola killing all whites who fell into their hands. Cacheu's garrison was also defeated by the Diola of Mata, and the commandant had to negotiate a settlement. Quatrim so antagonized neighboring Africans that Cacheu's landlord, the ruler of Mata, threatened to burn the settlement (Hair 1985, chap. 3: 8–9; Rodney 1970, 136).

In contrast, Quatrim's successor, António da Fonseca de Ornelas (1662–64), contrived to win the friendship of Mata's ruler, even serving as godfather at the latter's baptism. The ruler offered King Afonso VI a new (unspecified) site for the settlement that was "very cool and pleasant," but the offer was not accepted (Teixeira 1950, 100). Franciscans experienced failure as well as success. In 1664, when Father Sebastião attempted to stop a *chôro* in Banyun territory near Cacheu, he escaped with his life only by the intervention of several Christian converts. Chôros (from the Portuguese word for weeping) were wakes held to commemorate the deaths of elites. They lasted for days and sometimes for weeks and included feasting and dancing to musical instruments, the open-air eating and drinking being similar to Portuguese observances of All Souls' Day. Rulers were interred with cloth, iron, gold, and other valuable possessions, including slaves. A horse was buried alive near the grave. Like Portuguese, Christian converts continued to commune with their ancestors, including through the intermediation of *balobeiros* (or *valobeiros* [spirit mediums]) who were consulted about important matters such as commercial undertakings (Dias 1945, 161–62, 226–27; Carreira 1961, 514–15, 521–22, 533–36; Rema 1982, 150).

Portuguese merchants sought to take advantage of the improved circumstances in Guinea and the cession of Portuguese-Dutch warfare. In 1664, the brothers Lourenço Pestana Martins and Manuel da Costa Martins of Porto da Palmida founded the Companhia da Costa da Guiné for a term of eight years, but the firm had little success (Teixeira 1950, 110; Hanson 1981, 234). Francisco de Lemos Coelho, a Cabo Verdean from São Tiago whose years as a trader in western Africa spanned the mid-1640s to the mid-1660s and whose account incorporated additional information up to the time he completed his manuscript in the 1680s, described Cacheu as follows:

> [Cacheu] comprises two streets, the main one, where the houses of the inhabitants of most standing are situated, called Rua de Diante (Front Street); and another street behind this one, (the houses) right up against the fortifications of the town, called Rua de Tabanca (*Tabanca* Street). Apart from these two streets, the whole settlement is divided into two quarters. The first at the entry (to the town) is where the Commander lives, and where the parish church (*igreja matriz*) of Our Lady of Victory (*do Vencimento*) is situated, and this is called the quarter of Vila Fria (Cold Town). The other quarter, at the opposite end of town, has a chapel (*ermida*) dedicated to Santo António and is called Vila Quente (Hot Town). It has many houses of free blacks who work as *grumetes*, and it contains many heathen. Being a rare nest of thieves, it does a lot of harm to the town, hence many commanders have thought of razing it to the ground. To the same end, Commander Manoel de Almeida [1664–74] recently altered the fortifications, shifting the *tabanca* [stockade] to close up to the chapel of Santo António, which now forms the first point of this quarter of Vila Quente, putting the rest of the quarter and its inhabitants outside the protected part of the settlement, to live, as it were, on their own. (Hair 1985, chap. 3: 10–11)

Coelho's description was substantially valid for the next two centuries, as were his comments regarding the chronic disrepair of the fortifications and the diseased and dispirited soldiers of the garrison:

> The first house on entering the town through the quarter of Vila Fria, is the Strong House (*casa forte*). Its only resemblance to a fort is that it is made of

> stone and lime, that it belongs to His Highness and is maintained in his name, and that the Commander resides there with the twenty-five soldiers allocated to him, of which often, and even regularly, not as many as three are actually present. Overlooking the water, the Strong House has a terrace of stone and lime, (but one) so small that, in the rainy season, it is thatched over like the other buildings. On this platform some cannons are mounted according to the fancy and zeal of the commander who rules such a garrison. I have known it to the case—and I do not say when, lest I seem to censure the particular commander who was serving at the time—that it lacked a single gun that could be fired without risk, although the establishment had plenty of unmounted cannons, and any amount of timber to make carriages.
>
> Near this platform are the houses of the commander, which are made of sun-dried bricks and roofed with thatch, like the rest of the town. In the middle of them is a building with earth on top, this being the arrangement in the case of the other buildings (in the town) in which goods are kept, these buildings being called *cumbetes.* The *cumbetes* are the store-houses (which form part) of all residences, in order to counter the danger of fire. Because they have earth on top, even if the town is burned down, as very often happens, what is (stored) in the *combetes* is never burned. Below the houses of the commander is another terrace, also carrying cannons, their line of fire being inland, (hence directed) against the heathen. . . . All of this is surrounded by a stockade formed of pointed stakes with sharp tips, fastened together with crossbars, and it has two gates which are closed at night. . . .
>
> The settlement is completely surrounded on the landward side in the same way as the Strong House is. The stockade is constructed in the form and with the degree of strength (successive) commanders want it to be, and is often tumble-down, since the inhabitants share out the responsibility of building it, each individual taking so many yards (*braças*). This fortification is called the *tabanca.* I knew one commander who said that the only fortification he wanted was one of butts of wine to give to the blacks. Outside the *tabanca,* a good wide moat, full of water, used to be maintained, which canoes could enter and leave; today most of the moat is clogged with mud. (Hair 1985, chap. 3: 11–12, 14)

The anonymous capitão-mor's facetious remark acknowledged the fecklessness of Cacheu's inhabitants and their knowledge that the garrison was incapable of defending the settlement by military means. As mentioned, African landlords possessed numerous ways to compel submission, including stoppages of water and food and threats of setting fire to the traders' compounds. The latter menace was put into effect on more than one occasion, and Coelho helpfully specified where thatch was obtained in Banyun territory across the river to replace roofs after conflagrations (Hair 1985, chap. 4: 2). For centuries to come, the capitães-mores and members of the trading community at Cacheu had little recourse other than to try to maintain the status quo and keep rents and customary tolls as low as possible. When disputes arose, on occasion caused by arrogant and bellicose Portuguese commandants, resident traders intervened to restore peaceful conditions for commerce, offering African rulers wine, aguardente, and other presents.

On February 13, 1668, after decades of inconclusive border skirmishing, Spain recognized Portugal's independence and signed a peace treaty (Langer 1958, 453). Portugal was now at peace with all other European nations for the first time since the rupture with the Spanish monarchy in 1640. On September 26, 1670, when the Conselho Ultramarino took stock of the vicissitudes that Cacheu had experienced, it acknowledged that the maintenance of the praça had been almost a miracle (Teixeira 1950, 101).

Cacheu's "miraculous" survival derived not from soldiers and fortress walls but from Luso-Africans' commercial and kinship ties with neighboring African groups and the willingness of the latter to maintain commercial relations. Members of the Conselho Ultramarino addressed the humiliating circumstances whereby the king of Portugal was titled "Senhor da Guiné" but paid feudal duty to the ruler of Mata and Africans controlled the praça's water supply. The council recommended extending the praça's tabanca to the Bourganbor streamlet as the means to end this humiliation. No action was taken, however, and by 1671, the garrison had diminished to four men. In 1674, the residents of Cacheu were characterized as being "more like slaves to the insolence of blacks than their masters" [escravos da insolencia dos negros que conquistadores] (Teixeira 1950, 100, 112; Rodney 1970, 149–50).

Chapter 5
The Evolution of "Nharaship" in Senegambia

Apres luy avoir fait un present de corail et d'ambre, je me retiray de ce lieu comme Ulisse fit de la maison de Circé.

—Michel Jajolet de La Courbe, director of the Compagnie du Sénégal, after dining with the nhara known as La Belinguere (Cultru 1913, 198)

During the second half of the seventeenth century, western African commerce was fragmented into rival trading spheres as French and English companies established factors (traders) ashore to compete with Luso-Africans, Cabo Verdeans, and Portuguese. The European traders dispatched to western Africa found themselves constrained to accommodate to the long-established Luso-African commercial networks. For many French and English traders, it was Luso-African and African women who provided access to these networks, often profiting themselves and their kin.

The delimitation of commercial spheres in Sengambia that would endure for centuries began in 1638, when a French fleet dislodged Dutch traders from the island of Guet N'Dar at the mouth of the Senegal River. Fortification of the island, subsequently known as Saint-Louis, enabled French traders to monopolize the trade of the Senegal River. Once the dangerous bar at the mouth of the Senegal was crossed, the river was navigable for hundreds of kilometers in high water during the rainy season and for months thereafter. In a strategic follow-up, a French expedition captured Gorée in November 1677. From that point forward, Gorée became the French entrepôt for trade along the Petite Côte and in the Gambia River. Deprived of Gorée, Dutch vessels continued a coasting trade until the early eighteenth century, after which they concentrated their commerce on the Gold Coast and Angola.

French trading companies underwent a series of transmutations. In 1664, the Compagnie du Cap-Vert e du Sénégal, organized by Rouen traders, was incorporated into the Compagnie des Indes Occidentales, which lasted until 1674 when a second company of the same name was formed. Following the latter's bankruptcy, in 1681 the Compagnie du Sénégal was restricted to trade between Cape Blanco and the Gambia River. When this organization failed, it was succeeded by a new organization founded in 1696; that firm also lost money, however, and was sold in 1709 to a group of Rouen traders, who made profits until they sold the concession to the Compagnie d'Occident in 1718 (Cultru 1913, xxxi–xlvi).

During the 1650s, traders from the German duchy of Courland initiated commerce along the Gambia River, only to be driven away in 1661 by an English expedition dispatched by investors titled the Royal Adventurers of England Trading into Africa. Successive English trading companies thereafter strove to dominate the commerce of the Gambia River while expanding commerce in Serra Leoa. Portugal's role continued to decline, as the nation was reduced to a weak client state of England. English merchants supplanted Portuguese merchants in western African commerce, with English vessels trading at Cacheu and Bissau.

Luso-Africans contested with English traders for the Gambia's commerce, while maintaining, with Banyun collaborators, a monopoly of trade along the creeks and portages linking the Gambia, Casamance, and Cacheu Rivers. Luso-Africans continued to monopolize trade along the Geba, Corubal, and Grande Rivers and in the Bissagos Islands. Although increasingly challenged by English traders established in the Sierra Leone estuary and on the Iles de Los, Luso-Africans continued as the principal traders in the Nunez, Pongo, and Kolente Rivers.

Slave trading surpassed all other commerce from the early seventeenth century onward. Caravan routes connecting the Senegal, Gambia, and Niger Rivers took captives, gold, and ivory to the navigable reaches of rivers and estuaries for sale to Luso-African and European traders. Other commodities widely traded included kola, cotton textiles, hides, and beeswax. Besides ivory and slaves, the Sherbro River produced large quantities of camwood, used to make a valuable red dye. The Gallinas estuary and Cape Mount area supplied captives and large quantities of rice to provision slave vessels.

European cargoes bartered in exchange included wine, brandy, rum, and other spirits; tobacco grown by slaves in the Americans; textiles manufactured in Europe and India; iron bars that African smiths fashioned into agricultural implements, weapons, and tools according to local styles and preferences; knives, swords, and cutlasses (useful for clearing land for cultivation); firearms, gunpowder, and shot; kettles, pans, and brass basins (called "neptunes" and used for evaporating seawater to make salt); glass and amber beads; mirrors; and buttons, handkerchiefs, and other small haberdashery items. Less valuable items were useful as gifts and to close out barters, and along with cast-off clothing, empty bottles and the like were exchanged for fish, poultry, and foodstuffs of all sorts.

Luso-Africans successfully competed against—and cooperated with—European rivals, capitalizing on the advantages of their African kinship networks; their superior knowledge of African languages, cultures, and markets; their greater resistance to tropical diseases; and, always of paramount importance, their monopoly or near monopoly in kola trade and panos manufactured in Cabo Verde. Time and again, European traders suffered heavy losses during European wars and concomitant commerce raiding. Following the wars, Europeans reestablished their commercial spheres more or less as before.

The Evolution of Nharaship

The second half of the seventeenth century marked the rise to prominence of Luso-African women who acquired wealth and influence from their capabilities as translators and traders. Termed *nharas* in Crioulo, *signares* by Frenchmen, and, during the nineteenth century, *senoras* by English traders along the Gambia River, these women had wealth, property, and influence. The most renowned of these women possessed trading craft; numerous domestic slaves, including seamen and skilled artisans; European-style households and furnishings; beautifully crafted gold and silver jewelry; and prestige textiles and other splendid apparel.

The expansion of French and English commerce in western Africa offered greatly increased opportunities for Luso-African and African women to participate in commerce. European companies forbade employees from engaging in private trade, but private trade was potentially so lucrative that corrupt practices were endemic. Individuals intent on illegal self-aggrandizement found ready collaborators in Luso-African and African women who, as wives, translators, and business partners, provided access to African commercial networks through relatives.

French and English traders dispatched to western Africa confronted the same challenges and had the same liabilities as the first Portuguese lançados two centuries earlier—they lacked knowledge of African languages, trade networks, and political and social institutions. African societies treated these new strangers as they had the lançados: they were assessed tribute and taxes; they were not allowed to grow their own food or control wells and other potable water supplies; they were excluded from caravan routes linking interior markets; and they were allowed to marry women in the communities where they were permitted to settle.

What was different and what transformed previous African and Luso-African commercial and social patterns was the fact that many French and English traders cohabited with Luso-African, rather than African, women. They did so for many reasons. For instance, some Luso-African women had widespread kinship affiliations, both with Luso-Africans and with African traders and elites, and they could exploit these networks to their advantage. By contrast, African women's affiliations with elites and commercial networks were generally more restricted and localized. Luso-African women also spoke Crioulo, the lingua franca of commerce, and acquiring knowledge of Crioulo was essential for newly arrived Europeans. Luso-African women, like African women, knew local remedies for illnesses and which healers to consult. Moreover, they had some familiarity with European lifestyles, including food preferences and the domestic skills expected of wives. They were, in short, invaluable partners in commerce and in managing domestic affairs.

Inasmuch as Europeans of that era considered their religious beliefs of surpassing importance, Protestant Europeans may have rationalized that it was more appropriate and seemly to establish affiliations with Luso-Africans who professed Catholicism as opposed to African "pagans." English traders referred to "country-style" marriages, while French traders spoke of "mariages à la mode du pays." Racial attitudes indubitably were a factor; Luso-African women generally possessed lighter pigmentation than African women, and some European men no doubt allowed color prejudice to outweigh kinship and commercial advantages.

Lamentably for historians, information concerning nharas must be derived almost exclusively from accounts and records compiled by European, Cabo Verdean, and Eurafrican males. References to Luso-African women were usually limited to first names or sobriquets (for example, "Signora Pacha," "Seignora Catti," "Marie Mar," and "Belinguere"), with sparse, if any, details concerning their kinship affiliations. It is evident from the sources that will be discussed that there were significant differences in the experiences of Luso-African women living in stratified societies compared to those in acephalous societies. Europeans trading with stratified groups in Senegambia, such as Wolof and Mandinka, described Luso-African women as interpreters and commercial intermediaries facilitating commerce between Europeans and male traders and elites. The women might dispatch relatives and slaves on commercial ventures, but they did not themselves undertake trading voyages or travel into the interior. By contrast, Luso-African women living in the numerous acephalous groups south of the Gambia River engaged in commerce on their own account, as well as acting as partners in commerce with Portuguese and Luso-African men. The most enterprising Luso-African women owned trading vessels, exercised leadership roles in their communities, and were "chiefs" in trading settlements.

While particulars concerning nharaship differed according to African societies and Luso-African and European influences in an area, the principal features everywhere comprised patterns evolving from landlord-stranger practices. Marriages were pledged according to traditional rites, which might be modified according to circumstances as time passed. European traders were obligated to pay bridewealth and make other contributions to their wives' parents and relatives. Wives were obligated to adhere to norms of married behavior, and they expected the same of their husbands. In some instances, marriages were consecrated by Christian clergy, but African customs and practices regarding mutual obligations, responsibilities, and expectations always constituted the core of these relationships, and women and their relations possessed numerous sanctions to ensure their partners' adherence—not least of which was their vital role in commerce, including the secrets that an aggrieved woman might share with rival traders.

Luso-African and African women who married Europeans anticipated gaining access to European commodities and trade outlets, whether by means authorized by trading companies or otherwise. The merchandise obtained was traded by the wives, by their domestic slaves, or by relatives. Women who were successful entrepreneurs acquired increasing quantities of European merchandise and African commodities, owned numerous domestic slaves, lived in dwellings surrounded by large compounds, and flaunted their wealth with expensive gold and silver jewelry (readily negotiable assets), prestige clothing, and other forms of display.

Since Europeans suffered high mortality rates in western Africa and survivors eventually returned to Europe, the nhara frequently married more than one stranger, astutely improving her commercial opportunities with each change of partner. A successful nhara who had a command of local trade languages and had a well-furnished household, numerous male and female domestic slaves, and trading craft manned by skilled seamen and compradors was a prize to be competed for by the highest-ranked employees of trading companies and by military officers. Such a woman represented the best prospect for such men to acquire wealth, albeit by means of illicit commerce that they were charged with preventing or eradicating!

While a commercial nexus represented the core of these relationships, nharas provided their husbands with comforts and amenities of immeasurable physical and psychological importance. They and their domestic slaves supplied Europeans with the best available living conditions—a regimen of domestic life shared with women who spoke Crioulo, sometimes both French and English, and probably several African languages; who supervised the preparation of meals derived from both African and European cookery; and, crucial to the Europeans' survival in western Africa, who provided expert nursing and attentive care for their husbands when they were stricken with illness. Regarding the latter, Europeans living in western Africa were frequently ill and at times very sick for long periods, and the care provided by wives and domestic slaves could make the difference between life and death. And while incapacitated, these Europeans had peace of mind, knowing that their wives would carry on their commercial activities for mutual benefit; through such trials, women increased their capabilities to manage trade networks. Nharas' children bore their fathers' names, but they were raised in their mothers' societies and participated in the same socialization as their peers even as they observed and learned much that was advantageous for subsequent careers in commerce.

To achieve long-term success, it was crucial for the nharas to retain the possessions of their deceased or departed husbands, and this entailed contending with the rulers who claimed the property of deceased traders. Nharas' relatives had compelling reasons to support enterprising widows, anticipating benefits from their continued participation in commerce. And while women and their kinship networks were not always able to secure trade goods and trade slaves from grasping elites, widows' property rights over domestic slaves seems to have been respected. These considerations, together with the nharas' knowledge of Crioulo and European languages, their personal acquaintance of European and Eurafrican traders, and their proven trading experience, would be persuasive reasons to rally the support of influential relatives.

Luso-African women living in both stratified and acephalous societies were readily identifiable by the way they dressed and by their adherence to a lifestyle that combined European and African elements. Their clothing was a mixture of panos and European garments. They lived in distinctive, rectangular-shaped dwellings furnished with European articles. Their diet comprised both African and imported foods, condiments, and cooking styles, and through their cuisine, they contributed to the dissemination of European, American, and Asian plants, trees, and domestic animals. These included citrus fruits, poultry, and pigs from Portugal; pineapples, chilies, and peanuts from South America; and bananas, mangoes, and paddy rice from South Asia. Like Luso-African men, they wore crucifixes and rosary beads and insisted that they were Christian, white, and Portuguese. Where priests maintained churches or made itinerant pastoral visits, Luso-Africans baptized their children and sought Christian burial services, but until the nineteenth century, few sanctified their marriages or regularly attended mass. Such seems to have been the case both for the largest Luso-African communities in Cacheu and Bissau and for smaller settlements along the Petite Côte and the Gambia, Nunez, Sierra Leone, and other rivers that were sporadically visited by priests dispatched from the Cabo Verde archipelago.

One can only speculate about the extent to which Luso-Africans also identified themselves as members of their mothers' societies. We do know that they were often as dark-skinned as Africans, were raised in African societies, and were dependent on their relatives and other Africans for personal safety and the security of their possessions. Depending on circumstances, it would have been advantageous and perhaps even necessary for them to assert their "African" identities. Generally, it seems that western African societies treated Luso-Africans as if they belonged to an endogamous occupational group much like smiths, leather workers, and bards. Seemingly, this would explain why Luso-Africans dressed as they did. Their costumes comprising European clothing, crucifixes, and rosaries "advertised" their occupations as stranger-traders and grumetes or as wives of such individuals. These distinctive and highly visible identifiers afforded them personal protection and special privileges as people who promoted commerce and increased the rulers' revenues. Like hunters, bards, diviners, and Muslim clerics, traders and their entourages were readily identifiable by their apparel and accoutrements, and they were rarely molested. By contrast, strangers without credentials and kinship affiliations—such as escaped slaves, individuals made "displaced persons" by warfare or natural disasters, and people without kin to vouch for them—would have traveled the same routes in some peril.

Other than kin, the Luso-Africans' closest relationships were with grumetes and domestic slaves. Both groups shared the day-to-day activities of family compounds and trading communities, learned Crioulo, and contributed to many Luso-African lifeways. There were grumetes living in the principal trading settlements, but disappointingly little information about them is available. It is not known, for example, whether the men in such communities were long-term residents or whether they engaged in regular patterns of labor migration. Likewise, did grumetes bring women from their own villages, or did they take wives from local communities? To what extent did male children of Luso-Africans become grumetes (especially in stratified societies where they were denied the privileges of free persons), and did they marry the daughters of Luso-Africans, of grumetes, or of members of African communities? And what about the grumetes' daughters?

Many of the same questions are unresolved regarding the domestic slaves whom Luso-Africans acquired to perform a variety of trade-related and household tasks. Male slaves were expert sailors, smiths, woodworkers, or weavers or were trained in these and other skills. Women slaves were assigned household tasks, tended children, combed cotton, spun thread, and made pottery. It seems that some slaves and, more often, their children (who were frequently fathered by their masters) were absorbed into Luso-African and grumete communities. Little information was recorded concerning such matters, and research is made more difficult by the fact that both grumetes and slaves were given (or adopted) Portuguese first names and sometimes also acquired the surnames of their employers and owners.

Luso-Africans who were successful in commerce acquired large compounds with dwellings to house wives and children, relatives, grumetes, domestic slaves, and trade slaves. Constrained to adhere to African social patterns, they provided hospitality for African traders and members of their caravans, elites and their entourages, visiting Cabo Verdean and European traders, fellow Luso-Africans, and members of their wives' extended families and various hangers-on. Some of the latter might stay for long periods of time and might demand that their children or those of relatives reside as wards to learn commercial practices. At different times and seasons, Luso-Africans might host fishermen, hunters, medical practitioners, and oracles. Successful traders skillfully contrived to take advantage of reciprocal obligations. But Luso-Africans men living in stratified societies knew that wives and children generally could not save the possessions they had acquired from predatory elites, which was a crucial factor discouraging the development of "European" family patterns. It was not until the latter part of the eighteenth century that French control of Gorée and Saint-Louis ensured that the children of Luso-Africans and Franco-Africans could inherit their parents' dwellings and possessions, and not until the beginning of the nineteenth century did Luso-Africans living at Ziguinchor acquire rights to own land and bequeath property to their children.

Luso-Africans along the Petite Côte

Circumstances along the Petite Côte changed significantly during the 1620s, when the Dutch founded a permanent establishment on the islet of Ber, thereafter known as Gorée (a contraction of *Goède Reede,* the Dutch word for good roadstead, like the island of Goeree at the mouth of the Schelde River). Sheltered by the cradling arm of Cape Verde, Gorée's small cove had long been resorted to by mariners as a place to careen vessels for cleaning and repair. Several springs on Gorée provided only trickles of water, and the restricted space of the islet—a thousand meters long by several hundred meters wide, tapering to its northern point—allowed little room for gardens and keeping livestock. The Dutch and subsequent European inhabitants of Gorée constructed cisterns to collect water during the rainy season, but most of the residents relied on water and food supplies brought from Cape Verde, rendering them dependent on maintaining amicable relations with the ruler of Cayor (Knight-Baylac 1970, 406–7 and n. 6).

Despite growing European competition, Luso-Africans maintained an intermediary role along the Petite Côte, trading with the states of Cayor, Baol, Siin, and Saloum (Map 3.1). An abiding concern was the rulers' practice of confiscating the property of deceased traders. At Rufisque, the entrepôt for the Wolof state of Cayor, Luso-Africans carried on an extensive trade along with Dutch and French traders, all under the strict control of the alcaides and Wolof elites. The Cabo Verdean shipmaster Francisco de Lemos Coelho described circumstances during his visits in the 1640s and 1650s. The trade season began in "winter," that is, after the rainy season ended in October:

> Unless illness prevents them, the Portuguese who live here are obliged to visit the king of the land once a year and take him a very fine present, according to their means. This can sometimes cost more than 100 *mil-reis,* as it comprises very fine pieces of silver, brandy in barrels or flasks, fine coral, scarlet cloth, and other goods depending on what the donor possesses. The king thanks him for the gift and very often gives him back more than what he took was worth, but this depends on the king's attitude and his finances. The king's gift comprises blacks, hides, horses, and camels. The whites regularly use camels to transport the hides, and they buy more hides inland if they have the capital. A camel carries 40–50 hides. The blacks are very friendly towards the Portuguese, and more friendly to them than to any other nation. The coastal blacks, or most of them, speak our language, and also Dutch and French. A settler living here will have (as servants) (only) a few *grumetes,* this being what they call liberated blacks, since the local blacks will themselves do anything he orders them to do, provided they are paid; and as the land has so much trade, what is given them is hardly noticed. This land has very good tobacco, and a large quantity of the sort of cloth called Jalofo cloth, and also

> some other cloths called *bantans,* those obtained from this kingdom being the best (of this sort). (Coehlo 1684/1985, chap. 1: 6–7)

Coelho's references to "whites" were disingenuous, as revealed, for example, in his reference to Rufisque: "Here the Portuguese and white sons of the land live" (Hair 1985, chap. 1: 5).

Olfert Dapper, whose 1668 compilation of numerous sources incorporated information up to 1664, observed that traders from the Petite Côte visiting the ruler of Cayor might stop at the village of Endir, where four or five Portuguese families and several Luso-Africans engaged in commerce, or at Sanyeng, where two large Portuguese dwellings were sheltered beneath huge baobab trees (Thilmans 1971, 515, 523). Circumstances soon changed; Jean Barbot, a Frenchman from La Rochelle who visited Senegal in 1678 and 1681, related that the Portuguese and Luso-Africans had abandoned these villages in the interior (Barbot 1732, 1:26 and map in pl. A after p. 16; cf. Hair, Jones, and Law 1992, 1:69 n. 56).

The caravan routes linking markets along the Senegal River reflected the difficulty of sailing from Cape Verde northward against the Canary Current and prevailing north-northeast winds during the long dry season. It took two to three weeks to reach Saint-Louis by sea, compared to four days overland (Cultru 1913, 57), the latter being an experience that enthralled travelers over the centuries as an opportunity to view the flora and fauna of the African savanna.

Coelho noted that Luso-Africans living at Portudal, the chief place of trade for the Serer state of Baol, carried on an extensive commerce in hides, slaves, and cloth. Those living at Joal, in the neighboring Serer state of Siin, enjoyed more freedom than their peers in any other port along the Petite Côte, for only there could they move away whenever they desired without the ruler or inhabitants obstructing them or doing them any harm. The Saluum's ruler, the *bur,* permitted Luso-African and European vessels to sail up the Saloum River to his village, where he was the principal trader to the extent of purchasing entire cargoes. Coelho mentioned that Saluum's territory extended far along the north bank of the Gambia River to Nianija Bolon ("Rio de Nanhigega") and comprised many tributary states. He also remarked that many Luso-Africans had retired from Saluum with large fortunes, though they arrived with very little (Hair 1985, chap. 1: 8–13).

Luso-Africans retained their importance as middlemen along the Petite Côte in the decades that followed. Foremost among them was a Luso-African woman named Senhora Catarina ("Seignora Catti") who acted as commercial agent for the *damel* (ruler) of Cayor. In October 1664, after Admiral Michael De Ruyter's recapture of Gorée (which had been seized by the English the previous February), one of the Dutch vessels reconnoitered the Petite Côte. The alcaide of Rufisque who parlayed with the Dutch was accompanied by a Luso-African woman and a priest accompanied by another woman (Moraes 1998, 3:54). Doubtless, this person was the same woman whom the Frenchman Urbain Souchu de Renne-Fort described the following April as a clever "Portugaise" widow thirty-two years of age who was capable of carrying on the business of her deceased husband. The visiting Frenchmen were invited to Senhora Catarina's residence, where her two attractive adolescent daughters, "between white and black," hospitably served bananas and pineapples. The inhabitants of Rufisque included three Frenchmen trading for the Compagnie des Indes Occidentales, fifteen male "Portugais," and fifteen to sixteen hundred Africans (Boulèque 1989, 65–67; Moraes 1998, 3:78–79). Senhora Catarina may have been one of two "Caterinas" baptized by Fr. Alexis de Sainct-Lo at Joal in 1635 (Thilmans and Moraes 1973, 39 n. 6; Moraes 1995, 283).

Among those living at Rufisque in 1669 was a "Portuguese" known as Seignor Dom Joan (Juan), who entertained visiting Frenchmen in May 1669.

> [He] regal'd us with Rice, Palm Wine, meat & fish. He had several wives, by whom he had mulatto children. He pray'd two Missionaries, who were with us, to baptize his children, which they promis'd to do the next day. They warned him that, being a Christian, he ought to content himself with one wife, & that he ought not to have several like the natives of the country; that whomsoever he might choose he ought to marry in the face of the Church, in order not to live in sin; he promised to do so. I was astonish'd to see that this man was devout, having always a large Rosary in his hands, & several Images of Our Saviour, of the Virgin, & of the Saints, around his bed. The same with his wives or concubines, who carry'd also large Rosaries round their necks. For all that, this man could not be ignorant that he offended God in having so many wives. (Oliver 1897, 13)

Dom Joan's children were baptized the following day, as were several other children of "Portuguese" residents of Rufisque.

Sieur Du Bois related that while resting after a hunting trip in the countryside, he and a shipmate were offered lovemaking by two "very comely" young women with whom they shared their bread. Du Bois and his shipmate were embarrassed and hurried back to their vessel—but he recorded this experience and other observations of local women with a profusion of detail: "The dress and attire of these women is a petticoat with which they cover themselves from their waist to their feet; the remainder of their body is nude. They wear wristlets of gold, of silver, of brass, & tin on their arms, & have collars of coral, carnelian & grains of gold; they wear also earrings like their necklaces. These women are very shameless, & esteem it an honour to have to do with a white man, indeed their parents solicit them for the purpose: thus it happened to some of our folk who were solicited by the Fathers themselves for the girls of this country" (Oliver 1897, 14–15). A short-term visitor unfamiliar with local circumstances, Du Bois provided few clues concerning the social standing of the women he described or what their motives may have been.

The influence exerted by Luso-Africans along the Petite Côte was reflected in the privileged treatment accorded Lourenço de Mattos by French, Dutch, and Portuguese officials in a bizarre episode in 1670. Mattos was the son of the Luso-African Ambrósio Gomes, a former acting capitão-mor of Cacheu and husband of the nhara Bibiana Vaz; he was described in June 1671 by the governor of Cabo Verde as "the richest man in all Guinea" (Teixeira 1950, 107).

Ambrósio Gomes was the principal investor in a Portuguese slave ship that, with his son Lourenço de Mattos aboard, was captured illegally during peacetime by a French privateer in the West Indies. The vessel's crew and free blacks were set ashore on the Venezuelan coast, and after two months, they obtained passage to the Dutch port of Curaçao, then to Holland, and next to Portugal. On his arrival in Lisbon, Mattos sought redress from the French ambassador. The latter pledged his government's active efforts to make restitution, presented Mattos with twenty thousand reais for expenses, and arranged his passage to the Petite Côte on a French trading vessel in the expectation that Mattos and his father would promote French commerce in western Africa (Moraes 1978, 708–16). Evidently, one or both complied, for during the 1670s and 1680s, French traders were increasingly involved in trade at Cacheu and Bissau.

The French had an involvement of a different sort along the Petite Côte in 1679 when Captain Jean-Baptiste followed up on Admiral Jean d'Estrées's capture of Gorée two years earlier with attacks on Cayor, Baol, and Siin, compelling their rulers to sign treaties ceding to France the coastline from Cape Verde to the Gambia River, extending twenty-five kilometers into the interior. Recognizing that they had overreached, French authorities subsequently allowed the treaties to fall into desuetude (Curtin 1975, 122)—but the flouting of overbearing force surely had long-term consequences.

In 1680 and 1681, the French seized English vessels trading on the Petite Côte, but in both cases, the Royal African Company secured restitution, and its vessels subsequently traded without interference. In 1684, the company reestablished factories at Portudal and Joal and would trade until the War of the League of Augsburg began in 1688 (Gray 1940, 103–4; Davies 1957, 270).

French intentions toward Luso-African competitors were unequivocal. François de Paris castigated them as the "principal enemies" of French traders and recorded the fate of a Luso-African named André who sought reparations for losses inflicted by Admiral Ducasse's squadron at Sereine. In an attempt to obtain redress, André took hostage a French shipmaster. After escaping from confinement, the French captain landed thirty sailors, who massacred André and several others despite their pleas for mercy. André's head was taken to Gorée, where it was impaled on a stake under the flagpole (Boulègue 1989, 72–73).

François de Paris, who visited in 1682, recorded no names but characterized Luso-Africans at Joal as "all-powerful" (Thilmans 1976, 32). In their endeavors to compete with Dutch traders based on Gorée, French traders brought to the Petite Côte such luxury items as apples and fragrant herbs used by women to burn as incense ("brule-parfum") (Moraes 1972, 41). Coelho amplified Paris's information: for "whites" (that is, Luso-Africans), French vessels brought casks of wine and good brandy, cheeses, hams, oil, vinegar, sugar, different kinds of spices, and barrels of apples, onions, and garlic; enjoying such luxuries, Joal's inhabitants were referred to in jest as "the Bishops of the Coast" (Hair 1985, chap. 1: 11–12).

Jean Barbot, who visited the Petite Côte in 1681, published a panoramic depiction of Rufisque that showed Senhora Catarina's African-type dwelling with a large cross raised over the front gate of the compound (Barbot 1732, pl. 2 after p. 20; the picture is used for the dust jacket and frontispiece of this volume). Barbot described Senhora Catarina as "a black lady of a good presence, and a very jovial temper, widow to a *Portuguese* of note, and a Roman Catholick." She was also characterized as "a woman of high standing" (Barbot 1732, 1:38; Hair, Jones, and Law 1992, 1:123). Indicative of her wealth, she had presented the damel of Cayor with a horse valued at fourteen slaves (Hair, Jones, and Law 1992, 1:90). Senhora Catarina invited Barbot to dinner along with the alcaide of Rufisque and several of the damel's officials, but he later declared himself disgusted by the wooden platters of couscous, the "stinking boiled beef," and the tepid water provided for drink (Barbot 1732, 1:50; Hair, Jones, and Law 1992, 1:123–25). The African-style meal that Senhora Catarina served Barbot contrasted in every respect to the Luso-African cuisine that the nhara known as La Belinguere served La Courbe in Niumi, described on pages 150–51.

Coelho's Account of Trade in the Gambia and Casamance Rivers

Francisco de Lemos Coelho, who engaged in shipboard trade along the length of the Gambia River in the mid-seventeenth century, characterized Luso-Africans ("Portuguese") as the "intermediaries through whose hands the greater part of the trade passes" (Hair 1985, prologue 16 and chap. 2: 4). There was a settlement of Luso-Africans at Brefet in Foni, where Banyun traded "rice, many hides, many blacks, and much wax." Another Luso-African community, along with a group of Mandinka traders, resided at Bintang in the Banyun state of Jagra, trading hides, beeswax, and captives (Hair 1985, chap. 2: 4–5).

> The majority of the people in the village are Mandingas, and they are Mahommedans, so that this evil seed begins at this point (on the river); but they are good friends of the whiteman. Anyone living there should, however, be on good terms with the king of the land, and should not seduce the black men's wives or slave-women, seduction of the latter being the worse offense, because they value them more highly; the lightest penalty will be loss of property. Use civil words to all the blacks, and do note be deceived into thinking that they know no Portuguese because they do not speak the language, since most of them can understand it adequately. (Hair 1985, chap. 2: 5)

During the 1660s (and perhaps earlier), Bintang was the residence of two of the most important Luso-African traders in the Gambia—Capt. Manuel Vas de Franco and Manuel Alves de Brito, the former claiming to hold a commission as "commander-in-chief for the King of Portugal in the Gambia River" (Gray 1940, 26, 78–79).

Upstream along Vintang Creek was Geregia in the Banyun state of Jagra. Geregia was formerly the chief place for hides, wax, and captives, but contention between two Banyun factions and Diola banditry had diminished trade in the area and made the overland route to Cacheu, which Coelho traveled three times, less safe (Hair 1985, chap. 2: 4–6). Coelho's cautionary remarks notwithstanding, the route between Geregia and Cacheu continued to be used by strangers for decades to come, including Cabo Verdean priests, various English traders, and Jean Jajolet de La Courbe, director of the Compagnie du Sénégal whose 1686 journey will be discussed.

The most important place of trade along the upper Gambia River was Kassang on the north bank, entrepôt for the Mandinka state of Niani. Kassang was the head of navigation for large sailing vessels because the narrowing of the river and its reversal to the west hindered tacking against prevailing winds. Smaller craft might continue upriver to the shallows at Barracunda. At Kassang, Luso-Africans lived in a separate village; in Coelho's time, this was the only river port where that arrangement prevailed. Coelho described the circumstances:

> In this village the whites live in greater freedom than elsewhere. Only from this place can they remove themselves at any time they wish to do so, without the king impeding their removal or doing them any harm; and this freedom does not exist in the other ports of this river. In these, as in the ports on the coast, whites wishing to leave must act deviously, because if the blacks found out, they would rob them. Only in the port of Cação is this custom not followed. The blacks say that the white-man is like a fish—the water brings both, and the water takes both away again. Nevertheless, if a white dies in the land, the king is his heir and takes all. I resided at Cação for three years and actually lived there all the time I was not away on a voyage; and if I were to return to the river today, I would live nowhere else but here. For the blacks, the bravest and most spirited on the whole river are very affable and homely towards the whiteman, and his very good friends. The black females are the most beautiful women on the whole river; and are unsurpassed by any on the Coast of Guinea. Even if a white gets into trouble with one of these women—and may God deliver him from this—not even then will the blacks rob him. The land has much trade in hides, as well as in blacks, cloths and some ivory. Cola sells there extremely well. . . . There are very good facilities for repairing ships, because of the timber available in bulk at every point along the bank of the river, so that even if large numbers of ships were built here the timber would not run out for many years; and the islet, which is in sight of the port, can be used for the planking, the supply of timber again being immense. But above all, this is a very healthy land, well cleansed by the winds, and since it is sixty leagues from the mouth of the river seldom sultry. In all the time I lived there I never knew illness or fever, and in such remote parts this is not the least (blessing) one might desire. Cação also has the convenience that from there one can contact Farim or Cacheo quickly, as witness what once happened to me. I had a ship which was careened, in order to be freshly planked, when all the caulkers, carpenters, and deck-hands (*grumetes*) cleared out, leaving me without a single helper. Finding myself in this plight I sent a black to the land of Cacheo to find caulkers and deckhands, and within twelve days he had travelled there and returned with them. (Hair 1985, chap. 2: 14–15)

Coelho's last remark spoke to the safety of persons following the caravan routes linking the Gambia, Casamance, and Cacheu Rivers. Regarding Kassang, he made no mention of the Luso-African trade in tobacco related by Olfert Dapper. According to Dapper, tobacco was grown in great abundance around Kassang and upriver and was marketed sun-dried and green, for the growers did not know how to make rolls. The tobacco was purchased by Luso-Africans who came in chaloupes from Joal and Cacheu (Thilmans 1971, 511, 522–23).

Coelho cautioned that the Mandinka of Niani exacted the death penalty if lançados or Luso-Africans shed blood:

> A white living in this land must guard against killing or wounding anyone—spilling blood on the earth, as they say—because if he does this he will die. And if any slave of his does it, he will be robbed. I have had experience of this practice for when a black of mine who was held in chains killed his companion who was in the same chains, it led them to rob me. Only the fact that I was well liked enabled me to get my property returned; but I still lost a good amount. The king, with the nobles (*fidalgos*) and other people of the land, led away the killer, to wash off the blood, as they put it. It cost me more than three blacks, so you can see it is the greatest crime in the land. (Hair 1985, chap. 2: 15–16)

Coelho reported on numerous places of trade upriver from Kassang, but he mentioned no Luso-African settlements before the Mandinka state of Wuli on the north bank, where Luso-Africans ("whites") and their slaves could trade without being harassed. Elsewhere, he left *tavernas* (traders) ashore to barter salt for hides and cloth and other commodities while his vessel proceeded upriver. Coelho mentioned Luso-Africans ("filhos da terra") who traveled from place to place in pirogues (Hair 1985, chap. 2: 17–25).

The river port at Barracunda, so named because of the ledges of laterite rocks there that formed a barrier to navigation, was located in the Mandinka state of Wuli. Barracunda was the head of navigation for vessels drawing no more than "seven palm-spans of water" and was called Tubabo Sita (port of the whiteman). Coelho described trade with the annual Jahanke/Diahanke caravans comprising more than three thousand persons and two thousand donkeys, which arrived each July from the cotton-producing areas around Jahaba. These pacifist Muslims brought cotton textiles, slaves, ivory, and gold to barter with Luso-Africans and Europeans for glass beads and paper, the latter principally used by marabouts for writing passages from the Koran to insert into the amulets that commanded high prices from Muslims and non-Muslims alike. After nonstop, all-day and all-night trading, the Jahanke caravans continued along the north bank of the Gambia to Felam in Niumi, where they bartered cloth for sea salt. Coelho was informed that two more Jahanke caravans also set out each November, one to the Senegal River and one to the Pongo River, each with the primary goal of obtaining salt (Hair 1985, chap. 2: 2, 24–26). "The Jagancases are a very sincere people, and they take no revenge for any ill done to them, leaving it to God. They say that when they leave their land, their leaders [*solatiguis*] report to the king, who tells them to remember that they are going to alien lands and must instruct their people to keep their mouths shut and their trouser-slits sewn up; and that if anyone does to them any harm they should leave it to God (to act)" (Hair 1985, chap. 2: 26; cf. Sanneh 1989, 145). Coelho added sententiously that if Portuguese had kept this advice in mind, they would have avoided many disasters.

In contrast to the pacifist Jahanke, those in the caravans of "*Conjuros*" (a Portuguese word meaning incantation or magic charm), also comprising more than a thousand persons, bore weapons to defend themselves but principally relied on their reputation for possessing magical powers. "For all the Conjuros are great magicians (*feiticeiros*) and therefore very much feared by all the heathen, hence their property is sacred amongst all the blacks, and no one lays a finger on it against their will. But note that all the heathen of this river, especially those on the North side, take nothing from anyone and our goods can 'sleep in the street'" (Hair 1985, chap. 2: 26–27). Most likely made up of non-Muslim Soninke, these caravans also continued along the north bank of the Gambia River to Niumi to acquire salt. Numerous smaller caravans of forty to one hundred men brought ivory and slaves to Barracunda, principally to obtain salt (Hair 1985, chap. 2: 2, 27).

Coelho provided information concerning links between English traders in the Gambia, the Dutch establishment on Gorée, and traders in the Casamance and Cacheu Rivers. He related that during the period he lived in western Africa, only the individual leasing the trade monopoly from the commandant of Cacheu was permitted to sail a vessel into the Casamance River. Without acknowledging whether he had firsthand experience, Coelho described commerce along the river.

The Diola ("Felupos") living in Jame along the north bank were renowned for collecting large quantities of beeswax from hives of woven straw that they hung in trees. Coelho admiringly described the mead produced from the honey as "like the good wine of Portugal." Numerous Luso-Africans traversed Jame to trade for beeswax, principally bartering iron and small glass beads. The people of Jame also sold slaves, ivory, and rice (Hair 1985, chap. 3: 2–3).

Once past the "piratical" Diola group known as Sacalates, living along the south bank of the lower Casamance, one came to the Banyun of Bichangor and

Buguendo, who sold slaves, beeswax, and ivory and purchased large quantities of kola. Upriver on the north bank, the Banyun of Jase sold much beeswax, some slaves, and numerous animal skins in return for iron, textiles, kola, and beads. The famous hunters purchased muskets and gunpowder (Hair 1985, chap. 3: 3–5).

Coelho provided a detailed description of how to steer a vessel safely past the navigational obstacles at the mouth of the Cacheu River. He mentioned that Cacheu's traders sent vessels to the Gambia River for commerce with African and English traders and transported large quantities of wax and ivory to Gorée to barter for iron and other commodities with the Dutch residing there—except, presumably, during the 1657–61 war between Portugal and Holland over competing interests in Brazil (Hair 1985, chap. 3: 5–6, chap. 1: 2–3, chap. 2: 2; Langer 1958, 439; Rodney 1970, 161).

Gambia-Casamance-Cacheu Trade, 1650s–1680s

During the 1650s, Gambia trade was contested by Dutch, English, and Courlanders and, briefly, by a Danish trader. Dutch traders conveniently dispatched vessels to the Petite Côte and Gambia River from their base on Gorée Island. Beginning in 1651, Germans from the Baltic duchy of Courland initiated trade along the Gambia River. Duke James of Courland (1642–82) protected a considerable Jewish community, and through his association with members of the Nunes da Costa family in Amsterdam and Hamburg, he was associated with the Portuguese Brazil Company (Donnan 1930/1969, 1:135 n. 5; Gray 1940, 43; Israel 1989, 118–19, 139).

Despite the conflicts attending the English Civil War (1641–60), England's merchants continued to dispatch vessels to West Africa. In April 1651, Parliament awarded London entrepreneurs a patent granting them exclusive trade rights for fourteen years in an area extending from twenty miles north of Cormantine on the Gold Coast to within twenty miles of the Sierra Leone River (Zook 1919/1969, 6). Soon afterward, some of the merchants already involved in Gambia trade dispatched an expedition to trade for gold, beeswax, hides, ivory, ambergris, and other commodities, including "15 or 20 young lusty Negers of about 15 yeares of age" together with "Countrey provisions" to sustain them during the voyage to London. The principal trader was enjoined to recover debts from a previous voyage owed by Francisco Vaz de França, Andreas Perdegon (André Perdigão?), and other traders who had received Portuguese wine and other goods on credit (Donnan 1930/1969, 1:127–28).

When the English arrived in the Gambia, they found the duke of Courland's men building a fort on the small islet forty kilometers upriver known as Saint Andrew's Island, so called following the mid-sixteenth-century interment of a sailor who died on one of the first European voyages of reconnaissance. While some members of the London expedition prospected for gold along the upper river, others established a trading post at Bintang on Vintang Creek. Three more vessels were dispatched from London at the close of 1651, all to be captured by the royalist sea raider Prince Rupert a few months later (Gray 1940, 6, 31–33).

When Prince Rupert's squadron arrived off the Gambia River at the end of February 1652, Courlanders helped pilot the ships into the river and shared intelligence concerning the whereabouts of the Commonwealth vessels. Portentous for future English involvement in Gambia River trade, Prince Rupert's men were informed that near the head of navigation, there was a gold mine with "a firm rock of gold of a great bigness." They were also told of unicorns and many other wonders (Warburton 1849, 3:361; Gray 1940, 35–38).

Following the restoration of the Stuart monarchy in 1660, Prince Rupert and the king, queen, and other aristocrats organized the Royal Adventurers of England Trading into Africa to search for the "gold mountain." Members of an expedition dispatched in 1661 drove the Courlander traders from the Gambia River and undertook to fortify Saint Andrew's Island, which was renamed James Island. When apprised of these developments, the Dutch West India Company's commander at Gorée sent representatives to parlay with the mansa of Niumi about dislodging the English. The ensuing Mandinka attack was unsuccessful, and the Royal Adventurers and successor English companies barred rival European vessels from sailing upriver past James Island (Gray 1940, 52–53, 76–77).

During the 1660s, the Royal Adventurers founded trading establishments along the Gambia River in Combo, at Brefet in Foni, and at Kassang and other markets upriver. They also established factories along the Petite Côte at Rufisque, Portudal, and Joal and along the Grande, Nunez, and Sierra Leone Rivers—all long-standing places of Luso-African trade (Gray 1940, 84). English traders in western Africa came to be known as *factors* and their establishments as *factories,* terms derived from the Portuguese *feitor* (administrator, manager) and *feitora* (trading post); French traders termed their establishments *comptoirs* or *loges.*

The first ledger kept at James Island, begun in January 1664, listed thirty-one persons with Portuguese surnames who were hired as compradors or purchased goods from the company's agents. Among those hired in 1664 and 1665 were Dom do Alde[i]a (from the Portuguese words for village headman) to tend cattle (Wright 1976, 189; 1997, 123). Invoking landlord-stranger (*jati-suruga*) privileges, Niumi's mansas required all vessels to anchor at Juffure to pay customs and hire grumetes to supplement and, as needed, replace European crews stricken with disease. Grumetes included pilots, seamen to assist in navigating vessels and rowing small craft, and one or more "linguisters" (from the Portuguese *linguacista,* meaning linguist). These grumetes were Luso-Africans, free Africans, and slaves. Some of the latter were *mansajongs* (slaves of mansas); others belonged to Niumi elites and nharas. Grumetes who were hired out by nharas gave their mistresses half of their earnings and turned over some of the remainder to mansas and other officials (Wright 1976, 187; 1997, 123).

Fortunately for Luso-Africans, Cabo Verdeans, and Portuguese, their European competitors experienced chronic instability and great financial losses from commerce raiding during the European wars of the 1660s and 1670s. Holland and England were at war from 1664 to 1667, with France entering the war against England in January 1666; the combined Dutch and French forces reduced English naval power. In 1664, Lourenço Pestana Martins and his brother Manuel da Costa Martins attempted to take advantage of the circumstances, founding the Companhia da Costa da Guiné for a term of eight years, but the company had little success (Teixeira 1950, 110; Hanson 1981, 234).

In a shift of alliances, Holland fought England and France from March 1672 to February 1674, at which point it made peace with England, and with France until August 1678 (Langer 1958, 427, 439, 442–43). France's capture of Gorée in November 1677 deprived Dutch traders of the strategically located entrepôt with its warehouses and ship-repair facilities, and although Dutch vessels for decades afterward frequented Senegambia and the Upper Guinea Coast, the commerce of western Africa was increasingly aggrandized by French and English traders (Gray 1940, 128, 130).

In 1669, during the respite in European warfare that prevailed between 1667 and 1672, the Royal Adventurers leased the English monopoly of Gambian trade to a subsidiary group of shareholders known as the Gambian Adventurers for a period of seven years, beginning January 1, 1669. The agreement was subsequently extended to January 1, 1678, and the Gambian Adventurers continued to send vessels to the Gambia until 1683, more than a decade after the Royal African Company was chartered in 1672 (Zook 1919/1969, 22–23; Gray 1940, 84–87; Davies 1957, 43, 99–100).

Factors employed by the Gambian Adventurers dispatched vessels from the Gambia to Cacheu in 1670 and 1671, where they traded with the acting (?) capitão-mor Manuel Roiz de Mendonça, Vicente Rodrigues, and Ambrósio Gomes; as a consequence, Mendonça's arrest was ordered by the Conselho Ultramarino. To better conceal their activities, these traders later resorted to having their launches rendezvous with English traders off Cape Roxo (Rodney 1970, 137).

In September 1672, while England, France, and Holland were at war, English investors obtained a charter from King Charles II that granted the Royal African Company a monopoly of English trade between Cape Blanco and the Cape of Good Hope for one thousand years. No English vessel could intrude in this vast commercial sphere without the company's permission, and interlopers were subject to legal penalties. In return for its charter, the company was obligated to maintain forts in West Africa. During the 1670s and 1680s, the monarchy sporadically dispatched warships to West Africa to arrest unauthorized traders and protect the company's vessels.

In 1672, the garrison in the Gambia fort comprised some seventy men. Company sloops visited the Casamance, Cacheu, and Grande Rivers, and exports included slaves, gold, ivory, beeswax, and cowhides. The company had factories in the Sierra Leone River and the Sherbro, whence considerable quantities of camwood were exported (Donnan 1930/1969, 1:192–93; Davies 1957, 97–99; Kup 1961, 78–80; Rodney 1970, 163; Carlos and Kruse 1996, 292–305).

The Royal African Company sought to ensure reliable behavior on the part of its employees by means of contracts, oaths, bonds, and searches of vessels to prevent cheating by factors, officers, and seamen. To encourage good behavior and obviate "moral hazard," the security bonds ranged from six to ten times the factors' annual salaries, and they were secured by company-approved guarantors. Thus, newly hired factors with beginning salaries of forty pounds sterling a year were required to have guarantors give security for four hundred pounds sterling (Carlos 1994, 319–25). However, as related in instances that will be described, the circumstances in western Africa frustrated the company's efforts to monitor the behavior of its employees (let alone enforce its regulations), for once in Africa, newcomers were disheartened by the high mortality rates, corrupted by the dissolute lifestyle of their seniors, and seduced by the opportunities for personal enrichment provided by collaboration with Luso-African and African women. Regarding the bonding system, Kenneth G. Davies observed that there is little evidence that the company ever recovered from guarantors significant amounts from losses alleged against untrustworthy employees, and it seems that, in time, the bonds and oaths became little more than formalities (Davies 1957, 256).

Private traders were the bane of the employees of the Royal African Company, as was the case with all chartered companies, and not only for their competition but also for their arbitrary behavior. Some of the most competitive private traders were captains and ships' officers who had previously been employed by the company and thereby acquired trading expertise and valuable contacts both in Africa and in the West Indies. Private traders who had no expectation of returning to a place of trade might kidnap free persons or commit other crimes, causing the victimized African community to take revenge on the next vessel from the same nation or indiscriminately on whichever Europeans were next in their power; in the process, long-standing commercial and political relationships were threatened. When an interloper named Plowman kidnapped two people from Joal in 1692, John Booker, the Royal African Company's agent at James Island, urged the firm to recover them and return them home because their abduction would "endanger many men's lives" (Gray 1940, 94).

In 1678, the Royal African Company took over the factories of the Gambian Adventurers, adding, among others, Geregia along Vintang Creek where Dutch had previously carried on an extensive trade (Gray 1940, 69, 86–87, 92). Thomas Thurloe, who was chief factor for the Gambian Adventurers before serving as chief agent of the Royal African Company, advised his new employers about the middleman role exercised by Luso-Africans. He noted the prices paid to Luso-Africans for slaves, ivory, and wax were considerably higher than those paid to Africans, yet the former controlled the bulk of trade. Thurloe recommended a strategy of advancing Luso-Africans only limited quantities of company goods so that they could not accumulate capital on their own, for those who did so would became too independent and encourage interloper trade (Rodney 1970, 207–8). In Thurloe's words:

> To the natives wee give not so much but agree with them as wee can. But wee buy farr more of the Portugueze than of the Natives. If the Portugueze be kept poore then they will certainly bring their goods to the [James, Bunce, and Sherbro] Islands but if they begin to grow rich then they will stand upon high terms and carry their goods to any Interloper's Strange Ship that comes in unless wee comply with them in every particular therefore this method ought to be used, to lend the best of them soe much and no more as with the proffitt of the goods we lend them they may pay us againe and just maintaine their families soe that they wilbe allwayes in a necessity of borrowing and consequently only trade for us and not dare to sell what they gett to any strange Ship for fear wee should deny the lending of them. (Donnan 1930/1969, 1:234)

Obviously, the strategy would work only in the absence of competitors, specifically French factors at Albreda.

Thurloe promoted the practice of using shallow-draft sloops and yachts to shuttle between James Island and the main places of trade. The rationale he sent his superiors in 1679 gives a valuable insight into the circumstances along the Gambia River that challenged Luso-Africans no less than English traders:

> A factor once settled ashoare is absolutely under the command of the king of the country where he lives, and liable for the least displeasure to loose all the goods he hath in his possession with danger also of his life. Besides in case of mortallity it is very difficult to recover of the negroes any thing that was in the hands of the deceased. Whereas in a sloop if the factor die the vessell is soone brought down to [James] Island, and if he finds no trade in one port may goe to another and not b[e] liable to sell their goods at the pleasure of the kings. Besides a sloop will be in the way of all canoes which come down to the river and they will rather sell what they have there than be at the trouble to come to the Island, when it may be they would passe by a factory, knowing that if they goe ashoare they must pay duties either to the master of the town or to the king or both; & there is likewise this convenience in buying goods of the canoes that are coming down, tho' it may be with an intent to come to the Island, yet if any interlopers happen to be in the river (which they will heare of before they can arrive here) perhaps wee shall never see them, so that buying their goods above prevents this going to interlopers. (Davies 1957, 217–18)

Iron bars comprised one-fourth to one-half of the consignments the Royal African Company sent to the Gambia (Davies 1957, 234). Brandy was essential; as Thurloe wrote in 1680, "without brandy there is no trade" (Wright 1997, 121). Luso-Africans, for their part, could obtain iron bars fabricated in Futa Jallon and brandy from paths linking Ziguinchor and Cacheu.

During the time of the Royal African Company, Luso-Africans continued in their roles as middlemen along the Gambia River. Individuals frequently recorded in company ledgers included Anthony Diaz, Domingo Mora (Moura), and Manuel Noonez (Nunez) (Davies 1957, 218–19). Circumstances changed during the eighteenth century with the influx of private traders who established factories upriver, in competition with resident Luso-Africans.

By 1684, the Royal African Company had five sloops shuttling between James Island and other places of trade along the Gambia River and sailing to Cacheu and to Joal and Portudal along the Petite Côte (Davies 1957, 217). Cacheu was the chief place to obtain ivory and beeswax, but slave prices were high due to sales to Spanish vessels. To prosecute trade with Luso-African middlemen, the agents of the Royal African Company were obliged to extend credit and thereby incur numerous bad debts (Davies 1957, 217–18). In Cacheu, along the Gambia River, and elsewhere in western Africa, the inability of Luso-Africans to accumulate savings rendered them dependent on merchandise advanced on credit.

In 1681, the newly founded Compagnie du Sénégal established a factory at Albreda, five kilometers downriver from James Island. The French comptoir competed with English traders for the commerce of the Mandinka state of Niumi, for caravans coming down the river along the north bank, and for Africans and Luso-Africans engaged in riverine commerce. The competition engendered much intrigue and strife during the next two centuries. Successive mansas of Niumi (or Barra, as Europeans called it) opportunistically collected rents and customs from both English and French and otherwise profited from landlord privileges. With expanding trade and rising prices, Niumi's mansas contrived to quadruple English customs during the century after 1665 (Wright 1997, 115).

Besides competing with each other, factors for the Royal African Company and the Compagnie du Sénégal had to contend with European interlopers who offered higher prices to Luso-African and African traders and with piratical craft that preyed on shipping in western Africa. Corrupt factors colluded with rivals and took advantage of circumstances to exaggerate the exactions of African rulers and the pillage by African raiders and by pirates, with the alleged losses being sold for personal profit. One man who took advantage of such circumstances was Alexander Cleeve, chief agent at James Island during the 1680s. In 1683, Cleeve purchased a vessel from a pirate and goods allegedly plundered in the Cape Verde Islands (Wilkinson 1690, 10–11; Gray 1940, 95). He falsified his accounts using the Luso-African name Francis Lopuz. Cleeve subsequently left the company's employ and became an independent trader (Davies 1957, 219, 372).

Cleeve may have been the unnamed agent who, in 1681, derided the company employees and shipmasters who lobbied for a resident clergyman at James Fort. William Wilkinson, who supported this initiative, recorded that the agent (Cleeve?) responded, "Dam 'em, I hate the fulsom Company of those impertinent Fellows, who, perhaps, are in effect, no better than Butchers or Taylors Sons, yet value themselves upon their Habit and Order, that they expect the whole Respect of the Fort should be paid to their Persons. And besides, I love my Liberty to be merry with whom and when I will, which I cannot have, where these Insipid Fellows are" (Wilkinson 1690, 23). In his diatribe against the directors of the Royal African Company, Wilkinson contrasted circumstances at most of the

Portuguese and French forts and factories, which had "Priests and Almoners" who "often go about to Preach and Pray to those of their Religion." Portuguese, he related, referred to English as "DESALMADAS ENGLESES, which is to say, SOULLESS ENGLISH" (Wilkinson 1690, 21).

One longtime associate of the Royal African Company was António de Aguiar ("António Deagujar"), who, in March 1705, recorded that he was a native of Portugal who had married in the Gambia prior to 1684 and had been affiliated with the company "these twenty yeares" (Gray 1940, 13 n. 4, 139 n. 1). One of the company's factors had presided at Aguiar's marriage ceremony on James Island, perhaps similar to that of "Hope" Booker (as will be recounted in Chapter Seven). Aguiar had at least one son and seven daughters, for whom he provided fine garments and gold jewelry to assist them in making suitable marriages. By 1705, one daughter was married to a French trader, and the son was engaged in upper-river trade (Wright 1976, 187–88).

The First Companhia de Cacheu

In May 1676, while France and Holland were engaged in the war that lasted from 1672 to 1678, the Conselho Ultramarino sponsored the formation of a joint-stock company intended to revitalize Portuguese commerce and influence in western Africa. The Companhia de Cacheu, Rios e Comércio de Guiné was the first of a number of undercapitalized and ineptly administrated joint-stock companies organized in hopes of emulating the entrepreneurial successes of rival European nations. One of the company's most attractive prospects for investors was that it might compete with Luanda as the principal supplier of slaves for Brazil. Other anticipated sources of revenue for this first Companhia de Cacheu were duties imposed on kola and dyes obtained along the coast between the Nunez and Kolente Rivers, plus a portion of the tax on slave exports. The company's founding was opposed by merchants associated with Cabo Verde who profited from the resale of captives acquired from western Africa. In response to their lobbying, the Conselho Ultramarino directed that Cabo Verde's treasury was to receive full duties and that one-third of the cargo space in company vessels was to be reserved for Cabo Verdean shipments to or from western Africa (Rodney 1970, 139; Duncan 1972, 226–27; Hanson 1981, 234).

The Consello Ultramarino appointed António de Barros Bezerra the capitão-mor of Cacheu. Bezerra was a principal shareholder in the Companhia de Cacheu. Born in Madeira, Bezerra had thirty-five years of experience in western Africa, including residence at Cacheu, where one of his associates was Ambrósio Gomes, reputed to be the richest trader in Guinea. Bezerra proposed the conquest of Africans dwelling in the neighborhood of Cacheu as a means to advance Portuguese commercial interests, a strategy that the Conselho Ultramarino was unwilling to approve. The Companhia de Cacheu was, however, obligated to reinforce Cacheu's stockade, undertake further buildings and entrenchments, and maintain a garrison of fifty soldiers for the six-year duration of its contract (Hair 1985, chap. 3: 9–10; Teixeira 1950; Rodney 1970, 135–40; Duncan 1972, 227; D. A. Pereira 1993).

Following his arrival in Cacheu, Bezerra used the garrison's soldiers to defeat the Diola of Mata who controlled the Bouganbor streamlet and spring, but the garrison's ascendancy was temporary; after Bezerra's period of command, Cacheu's inhabitants were again harassed when drawing water (Hair 1985, chap. 3: 9–10).

Bezzera's experience and purposefulness during the time he was capitão-mor of Cacheu (1676–82) were reflected in the English traders' complaints about increased competition along the Gambia River and the Sierra Leone estuary. Nonetheless, the Companhia de Cacheu failed to attract significant investments from Portuguese mercantile interests and was so poorly financed that it was able to dispatch only one vessel a year from Portugal, instead of the six pledged the Conselho Ultramarino.

Consequently, the undercapitalized company's business during its four years of existence was effectively limited to acting as a commercial intermediary for English interests while striving to maintain a middleman role with Luso-Africans and Africans. Both these groups vigorously opposed the situation, for they were united by common interests. In 1680, the Companhia de Cacheu failed and was incorporated into the Companhia Geral do Comércio do Brasil, founded in 1649 with considerable funding from New Christians who were promised immunity from having their property seized by the Inquisition (Kup 1961, 11; Rodney 1970, 140–41; D. G. Smith 1974, 237–38; Hanson 1983, 497; Blackburn 1997, 200).

During the 1670s, cooperation between the residents of Cacheu and English traders in the Gambia was promoted by representatives of both the Companhia de Cacheu and the Gambia Adventurers. In 1678, Capitão-Mor Bezerra offered Thomas Thurloe, the chief factor for the Gambia Adventurers, a long-term agreement by which English traders would be supplied with ivory and camwood at twenty-four and twenty bars a hundredweight, respectively. Thurloe did not take up the offer, considering the prices excessive at a time when the Royal African Company was about to supplant the Gambian Adventurers. In February 1683,

Bezerra's and Thurloe's successors, José Gonçalves Doliveira and John Castle, negotiated a similar arrangement, with the price of ivory reduced to twenty-two bars a hundredweight and the price of beeswax set at sixteen bars per hundredweight. The English thereby obtained the advantage of acquiring commodities in bulk instead of piecemeal (Gray 1940, 88, 91; Rodney 1970, 208).

The Royal African Company's factors in the Gambia may have sought collaboration with traders in Cacheu as a consequence of growing competition from English interlopers and from traders of the French Compagnie du Sénégal, established at Albreda from 1681 onward. Niumi's mansas exploited the European rivalry to considerable advantage. The English and French factors at James Island and Albreda were compelled to negotiate annual customs payments to renew the landlord-stranger relationship, and they had to negotiate specific agreements on tolls, rights, and privileges as well. Vessels entering the Gambia River were required to anchor at Juffure or Albreda, where alcaides collected duties and presents for mansas, themselves, and lesser officials. Fees also had to be paid for the privilege of obtaining wood, water, and provisions. The Royal African Company's agents negotiated standard payments for company vessels, while ships owned by private traders were obliged to pay significantly higher tolls and charges (Wright 1976, 247–48).

Numerous Luso-Africans were attracted to Juffure and Albreda, including the nharas who were associated with Europeans in trade, sold provisions to factors, and hired grumetes to work on vessels. It is likely that many of the grumetes were Luso-Africans, not all of them free men: some Luso-Africans belonged to the Mandinka *jongolu* (slave) social category. When Luso-African men married royal slaves, their children were considered slaves whose possessions would be inherited by the rulers (Boulègue 1989, 63). At the close of the seventeenth century (if not earlier), Luso-Africans residing at Juffure paid the mansa an annual rent of 50 ecus (equal to 150 francs) and had to render a tax of one-tenth of the value of all commodities traded (Wright 1976, 188–90; 1997, 86).

Among Luso-Africans who profited from Anglo-French competition was a shipmaster named François Basse Cogneu, who traded at Albreda in April 1685 with a bark flying a Portuguese flag (Ly 1964, 30); this was probably Francisco Vaz Coelho, a Luso-African residing at Geba mentioned in chapter 6 who, in February 1687, offered hospitality to Jean Jajolet de La Courbe, the director of the Compagnie du Sénégal (Cultru 1913, 248).

Doliveira and Castle's February 1683 commercial agreement lasted only a few months. In mid-1683, Doliveira instituted new policies that excluded foreign vessels from trading at Cacheu and sought to diminish the middleman role exercised by local traders. These appealed to the governor of Cabo Verde, and when this effort proved unavailing, they made common cause with Papel who were determined to ensure the admission of English vessels (Rodney 1970, 209). Following an unsuccessful attempt on Doliveira's life in February 1684, Cacheu's trading community, with the collaboration of a resident Spanish Capuchin, captured Doliveira and compiled charges of fraud and corrupt practices against him. Doliveira was taken to Farim, where he was incarcerated at the residence of Bibiana Vaz, a rich and influential nhara.

Bibiana Vaz was a Luso-African who married Ambrosio Gomes, a former acting capitão-mor and one of the most successful traders of his time. When Gomes died in 1679, Vaz acted as an African ruler would and took possession of her husband's property to the exclusion of his son by a previous marriage, Lourenço Matos Gomes. Possessing a two-masted vessel and other trading craft, she exploited an extensive commercial network that included Niumi, Cacheu, Farim, and Guinguim and extended as far south as the Sierra Leone estuary, where she traded with the English on Bunce Island. Testifying to Bibiana Vaz's enterprise, her trade network extended from the Gambia River to the Sierra Leone estuary and encompassed the Banyun-Bak and Biafada-Sapi commercial spheres (Rodney 1970, 209–10; Wright 1976, 195; Havik 2001, 24–25).

Bibiana Vaz and her brother Ambrósio Vaz, who lived at Cacheu, as well as her nephew Francisco Vaz, who was a leading trader in the Nunez River, were probably related to the previously mentioned Manuel Vaz de Franco of Bintang. More speculative are questions about whether Bibiana and Ambrósio were full or half siblings (same mother?), whether Francisco Vaz was in fact a nephew, and what kinship affiliations the three may have had with other Luso-Africans and Africans. Such relationships are unknown, due to Luso-African males' disdain for Christian marriages, their victimization of female slaves, and the absence of birth registers.

Doliveira was held captive at Farim for fourteen months before he effected an escape. Meanwhile, Cacheu's trading community established a "republic" ruled by an elected triumvirate that enacted decrees "in the name of the people." The three leaders were Santos de Vidigal Castanho, Manuel de Andrade from Farim, and Ambrósio Vaz, brother of Bibiana Vaz. Luso-Africans along the Casamance River were represented by António Duarte. Members of the trading community expressed their hostility to a proposed government-sponsored trading company, and it was decreed that in the future, Portuguese could trade with Africans only through the agency of resident traders (Rodney 1970, 209–12). This self-promoting edict likely did not have the support of Papel and Banyun allies, and it probably contributed to the republic's collapse. In May 1685, the Luso-African republic was terminated by the arrival of an expedition from Portugal commanded by the former capitão-mor António de Barros Bezerra, reinforced with a hundred militia from São Tiago. The republic's leaders surrendered with the promise of clemency, and Ambrozio Vaz was taken prisoner to São Tiago. The third member of the ruling triumvirate, Santos de Vidigal Castanho, was not apprehended, nor was Bibiana Vaz until two years later (Rodney 1970, 209–12).

One Luso-African woman living in the Gambia, a contemporary of Bibiana Vaz, was known to Europeans by several sobriquets: Marie Mar (in 1682), La Belinguere (in 1686), and Maguimar (in 1687). The daughter of a former ruler, she was considered the most influential person in Niumi after from the mansa and reputedly possessed a fortune worth more than forty thousand livres in gold, slaves, and cattle. She was renowned for her openhanded hospitality to European traders.

"Belinguere" apparently was a Wolof title of respect applied to this influential Luso-African woman. In Cayor, the bur's mother (or in some instances his sister) held the title of "linger." She controlled a number of villages whose inhabitants cultivated her lands and paid tribute to her and members of her personal entourage. A linger presided at her own court, which dealt with women's matters, such as cases concerning adultery (Gamble 1967, 58). The title "belinguere" was found in James Fort's "Accounts and Charges for 1734," which recorded two payments made to "Belinger, Queen of Barra, a person of power and a good friend" (T70/1451, 232–58; Wright, personal communication).

Michel Jajolet de La Courbe, the director of the Compagnie du Sénégal who visited the Gambia in June 1686, characterized La Belinguere as the "reef" on which numerous whites from different countries had "shipwrecked" (François de Paris 1682, cited in Thilmans 1976, 26; Cultru 1913, 196–98). That La Courbe and his colleagues were enthralled by her is evident from his account of a banquet served on mats on the verandah of her Luso-African-type dwelling.

> [The meal] included two boiled chickens and rice that was very well prepared with a considerable amount of *piment,* which is a type of red and green fruit shaped like a small cucumber having a taste very similar to pepper; next, we were brought *galine pecade,* which is to say a fowl cut up and seasoned and put back in its skin for boiling, giving it a taste something like spiced cervelas sausage. I ate, also for the first time, *batangue,* which is a bread made from millet flour, round and flat like a very thin cake, which is served very hot, and is not at all bad. We were also served a dessert which I had never previously

> eaten: it was a pineapple, an excellent fruit which has a taste somewhat like a sugared rennet apple, but much better; it is, however, very dangerous, and if you insert a knife in one for two days it completely corrodes the blade; to prevent this, it is consumed with wine and sugar. We were also served bananas, which is a yellow fruit shaped like a cucumber, except it is thinner; it has strong flesh, is very sweet, and extremely good. For drink, we were served palm wine and we had brought brandy, of which the lady drank a little. She was garbed in a very elegant man's shirt and a small Portuguese-style corset which emphasized her figure, and for a skirt she wore a beautiful African cloth which they call a pagne alse, that is to say a prestige cloth which comes from Sao Tiago in the Cape Verde Islands. She had a very fine muslin coiled around her head in the shape of a turban raised a little in front. She had a gracious manner and a gift for conversation, and spoke Portuguese, French, and English well, indicative of the extensive commerce she carries on with all nations. (Cultru 1913, 196–98)

After giving La Belinguere a present of coral and amber, La Courbe reluctantly departed, "like Ulysses leaving Circe's home," he added.

As La Courbe's description of the repast showed, the Luso-African cuisine incorporated foods from four continents. La Belinguere's dinner comprised western African millet, rice, and palm wine; sugar that was probably grown in the Cape Verde Islands; Portuguese wine; chilies and pineapples from South America; and bananas from South Asia. It is little wonder that in addition to adopting other attributes of the Luso-African lifestyle, many African elites sought cooks who knew how to prepare Luso-African dishes.

La Belinguere's personal ensemble was a precursor of a style refined to a renowned elegance by the signares of Gorée and Saint-Louis that will be described in Chapter Nine. Noteworthy is her turban, an elegant headdress probably derived from a long-standing practice of wearing cotton cloth to adorn hair plaited into towerlike coils (Moraes 1993, 72 n. 41). Signares living in Senegambia during the eighteenth and nineteenth centuries flaunted cone-shaped turbans contrived from a number of colored kerchiefs.

One of La Belinguere's contemporaries in Niumi was Lucia, also a Luso-African woman of considerable influence ("une grande dame du pays"). She became associated with a French factor named La Coste, whom La Courbe assigned to Albreda in 1686. Lucia allegedly partnered with La Coste in embezzling gold belonging to the Compagnie du Sénégal. Two employees of the company were dispatched from Gorée to investigate the matter, but when they attempted to search Lucia's dwelling for the missing gold, her entourage caused them to desist for fear of their lives (Cultru 1910, 115–16, and 1913, 270; Gray 1940, 92–102). Residing in Niumi, La Coste would have been more vulnerable to Circean enthrallment than the transient La Courbe.

The Compagnie des Indes Occidentales sought to address this and other problems by introducing rigorous new regulations in January 1688. Among various requirements, new employees had to swear they would not maintain African women, allow African women to enter their quarters, or visit African villages without permission—regulations that doubtless were ignored after the men arrived in western Africa. The same year, Louis Moreau de Chambonneau, the commandant and chief agent at Saint-Louis, proposed that the company establish an agricultural colony along the Senegal River—or, alternatively, on the Cape Verde peninsula, along the mouth of the Gambia River, on Ilha de Bissau, or in the Bissagos Islands. To perpetuate French interests, it would be essential to send French women to the area and to prevent male colonists from marrying African women. Otherwise, Chambonneau warned, the company risked a repetition of the Portuguese experience: mulatto children whose descendants would become darker and darker, ending up completely black (Cultru 1910, 74, 115–18; Ly 1958, 257–64).

It is worth noting that La Courbe's laudatory description of La Belinguere was strikingly at odds with his derisory account of male Luso-Africans living along the Gambia River. La Courbe was informed that Luso-Africans in Niumi controlled "almost all" Gambia River commerce using large dugout craft but were always indebted to French and English traders who advanced them European merchandise on credit. Luso-Africans traded upriver for captives, ivory, and gold, later dissipating their earnings on women and drink (Cultru 1913, 192–93)—a lifestyle that reflected the intractable problems of accumulating capital, given the demands of kinfolk and local elites and the African rulers' practice of confiscating strangers' property on their deaths. La Courbe derided Luso-Africans' strategy of professing Christianity when with Europeans and Islam when among Muslims. The latter accommodation was doomed to failure, for during the eighteenth century, Muslim traders supplanted Luso-Africans along the Gambia River.

> [Residing among the Mandinka of Niumi] are certain blacks and mulattos who call themselves Portuguese because they are descended from Portuguese who formerly lived here; these latter, besides the local language, continue to speak a certain jargon which has only a little resemblance to the Portuguese language and which is called the Creole language, like the lingua-franca in

> the Mediterranean Sea; they always wear a large crucifix around the neck and call themselves by a saint's name, although for the most part they are neither baptized nor show any evidence of the Christian religion. They usually wear a hat, shirt, and breeches like Europeans, and although they are black, they nevertheless assert that they are white, trying to show that they are Christians like white people. Most of them neither offer prayers nor *rakah,* and some do both: being with blacks they perform rakah, and when they see whites, they take their rosaries and copy them; they usually live in dwellings made of earth Portuguese-style, and for the most part arm themselves with guns; it is they also who undertake most of the commerce of the country, having large canots made from a single log, which carry more than ten tons, in which they engage in commerce; but inasmuch as they are extremely debauched, and consume all they earn, either on women or drink, they are always in debt, either to the French or the English who advance them merchandise to undertake trade in the upper river and tributary streams, to return and sell what they have acquired at more than half profit. (Cultru 1913, 192–93)

François de Paris, whose visit to the Gambia preceded La Courbe's by a half dozen years, similarly disparaged Luso-African men:

> These Portuguese are as black as the Africans themselves. . . . They declare themselves good Christians, notwithstanding that most of them know nothing more than the sign of the cross and engage in all the vices of the Africans, especially lasciviousness, to which everyone in this land, both men and women, are excessively addicted, and like them, possess many women. They are useful for manning vessels in the river from October to June, which is this country's good season. (Paris 1682, quoted in Thilmans 1976, 26)

La Courbe's Reconnaissance of the Banyun Trade Network

In June 1686, after visiting Albreda and Geregia (where he later installed a French factor), La Courbe followed the Banyun trade route overland to Cacheu, visited Ilha de Bissau and the Grande River, and then returned to Cacheu for several months (October? to December 1686). Pierre Cultru's publication did not include the pages of La Courbe's journal recounting his travels between Geregia and Bissau; these were not part of the La Courbe manuscript found in the Bibliothèque Nationale, nor were they in the material deposited in the

Archives Nationales. However, a pirated version of La Courbe's journal, including the missing section, was published in 1728 by Père Jean-Baptiste Labat, who, for reasons unknown, attributed La Courbe's travels to Andre Brüe, the director of the Compagnie du Sénégal from 1697 to 1702 and from 1714 to 1720 (Cultru 1913, IV–IX; Boulègue 1993 and 2001). Labat's numerous modifications of La Courbe's journal can be checked against the manuscript published by Cultru and other extant sources—except the section covering the Banyun trade network for which other sources are lacking. Unresolved is the question of whether Labat had access to a different version of La Courbe's journal than the two parts located by Cultru.

On learning from the Royal African Company's factor at Juffure ("Gilfroid"/ "Jillifry") that several English traders had traversed Banyun territory to Cacheu, La Courbe resolved to do likewise. At Bintang in Foni, he met an influential Luso-African woman who, after being widowed, had married the English mariner Capt. Cornelius Hodges ("Agis"), with whom she had several children. In response to La Courbe's inquiries regarding the kola she offered him, she replied, preposterously, that they came from more than three hundred leagues upriver and that those most esteemed came from Serra Leoa (Cultru 1913, 198–204)—Luso-Africans were always determined to protect their chief trade by spreading misinformation or other means.

Five years earlier, in 1681, Captain Hodges had made a reconnaissance voyage along the upper Gambia on behalf of the Royal African Company, and he made another between 1689 and 1690, guided by Luso-Africans (Stone 1924; Gray 1940, 184; Curtin 1975, 277; Boulègue 1989, 48–49). When his wife gave birth to a black baby, he accused her of committing infidelity, and, in a violent rage, he crushed the baby in a mortar and fed it to dogs. Despite this atrocious act, however, Hodges later reconciled with his wife because she was invaluable in terms of his commercial affairs (Cultru 1913, 201–4; Gray 1940, 96 n. 1).

La Courbe next visited Geregia, the chief Vintang River entrepôt for wax, captives, and other commodities brought from Casamance. At Geregia, where he stayed at the Royal African Company factory managed by the Irishman William Quinn ("Gouin"), La Courbe learned that resident Luso-Africans dispatched African compradors to Diola settlements to trade for beeswax, hides, ivory, slaves, and gold in small quantities. Their principal trade was in beeswax, which they made into cakes ("en pain") for sale to the English factory and French trading craft. The Luso-African influence on the Banyun ruler of Jagra who lived a quarter of a league from Geregia was evident, for he wore a Portuguese cap with African garments, and his dwelling was furnished "Portuguese-style" (Cultru 1913, 204–6; Gray 1940, 102).

A Spanish trader named Juan Filipe ("Jean-Philippe") was married to a young daughter of the Banyun ruler, and La Courbe noted that male and female Africans bowed to this man as though he were the ruler himself. The Spaniard had instructed his wife and her father in Christianity, but the latter refused to change his religion lest he antagonize his restless Diola subjects. The Banyun ruler was frequently at war with Diola, selling those who were captured. He was well supplied with arms and powder and had many men skilled in their use. Filipe disparaged the local Luso-Africans as mostly descendants of Jews who disdained his proposal for the collective maintenance of a priest (Cultru 1913, 207–8).

As a sidebar, it should be noted that the first part of La Courbe's journal deposited at the Bibliothèque Nationale ends at this point (Cultru 1913, 210); the part from the Archives Nationales begins at Bissau. The information in the following passages is derived from Labat's publication.

According to Labat's account (1728, 5:18), La Courbe was informed that the numerous Luso-Africans living in Gereges paid the ruler an annual contribution or head tax. Furthermore, the ruler inherited the property of those who died without children — a significant difference from circumstances along the Gambia River, where rulers of stratified societies confiscated the property of deceased Luso-Africans regardless of offspring.

Labat contrasted the "civilized" Banyun, who welcomed commerce with strangers, with the "savage" Diola ("Feloupes"). So threatening were the latter that Pasqua, the village of the Banyun ruler along the Songrougrou River, was surrounded by six rows of palisades and garrisoned by a hundred fusiliers. La Courbe was cordially received by the Luso-Africans living there. Some distance from Pasqua was the large compound of a Spaniard from Cuba who titled himself "Signor Dom Juan Maldonado." His large compound was surrounded by four palisades and defended with cannons (Labat 1728, 5:39–41).

At the village of James, Luso-Africans acquired large quantities of beeswax from Diola ("Feloupes") at biweekly markets. By contrast, Feloupes living along the Casamance River reputedly rejected any contacts with "whites" and neighboring groups were "continually" at war (Labat 1728, 5:43, 45).

According to Labat, La Courbe crossed the Casamance River upstream from the Portuguese praça at Ziguinchor, which, significantly, he did not visit. He was informed that the fort had two half bastions with cannons facing the river and two full bastions on the land side consisting of double palisades with earthen ramparts (Labat 1728,5:46). La Courbe's party followed a marigot to Baito, where there was a small fort consisting of a palisaded compound, huts for soldiers, and seven or eight cannons. The sickly-looking detachment comprised an officer, two sergeants, and fifteen soldiers. The garrison was charged with preventing Africans and Luso-Africans from carrying wax to Cacheu for sale instead of to Ziguinchor because the king of Portugal derived considerable revenue from the latter (Labat 1728, 5:46–47).

La Courbe visited the village of the Banyun ruler of Buguendo and then continued on to Guinguim, which had a large Banyun community and a number of Luso-Africans ("Portugaise") who resided there during visits to collect the large quantities of wax obtained in Banyun villages by their grumete compradors. La Courbe recorded that Luso-Africans paid customs to the Banyun ruler, but he remarked that they were as much masters of the country as he was (Labat 1728, 5:49–50).

At Cacheu, La Courbe found an English vessel commanded by John Booker ("Mestre Bocher"), the Royal African Company's chief agent at James Island who had visited Lisbon and São Tiago en route—attesting to the collaborative commercial arrangements negotiated in 1683 by Doliveira and Castle for the Companhia de Cacheu and the Royal African Company, respectively. La Courbe's host in Cacheu was Manuel Pereira ("Dom Manuel Perera"), whom he described as a friend of the Compagnie du Sénégal and with whom he engaged in contraband trade. La Courbe mentioned without comment the former capitão-mor, Antonio de Barros Bezerra (Labat 1728, 5:54, 56).

La Courbe's description of Cacheu's fortifications and dwellings differed little from that written by Francisco de Lemos Coelho. He observed that the inhabitants owned no land outside the stockade; hence, they could not keep domestic animals, grow rice or other foodstuffs, or engage in fishing; all such commodities had to be purchased from neighboring Africans or imported at considerable expense. The garrison of thirty soldiers was composed of criminals exiled from Portugal for three years of service. The men were so wretchedly provided for that they needed to practice a trade or find some other means of support. Not surprisingly, La Courbe dwelled on the nighttime insecurity of persons and property (Labat 1728, 5:58–66, 68–70).

According to Labat's rendition of La Courbe's account, there were "very few" European-born Portuguese at Cacheu, with the greater number of "Portuguese whites" being "so dark that one must have a great knowledge of colors and their different shades to distinguish them from the blackest Africans" (Labat 1728, 5:66). Wives were restricted to compounds and lived circumscribed lives: "These white Portuguese, tan, mulatto, or black, keep lawful wives and those with this claim are closely guarded in their dwellings. White women never leave their dwellings during the daytime, not even to go to mass. . . . Portuguese women of other colors have a little more freedom, going out in the daytime, but so covered-up that one can see only their feet and one of their eyes" (Labat 1728, 5:66–67). That "lawful" wives were subjected to close confinement presumably derived from the husbands' obsession with adulterous liaisons and illegitimate children—and from fears of contracting venereal diseases, allegedly "so commonplace and so ordinary as to cause neither shame nor embarrassment." In fact, husbands were so jealous that suspected rivals were challenged to duels, and wives risked being stabbed or poisoned. Papel women and slave girls performed the housework, went to the market, and fetched firewood and water from outside the palisades, often under armed escort so that they would not be accosted or carried off by the Diola of Mata (Labat 1728,5:67–69, 73).

The observation concerning "white women" being "lawful wives" related to the exceptional status of a consecrated Christian marriage. Nearly all Portuguese and Cabo Verdeans married "country-style," and official documents recorded their social status as *solteiro* (single)—their intention being to reserve the option of a Christian marriage when they returned to Portugal or Cabo Verde.

La Courbe did not visit Farim, and he was doubtless prevented from learning about the principal source of Cacheu's trade. Subsequently, traders in Bissau informed him that all the traders at Cacheu had factories ("cases") in Farim, leaving grumetes in villages along the Cacheu River to trade for beeswax with people living in the hinterland (Cultru 1913, 232). La Courbe rendezvoused with a French vessel at Cacheu and sailed to Bissau to make a reconnaissance of the Geba-Grande commercial sphere discussed in chapter 6 (Labat 1728, 5:55).

La Courbe revisited the Cacheu River in February 1687 en route to the Petite Côte. The Diola living at Cajegute were hostile to Europeans, having recently pillaged a Dutch vessel and massacred its crew, but those at Bot engaged in peaceful trade. So did the Diola at Bolale at the mouth of the Cacheu River, who produced large quantities of rice and welcomed European traders. At Bolale, La Courbe encountered an English trader who related that he had been installed there by John Booker and Alexander Cleeve, the chief agent of the Royal African Company, because he had informed the company's directors of numerous embezzlements of funds. The English factor soon departed for Europe via the Azores on a Portuguese vessel. La Courbe remarked that the Diola inhabitants of Bolale possessed a hundred canoas ("canots") of all sizes, in which they transported rice to Cacheu for sale. Most of the men emulated Luso-Africans in having saints' names but were not practicing Christians (Cultru 1913, 258–61).

After departing from Cacheu, it took La Courbe's vessel two weeks to navigate the three hundred kilometers up the coast to Joal against prevailing north-northeast winds and the flow of the Guinea Current. The shipmaster had no alternative but to anchor for a week at Cape Roxo until the wind changed (Cultru 1913, 262–63). At Portudal, a Luso-African employee named Pinheiro ("le seigneur Pigniere"), who had shipwrecked at the mouth of the Cacheu River, was left to have a venereal disease treated by a "black Portuguese" reputed to be a good healer. La Courbe stated that Pinheiro was "tout gaste" by the venereal disease, "like most Luso-Africans in this country" (Cultru 1913, 261, 263). It is noteworthy that the verb *gastar* (to wear out, consume, or waste) is not French but Portuguese and Crioulo. That Pinheiro sought a reputed Luso-African healer seems a sensible choice, inasmuch as the medications brought from Europe to treat venereal diseases included sarsaparilla, china-root, and gayac—none of which possessed curative powers (Labat 1728, 5:72–73; Hair, Jones, and Law 1992, 1:576 n. 1).

European Competition in the Aftermath of La Courbe's Reconnaissance

La Courbe's intrusion into the Gambia-Casamance-Cacheu trade network, together with the expanding English shipboard trade in the Geba-Grande-Serra Leoa commercial sphere promoted by John Booker, seems to have provoked countervailing measures by Capitão-Mor José Gonçalves Doliveira. In September 1686, Doliveira allegedly connived in the attack on an English trading vessel from the Gambia, in which the master and a crew member were killed (Gray 1940, 98). Nonetheless, when La Courbe returned to Cacheu in October (?), to reside there until December 20, he was hospitably received by the residents, including the *feitor* (royal customs collector) Capitão António Semedo de Fonseca ("António Zenedo de Fontra"). La Courbe made no mention of Doliveira, but it is noteworthy that he did not visit Farim; it is likely that the capitão-mor refused permission. La Courbe recorded only that Cacheu's resident traders had factories at Farim, leaving grumetes at villages along the Cacheu River to trade for wax (Cultru 1913, 230–32).

Doliveira's aggressive strategy was short-lived. He was succeeded by António de Barros Bezerra (1687–88), who had initiated negotiations with English traders in the Gambia during his previous service as capitão-mor. Foreign traders were made welcome, as evidenced by the two French traders living at Cacheu and Bissau in 1687 (the Bourguignon brothers) and by the French and English vessels frequenting Cacheu, Guinguim, Bissau, Geba, and the Grande River in 1686 and 1687 (Cultru 1913, 257; Labat 1728, 5:73; Ly 1964).

Bibiana Vaz was apprehended in 1687 and taken prisoner to São Tiago, where leading Cabo Verdean traders vouched for her security and maintenance. To the frustration of the Portuguese authorities, her property was in African territory and therefore could not be confiscated. To resolve the standoff, Bibiana Vaz was granted a royal pardon after paying a symbolic indemnity for expenses incurred by the Crown and promising to make substantial payments when she recovered her property. She also agreed to construct a fort at Bolor on the north bank of the Cacheu River, an enterprise she never undertook. Meanwhile, both her brother and cousin received royal pardons (Barcellos 1899–1913, 2:83, 102, 170; Rodney 1970, 211–12; Havik 2001, 26–29). Santos de Vidigal Castanho, the member of the triumvirate who escaped capture in May 1685, was pardoned after a fine was assessed. Subsequently, he became the capitão-mor of Cacheu (1691–1707), serving during the time of the second Cacheu Company (Rodney 1970, 147, 210–12). Castagno's appointment attested that accommodation to the interests of Luso-Africans and Africans was indispensable to the furtherance of commerce.

When La Courbe returned to the Gambia in April 1687 to load a cargo of slaves for Santo Domingo, Niumi's trade with the Royal African Company was stopped due to an altercation involving La Belinguere and Capt. Cornelius Hodges. La Belinguere and other women had attended a boisterous party at James Fort. Something said to one of the women provoked a brawl, and an inebriated Hodges had wounded the woman with a knife. As a consequence, the mansa of Niumi, Jenung Wuleng Sonko, seized the English factor at Juffure and confiscated all his trade goods as compensation. When the chief agent, Alexander Cleeve, went ashore to parlay, he was seized by the mansa's entourage. To obtain his release and reclaim the confiscated merchandise, Cleeve paid two hundred bars on behalf of Captain Hodges, which caused a falling-out between the two men and a cession of English commerce to the benefit of French traders. La Belinguere and the French agent La Coste colluded to great advantage, earning the rancor of the notables at Juffure, who became incensed by her behavior toward them (Cultru 1913, 270–72; Gray 1940, 96–97; Thilmans 1976, 49 n. 71; Wright 1997, 109–10).

Eventually, the Banyun ruler of Foni negotiated an accommodation between the English and the mansa of Niumi. The Compagnie du Sénégal meanwhile made the most of the circumstances and recruited a network of Luso-African compradors to exploit the upper river trade, which had previously been monopolized by the Royal African Company. Shipmasters were provided formal documentation: a commission dated March 24, 1689, issued by José Pereira da Silva, clerk (*commis*) for the Compagnie du Sénégal at Albreda, engaged Diogo Rodrigues to trade along the upper Gambia River, flying the French flag (Ly 1958, 277; Boulègue 1989, 76). These initiatives, together with French enterprise elsewhere in western Africa, were ruined by destructive commerce raiding after England entered the War of the League of Augsburg in 1689.

By the close of the 1680s, the directors of the Royal African Company decided it was uneconomical to purchase slaves in the Guinea-Bissau region in competition with Spanish, Dutch, and Portuguese traders, plus English interlopers. Consequently, in 1688, John Booker, the chief agent at James Fort from 1688 until his death in 1693, was instructed to ship only wax and ivory and to reexchange slaves for these commodities (Davies 1957, 236, 272). This policy proved counterproductive. John Booker subsequently reported that, in accordance with his instructions, he had refused to buy several hundred slaves, and that as a result African traders had not brought other commodities downriver. It was necessary, he informed the directors, to buy slaves in order "to keep up the credit of the trade," even though they might be obtained more cheaply elsewhere (Davies 1957, 236). The Royal African Company's directive was especially inopportune, for in 1689 and 1690, there were famine conditions in the interior of Senegambia—circumstances that always advantaged the slavers (Stone 1924, 91–92, 94; Curtin 1975, app. 1:3; Becker 1985, 169). The "symbiosis" of slave and nonslave trades would become a thorny issue during the suppression of the slave trade.

Chapter 6
Trade with the Kaabu Empire and Serra Leoa

[The ruler of Kaabu] is capable of killing a man like a mosquito. He makes war on his neighbors without cause.

—Cultru 1913, 252

Every man hath his whore for whom they steale.

—Davies 1957, 257

During the second half of the seventeenth century, Luso-Africans struggled to retain commercial ascendancy at Geba and Bissau and in the rivers of Serra Leoa, competing and cooperating with traders affiliated with the Compagnie du Sénégal and the Royal African Company. Meanwhile, English and Anglo-Africans progressively aggrandized more and more of Serra Leoa's trade. Crucial to their competitiveness, Luso-Africans and their associated African grumetes maintained a monopoly or near monopoly in coastwise commerce in kola. In 1688, the outbreak of the War of the League of Augsburg greatly diminished French and English competition in western Africa, to the Luso-Africans' advantage.

Geba-Grande Competition, 1650s–1680s

Apart from Cacheu, the principal Luso-African settlement was Geba, located some one hundred kilometers up the Geba River at the head of navigation for sailing vessels. Geba was the entrepôt for Mande traders traversing Kaabu territory. Only one hundred kilometers distant from Bissau as the crow flies, though farther by a fifth via the coils of the Geba River, Geba has a drier and more salubrious climate due to its higher elevation and lower rainfall (about 1,500 mm versus 2,000 mm annually), lower humidity, and no mosquito-infested mangrove swamps. The savanna-woodland zone extending east of Geba was relatively free of tsetse infestation during the c. 1630–c. 1860 dry period, so its inhabitants and visiting traders could maintain horses and donkeys, in contrast to the situation at Bissau, where the animals soon succumbed to trypanosomiasis (Mota 1954, 1:33; Beaver 1805, 359).

Bissau gradually superseded Geba because its port could accommodate larger vessels, which enhanced its value as an entrepôt for trade with the Geba and Grande Rivers and the Bissagos archipelago, as well as trade southward along the Upper Guinea Coast. Ilha de Bissau extends some fifty kilometers along the Geba River and is bounded on the east by Impernal Channel, which separated Papel and Balanta territories. The port of Bissau was the northernmost entrepôt of the Biafada-Sapi trade network. Three Papel communities shared the southeastern part of Ilha de Bissau neighboring the principal anchorage: Intim controlled the port and trading settlement, Antula territory began a few hundred meters to the east of the port, and Bandim land started a few hundred meters to the west. The ruler of Intim was the principal landlord, receiving tribute from the rulers of Antula, Bandim, and other Papel groups living on Ilha de Bissau (Hair 1985, chap. 5: 5–9).

Balanta territory extended eastward from the Impernal Channel to the end of the Geba estuary and northward to the Casamance River. Balanta refused to trade with whites, and they allowed none in their territory. They restricted their commerce to one port along the Impernal Channel, bartering large quantities of foodstuffs with visiting trading craft. Balanta indiscriminately pillaged Europeans and other African groups along the Geba River, conducting their raids in large dugouts. African captives were sold as slaves, but whites were reputedly slain. Balanta who were taken captive killed themselves or fasted to death rather than remain slaves (Hair 1985, chap. 5: 7–8; Cultru 1913, 257–58; Rodney 1970, 82, 110).

Coelho and other strangers were informed, wrongly, of the existence of a waterway connecting the Mansoa and Cacheu Rivers and controlled by the Naga group of Papel, but they dared not reconnoiter for fear of being captured by Balanta (Hair 1985, chap. 5, 7). Information concerning commercial links between the rivers was kept secret from Portuguese and Luso-Africans alike, as acknowledged in 1856 by Honório Pereira Barreto, the best-informed and most influential Luso-African of his era (Barcellos 1899–1913, 6:86–87).

Traders living in Bissau frequented the lower Mansoa River. Vessels bound for Serra Leoa loaded large quantities of salt bought at inexpensive prices at Bujamata in the Papel state of the same name on Ilha de Bissau. Bula (Bole), a Papel community at the head of a marigot entering the Mansoa River from the north, was a noted market for rice (Mota 1972, map facing p. 288; Hair 1985, chap. 5: 7). During his visit in 1687, La Courbe commented on the ruler's "labyrinth-like" dwelling where he was entertained at a memorable banquet, without appreciating that the building was designed for protection: in the event of a surprise attack, the inhabitants could flee assailants, a defensive measure widely adopted during the sixteenth and seventeenth centuries by groups living in areas raided by Bijago (Cultru 1913, 237–40; Mota 1974a, map facing p. 262). Trading craft bound from Bissau to Cacheu followed the Mansoa River west to its mouth, then north via the Canal de Pecixe and Canal de Jeta.

The lower course of the Geba River is an enormous, uterine-shaped estuary. The Geba actually begins upstream from its confluence with the Corubal River. The narrowing, serpentine channel is only navigable by small sailing vessels with shallow drafts and by canoas, with mariners utilizing successive tides to propel their craft upriver. La Courbe, who visited the Geba River in February 1687 at the end of the dry season when the flow of the river was greatly diminished, graphically described the remarkable force of the tidal bore sweeping up the estuary; his trading craft was anchored at the head of the estuary near the entrance to the river proper: "When the tide began to rise, we heard a great noise of turbulent water and saw at a distance the *mascaret* which seemed to engulf us; we immediately raised anchor and bent to the oars; entrapping us the *mascaret* raised us like a mountain [of water] and bore us along with astonishing rapidity" (Cultru 1913, 247; cf. Hair 1985, chap. 6: 2–3).

During the dry season — the trading season — Geba was the head of navigation for sloops and schooners drawing less than a meter and a half of water. The settlement was on rising ground on the right bank of the river. Dugout craft might continue upstream as far as Bafatá (from the Mandinka word *ba-fatá,* meaning divided river), which was at the confluence of the Geba River and the tributary Colufe River (Bertrand-Bocandé 1849, 288–89; Labarthe 1802, 139). Geba was a principal entrepôt of the Kaabu Empire, where cargoes of kola brought from Serra Leoa were bartered for captives, ivory, and wax. In addition, caravan routes linked Geba with markets along the upper Cacheu, Casamance, and Gambia Rivers. During the time of the joint Spanish-Portuguese monarchy (1580–1640), Geba had the largest Portuguese and Cabo Verdean community in western Africa and supported a parish church and a chapel (Hair 1985, chap. 4: 8–9, chap. 6: 4).

Following the rupture of the Spanish-Portuguese union, Gonçalo de Gamboa de Aiala, the capitão-mor of Cacheu, ordered traders established at Geba to move to Farim at the head of navigation on the Cacheu River, where he could more easily supervise their activities and prevent them from trading with foreign vessels. Aiala granted a monopoly of Geba's trade to the highest bidder, but Coelho related that the (unnamed) monopolist dispatched only one vessel a year to Geba with iron and other commodities and made little profit. Geba's kola trade remained in the hands of the considerable community of Luso-Africans, whom Coelho termed "native-born white Christians" (*brancos cristãos filhos da terra*). These individuals were regularly visited by priests dispatched by the bishop of Cabo Verde, who realized "a very good profit" from their pastoral offices (Hair 1985, chap. 6: 4–5; Rema 1982, 89–90, 122).

Capitão-Mor Gamboa de Aiala tried unsuccessfully to impose his authority at Bissau, where traders and Papel leagued against him. In 1647, when he ordered two Spanish vessels seized, the ruler of Bissau protected them, and Aiala was powerless to force compliance (Rodney 1970, 131–32). In fact, the inhabitants of Bissau were so accommodating to traders that Coelho recommended that Cacheu's inhabitants move to Bissau (Hair 1985, chap. 5: 10–11). The situation changed greatly during the 1670s, as Cabo Verdeans and Portuguese residing at Bissau experienced growing competition from French and English rivals, to the advantage of Papel landlords and traders. In the circumstances, Catholic priests time and again proved to be the most effective agents of Portuguese interests, exercising substantial influence in matters both spiritual and temporal.

A Portuguese Franciscan priest who moved to Bissau from Cacheu in 1681 is credited with blocking the establishment of an English factor and preventing French traders from obtaining interpreters to engage in commerce in the Bissagos archipelago (Rodney 1970, 143–44). By contrast, three Spanish Capuchins who maintained a mission at Bissau from 1683 to 1686 proved inimical to Portuguese interests because they condemned the consequences for African societies of unrestrained slave raiding. In particular, the Capuchins attributed the Bijagos' depredations on the calculated and insidious blandishments of slavers: "When slavers found few or no slaves, they would reproach the islanders, insisting that this was a stain on the latter's good name. Other Europeans, they said, would ignore the Bijagos on hearing that these famous warriors had become decadent. Such appeals, accompanied by the liberal distribution of alcohol, usually achieved the purpose of inciting the Bijagos to go out and bring in more victims for the slave merchants." The Capuchins so enraged slavers at Bissau that when they set off on slaving expeditions, they demanded the priests' blessings and threatened to hang them if they refused. Responding to the traders' remonstrances, the Conselho Ultramarino obtained the recall of the Capuchins in 1686; they would be replaced by more compliant Portuguese Franciscans (Rodney 1970, 104–5, 143–44).

French trade in the Geba-Grande area expanded greatly during the 1680s, following the capture of Gorée Island from Holland in November 1677. Jean de la Fond settled at Bissau to be joined by brothers named Bourguignon. There were no resident English traders at Bissau, but ship-borne commerce was directed by John Booker, the chief agent of the Royal African Company in the Gambia (Cultru 1913, 212–13, 257). French initiatives in the Geba-Grande area intensified following a reconnaissance in 1686 by Sieur de la Courbe, director of the Compagnie du Sénégal.

Coelho's Account of Trade between the Geba and Sierra Leone Rivers

Traders established at Bissau and along the Grande River engaged in shipboard commerce with the Bissagos Islands after lançados devised effective countermeasures against predatory Bijago attacks. Bijago raids along the Grande River diminished by the 1630s because the lançados built *casa fortes* (strongholds) protected by cannons and launched ruthless counterraids in the archipelago. In Coelho's words, these tactics rendered the Bijago—for a time—"the most well-behaved and the most friendly towards the Portuguese of all the blacks throughout Guinea." However, with their raids against other groups curtailed, Bijago engaged in ruinous interisland strife—internecine conflicts that Coelho attributed to high birthrates in the area: "Were it not for the wars and their being sold as slaves . . . there would no longer be room for them all on these islands" (Hair 1985, chap. 7: 4).

Trading vessels frequenting the Bissagos archipelago obtained large numbers of war captives and accused sorcerers (*feiticeiros*). Coelho made more than two dozen voyages from Bissau during the 1640s and 1650s (?), purchasing the "best part" of one thousand slaves. Some village headmen who hosted visiting traders entrusted their sons to shipmasters to learn European ways while serving as seamen and *linguas* (interpreters and spokesmen), and the son of the ruler of Ilha da Caravela (Carraxa) was a Christian and master of a small vessel (Hair 1985, chap. 7: 6, 8–9, 15–16).

Coelho extolled Bolama Island's strategic location for commerce and its potential for a colony, relating that Biafada had once inhabited the island but had been driven away by Bijago raids: "Settlers would immediately become lords of the land and could form great estates on the island; while at Cacheu, not only do they not own an inch of land, but they lack even water for drinking, which sometimes involves great expense since they have to buy it so dearly, like the soldiers of David at the well of Bethlehem. . . . Bolama is well equipped for the building of ships, and possesses a fine river for wintering in, and splendid beaches for careening ships on" (Hair 1985, chap. 8: 1–3). Coelho was one of many who advocated founding a settlement on Bolama, making the island the cynosure of competing imperialisms — African, Eurafrican, and European — for centuries.

Coelho related that Portuguese and Luso-Africans living along the Grande River traded south along the Upper Guinea Coast as far as the Sierra Leone River. He was informed that Africans journeyed overland between the Grande and Nunez Rivers in four days and from the Nunez to the Sierra Leone estuary in eight days (Hair 1985, chap. 8: 12–14). Since the distance between the Grande River and the Sierra Leone estuary is more than four hundred kilometers, that was surely a challenging journey in a dozen days. Nonetheless, the overland trail would have been the most reliable route during the dry season when the Guinea Current and prevailing winds impeded northward passage by sailing vessels.

Regarding Nunez River commerce, Coelho reported that war captives, salt, and rice were purchased from Baga living at Benar at the mouth of the river — the salt intended for trade along the upper Nunez River and the rice for trade in the Pongo River. Three tides up the Nunez River was a settlement at Kakundy (Cangande) inhabited only by traders and their slaves, each compound having a wharf along the river. There was also a chapel that was sporadically visited by priests from São Tiago. Resident traders dispatched canoas on weeks-long expeditions along the Nunez's tributaries to purchase slaves, ivory, and rice from Nalu groups. They also sent trading craft into the Kapatchez River to trade with Baga for rice (Hair 1985, chap. 9: 6, 8, 10).

Traders at Kakundy lived in separate compounds but adhered to at least one mutually self-serving practice:

> The whites who live in this village are not united, for each one, with his household, forms a separate settlement by the river; so that there are as many settlements and ports as there are whites, each port being called by the name of the master of the settlement. But nevertheless the whites observe a courteous convention among themselves for the purposes of trade, as follows: once a commodity has entered the house of a resident, be the commodity a slave

> or ivory or dyes, its owner must either sell it (to the house-holder) or have it carried back up-river again, because no other resident will buy it back from him, even if the owner offers it for less than he offered it at first. This convention is never violated. (Hair 1985, chap. 9: 6–7)

Africans conversant with the practice likely confirmed purchase prices before taking their possessions into a resident's compound.

Besides ivory, the main trade along the Nunez River was for cakes of indigo dyestuffs, which the resident traders resold to vessels dispatched from Cacheu for sale at Cacheu and Banyun ports. Coelho asserted that one hundred thousand indigo cakes were exported one year when he traded in the Nunez (in the 1640s?) (Hair 1985, chap. 9: 9). Chance finds of ambergris were bonanzas for traders, who purchased it at derisory prices: not knowing its value, Africans used ambergris for caulking canoas. Coelho noted that substantial quantities of ambergris found along the river and purchased by the resident traders Luis Francês of Lisbon and Vicente Rodrigues Duarte of Monte Maior o Novo, São Tiago (?), were resold to English traders in the Sierra Leone estuary. Musk from captive civet cats was another exotic export from the Nunez River. The principal imports were different types of cloth, wine, cowries, iron, beads, and provisions for the trading community (Hair 1985, chap. 9: 8–9).

Susu encouraged traders to visit their lands and escorted them on the six- to eight-day journey there in caravans, providing hospitality (including the companionship of their daughters and wives) at villages en route. Susu were well armed and constantly on guard, for Fula living inland in Futa Jallon frequently raided the caravans. Both groups used poison arrows and antidotes, the latter of which Susu supplied to white traders venturing inland. Coelho observed, "Those whites who go there with little wealth get a lot, but it is hard work" (Hair 1985, chap. 9: 7–8). When Fr. André de Faro visited Kakundy from April to June 1663, he reported finding more than 150 Christians, and he baptized 54 persons (Hair 1982, 25).

Coelho acknowledged that he personally had never traded along the coast and rivers between the Nunez River and the Iles de Los, but he reported what he had learned from "many individuals who have traveled on this coast, by land as well as up the rivers." The Pongo River marked the beginning of the "Sapes nation" (that is, Bullom and Temne groups) and the start of kola trade. Prior to 1658, "white" traders carried on a considerable business at Dizo, on the northern branch of the river known by the same name. But in 1658, a "king of the land" attacked the village and killed all the whites who could not escape to their vessels. Traders continued to reside at Deponga along the southern branch of the Pongo, where they purchased ivory and cloth brought by Susu caravans and traders bound for Susu country disembarked. As was the case along the upper Gambia, gold was brought to Deponga by Jahanke ("Jagancazes") who came to purchase salt from the resident traders; the traders had obtained it by bartering rice and iron with Baga salt producers living in the Kaxas ("Cagacaes") Islands in the estuary. Traders established at Deponga removed themselves to the rivers and bays near the Iles de Los to spend the "winter" (meaning the dry season), living aboard their vessels and purchasing slaves, cloths, and ivory brought by Susu caravans (Hair 1985, chap. 9: 10–14).

The Iles de Los were a haven for shipping, for they were conveniently located for provisioning and afforded safe anchorage for ship repairs. Tamara and Kassa Islands were inhabited by Bullom, the former having the larger population and a stream of delicious water used for supplying vessels. The abundant provisions for sale included rice, sun-dried fish, dried bananas, tasty pumpkins that were renowned in western Africa, and palm wine made into a drink "like malmsey wine." The kola from the trees in this area were larger and harder and kept fresh longer than those from trees elsewhere, and they sold at premium prices (Hair 1985, chap. 9: 14–15). Twelve kilometers ("two leagues") south of the Iles de Los was the Forékariah River ("Rio dos Samos"), resorted to by Luso-Africans as the closest port of entry to Susu country. The ivory they obtained there was purchased by English and Dutch traders who visited the river in launches (Hair 1985, chap. 9: 21).

In Coelho's time, Serra Leoa was well known for having kola and rice in such abundance and at such reasonable prices that they were transported to windward markets by the shipload. In addition, the area had ivory, malaguetta pepper (called *cacião*), and a saffron-colored pepper known as *mantubilha*—spices sought by English and Dutch traders. English purchased large quantities of camwood (*pão camo*) at prices "as cheap as firewood" in Europe. Vessels were provisioned inexpensively with citrus fruit, dried bananas, pineapples, and sugarcane. Coelho extolled the hospitality of Temne, who offered traders residing in their dwellings the choice of their wives or daughters (Hair 1985, chap. 9: 16–18). In regard to this custom, Coelho mentioned a case in which stranger privileges were maliciously abused for personal gratification:

> This man went to a village called Cacheo, having learned that the king of the village had a very beautiful wife and being attracted more by the reputation of the black woman than by trade, and he said that he wanted to stay there

> for a time. When the king arrived he welcomed the man with remarkable benevolence, making him master of everything and being content to remain himself merely king in name. He showed the man all his wives, numbering more than 20, so that he could choose from among them the woman he thought the best. However, he concealed from him the wife whom the white man sought and fancied. The white man then expressed annoyance rather than gratitude; and he told the king that he was not his friend, for he was hiding from him one of the wives he knew he had, she not being present, and this being the case she must be beautiful, since he did not show her to him. On reflection, if the king did not care to offer him this wife, then he could not accept any of the other women, and he would go to another village where they would deny him nothing. The king answered that what he said was true. He had not shown him this particular wife because he himself was old, as he could see, and this wife was the daughter of the king of Caricolli, a great king of the land, and was his whole mainstay, and he could not be without her; but if the man was not satisfied with the wives he had shown him, then he would show him his daughters and nieces, who were beautiful and numerous, and from these he could choose any woman he wished, and the one he chose he would give him. The white man, provoked by some evil spirit, insisted that either the king must give him the wife he was refusing, the one whose beauty he had heard about, or else he would take none of the others but instead would have to go, as he had threatened, to another village. The king said to him in reply: "White man, you are the son of God, I cannot deny you anything. There, have the wife you ask for, I shall send her to you. I request you treat her well, since she is the daughter of a great king of the land." This story indicates how good-natured these heathen are. (Hair 1985, chap. 9: 19–20)

One supposes that, despite their indulgent behavior, the village leader and his wife were not without recourse to even the score with the despicable visitor. The town mentioned in this passage, "Cacheo," was a Bullom village located a short distance south of the Kolente River in the Bullom state of Caricolli/Carecoulis (Hair 1985, chap. 9: 31, 36). Coelho did not remark on the village's name, but it likely derived from the fact that traders from Cacheu has visited the area over many years.

The Kolente River ("Rio dos Cazares") was the principal market for the annual kola fleet from the Guinea-Bissau region. An islet in the lower reaches of the river was called Dona Genebra (from the Portuguese word *gin*), named for a Luso-African woman trader whose vessel had wrecked there. Following celebrations that included much eating and drinking and a ceremony during which the Mani ruler received a "donation" worth forty milreis from the owners of the ships of the kola fleet, vessels were escorted by subordinate Temne rulers to ports extending fifty kilometers along the river. Crews lived ashore for weeks. Temne offered traders residing in their dwellings the choice of their own wives and daughters (Hair 1985, chap. 9: 24–26).

Rice was purchased along the Kolente River from elite noblewomen who traveled inland to purchase it. The women were famous for their commercial skills: "[They] are so practiced in trading that even if given a variety of measures for different commodities, not a single one of them makes a mistake, nor is there ever any doubt (about their calculations), because they are completely trustworthy." The fidalgas also procured young women for the sailors (Hair 1985, chap. 9: 28).

Besides shiploads of kola, traders purchased captives and ivory, principally in exchange for cotton textiles—either Farim cloth purchased along the upper Cacheu River from Mande traders or *roupa alta* (prestige cloth), which were panos from São Tiago in Cabo Verde. Some of the slaves purchased to windward were sold to Temne, who prized them as palm-wine tappers. Coelho mentioned no resident traders, nor any offspring—but one may speculate concerning Luso-African children resulting from the visits of annual kola fleets (Hair 1985, chap. 9: 24–30).

Elsewhere in his narrative, Coelho detailed how kola seeds were removed from pods, selected, sorted, and transported, and he raved about the enormous profits derived from exchanging kola and cotton textiles. Africans along the Kolente River routinely bartered three baskets containing four hundred to five hundred kola for one ordinary white cloth and even more for better-quality textiles. Indeed, an especially valued pano might fetch as many as five thousand kola. At Farim, Mande traders generally sold a pano for one hundred kola and sometimes only fifty; in times of shortage, that figure might be as low as ten (Hair 1985, chap. 9: 12–13).

From the Kolente River, vessels of the kola fleet sailed southward to the Sierra Leone estuary to fill barrels at the renowned watering place and load provisions before commencing the return voyage. Coelho wrote that eight to ten Englishmen, together with skilled domestic slaves (*escravos ladinos*), resided on Tasso Island in a factory built of brick and lime. The English factors used launches to trade northward to the Forékariah River for ivory and southward to the Sherbro River ("Rio de Magrabomba") for camwood and ivory (Hair 1985, chap. 9: 36–37). Coelho's information dated to some time between 1662 and 1664. In 1663, two years after inaugurating trade along the Gambia River, the

Royal Adventurers established factories on Tasso Island in the Sierra Leone estuary and along the Sherbro River. In September 1664, the factory on Tasso Island was destroyed by Admiral de Ruyter in a preemptive strike before the beginning of the Anglo-Dutch war of 1665–67 (Kup 1961, 50, 96; Fyfe 1962, 4).

Coelho also stated that eight to ten Dutch traders were living in houses made of planks located a tide's travel upriver on the south bank of the Sierra Leone estuary in the Bullom state of Baka. Like the English, they had skilled domestic slaves and launches to transport ivory, which Luso-Africans living along the estuary sold to whomever paid the highest price. Half a tide farther up the estuary was Tombo Island, where there was a Luso-African settlement with a church. Visiting priests stayed at the very large house owned by Matias Fernandes, a Luso-African. Coelho characterized Fernandes as a filho da terra of the Bullom people "but a Christian who behaved like a whiteman." One of Fernandes's daughters was married to a rich Cabo Verdean. When Coelho visited Tombo, the English had temporarily moved their factory there, having been expelled from Tasso Island by the Bullom ruler of Caracolis (Hair 1985, chap. 9: 37–38).

At the head of navigation of the Mitombo River was Port Loko, which attracted African traders from the states of Grand Limba and Grand Concho, including Fula from Futa Jallon. When Coelho visited in the 1640s, Port Loko's importance had diminished from former times, when "whites" (that is, Cabo Verdeans) had lived there surrounded by groves of citrus trees, bananas, and pineapples. Only Luso-Africans remained; their principal commerce was in ivory, kola, and straw manufactures that Coelho characterized as "curiosities" (*corosidades*). They were served by Fr. Seraphim de Leão—a Spanish Capuchin (Franciscan of new rule of 1528) who ministered to Christians at Port Loko and Tombo Island from the end of the 1640s to the mid-1650s—and by secular clergy who made sporadic visits from Cabo Verde (Hair 1985, chap. 9: 38–39).

Capuchin missionaries who visited Port Loko in 1654 described the Luso-Africans as suppliant to the Mani ruler Bolofare, who made arbitrary demands on them for trade goods. After he converted to Christianity, he was persuaded to accord them better treatment. Fr. Agostino de Ronda and Fr. João de Peralta arrived in western Africa in 1658. Father Peralta served for a time at Port Loko, spent two years in the Nunez River, and afterward moved to Bissau; Father de Ronda meanwhile served the Port Loko and Tombo Island churches from 1658 until his death in 1665. Other Capuchins followed and maintained the Serra Leoa mission through the mid-1680s, including Padre Salvador de Taveiro, who lived in the Nunez River in the 1660s. In all, some twenty-five Capuchins served in Serra Leoa between 1650 and 1686, most of them for short periods of time. Then, except for sporadic visits by ships' chaplains, the Tombo and Port Loko churches were without a priest until the arrival of the African missionary priest Signor Joseph in 1715 (Hair 1985, chap. 9: 46–55, 1988, and 200c, 412–13; Kup 1961, 67–68; Rodney 1970, 215). The contributions of Capuchins during these decades must be considered of signal importance for sustaining Luso-African lifeways during an era of growing competition from Protestant English and Dutch traders hostile to Catholicism. For their part, the Eurafrican descendants of English and Dutch traders were disadvantaged by the absence of resident Protestant clergy.

English Competition in Serra Leoa, 1660s–1680s

Following the destruction of their factory on Tasso Island by Admiral de Ruyter in September 1664, officials of the Royal Adventurers moved the factory to Konkaw Island (then called Cogu), also in Bullom territory. Abraham, the Royal Adventurers' agent, had a fine house protected by four cannons and the friendship of his landlord. The French trader Nicholas Villault, Sieur de Bellefond, who visited the Sierra Leone estuary in December 1666, recorded evidence of power shifts that would diminish the influence of Luso-Africans. The *Europa,* a Dutch vessel from Amsterdam, displayed the "flag of Ostend" of the Spanish Netherlands—a subterfuge to fool the residents of the English factory. Holland and England were at war from 1665 to 1667, and France had entered the war on the side of the Dutch in January 1666 (Langer 1958, 427; Kup 1961, 96; Astley 1745–47/1968, 2:377).

Two of the *Europa*'s officers were dispatched with gifts "ten leagues" up the estuary to inform Farim Buré that the vessel intended to trade and load water and firewood. While members of the crew began to take on water and cut down trees, four or five canoes arrived, commanded by John Thomas, described as "captain of one of the islands in the river." When the *Europa*'s captain rejected the ivory that Thomas offered to sell him, claiming it was overpriced, Thomas's men attacked the seamen on shore. The next morning, the sailors retaliated and drove away Thomas and his men. When Farim Buré's brother arrived to collect the dues for wood and water, he was accompanied by a Luso-African ("Portuguese") trader and an entourage that included musicians playing a trumpet and a drum. During the banquet held in his honor, the ruler's brother condemned John Thomas as "a Rebel and a Mutineer" and wished for his capture. Over the days that followed, Africans and Luso-Africans went aboard the *Europa* to trade.

The subsequent behavior of the Dutch captain was as reprehensible as that of John Thomas. He assured Abraham, the English factor, that he could trade in safety aboard the *Europa,* only to kidnap him and three others, including a Luso-African. After a Dutch attack on the English factory was repulsed, a son of the Bullom ruler ransomed Abraham for nine hundredweight of ivory and two civet cats (Astley 1745–47/1968, 2:377–78). Two months later, in February 1667, Abraham himself resorted to treachery: with the assistance of Luso-Africans, he seized a longboat and its nine-man crew and held them for ransom. In retaliation, the vessel destroyed the English factory, causing Abraham to move to Rotumba on the south bank of the estuary (Kup 1961, 97).

Two years later, the English factory passed into the hands of the Gambia Adventurers, who leased western African trade from the Royal Adventurers for the period January 1, 1669, to January 1, 1678. It was probably in 1672 that the Gambian Adventurers leased the island that was alternately known as Bence (named for one of the directors of the Royal African Company), Bance, and Bunce in later years, where the company began to construct a stone fort with the help of imported carpenters, masons, and shipwrights (Davies 1957, 99; Fyfe 2000, 16). Bunce lacked a source of freshwater, which had to be brought from neighboring Tasso Island until a well was cut deep into rock. The fort became the property of the Royal African Company in 1678, and Zachary Rogers, who had been the agent for the Gambia Adventurers in the Sherbro River since June 1668, was stationed there as a factor by the company (Kup 1961, 50, 96–97, 143; Davies 1957, 99, 215 n. 3; Adam Jones 1985, 27).

In June 1678, Edmund Pierce, the Royal African Company's first chief agent on Bunce Island, deplored the paucity of trade along the estuary, asserting, "I never knew a Ton of Teeth [ivory] brought down this river in my life, yet I hope in time we may procure a trade of Redwood." Pierce recommended moving his headquarters to the Iles de Los, which he characterized as the "heart of the trade" (Kup 1961, 49, 97–98). In December 1678, indicative of the difficulties of competing with Luso-African traders in the area, Pierce recommended countering their ascendancy by importing forty or fifty English-speaking slaves from Barbados. No action was taken on the proposal, however. The following year, Pierce dispatched two Africans from Bunce to England to learn a trade. English traders in Serra Leoa were disadvantaged by location, for the company's vessels supplied the Gambia factors en route to Bunce Island. In August 1679, Pierce complained that Thomas Thurloe, the company's agent at James Island, had kept all the best goods sent from London and "hath sent us a percell of old refuse in their steed, as old small Bells without Clappers, Pistolls and Fowling peices old and damnified" (Kup 1961, 69, 77, 98 n. *).

During the decade following Villault de Bellefond's visit, John Thomas evidently consolidated his circumstances in the estuary, regarding both overlords and Luso-Africans. Bunce Island accounts for August 1678 record that brandy was paid to John Thomas, who was living on the south bank of the estuary, and to his overlord, Bai Samma, on the north bank (Kup 1961, 150). When Jean Barbot visited the Sierra Leone estuary three months later on a French vessel from La Rochelle, he reported that Thomas was the "captain" who collected dues for water and wood, but he made no reference to an overlord. Thomas's "dues" comprised "an old musket, a small barrel of brandy, 3–4 lbs of powder, a dozen second-hand knives and some old clothes, but no more; though, if he were to be believed, he ought to be given three times as much." Barbot related that he spent a day ashore as a hostage, during which Thomas offered to feed him boiled monkey. The French vessel traded both with the English factor Humphrey Yard at Bunce Island and with Africans in the estuary, but Barbot made no mention of encountering Luso-Africans during his nine-day stay (Hair 1981c; Hair, Jones, and Law 1992, 1:184, 186–89, and illustrations 13 and 16 for John Thomas's residence).

In August 1679, in an initiative intended to compete with the long-standing Luso-African trade in textiles, Edmund Pierce asked to be supplied with Senegambian cloth, especially the types known as *barafulas* and *golozans*. Two years later, in August 1681, Joshua Platt, the company factor in the Sherbro, acknowledged receipt of 1,413 cloths (Rodney 1970, 182). Another company initiative during the 1680s was an unsuccessful undertaking to grow indigo in the Sherbro. Both initiatives were disrupted by the nine-year War of the League of Augsburg, which commenced in 1688. During the decades that followed, the Royal African Company increasingly relied on English-manufactured cloth, which became progressively cheaper and more competitive in African markets (Davies 1957, 175–76, 220–21).

In 1680, the Royal African Company expressly forbade private trade. The regulation was honored in the breach, as attested by Henry Clark, a factor on Bunce Island during the 1680s. "Every man hath his whore for whom they steale," he remarked (Davies 1957, 257). As elsewhere in western Africa, interlopers confounded the operations of the Royal African Company. In 1680, English private traders carried off a member of a ruling family in the Nunez River, with the consequence that all Englishmen were threatened with death. Fortunately for the company's operations, the private traders transported their captive to the Sherbro, where Edmund Pierce purchased him and returned him to the Nunez (Rodney 1970, 115).

Prior to his death in May 1682, Pierce established factors at Port Loko, at a site known as "Jassily" (which perhaps was in the Iles de Los), at Samo on the Forékariah River, and in the Nunez River (Kup 1961, 89, 98). A trader named Porter, dispatched to the Nunez River in 1681, soon began trading on his own account, selling ivory to Dutch vessels and other interlopers (Kup 1961, 98). According to Coelho, Porter became the ultimate purchaser of all ivory obtained from Nalus, Landuma, Cocolis (Northern Landuma), and Susu (Hair 1985, chap. 9: 7). Not to be excluded, the Royal African Company established another factor along the Nunez River in July 1687 (Kup 1961, 101).

Peter Kup recorded the European and African commodities traded in Serra Leoa. He noted that the Royal African Company's traders purchased little kola, although they were well aware that Luso-Africans obtained huge quantities at Balansera, Mambolo, Rokupr, Katimpi, Rotun, Tauyia, and other villages along the Kolente River, which they used to purchase slaves elsewhere, that is, to the north in the Guinea-Bissau region and Senegambia (Kup 1961, 78, map 1 on p. 5). Lacking Cabo Verdean panos and Farim cloth, the textiles Luso-Africans purchased from Mande traders along the upper Cacheu River to barter for kola with Temne living along the Kolente River, English traders would have traded at considerable disadvantage.

Pierce was succeeded by John Case, who commanded Bunce Island during most of the years between 1682 and 1690 (Adam Jones 1985, 26 n. 7). John Thomas maintained his situation as "Water Captain," as noted by Otto Friedrich Von der Groeben of Brandenburg, who visited the Sierra Leone estuary in 1682. Groeben stated that while the crew loaded water and firewood, Thomas, together with some forty men and thirty women from the nearby village, drank brandy and danced to musical instruments played by the Germans. Thomas's command of German was limited to short phrases, for example (as translated by Adam Jones), "Thunder [and] sacrament! To me, Captain Jan Thomas, must pay for wood and water!" The payment made to Thomas aboard ship was a quarter (barrel) of brandy and several bottles of wine (Jones 1985, 24, 26).

Groeben's account is noteworthy as one of the earliest to describe Africans' use of written testimonials. "To demonstrate how respectable a man he was, [Thomas] showed us various notes of recommendation from different ships, of which I shall quote the one with the highest recommendation: 'The wind blows from East and West. Be on your guard against the black dogs; they are not to be trusted, as they are false rogues. Take note: for water and firewood, gave one musket, 3 lb. gunpowder, 3 bottles of brandy. Sierra Leone, The ship NN'" (Adam Jones 1985, 26). The use of testimonials became an established practice. Vessels arriving in the Sierra Leone estuary were accosted by entrepreneurs in watercraft who presented written credentials and offered their services as interpreters and middlemen (Kup 1961, 92). During the nineteenth century, such certificates (or "books," as they came to be called) were extensively used by Kru mariners seeking employment on European vessels. And like John Thomas, illiterate Kru were vulnerable to false and derisive statements (Brooks 1972, 14, 26–28 passim). Unfortunately for historians, the imposition, often frivolous and arbitrary, of "European" names such as John Thomas frustrates the identification of individuals and their kin.

Groeben published four sketches made during his visit to the Sierra Leone estuary: one of an African village, another of the English establishment on Bunce Island, and two depicting the dress of male and female Africans—one labeled "slave, commoner, officer" and another labeled "common woman, officer's wife, Christian's concubine" (Adam Jones 1985, pl. 3 after p. 348). The contrasting quantities and qualities of their garments were graphic status markers. The African "officer" was outfitted in matching shirt and knee breeches, and he carried a sword. All the men and women in these images were depicted barefoot, but the woman affiliated with the "Christian"—that is, the European—wore a blouse covering her breasts and a narrow strip of cloth tied around her head. None of the men or women was shown wearing a crucifix or rosary, like those Luso-Africans commonly wore. According to Groeben's report, the chief factor's woman and the women of the ship captains lived in two little huts separate from other dwellings. He added, "These concubines go around wearing silks and do not allow any part of their body to be seen naked" (Adam Jones 1985, 27).

While visiting the dwellings of the "castle slaves"—the domestic slaves working on Bunce Island—Groeben encountered the concubine and children of the previous chief factor, Edmund Pierce, whose little boy and girl both had long yellow hair. They were called "mulattos," while children of a black man and a mulatto woman or a mulatto man and a black woman were called "castise." Before the Germans departed, John Case assembled concubines and other Africans and ordered them to *bajaran* (from the Portuguese word *bailar,* meaning to dance) to the music of a xylophone and bells (Adam Jones 1985, 27 and n. 9).

Groeben's designation of women as "concubines" is noteworthy. The women on Bunce Island lived in segregated quarters, in contrast to the circumstances in Senegambia and the Guinea-Bissau region where nharas resided with their spouses and children. Groeben did not record the women's names, nor did he relate those of their children. Were they given their fathers' surnames? Unlike nharas or the elite women in the Sherbro, who will be discussed, the women of Bunce Island evidently had no role in the prosecution of commerce, and it may be that they were brought to the island as slaves.

Groeben left unmentioned any sexual liaisons between defenseless female captives and the dozens of English traders, clerks, artisans, and soldiers living on Bunce Island, and he said nothing about what became of their offspring. In 1704, the Royal African Company employed forty-six white men on Bunce Island; in addition, there were forty-five whites on York Island in 1688 and about thirty by 1708 (Kup 1961, 71). Unless aborted by the victimized women, the children produced by liaisons between these men and the captives would have been born aboard slave vessels crossing the Atlantic or in captivity in the Americas.

Royal African Company records distinguished between "sale" slaves, "castle" or "factory" slaves, and "gromettoes" (grumetes). Castle slaves labored at Bunce Island and in factories, and they manned trading vessels. Grumetes included the sons of African elites sent to learn about the company's operations. One notable grumete was Sephalo, son of the Bullom ruler known as King Harry, whom he succeeded as chief around 1730 (Kup 1961, 88). Castle slaves were branded and were subjected to brutal punishments for theft and insubordination. When "old and useless," they might be freed. In 1702, the directors of the Royal African Company instructed that castle slaves should be converted to Christianity, given names, taught to speak English, and allowed to marry other castle slaves (Rodney 1970, 267–68). Whether and to what extent the company's agents addressed the directors' instructions was not recorded.

During the two years following Groeben's visit to Serra Leoa, John Case and his associates at Bunce Island, together with their trading partners, were afflicted by a spate of piratical depredations. Most destructive was the French pirate Jean Hamlin, who cruised Serra Leoa waters for seven months in 1683. Disguising his vessel to look like a Royal Navy ship, Hamlin captured seventeen Dutch and English vessels. Other pirates scourged the coast in 1684 (Kup 1961, 53).

From the latter part of the seventeenth century on, the Sherbro area came to be dominated by Anglo-Africans, who controlled trade and acquired growing power among the coastal groups. The first English trader to found an influential lineage was Zachary Rogers, who arrived in western Africa in 1668 as an employee of the Gambia Adventurers. A decade later, he was hired by the Royal Africa Company. Rogers had meanwhile married a woman related to the Sherbro ruler (possibly his sister)—a woman of such authority that Joshua Platt, the factor who succeeded Rogers following his death in 1681, referred to her as "the great woman." After her husband died, this woman insisted on receiving the salary due him, stopping camwood trade until her demands were met (Kup 1961, 101; Rodney 1970, 219–20; Day 1983, 95–96).

Thomas Corker, one of Zachary Rogers's successors in the Sherbro, likewise founded an Anglo-African lineage that augmented its influence generation by generation. After he arrived in the Sherbro in 1684, Corker married a Bullom woman from the Ya Kumba family, which ruled the shores of Yawry Bay between the Sierra Leone peninsula and the Sherbro estuary. This influential woman, who lived until 1722, was known to the English as "Senhora Doll, Dutchess of Sherbro." Corker and Senhora Doll had two sons, Stephen and Robin, before the Royal Africa Company transferred Corker to the Gambia River as chief agent in 1699 (Gray 1940, 122; Fyfe 1962, 10). The title "Senhora Doll" suggests that the woman was a Luso-African; the "Doll" may have been derived from *dolo,* the Portuguese word for fraud, deceit, or deception, and perhaps she was so named by exasperated English traders. The Caulkers, as Senhora Doll's descendants came to be called, expanded their hegemony coastwise, including control of the Plantain and Banana Islands (Fyfe 1962, 10).

Rogers and Corker obliged the Royal African Company to employ their sons, and they used company slaves to work on their plantations. It is not surprising, then, that individuals named Zachary, Samuel, Larne, Simon, and John Rogers were mentioned in company records until the firm ceased operations in 1723 (Rodney 1970, 216–17, 219; Day 1983, 88–90, 96). Company employment provided privileged access to European trade goods, enabling the acquisition of wealth and political influence. A third lineage of Anglo-Africans who acquired wealth from the slave trade and growing influence in the Sherbro area was founded by Peter Tucker, a company agent at York Island in the 1680s. Sources mentioned a mulatto named Joseph Tucker in 1697, and at least four different Tuckers were independent traders in the Sherbro (Day 1983, 98).

In 1690, two years after the outbreak of the War of the League of Augsburg, Bunce Island's garrison was evacuated to reinforce James Island in the Gambia River. A few traders who remained were placed under the authority of Thomas Corker, the company's factor at Sherbro (Davies 1957, 219; Kup 1961, 70–71).

La Courbe's Survey of the Geba-Grande Trading Sphere

Following his reconnaissance of the Banyun trade route linking Geregia and Cacheu, Sieur de la Courbe visited Bissau from July 1686 until February 1687. During this period, he also made trips to the Bissagos archipelago, to the Geba, Mansoa, and Grande Rivers, and to Cacheu, accompanying Jean de la Fond.

In October and November 1686, prior to the beginning of the trading season, La Courbe spent several weeks at Bissau. One of the purposes of his visit was to negotiate with Bacampolco Có, the Intim ruler, for permission to construct a fort. The ruler refused his request but welcomed French traders to establish a factory at Bissau (Rodney 1970, 143). Bacampolco Có exercised authority over the other Papel rulers of Ilha de Bissau—who numbered nine, according to La Courbe, or six, according to Coelho and the Portuguese priest Francisco da Guarda—and his influence extended across Papel territory as far as Cacheu (Cultru 1913, 222; Hair 1985, chap. 5: 7; Barcellos 1899–1913, 2:113). Bacampolco Có lived "a good half league" distant from the port and was guarded by twenty or thirty men (Cultru 1913, 220).

La Courbe wrote about the Luso-African and Portuguese traders at Bissau idling their days away smoking tobacco and chewing kola on the verandas of their houses. Married men kept their wives secluded in their compounds, allowing them out only to go to confession, while they themselves consorted with African girls (*raparigues*)—probably virgins sought out in order to avoid venereal diseases. La Courbe mentioned the name of only one Bissau trader, Manuel Nunez (Cultru 1913, 231–32, 237). Much of what he recorded concerning economic and social circumstances at Bissau was probably information acquired from La Fond.

> The Portuguese who inhabit this island are very displeased with this ruler and the notables of the country, for he often demands what he wants of them, and they dare not refuse him. Vessels that stop here for commerce pay him tribute, besides which it is necessary to pay for water and wood. There are nine rulers on the entire island, of which this one is considered like an emperor: he has an idol called *Chine,* which he consults concerning all his affairs and which it is believed lets him know what he desires; he sacrifices to him dogs, roosters, and bulls, and they place the horns and bones in the trunks of trees near the sea which are sacred to them. When the ruler dies, his favorite wives and the house slaves are sacrificed on his tomb, and, when he is dead, they place his body in a wicker bier borne by notables who make it spring into the air and the person on whom it falls is chosen ruler according to the will of the deceased, whom they then inter underground.
>
> There is an islet vis-a-vis Ilha de Bissau about a cannon shot distant, which is entirely covered with trees that we call Sorcerer's Isle because every year the ruler goes there to make an important sacrifice to his idol. (Cultru 1913, 222–23)

La Courbe accompanied Jean La Fond on a trading voyage to Guinala in September 1686. Their vessel stopped at Bolama en route. La Courbe was informed that the island was uninhabited, but, unlike Coelho, he reported that Bijago cultivated rice during the rainy season. Bolama's timber and other resources for boat-building were being exploited by the traders living along the Grande River. Besides Luso-Africans living at Guinala, La Courbe met a Catholic English ship-master whose African wife controlled an island in Serra Leoa ("Serrelione") where the man's forty- to fifty-ton vessel was constructed. La Courbe mentioned only one of Guinala's traders by name—Patrisio-Perese (Patrício Peres/Pires?), whom he described as "a white Portuguese, son of a Dutch man and a mulatresse" who was the daughter of a Biafada notable. The Biafada ruler lived about a league distant, near a marigot flowing into the Corubal River (Cultru 1913, 227–29). The Guinala trader's father may have been a New Christian who moved to Holland. Too few in western Africa to sustain a "Dutch presence," the descendants of Dutch traders became identified as Luso-Africans.

La Courbe did not travel beyond the Grande River, but he did relate what he learned about commerce southward in Serra Leoa. He stated that vessels from Cacheu and Geba (not Bissau, as in Coelho's time four decades earlier) made annual voyages for kola. He also learned that only Luso-Africans and English traded in the Nunez River, where Fula from Futa Jallon brought numerous captives, much ivory, and some gold. (Four decades earlier, Coelho had reported that Susu-Fula warfare prevented Fula from gaining access to the Nunez River.) Indigo was the only other commodity La Courbe mentioned, and João Rodrigues ("Jean Rodrigue"), a "white Portuguese," was the only trader he identified. Rodrigues was perhaps a Luso-African and the son of Manuel Rodrigues, a New Christian who was interim capitão-mor of Cacheu in 1657. La Courbe alluded to a small English fort (meaning Bunce Island) in the Sierra Leone estuary, from which English traders traveled overland to the Pongo and Nunez Rivers (Cultru 1913, 254, 256–57; Moraes 1972, 40).

La Courbe visited Geba in early February 1687. En route, he was informed that a great deal of ivory was obtained along the Corubal River but that grumetes excluded foreigners, presumably acting on behalf of Bissau traders to prevent access to Mandinka trade at the Courubal market reported by Coelho (which may have been at Xitoli) (Cultru 1913, 246). La Courbe arrived at Geba a short time after the death of Manuel Alves (Alvares?), the Luso-African commandant of Geba, whom he described as a Christain African and a man highly esteemed for his liberality to visitors: "No one left him without his making a present of one or several ounces of gold, according to his rank." La Courbe visited the man's wake, where, according to local custom, numerous women congregated with the widow for a week or two of lamentations sustained by brandy and palm wine; he also attended the burial service, where the members of the trading community were dressed in long black cloaks (Cultru 1913, 248–50).

La Courbe mentioned only one other trader by name—Francisco Coilleau, the "Portuguese" trader he stayed with whose African wife he described as very civil and highly intelligent. Coilleau was possibly a son of the Cabo Verdean Francisco de Lemos Coelho (Cultru 1913, 249–50; Ly 1964, 30). La Courbe did not indicate whether the African wives of "Portuguese" traders were involved in commerce. Yet somewhere around the time of his visit, there was at least one nhara at Geba comparable to Cacheu's Bibiana Vaz: a Luso-African named Maria Soares who owned a vessel that transported kola from Serra Leoa to Geba in 1699 (Rodney 1970, 149).

Geba's trading community was sited on a hill "a musket shot distant" from the river. Although the commandant's dwelling had eight bronze cannons displayed in front, there was no wall or palisade surrounding it; the trading community lived under the protection of Mandinka authorities. La Courbe was informed that Geba had three thousand to four thousand inhabitants but remarked that there were no more than ten to twelve dwellings inhabited by "whites" (*blancs*); however, he implied that he meant Luso-Africans: "They all say they are Portuguese and Christians" (Cultru 1913, 251). Geba's principal commerce was in slaves and wax. Many of the captives were supplied by the ruler of Kaabu, while the beeswax was obtained by grumetes trading with neighboring Mandinka communities (Cultru 1913, 250–52).

Geba's Mandinka landlord, known as *roy* (king), lived in a large village a half-league distant, which, in contrast to Geba, was protected by palisades. La Courbe remarked that the floodplain along the river was suitable for rice growing but that no one in Geba engaged in cultivation, being exclusively occupied with commerce. Upon expressing astonishment that the residents kept no cattle, he was told that neighboring Africans would steal them (Cultru 1913, 250–52). Manifestly, the Mandinka landlord denied Luso-Africans protection of livestock and refused permission for cultivating crops: strangers were dependent on the landlord for food supplies.

The mansa of Kaabu lived in the direction of the Gambia River at a distance that could be covered in four to five days of travel. He was reputedly "very powerful, very rich, and very generous" (Cultru 1913, 250–52). Luso-African, English, and French traders competed to bring him novelties—the type of items for which he had once compensated givers a hundredfold. But because his dwellings were filled with curios for which he had no use, the mansa had recently become less generous and reciprocated more appropriately to the value of gifts (Cultru 1913, 252). Kaabu's mansa was said to be as ruthless toward African adversaries as he was hospitable to Luso-African and European traders:

> He is capable of killing a man like a mosquito. He makes war on his neighbors for no cause. Having laid siege for six years to the town of Cantor which was heavily fortified with palisades in the manner of the country, on taking it he utterly destroyed the town and took captive all its inhabitants which he entrusted to his followers until he had need of them. If one died or escaped, those who guarded them were obligated to find them, or give others, or themselves become captives. He sends his warriors into the lands of his neighbors to seize all the people they can capture and brands them for sale at the first opportunity. He exercises unspeakable cruelty, of which one example: he had two babies torn from their mother's womb, pounded in a mortar before her eyes, and incorporated them into a poison to rub on his arrows which is reputed quickly effective. He is an animist, and his people also, but the Mandinka living around Geba are Muslim. (Cultru 1913, 252–53)

The abominable slaying of a mother to use an unborn baby as a sacrifice to a "fetish" was also attributed to Sundiata, the thirteenth-century founder of the Mali Empire (J. Johnson 1986, 147, lines 1725–45). That the Mande trading community at Geba was Muslim correlated with Coelho's description of the African trading community at Farim as being Muslim Soninke.

La Courbe departed Bissau for Cacheu on February 20, 1687. He was accompanied by Jean la Fond and one of the Bourguignon brothers, the other remaining at Bissau (Cultru 1913, 257–63). Intelligence concerning commerce and geography acquired by La Courbe and other Frenchmen trading in western Africa was used to advantage the following year when a French squadron of five vessels raided English establishments in western Africa, anticipating the outbreak of the War of the League of Augsburg. In May 1688, French warships captured the Royal African Company's ship *Lady Mary* at Gossanda (Guinala?) in the Grande River, and three other vessels were taken in the Nunez River several weeks later. The *Lady Mary* alone was valued at nearly five thousand pounds sterling. The Royal African Company's negotiations with the French government for the return of the vessel and its cargo terminated with the onset of war (Gray 1940, 105–6; Davies 1957, 271–72).

The War of the League of Augsburg, involving France and England but not Portugal, provided a much needed respite for Luso-Africans, Cabo Verdeans, and

Portuguese whose commerce had been so aggressively challenged during the 1680s by the factors of English and French trading companies. The conflict was closely followed by the War of the Spanish Succession (1701–14)—an even wider war that involved Portugal in costly hostilities with Spain that contributed to increased economic subordination to England.

Chapter 7
Era of the Second Cacheu Company

> Wee are fully assured that if our Agents and Factors did truly espouse and mind our Interest as they ought to doe, wee might have the choice of the Commodities of those countries at the best hands and not be beholding to Robert Gun or any others who make great advantage by buying of the Natives at the best hand and selling to you at much higher prices, though (wee understand) they purchase them with the same goods wherewith you trust them.
>
> —Royal African Company to Thomas Corker (Fyfe 1964, 65)

Commercial relationships in western Africa were significantly affected by two protracted European wars. The first, the War of the League of Augsburg (1688–97), involved a coalition of German states, Sweden, and Holland against Louis XIV (1661–1715) of France. England experienced the tumultuous events of the "Glorious Revolution," which put William of Orange on the throne and caused England to join the alliance against France in May 1689 (Langer 1958, 429–30, 443–45). Portugal did not participate in the long war, to the considerable advantage of its commercial interests.

The involvement of France and England in the War of the League of Augsburg gave impetus to the Portuguese government's sponsorship of a joint-stock trading company, the Companhia de Cacheu e Cabo Verde (1690–1706). This second Cacheu company had significantly greater success that the first, benefiting both from European rivals being embroiled in war and from acquiring the coveted *asiento*—the contract for supplying slaves to Latin America—from 1696 to

1701. The company focused its resources on Bissau instead of Cacheu, and its endeavors were ably seconded by Portuguese Franciscan missionaries, who had replaced Spanish Capuchins in 1686.

The War of the League of Augsburg was closely followed by the War of the Spanish Succession (1701–14), which involved Portugal along with Spain, France, England, and other European states. During this period, besides the commerce raiding conducted by the ships of war and privateers of the belligerents, piratical vessels pillaged indiscriminately and menaced western African trade, as they would for decades afterward. Any continuity of commercial networks that existed during these unpredictable times was principally due to Luso-Africans, who reasserted their middleman role vis-à-vis European traders and African traders and elites in many areas.

The War of the Spanish Succession was disastrous for Portugal due to the financial and military losses sustained during the war as well as the economic concessions that mortgaged Portugal's future by making it a client state subservient to English interests. Portugal's alliance with England drew it into the war and provoked a Spanish invasion. The Methuen Treaty, negotiated by the English ambassador to Portugal in December 1703 on the eve of the Spanish invasion, exacted the preferential admission of English textiles to Portugal and its overseas dominions in return for the unequal concession that Portuguese wines be admitted to England at a reduced tariff. This agreement resulted in the progressive subordination of Portuguese commerce to English interests. The Spanish invasion in May 1704 was expelled with the assistance of an English expeditionary force. The allied armies captured Madrid in June 1706, but following reverses in the spring of 1707, the Portuguese army was little involved for the duration of hostilities (Livermore 1963, 204–7; Langer 1958, 445–47, 453; Hanson 1981, 264–76; Blackburn 1997, 484–85).

The second Cacheu company was terminated in 1706, one of the economic casualties of the War of the Spanish Succession. The decades that followed marked the nadir of Portuguese commerce and influence in the Guinea-Bissau region. Portugal's "English connection" was never more evident, as English merchants' affiliations with Lisbon firms enabled them to dispatch vessels to Cabo Verde, Cacheu, and Bissau for licit and illicit commerce—generally, to the detriment of Portuguese, Cabo Verdean, and Luso-African trading interests and to Portugal's customs revenues. English traders who obtained panos, salt, and other commodities from the Cape Verde Islands could compete with Cabo Verdean and Luso-African traders in western African markets. Not until the 1750s did Portuguese merchants reestablish significant commercial links with the Guinea-Bissau region. Meanwhile, French and English traders expanded their commerce in western Africa, founding Franco-African and Anglo-African families whose networks competed with those of Luso-Africans.

During the decades of warfare in Europe and with the consequent unpredictability of European commercial ventures, Luso-Africans opportunistically collaborated with French and English traders whenever it served their interests, at the same time tenaciously defending their middleman position in regard to African commercial networks. Luso-African links with Cabo Verde were sustained by shared commercial, social, and cultural ties. Portuguese missionary endeavors diminished along with Portugal's economic decline, but a few priests maintained the churches at Cacheu, Bissau, and Ziguinchor. Sporadic visitations by Cabo Verdean priests to trading communities along the Gambia and the rivers of the Upper Guinea Coast contributed in important ways to Luso-Africans' adherence to Catholicism as an integral component of their lifeways. Portuguese and Cabo Verdean priests, moreover, made notable contributions as chaplains and advisers to African elites, as mediators of conflicts on behalf of Portuguese and Luso-African traders and officials, and as acting commandants of Cacheu, Bissau, and other praças.

Senegambia, 1690s–1710s

The first years of the War of the League of Augsburg went well for the Royal African Company's interests in western Africa. In 1689, when John Booker, the company's agent at James Island, learned that England and France were at war, he informed the mansa of Niumi, who immediately pillaged the French comptoir at Albreda (Gray 1940, 108). Claiming the exigencies of wartime, Booker detained employees whose term of service had expired. In response to their angry complaints, he compromised by allowing them to live among the Luso-Africans at Brefet in Foni; they could also engage in private trade and yet still be available to defend James Fort in case of a French attack (Gray 1940, 108–10).

In 1692, Booker organized an expedition that captured Saint-Louis in January 1693 and Gorée the following month. He left a small number of men at Saint-Louis and abandoned Gorée after demolishing the fort. Circumstances were reversed the following summer when French forces reoccupied Saint-Louis and Gorée, and La Courbe was dispatched from France to reestablish French commerce. In July 1695, a French squadron captured James Island and demolished the fort. The English taken prisoner were transported to the West Indies, except for married men, who were permitted to remain with their wives (Froger

1699, 21–29; Gray 1940, 111–18). Following the capture of James Island, the commander of the French squadron entertained the alcaides of the Petite Côte, together with the governor of Gorée. The alcaide of Rufisque was accompanied by Senhora Catarina, described in chapter 5. On this and similar occasions, Senhora Catarina evidently acted as an interpreter (Froger 1699, 8).

Investors in the new Compagnie du Sénégal, which had been organized in 1681, went bankrupt, and in January 1696, they sold the nineteen remaining years of the company's charter to another group of speculators (Gray 1940, 119; Cultru 1913, xliv–xlvi). The directors of the Royal African Company also experienced reverses. English commercial monopolies were challenged in the wake of the Glorious Revolution of 1689 that installed William of Orange on the throne, and Parliament suspended the Royal African Company's monopoly in 1696 and abolished it two years later. Thereafter, private persons could engage in West African trade if they paid the company a 10 percent duty on the value of goods exported from England; the payments were intended to defray the costs of maintaining the company's forts. After 1712, this requirement lapsed, and trade was open to all, without restriction (Davies 1957, 100–101; Kup 1961, 79–81, 100).

Andre Brüe, who served as the director of the Compagnie du Sénégal from 1697 to 1702 and from 1714 to 1720, energetically promoted French trade in Senegambia. In 1697, he visited Rufisque, where he met the damel of Cayor and Senhora Catarina, who acted as the damel's commercial agent. Brüe lodged in Senhora Catarina's dwelling; awakening in the night, he found her lying beside him. A professed Christian who followed Luso-African lifeways in dress and other matters, Senhora Catarina nonetheless had recourse to the ministrations of the "grand marabout" (chief muslim cleric), justifying her behavior as a common practice among the inhabitants of Rufisque (Labat 1728, 4:152, 172–73).

Brüe accompanied Senhora Catarina in a caravan of camels and horses to visit her place of trade near Macaye, where the damel of Cayor resided. He described Senhora Catarina's dwelling as a sort of "Métairie" where several slaves traded on her behalf (Labat 1728, 4:175–76). *Métairie* derives from the word *métayage,* meaning land leased on the condition of sharing the production with the owner—and the use of the term in Brüe's account indicates that, notwithstanding her many years of service to the damel, Senhora Catarina, like other Luso-Africans, was not allowed to own property.

Senhora Catarina was probably one of the Luso-African traders alluded to in an anonymous source that noted that Luso-Africans living along the Petite Côte dispatched domestic slaves and grumetes to trade in the interior as far as the Lac de Guiers in Walo (Boulègue 1989, 45). Another trade route used by Luso-Africans linked Rufisque with Kawon, the capital of Saluum, and Mansagaar near Kau-ur along the north bank of the Gambia River. Kau-ur was an entrepôt for trade with caravans coming from the far interior, and twice annually, Luso-Africans went to Mansagaar, planted a market cross, and organized a fair to engage in trade with Saluum (Curtin 1975, 98–99 and map on p. 97). Luso-Africans living at Joal traded in canots along the Saloum River, especially at Kawon (Boulègue 1989, 79).

Commerce along the Petite Côte in both cowhides and panos greatly diminished at the close of the seventeenth century. European accounts attributed various reasons for the falloff of the once thriving trade, but the ongoing desiccation during the c. 1630–c. 1860 dry period seems the most likely explanation (Moraes 1972, 41–42, and 1973, 73–74). By the latter part of the c. 1630–c. 1860 dry period, the principal source of hides was the highlands Futa Jallon, hundreds of kilometers to the south. Luso-African caravan trade in the hinterland of the Petite Côte ceased due to the depredations of Lat Sukaabe, who ruled both Cayor and Baol (Boulègue 1989, 71–72). Brüe and the Companie du Sénégal encountered competition along the Petite Côte after April 1699, when the Royal African Company reoccupied James Island and Thomas Corker, the head agent, established factories at Portudal and Joal, the entrepôts for Baol and Siin, and sent traders to Saluum (Gray 1940, 123).

Rufisque continued to prosper as Cayor's principal trade center. Père Godefroy Loyer, who visited the Petite Côte in either May 1701 or May 1702, described Rufisque as having two hundred to three hundred dwellings, with those of the notables being especially large. He considered it admirable that Luso-Africans identified themselves as Christians by wearing large rosaries around their necks, by reciting prayers in Crioulo, and by baptizing and instructing children themselves, having neither priest nor chapel. Père Loyer visited the dwelling of a Luso-African family, where he interrogated them concerning the "Mysteries of our Religion," and reported that they acquitted themselves "fairly" (Roussier 1935, 137–38). He did not include any personal observations concerning Luso-Africans' commercial activities.

In September 1697, Andre Brüe sent an agent to negotiate treaties with the mansa of Barra and other Gambian rulers. But not until April 1698 did he dispatch a chief factor and fourteen other Frenchmen to reestablish factories at Albreda and Geregia, at the head of the Banyun and Luso-African trade route linking Ziguinchor and Cacheu. The Royal African Company did not reoccupy James Island until a year later, in April 1699—two years after peace was made between the warring factions. During the intervening period, Dutch and English private traders frequented the Gambia (Cultru 1910, 153; Gray 1940, 111–12, 122–23, 128; Davies 1957, 272–73).

Thomas Corker had previously been the Royal African Company's agent in the Sherbro, where he founded the Corker/Caulker lineage. He acted expeditiously to counter Andre Brüe and the Compagnie du Sénégal. He established a factory at Geregia near the French factory and vigorously contested the Compagnie du Sénégal's "right" to travel upriver past James Island, notably, to Mansagaar/Kau-ur, the Luso-African entrepôt for trade with Saluum and with long-distance caravans. Corker, moreover, challenged the Compagnie du Sénégal along the Petite Côte, establishing factories at Portudal and Joal, the trade centers for Baol and Siin.

Corker's initiatives were contested by Brüe, resulting in much acrimony and the seizure of trading vessels (including those of independent traders)—all of which continued until the War of the Spanish Succession interrupted the commercial operations of both companies. England and France declared war in May 1702. Meanwhile, the Royal African Company recalled Corker to England to address a plethora of charges related to embezzling company property; trading privately, including seizing a Dutch vessel and dispatching it on a trade voyage to the Nunez and Pongo Rivers on his own account; and engaging in other corrupt practices that had enabled him to amass a considerable fortune. Corker died soon after his arrival in England in the fall of 1700 (Gray 1940, 123–32).

As a consequence of its losses during the War of the League of Augsburg and the deprivation of its African trade monopoly, the Royal African Company negotiated with the Compagnie du Sénégal for several years concerning conflicting claims in the Gambia River and along the Petite Côte. The two firms also conducted negotiations to address their mutual interests in setting prices on European and African commodities and excluding private traders. These negotiations continued after the outbreak of the War of the Spanish Succession, in which England and France did not become adversaries until 1702, and concluded in June 1705 with an agreement to observe neutrality, signed by the directors of both companies—which proved of little consequence in terms of the circumstances in western Africa (Gray 1940, 124–31, 143–46, 148; Davies 1957, 272–73).

During the War of the Spanish Succession, the Royal African Company suffered significant losses in the Gambia. In November 1702, French privateers captured James Island and exacted a large ransom. This action was repeated in 1704 and again in 1708. English factors made the most of circumstances, embezzling goods for personal advantage by exaggerating the company's losses. Two fires that allegedly destroyed records as well as goods rendered hopeless any possibility that the company could order its Gambian accounts. An anonymous commentator reported that the company's employees overstated losses to conceal their own peculations: "[James Fort] has several times been plundered by the French in the late warr and severall times the storehouses (which are usually covered with thatch instead of tile) have been set on fire and have served to balance their accounts, which could not otherwise have balanced" (Gray 1940, 150–51). In 1709, the few remaining employees of the Royal African Company abandoned James Island to engage in private trade. The Compagnie du Sénégal went bankrupt the same year and sold its privileges to Rouen merchants, who took few initiatives before the making of peace in 1713 (Gray 1940, 131, 133–34, 139, 141–42, 147–49; Davies 1957, 273–74).

During and after the war years, there was ruthless competition between opportunistic privateer-traders. Jean Barbot wrote of a sanguinary encounter that involved the Luso-African community at Kau-ur ("Liahor"), as related to him in England by a French prisoner. On Christmas Eve 1710, a French corvette attacked a British vessel anchored at Kau-ur, the entrepôt for trade with Kawon, which was the capital of Saluum. Some one hundred Luso-Africans—this (possibly inflated) number presumably including grumetes and domestic slaves—went to the aid of the English, of whom seventeen were killed before the French were driven off. The Frenchman described Kau-ur as "a great mart of gold, wax, ivory, and some slaves." The Luso-African community comprised several families carrying on a considerable trade along the Gambia River and adjacent territory (Hair, Jones, and Law 1992, 1:153; Gray 1940, 149).

The surpassing importance of Luso-African women during this period is revealed by the saga of the nhara Esperança Vaz, called "Hope" and "Sperance" by English traders. After her husband, John Booker, died in June 1693, Esperanca married his successor as chief agent, William Heath, in October of the same year. Heath sent Esperanca to England in 1694, expecting to follow soon after but only to die in Africa the next January. Their daughter, Elizabeth, born in November 1694, was recognized as Heath's heir despite a legal challenge by Samuel Heath, William's brother (Wright 1976, app. B: 277). Samuel Heath's lawsuit was the subject of a document that described the circumstances of Esperanca's marriage to William Heath:

> WILLIAM HEATH Agent for the Guinea Company at James Island in the River Gambia in Guinea, being a Batchelor and having a mind to marry one

> Speranca, alias Hope Booker a Black Then in said Island, a Spinster in October 1693; invited several Persons belonging to the Factory on the Said Island, military officers these, to a Supper or Entertainment and acquainted them with his Intention of taking the said Sperance, alias Hope Booker to be his Wife, and immediately before Supper the said William Heath speaking to the Company then present said, Gentlemen, I declare before God and you all that I take Sperance to be my lawful wife and do promise never to take any other, as long as she lives: and the said Sperance then consented thereto, and taking him by the hand, declared that she took the said William to be her lawful Husband. (Quoted in Wright 1976, app. B: 277)

How long Hope and her daughter stayed in England is unknown, but they may have remained there until peace was concluded at the Treaty of Ryswick in September 1697. Esperança was mentioned in Royal African Company dispatches in 1702, when a new chief agent, Humphrey Chishull, was charged with embezzlement and fostering "strange divisions" among resident English traders. Chishull forsook James Fort to reside at Juffure, where his trading partner was a "Madam Esperance." He was replaced as chief agent in December 1703 by Capt. Thomas Weaver, whose efforts to improve company administration and curtail corrupt practices abruptly ended when he was shot dead in September 1704 in circumstances that were not communicated to the company's directors (Gray 1940, 134–39).

Captain Weaver's successor was John Chidley, whose term ran from 1704 to 1706. While a company factor at Joar (which was near Kau-ur), Chidley had censured his fellows for living "more like heathen than Christians," castigating their marriages with Luso-Africans and their embezzlement of company goods for private trade. Company officials did not respond to Chidley's appeal to send a parson, but in a September 1704 dispatch, they wrote, "We agree intirely with you in opinion that the greatest reason why our servants wrong us is their taking women, who oblige them to live extravagantly and waste our estates in presents, and hope you will by your example depress such debauched practices" (Gray 1940, 140). J. M. Gray commented, "The extent, to which Chidley fulfilled those hopes, may be gauged by the fact that he was himself the father of a child by a female slave on whom he bestowed large quantities of the Company's property including some gold, slaves, 'and a great deal of brandy, wine, beer, and severall other things' and that he had acquired the mother in exchange for two of the Company's slaves" (Gray 1940, 140). Chidley's association with a slave woman must be reckoned an infatuation. A female slave, especially one from another society, lacked kinship affiliations, especially with Mandinka elites, and her value as a translator or trader was likely inferior to that of a grumete.

Cacheu-Casamance, 1690s–1710s

The Companhia de Cacheu e Cabo Verde (1690–1706) was inaugurated January 1, 1690, at a propitious time, for Portugal was at peace and England and France were engaged in the War of the League of Augsburg. This second Cacheu company received strong support from the monarchy, including one-third of its financing. The company's chief slaving entrepôt was the island of Príncipe, with ancillary places of trade in Angola and western Africa, notably Bissau.

In 1693, the Companhia de Cacheu e Cabo Verde secured a contract with the Spanish holder of the asiento to supply four thousand slaves annually. Three years later, it was awarded the asiento itself, which it held until 1701, to the considerable profit of its investors (Hanson 1981, 242–44). In 1701, France obtained the asiento, and the Companhia de Cacheu's fortunes were ruined by the outbreak of Portugal's conflict with Spain during the War of the Spanish Succession.

Cacheu's Luso-African trading community prospered during the War of the League of Augsburg as English and French captured each other's vessels and factories. Indicative of the circumstances in those times, the ouvidor geral of Cabo Verde appointed the Luso-African Santos de Vidigal Castanho capitão-mor of Cacheu in May 1694 (Barcellos 1899–1913, 2:113). A decade earlier, Castanho had been part of the ruling triumvirate of the Luso-African "Republic" of 1684–85, along with Manuel de Andrade and Ambrósio Vaz, brother of Bibiana Vaz. Vaz and Andrade were taken prisoner and sent to Cabo Verde, but Castanho was released after forfeiting four thousand panos and promising to maintain two bastions of Cacheu's fort (Rodney 1970, 211). In 1697, under the favorable circumstances for Portuguese commerce afforded by the War of the League of Augsburg, Castanho lobbied the government to reassert Portuguese influence along the Gambia River. He sent communications to Lisbon from the ruler of Niumi on the Gambia's north bank and the ruler of Foni at the terminus of the Banyun and Luso-African trade route on the south bank, both of whom were expressing support for his initiative, but the Portuguese government refused to challenge English commercial interests (Rodney 1970, 131).

During the War of the Spanish Succession, the Royal African Company restricted the activities of the Companhia de Cacheu in the Gambia River, although Portuguese traders were, for a time, permitted to purchase slaves from its factors in the river. Cacheu's trade declined, as its traders could not compete for wax and other Casamance products with Europeans making purchases along the Gambia. In June 1707, Capitão-Mor Paulo de Abreu e Lima reported that the trading community could barely acquire one shipload of captives a year (Rodney 1970, 241). The same year, during a period of dispute with the Banyun ruler of Bichangor that disrupted beeswax trade with Cacheu, João Baptista, a son of a former capitão-mor of Cacheu, was appointed commandant of the presidio at Ziguinchor in hopes of improving relations (Rodney 1970, 162). To what extent Baptista succeeded is not known.

Bissau and Geba River Trade, 1690s–1710s

Belying its title, the Companhia de Cacheu e Cabo Verde concentrated its operations at Bissau, not Cacheu. Vessels found it safer to enter the Geba River rather than crossing the dangerous bar at the mouth of the Cacheu River, which became more challenging as the years passed with the dispatch of larger European vessels and lower river levels due to diminished rainfall during the c. 1630–c. 1860 dry period.

Circumstances at Bissau significantly changed at the close of the 1680s, with the arrival of Portuguese Franciscan missionaries and the outbreak of the War of the League of Augsburg that disrupted French and English commerce with West Africa. Padre Francisco de Pinhel, one of the Portuguese Franciscans sent to Bissau following the recall of the Spanish Capuchins, arrived early in 1687. He bore gifts for Bacampolco Có, the principal ruler of Ilha de Bissau, and in return accepted, on behalf of King Pedro II, three slaves, a male, female, and a child (Rodney 1970, 142).

During the years that followed, Padre Pinhel and his fellow Franciscans succeeded in converting Bacampolco Có and numerous other Papel to Christianity. In this endeavor, they had the assistance of the Luso-African community, one of whose leaders, Barnabé Lopez, was related to Bacampolco Có and held a royal commission as a lieutenant captain, representing Portuguese interests at Bissau. By 1694, when D. Frei Vitoriano Portuense, the bishop of Cabo Verde, visited Guinea, priests counted some seven hundred Christians at Bissau, twelve hundred at Geba, seven hundred at Cacheu, and six hundred at Bolor. The bishop was especially concerned about the sinful state of unmarried Christians.

Bacampolco Có entrusted eight of his sons to the bishop. The eldest, Batonto, was subsequently sent to Lisbon, where he was baptized with King Pedro

II as his godfather. Pledging sons for political ends and commercial objectives was widely practiced in western Africa, and Bacampolco Có had previously sent one of his sons to the court of the mansa of Kaabu, through whose territory passed much of the trade that brought prosperity to Bissau (Rodney 1970, 142–45; Mota 1974b, 15, 69–71; Rema 1982, 202–3).

The ascendancy of Portuguese interests in the following years was due, in large part, to the duration of the War of the League of Augsburg and the curtailment of French and English competition. Prior to Bacampolco Có's death in 1696, the Franciscan priests persuaded the ruler to grant Portugal permission to construct a fort and to exclude rival European traders—privileges repudiated by his successor, Incinhate (who ruled from 1696 to 1701). Toroco, Incinhate's rival in the contested succession, was a Christian convert favored by the Portuguese, but Incinhate had the support of the Biafada ruler of Guinala as well as Barnabé Lopez and most of the Luso-African trading community (Rodney 1970, 144–46).

Incinhate was subsequently persuaded to become a nominal Christian and to allow construction of a fort named Nossa Senhora de Conceição (Our Lady of the Immaculate Conception), but this accommodation was undermined by the ending of the War of the League of Augsburg and the return of rival European traders to western Africa. Papel-Portuguese relations were ruptured in December 1696 when the first capitão-mor appointed for Bissau, José Pinheiro de Camara (1696–99), refused to allow two English vessels to trade at Bissau. Papel were enraged by Pinheiro's arrogation of landlord rights—"Are you the *Senhor da Terra?*" they demanded—and lay siege to the unfinished fort, cutting off food and water. Santos de Vidigal Castanho, the capitão-mor of Cacheu, brought a relief force of some one hundred traders and two hundred grumetes and negotiated a truce, but the dispute was renewed with the arrival of another foreign vessel. Pinheiro died after being beaten and imprisoned by Incinhate (Rodney 1970, 145–47).

Neither the company's officials nor the Franciscan priests could prevail against Papel intransigence. Meanwhile, French and English vessels purchased large quantities of wax and ivory at Bissau. In 1698, Incinhate allowed a French trader named Castaing to reside in Bissau, and one year later, an English trader described "'quick despatches with 20 or 30 tons beeswax and 20 to 30 tons of elephants teeth per each ship'" (Cultru 1910, 153; Rodney 1970, 161). Portuguese authority was challenged in April 1699 when Pinheiro's successor, Rodrigo Oliveira da Fonseca (1699–1707), ordered Maria Soares to pay duties on a cargo of kola she was transporting in her vessel from Serra Leoa to Geba. She refused and appealed to Incinhate, and Fonseca was compelled to acknowledge

Incinhate's prerogatives as landlord and forego Portuguese claims. As Fonseca candidly acknowledged in November 1699, "[The Papel] do not want to lose their freedom" (Rodney 1970, 147, 149–50).

André Brüe, director of the Compagnie du Sénégal from 1697 to 1702, visited Bissau in February and March 1700, and despite Portuguese protests, he obtained Incinhate's permission to establish a comptoir. Brüe also obtained permission from the Biafada ruler of Guinala to establish a factory on Bolama, in part motivated by Biafada hopes that the French would drive away the Bijago who cultivated rice on the island during the rainy season (Cultru 1910, 153; Berlioux 1874, 143, citing Labat 1728, 5:164). Brüe may have visited Bolama on this occasion, or he may have learned about the island from La Courbe's account. In any case, he recommended founding a trading establishment on Bolama, but the company's directors rejected his proposal, citing financial exigencies (Hair 1990, 5–6; Jore 1965, 111–12).

During the following year, French and other European traders so dominated the Geba-Grande commerce, in competition with the struggling Companhia de Cacheu e Cabo Verde, that the Conselho Ultramarino decided to concentrate its limited resources at Cacheu. In 1701, the praça Nossa Senhora de Conceição was abandoned. So too was the factory of the Compagnie du Sénégal with the onset of the War of the Spanish Succession. The Companhia de Cacheu e Cabo Verde was barely able to maintain Cacheu until it went bankrupt in 1706 (Rodney 1970, 151; Marques 1972, 1:467).

Incinhate died in 1701 (Rodney 1970, 151). Papel and Luso-African traders continued to welcome traders of all nations, but after the outbreak of war, fewer vessels arrived, especially from Portugal, which was invaded by Spanish forces in 1704 and was heavily involved in fighting for several years thereafter (Langer 1958, 453). When Michel Jajolet de la Courbe was appointed director of the Compagnie du Sénégal in 1705, he recommended establishing a factory in the Geba River, built either on the remains of the Portuguese fort at Bissau or on Ilha do Rei/Sorcière. However, nothing could be done during wartime, and the Compagnie du Sénégal foundered in 1709 (Cultru 1910, 161–63).

Serra Leoa, 1690s–1710s

In 1690, following the outbreak of the War of the League of Augsburg, two years earlier, the Royal African Company evacuated Bunce Island's garrison to reinforce James Fort in the Gambia River. A few traders who remained were placed under the authority of Thomas Corker, the company's factor at Sherbro (Davies 1957, 219; Kup 1961, 70–71). In September 1692, Corker's letter of appointment, quoted at the beginning of this chapter, cautioned him against collusion with interlopers, of whom Robert Gunn and Francis Vass were specifically named. The latter probably was Francisco Vaz, who may have been related to the redoubtable Bibiana Vaz, a leading trader in the Nunez River (Fyfe 1964, 65; Rodney 1970, 209). Wartime exigencies fostered opportunistic collusion between the Royal African Company and independent traders: three years after warning Corker about associating with interlopers, the directors of the Royal African Company wrote to Gunn to solicit his cooperation for mutual advantage (Davies 1957, 220; Kup 1961, 59). Seemingly, the company found such middlemen indispensable.

Advancing—the practice of "trusting" goods to independent traders, whether Europeans, Eurafricans, or Africans—was the bane of European trading companies, producing much uncollectible debt. Credit was always a contentious issue between merchants safely ensconced in counting houses in Europe and factors, shipmasters, and supercargoes, the latter of which had to accommodate to customary practices in western Africa.

The English traders who remained on Bunce Island were pillaged by a French filibuster in 1692 and a French squadron in 1695. A new establishment was built in 1700, on the eve of the War of the Spanish Succession. As mentioned earlier, when Parliament abolished the Royal African Company's monopoly in 1698, private traders could freely trade on payment of a 10 percent duty on goods exported from England, with the tax designated to pay for the maintenance of the company's forts. In an attempt to increase returns, the Royal African Company changed its compensation policy in 1700, paying factors commissions for purchases of slaves, gold, ivory, and other commodities (Kup 1961, 77).

An ill-conceived initiative in 1702 allowed employees to take wives from England to Bunce Island and the factory on York Island in the Sherbro, with the company providing allowances for their maintenance (Davies 1957, 257 n. 3). Dispatching English women to western Africa in no way addressed the company's concerns about factors consorting with Eurafrican and African women. In the unlikely circumstance that an English woman could maintain her health and surmount the challenge of learning African languages and social practice, she would nevertheless lack the kinship affiliations that made Eurafrican and African women invaluable to European traders.

In 1703, a Susu ruler, probably from Futa Jallon, journeyed to the Sierra Leone estuary to meet the chief factor at Bunce Island and propose the opening of direct trade, bypassing the Luso-African middlemen. The factor temporized, for the meeting aroused the enmity of Luso-Africans, and such an initiative was made the more problematic by the uncertainties of wartime (Rodney 1970, 213–14). Whatever the factor might have decided was soon rendered irrelevant, however, for in July 1704, a French squadron bombarded and pillaged the factory on Bunce Island (Ly 1958, 288; Kup 1961, 100, 103).

The French vessels were piloted up the Sierra Leone estuary by John Leadstone, a former employee of the Royal African Company who had deserted with eleven hundred bars of iron to become a private trader. Prior to his employment with the company, Leadstone had been taken captive by an African ruler. He was ransomed by a Luso-African trader, who took him to Cacheu. Leadstone ingratiated himself with Cacheu's commandant, who advanced him trade goods that he did not repay. Before fleeing to Sierra Leone and employment with the Royal African Company, Leadstone stole trade goods and murdered the commandant's surgeon. By 1715, he had become a pirate, and in 1721, he "retired" to settle at Whiteman's Bay on the south side of the Sierra Leone estuary, along with other brigands and their African women; there, he became known as "Old Captain Cracker" (PRO T70/2, 39–40, 55–57; Kup 1961, 50, 52–53, 56, 71).

The Royal African Company abandoned Bunce Island after the French warships destroyed the fort in 1704. The island was not reoccupied until 1713, as a subfactory under the chief agent residing at York Island in Sherbro. When York Island proved too unhealthy, Bunce Island was again made the company's headquarters (Fyfe 1962, 4; Hair, Jones, and Law 1992, 2:189). The brief report on the death of John Clark, the agent at Sherbro, on October 3, 1714, said much about local circumstances: "'He having no Will but Verball which was to his Woman and her Friends. They together rifled all his Effects'" (Kup 1961, 104 n.). Assessing this era in the history of the Royal African Company in western Africa, K. G. Davies commented: "In war the forts were a temptation to the enemy, who systematically plundered James, York, and Bence Islands, and in peace they invited and suffered from the embezzlements of the company's own employees" (Davies 1957, 261).

Chapter 8
Expanding Slave-Trading Networks and the Corruption of African Social and Cultural Patterns

> Ships of all Nations, English, French, Dutch, etc. shall have free Liberty of trade in the river and the utmost safety, Except those belonging to the Royal African Company of England.
>
> —Posted on a tree at the watering place in the Sierra Leone estuary in October 1728 by José Lopes de Moura after driving the Royal African Company's employees from Bunce Island (quoted in Kup 1961, 84)

Following the War of the Spanish Succession (1702–13), Luso-Africans contended with growing competition from French and English joint-stock trading companies, from European independent traders, and from Franco-Africans and, especially, Anglo-Africans. During this period, the corrupting influences of the slave trade became increasingly manifest. Rulers and predatory elites in stratified societies violated judicial processes to condemn people for sale as slaves, and some rulers raided and enslaved the inhabitants of their own states. Luso-Africans progressively lost trade and political influence, especially where elites in stratified societies came under the influence of Muslim clerics. From Senegambia to Serra Leoa, small groups of Mande and Fula traders, including marabouts in growing numbers, infiltrated acephalous societies and were allowed to reside in separate quarters of villages or in neighboring settlements of their own: Fulas founded Fulacundas, Mande had Tienecundas, and Muslim Mande lived in Morocundas (Mota 1954, 1:157–58).

The Treaty of Utrecht, signed April 11, 1713, concluded peace between Spain, Portugal, England, and France, but France remained at war with Austria for another year. In one of the provisions of the treaty, Spain granted England the asiento, an exclusive contract to supply four thousand slaves annually to Spanish America for thirty years—an allotment that the Royal African Company found impossible to fulfill, despite the fact that its commercial network extended from Senegambia to the Gulf of Guinea. There were, however, other advantages: until the asiento was suspended by Spain in 1739, English merchants utilized slaving voyages as a means to engage in a remunerative contraband trade in English manufactures (Langer 1958, 432–33, 446–47, 450; Davies 1957, 152; Blackburn 1997, 495).

From the 1720s to the 1750s, English and French merchants expanded their slave trade in western Africa (Curtin 1969, 150, table 43, 170, table 49). This period marked the nadir of Portuguese commerce and influence in western Africa. The government of Portugal did not replace the defunct Companhia de Cacheu e Cabo Verde, which had been dissolved in 1706. As a consequence, the Royal African Company, the Compagnie du Sénégal, and independent English and French traders dominated the trade of Cacheu and Bissau. Portuguese missionary endeavors diminished along with Portugal's economic decline, but Franciscan priests continued to serve at Cacheu, Bissau, Ziguinchor, and Geba. Links with Cabo Verde were sustained and strengthened by shared commercial, family, and cultural ties, including sporadic visits by itinerant Cabo Verdean priests to Luso-African communities in western Africa. And, on occasion, Cabo Verdean and Portuguese priests acted as chaplains and advisers to African elites, functioned as mediators during conflicts and negotiators of truces and treaties, and served as acting or de facto commandants of the praças of Cacheu and Bissau.

During the 1710s and the early years of the 1720s, western African commerce was plagued by piracy. Most of the pirates were English seamen, many of them coming from the ranks of the forty thousand sailors discharged by the Royal Navy after the War of the Spanish Succession. Due to the huge numbers of unemployed individuals and the depressed wages for available berths, many seamen turned to piracy to, as one sailor expressed it, "revenge themselves on base Merchants, and cruel commanders of ships" (R. Ritchie 1986, 234). Thousands of pirates roamed the seas during the period between 1680 and 1725 (Rediker 1987, 256–57; Webster 1999, 74). Those frequenting western Africa, especially along the Sierra Leone estuary, were not routed out until the 1720s.

After the 1713 Treaty of Utrecht accorded England the asiento, the British government awarded the contract to the South Sea Company, which in turn contracted the Royal African Company to supply an annual quota of slaves. These slaves were to be transported across the Atlantic in vessels belonging to the South Sea Company. Also in 1713, Parliament opened West African trade to all Englishmen willing to pay a license fee. The Royal African Company soon proved unable to compete with independent traders and meet its quotas with the South Sea Company. The factory on York Island was abandoned in 1726, as was the fort on Bunce Island in 1728. Two years later, the conditions of James Fort in the Gambia and the company's forts along the Gold Coast were so deteriorated that to maintain them in a defensible condition the British government granted the company an annual subsidy of ten thousand pounds sterling. Deprived of its subsidy in 1746, the company was terminated four years later. In that same year, 1750, Parliament created a regulated company—the Company of Merchants Trading to Africa—that was open to any shipper who paid a low fee for membership. This company's sole purpose was not trade but the maintenance of fortified trading posts in West Africa, aided by an annual grant from Parliament. The Company did not take responsibility for Bunce Island in the Sierra Leone estuary, where London merchants had established a factory after the island was abandoned by the Royal African Company in 1728. The only establishment in western Africa that lasted until 1765 was the fort on James Island in the Gambia (Gray 1940, 217–18; Davies 1957, 152, 344–45; Rodney 1970, 248–49; Curtin 1975, 104).

Slave trading in western Africa significantly increased after the founding of the Fula almamate—a state founded on Islamic principles—in Futa Jallon during the 1720s and its subsequent conquests of groups living in the hinterland of Serra Leoa and the Guinea-Bissau region. A combination of factors enabled Fula to supplant Mande ascendancy in Futa Jallon. During the long c. 1630–c. 1860 dry period, Fula pastoralists herded their livestock southward into the Guinea-Bissau region and the Futa Jallon massif. In both areas, these Fula became interspersed with Mande cultivators who, as landlords, ruled and taxed the newcomers. Growing tensions between Fula strangers and Mande landlords were skillfully exploited by militant *torodbe* marabouts who forged alliances with Muslims belonging to trading and farming groups. Originating in Futa Toro along the middle reaches of the Senegal River, torodbe were clerics renowned for subordinating their ethnic and kinship ties to their commitment to Islam. Some were cultivators serving as village marabouts; others earned their livelihoods in itinerant trade, accompanied by *talibés*—youths studying the Koran under their supervision (Willis 1974, 2; Wright 1997, 80–81, 140–44).

A fundamental goal of the torodbe and other Muslim clerics was to create states ruled by Islamic law where they could implement the pervasive changes they believed were needed to "purify" the practice of Islam across West Africa. During the 1720s, a torodbe-led jihad succeeded in gaining control of the highlands surrounding Labé and Timbo. With the founding of an almamate, Futa Jallon became a lodestar for Muslims all over western Africa and a base of operations for those involved with new initiatives elsewhere. As torodbe-led Fula expanded their territorial conquests, they enslaved prisoners who refused to convert to Islam. Some captives were compelled to live in slave villages (*remaibe*) to grow food and practice crafts for Fula masters; others were sold into transatlantic slavery. During the second half of the eighteenth century, the almamate gained ascendancy over Landuma and Nalu living along the Nunez River and Susu along the Pongo River, compelling them to pay tribute and to allow Fula caravans to engage in direct trade with Europeans, Luso-Africans, and Anglo-Africans.

England and France were adversaries during the War of the Austrian Succession (1740–48), causing Portuguese merchants to reevaluate western African's potential for supplying large numbers of slaves to Brazil. In 1752, the Portuguese government was persuaded to build a new fort at Bissau, an initiative later taken over by the Companhia Geral do Grão Pará e Maranhão, founded in 1755 by the marquis of Pombal The new company prospered while France and England engaged in global conflict during the Seven Years' War (1756–63).

Drought and famine conditions caused by increased desiccation during the c. 1630–c. 1860 dry period exacerbated conflicts between groups in western Africa — conflicts that increasingly involved slave raiding and trading. Philip Curtin evocatively portrayed what happened in Senegambia during the 1750s when locust swarms and tropical diseases compounded famine conditions:

> [The crisis] began with three inadequate rainy seasons in 1746, 1747, and 1748. The year 1749 brought a normal harvest along the lower Senegal, but grain reserves were not yet replenished by 1750, when the rains were again insufficient on the lower river. The famine could be relieved in part by importing grain from the upper Senegal, which had a normal harvest in 1750, but now even the Gambia was brought into the disaster area by swarms of desert locusts, which remained a danger here and there in the region during most of the next decade, with an especially severe attack on Waalo in 1758. Harvests in Wolof country were again bad in 1751 and terrible in 1752, so that people began to slaughter and eat their reserves of cattle. Slaves held in Saint-Louis awaiting shipment began to die of malnutrition. . . . The

> Compagnie des Indes [in 1754] shipped more slaves than it had ever done before, though slaves and traders at the entrepôt had to be kept alive by food imported from France. In 1755, the harvest was again sufficient for current needs in the northern Wolof country, though reserves continued dangerously low. Saint-Louis was especially hard hit when the British blockade began in 1757. The French commander finally drove some five hundred slaves out of the fort to fend for themselves, rather than let them die of starvation in captivity. Even after the British captured the island in May 1758 and the rains came again, desert locusts prolonged the famine. By the end of the year, the British themselves were forced to send a ship to the Cape Verde Islands in hope of buying provisions that were unavailable on the mainland. After that, the worst was over, but the natural catastrophe must have been far more serious across the whole northern belt of savanna than the European records could possibly indicate. (Curtin 1975, 110)

Tragically for the peoples of western Africa, this era of droughts, famines, and deteriorating economic and social circumstances coincided with accelerating demands for labor on American plantations and rising prices paid for slaves. As slaving intensified, so did the corruption of judicial processes, with the result that innocent persons, along with criminals and deviants, were sold into transatlantic slavery.

Generally, there was a southward progression of slave trading during the eighteenth century. In the first part of the 1700s, more captives were shipped from Senegambia and the Guinea-Bissau region; thereafter, more were taken from along the rivers of Serra Leoa that linked to caravan routes connecting the expanding Futa Jallon almamate (Curtin 1969, 150, 170, 266; Lovejoy 1982, 485). In addition, African traders exacted higher prices from Europeans for slaves and other exports as time passed. Analyzing sources for the period from the 1680s to the 1830s, Curtin demonstrated that net barter terms of trade in Senegambia shifted consistently in favor of Africans: "As a median estimate, the Senegambians at the end of the period received about ten times as much as they had received 150 years earlier for the same quantity of goods exported (Curtin 1975, 340). Christopher Fyfe described the same price inflation a thousand kilometers to the south: at Bunce Island, male slaves cost eighteen to twenty-four bars in 1678 and forty to sixty in 1725, and by 1787, the price of a slave in sterling was over five times what it had been a century earlier (Fyfe 1962, 9). Davies reported on similar trends in different parts of West Africa as well (Davies 1957, 236–38).

The Mandinka-ruled state of Kaabu and the Fula almamate in Futa Jallon engaged in almost continuous warfare to acquire captives for sale into the Atlantic slave trade. So did the rulers of numerous states, for they and their entourages were avaricious for European spirits and other imported goods. Senegambian rulers became notorious for raiding people in their own states as well as those of neighboring states, thereby earning the epithet "devourers of men" (Prélong 1793, 302–3). The damels of Cayor and other rulers in stratified Senegambian societies were obligated to share their pillage among their retinues, and once the commodities obtained from the sale of slaves were consumed, they had to undertake new raids and new wars (Collier 1824, 39). Conspicuous consumption of European imports and redistributive obligations were likewise incumbent on Eurafricans in Serra Leoa who arrogated chiefly powers and acquired numerous dependents. Henry Smeathman, who gathered botanical specimens from 1771 to 1775, trenchantly discoursed on what he observed:

> The law of hospitality is destructive of industry. If there is provision in the country, a man who wants it has only to find out who has got any; and he must have his share. If he enter any man's house during his repast, and gives him the usual salutation, the man must invite him to partake. Thus whatever abundance a man may get by assiduity, will be shared by the lazy; and, hence they seldom calculate for more than necessaries. . . . Hence also they seldom live in large communities. Industrious men, who have wives, children and domestics about them, retire to some sequestered creek to avoid these interlopers, who lounge in every small town. Here they may thrive; but are often exposed to the dangers of slavery, from some neighbouring tyrant. But the laws of hospitality are not restricted to diet. A common man cannot quietly enjoy a spare shirt or a pair of trousers. Those who are too lazy to plant or hunt are also too lazy to trade, and begging is not disgraceful; . . . The rich are continually plagued with such requests, and are in fact but stewards for the rest. As they are constantly drained by their dependents, and are themselves both improvident and extravagant, they often suffer a total want of European luxuries. A great chief who sells 20 or 30 slaves for cloths, laced hats, beds, rum, tobacco, gun-powder (chiefly for salutes), salt beef, pork, hams, butter, flour, biscuits, porter, wine, tea, coffee, chocolate, sugar, spices, etc., as they affect very much to live in the European manner, shall, in 6 or 8 weeks, be entirely exhausted, and be obliged to live on rice and cassava, and take his chance of fishing or hunting. What a dreadful trade, and how weak must be societies, where they part with those who constitute the wealth of other

> countries, for articles, from which they derive as little benefit as we do from the West Indian turtle! (Fyfe 1964, 98–99)

Whether in the stratified societies of Senegambia or the acephalous groups of Serra Leoa, manifestly redistributive obligations were of surpassing importance.

Another resilient social practice that spanned a thousand kilometers of western Africa was the personal security accorded domestic slaves. In an era of increasing slave raiding and slave trading, societies generally adhered to their traditional values in refusing to sell domestic slaves unless they attempted escape, threatened the life of a free person, or engaged in incorrigible behavior. This principle was frustrating to European slavers anxious to complete their cargoes and depart the coast. F. Saugnier and P. R. de Brisson described the calamitous consequences that would ensue at Saint-Louis if a shipmaster attempted to collect debts owed by resident traders by seizing their domestic slaves: "Whoever should dare, either from a spirit of vengeance, or by way of bravado, to embark the Tapades' captives, would run the greatest risk, nor could he escape being stabbed or poisoned but by miracle: at the best he would be sure to lose his merchandize, and to be reduced to slavery among the negroes or the Moors" (Saugnier and Brisson 1792/1969, 277–78).

Exceptions there were. As the prices of slaves escalated, for example, slave owners were tempted to condemn domestic slaves for petty theft and other misdemeanors. C. B. Wadstrom, who visited Gorée in 1787, observed young women being publicly sold for acts of petty larceny (Wadstrom 1789, 28–29). And John Matthews wrote of similar practices in Serra Leoa as well, making a trenchant comparison to English practices in times past:

> Notwithstanding the almost absolute power which the master has over the life and property of his slave, he cannot sell any who are born his slaves, or who, though purchased, have resided twelve months in his possession, without accusing them of some crime; but for an accusation they are never at a loss. Witchcraft is the most general charge, and such is the astonishing folly and superstition of these people, whether a slave or freeman, that they generally acknowledge themselves guilty of the crime of which they are accused; but if a slave should plead not guilty, it would little avail him, as, on these occasions, the master is both the accuser and judge; and, if a freeman, he would be obliged to drink red water, which is a poisoned liquor prepared on the occasion. The analogy between this mode of trial and those which formerly obtained in England is very striking. (Matthews 1788/1966, 153–54)

Gorée and the Petite Côte, 1710s–1750s

After the War of the Spanish Succession concluded in 1713, French trade with western Africa was reorganized under new auspices. In 1719, the Compagnie Française des Indes incorporated a number of privileged companies, including the Compagnie du Sénégal, which had gone bankrupt in 1709. The name "Compagnie du Sénégal" continued in use in western Africa, and will be employed following. From 1725, the company's directors sold trading permits to independent businessmen to engage in the slave trade, which licensing practice continued until the French Revolution. Some of the businessmen involved were Portuguese Jews who settled in France, notably members of the Gradis and Mendez families of Bordeaux. André Brüe, who had directed the Compagnie du Sénégal from 1697 to 1702, was dispatched to Saint-Louis to reestablish French trade in Senegambia and the Guinea-Bissau region. During his second administration, from 1714 to 1720, Gorée Island was made the headquarters of a "governor" who supervised trade along the Petite Côte, in the Gambia River, and in the Guinea-Bissau region (Stein 1979, 18–19, 159, 186–87; Lacroix 1986, 32–33). French traders established in factories at Gorée and Rufisque in Cayor, Portudal in Baol, and Joal in Siin sought to monopolize trade along the Petite Côte. Their efforts engendered resentment and sporadic strife with Africans, Luso-Africans, European independent traders, and English traders of the Royal African Company based at James Island in the Gambia.

The activities of Luso-Africans along the Petite Côte during these decades were seldom mentioned in French and English reports. One exception involved an incident in 1714, when, as the arrival of an enemy vessel threatened, the master of an English vessel precipitately sailed from Portudal before paying for the fifty slaves loaded on board. The supercargo left behind onshore was permitted to go to Joal, having assured his creditors that payment would be forthcoming—which did not happen. An opportunity for retribution came in 1722 when goods landed at Joal by William Ramsey of the Royal African Company were confiscated and Ramsey was threatened with seizure. Subsequently, a Luso-African who traded with the Royal African Company was detained for payment of the debt (Gray 1940, 180–81).

Royal African Company vessels dispatched from James Island to Portudal and Joal were not molested in 1714, but the following year, two vessels of English independent traders were seized at Portudal, allegedly with the collusion of the ruler of Baol (Gray 1940, 154–55). A decade later, in 1724, when English and French traders along the Gambia came into conflict, a French sloop captured an English sloop at Portudal. Charles Orfeur, the Royal African Company agent, was at first protected by Baol's ruler, then by means of bribes and coercion, he was induced to surrender to the French. Subsequently, French and English traders cooperated for mutual interests. Not wanting to jeopardize their trade at Albreda, the French ceased to interfere with Royal African Company vessels trading along the Petite Côte (Gray 1940, 187–88, 207).

Disagreements between French traders and African rulers along the Petite Côte concerning customary payments and other matters sporadically escalated to strife. For instance, disputes over customs at Rufisque resulted in the death of a French shipmaster in 1729 and a seaman four years later. And in February 1729, the governor of Gorée, a French trader, a sailor, and three soldiers were killed at Joal (Lacroix 1986, 32–33). In the meantime, the trading community accommodated to circumstances as in times past. French employees of the Compagnie des Indes who resided along the Petite Côte formed alliances with Luso-African and African women, and they and their descendants maintained close links with the inhabitants of Gorée.

Gorée and Saint-Louis: From Nharas to Signares

During the eighteenth century, Gorée and Saint-Louis were renowned for their African and Eurafrican signares. Like *nhara,* the word *signare* is derived from the Portuguese *senhora,* denoting a free woman of property and social consequence. Signares collaborated with Frenchmen and Englishmen in marital and commercial alliances for mutual advantage. They exploited their privileged access to African and European trade networks, possessed households and skilled domestic slaves, and were indispensable to Europeans as interpreters of African languages and cultures. Renowned for their beauty and feminine artifices as well as their entrepreneurship and business acumen, signares were reputed to have been irresistible to European men and ruined many careers.

That the largest number of influential Eurafrican women in western Africa during the eighteenth century lived at Gorée and Saint-Louis is not surprising, since more Europeans lived at these two commercial entrepôts than elsewhere—French and English both, according to the fortunes of war. The island of Guet N'Dar is a sandbar near the mouth of the Senegal River some two kilometers long and two hundred meters wide. Gorée (Bir) is nine hundred meters in length and a few hundred meters in width, tapering to its northern point. These restricted—and, for Europeans, relatively healthy—island milieus fostered sustained social interaction and cultural exchanges between Africans and Europeans.

Guet N'Dar was part of the territory of the damel of Cayor, the Wolof ruler whose lands extended from the Senegal River along the Atlantic coast past Cape Verde to Baol. The damel extracted substantial tribute from the Compagnie du Sénégal for the privilege of engaging in commerce and to ensure that the settlement of Saint-Louis received the large quantities of millet and other provisions required by the burgeoning population, in addition to potable water, firewood, and other necessities. Saint-Louis throve on the commerce of the Senegal River, which was navigable for hundreds of kilometers to the Soninke state of Gajaga (called "Galam" by the French). The crews aboard watercraft congregated with Moors at river ports (*escales*) along the middle reaches of the river to trade for the globules of gum the Moors harvested from acacia forests from December to February; that was the season when the harmattan's desiccating winds caused the trees' bark to crack open and the sap to collect in golden balls. Acacia gum had a variety of uses in Europe, notably in glazing textiles. During the annual "voyage de Galam," vessels from Saint-Louis rendezvoused with Fula and Mande caravans along the upper river to barter salt, European cloth, and other merchandise for slaves and gold from the fabled mines of Bambuk. Many of the boatmen known as *laptots* (from the Wolof word for sailor) were domestic slaves belonging to signares who hired them out to the Compagnie du Sénégal in return for a half share of their wages, the men receiving the remainder (Curtin 1975, 113–14, 229).

The commerce of Saint-Louis was inhibited and made more costly by the dangerous bar at the mouth of the Senegal River. The interaction of ocean tides and river currents caused the bar to continually shift, making the passage risky at best and extremely dangerous at worst for most of the year—although less so during the rainy season extending from July to October, when winds and currents shifted from the north-northeast to the south-southwest. Sloops, schooners, and other small craft could generally cross the bar if reasonable precautions were taken, but larger vessels arriving from Europe had to anchor in the insecure roads offshore while cargo was transferred to lighters. The job of piloting vessels across the bar and the laborious work of lading and off-loading ships that were pitching and rolling in the roads were done by the intrepid Lébou seamen inhabiting Gandiole at the mouth of the river. Saint-Louis's prosperity rested on the skills and hardihood of these men and their appeals to the powerful spirit whose protection they invoked by praying and whistling as they maneuvered their craft. Nonetheless, the unpredictable currents and waiting sharks exacted a fearsome toll on ships and men alike: during S. M. X. Golberry's residence in Senegal from 1785 to 1787, four vessels, twenty-two launches, and 119 men perished at the mouth of the Senegal River (Golberry 1802, 1:141–48, 163; Durand 1806, 110–12; Frey 1890, 4–10).

The extensive salt pans at Gandiole were controlled by the wife of the damel of Cayor, and the officers of vessels loading salt for trade along the Senegal River negotiated a customs duty with her representative. Salt was loaded aboard the ships by the women of Gandiole, who were paid in coral, beads, and iron (Durand 1806, 1:34).

The most numerous inhabitants of the island of Guet N'Dar were Wolof from neighboring Cayor and Walo, along with Fula-speaking Toucouleurs from communities along the lower Senegal. Many of the domestic slaves came from societies along the upper Senegal River and lands beyond. Until the mid-eighteenth century, there were two communities on either side of the French fort, one predominantly Muslim and the other Christian. This bifurcation of groups gradually disappeared, with the several communities dwelling interspersed with mutual tolerance, syncretistic religious observances, and an ambiance admired by numerous visitors (Pruneau de Pommegorge 1789, 2–3; Lamiral 1791, 43).

Gorée's size, number of inhabitants, and trade were all much smaller than those at Saint-Louis. The *castel,* the remnant of an ancient volcanic cone that comprises the southern third of the island, was reserved for military purposes and had no civilian inhabitants—other than Mam Coumba Castel, the beneficent genie who was believed to protect the inhabitants while on the island and when fishing in surrounding waters. Successive European garrisons constructed forts to defend the cove on the northeast part of the island and on the castel to command the roadstead between Gorée and the cradling arm of Cape Verde.

The Compagnie du Sénégal maintained comptoirs at Hann, the chief source of potable water for Gorée and vessels anchored in the roads, and at Rufisque, Portudal, and Joal along the Petite Côte, where employees traded for livestock, fish, poultry, millet, palm oil, and other foodstuffs but obtained few captives. Restricted to the one comptoir at Albreda in the Gambia River, the French obtained only a few hundred slaves but considerable amounts of beeswax (Pruneau de Pommegorge 1789, 119–20, 126–27).

The African inhabitants of Gorée were principally Lébou—Wolof-speaking residents of the Cape Verde peninsula who, over centuries, had developed a distinctive culture combining some of the attributes of their Serer neighbors and who had asserted a measure of independence from the rule of the damel of Cayor. Gorée's inhabitants and the Lébou living on Cape Verde had a symbiotic relationship: Goréens relied on the inhabitants of the mainland, some of whom were kinfolk, for water, foodstuffs, and wood for construction and fuel, while Lébou living on Cape Verde depended on Gorée's European, Eurafrican, and

African inhabitants for trade goods, weaponry, and a place of refuge during conflicts with the damel of Cayor (Demanet 1767, 106–7).

There were several small springs on Gorée, the most productive of which were preempted by successive commandants for their personal use. Wells produced brackish water that could be used for some domestic purposes but was unfit for human consumption. The principal source of potable water for the inhabitants of Gorée and for vessels anchored in the roads between the island and the mainland was near the village of Hann, the usual place of embarkation for Gorée. The water was collected from holes dug in the sand near a swampy area, and it needed filtration to improve its taste. During the dry season extending from November to June, traders from the mainland visited Gorée daily, bringing casks of water, fish, vegetables, firewood, and charcoal. Sheep, goats, and poultry trussed in the bottom of pirogues were often awash in water shipped during crossings in rough seas, and cattle towed behind the pirogues arrived exhausted and more than half drowned. Goréens paid for these necessities by bartering European goods of all sorts. The loading and unloading of pirogues and other vessels, the transporting of foodstuffs, water barrels, and merchandise around the island, the breaking of stone for construction, and other rough labor was done by the trade slaves held in the fort awaiting embarkation. These individuals worked two by two, wearing iron collars linked by chains five to six feet in length (Pruneau de Pommegorge 1789, 103–4, 118–19; Saugnier and Brisson 1792/1969, 257–58; Roussin 1819, 63–65; Knight-Baylac 1970b, 407).

Gorée was reputed to be the healthiest environment for Europeans in western Africa—except during the rainy season. Notwithstanding the fact that Gorée was separated from Cape Verde by more than three kilometers of open sea, its inhabitants were sporadically subject to epidemics of malaria during the *hivernage,* the four-month rainy season from June and July to October when winds carried mosquitoes from Cape Bernard to the southern ramparts of the island; there, the insects found moisture and sustenance in fissures of the castel's volcanic walls. During the hivernage, Gorée was periodically cut off from the mainland when tornadoes and contrary winds made the crossing more difficult and frequently dangerous, risking the ruin of foodstuffs and merchandise. Meanwhile, the inhabitants of the mainland cultivated their fields. Gorée's inhabitants could store rainwater in cisterns, and they husbanded food supplies by using nets and hooks and lines to catch the species of fish swimming in the northward-flowing warm currents. During the hivernage, livestock could forage grass growing in uninhabited spaces, including unfortified areas of the castel. The inhabitants of the larger compounds on the island cultivated vegetable gardens and fruit trees (Demanet 1767, 98–99; Pruneau de Pommegorge 1789, 118–19; Saugnier and Brisson 1792/1969, 258).

"Signareship" evolved during the French occupation of Gorée and Saint-Louis, despite the regulations promulgated by the directors of the Compagnie des Indes forbidding employees to engage in private trade or traffic with African women. The company's directives were flouted by employees of every rank and by soldiers and sailors, as well. While director of the Compagnie du Sénégal from 1688 to 1690, La Courbe fulminated against the flagrant cohabitation practiced by every Frenchman at Saint-Louis, including the priests sent out by the company.

Women traders carried on most of the local commerce, dispatching domestic slaves to purchase hides, millet, and cotton cloth. A few men were involved in commerce, mainly in trading slaves, but most males were occupied with fishing and agriculture (Cultru 1910, 113–14; 1913, 25–26, 28–29). Confronted by local realities and the need to accommodate to circumstances, successive governors residing at Saint-Louis sought authorization for the company's employees to marry local women. Gov. Julien du Dubellay (1722–25) argued that such a policy would encourage long-term service and reduce the turnover of employees. Remarking that there were only five Eurafricans aged twelve to fifteen who were suitable for marriage at Saint-Louis, Dubellay suggested that the company annually dispatch six to eight *parisiennes* aged fifteen to sixteen so that employees might have French wives. The company's directors rejected both proposals and expressly forbade marriages between Frenchmen and women of color (A. Delcourt 1952, 95, 123).

The company's directives were honored in the breach. Frenchmen living at Saint-Louis and Gorée married African and Eurafrican women—a few before a priest but most à la mode du pays ("country-style," in English usage)—accommodating to Wolof and Lébou marriage and inheritance practices, with the responsibilities and obligations they entailed. Frenchmen, like Portuguese and Luso-Africans before them, insisted that wives and children take their surnames and French given names, for example, Maria was replaced by Marie and Pedro by Pierre (A. Delcourt 1952, 95–123; Prélong 1793, 299–300; Golberry 1802, 1:157; Villeneuve 1814, 1:68–70). The replacement of Portuguese names by French names accounts for the rapid "disappearance" of Luso-Africans at Gorée and Saint-Louis. For example, André Brüe's listing of employees of the Compagnie du Sénégal at Gorée in April 1720 included "Paula de Rufisk, Veuve du sieur Charles Cavillon." Whereas the Portuguese *Paula* had not been transformed to *Paule,* reflecting the proximity of long-standing Luso-African communities along the neighboring Petite Côte, the names of women listed at Saint-Louis adhered to French usage: "Marie Charron, Mûlatresse, fille de Pierre Charron en son vivant matelot . . . Marie-Thérèse Yacam Semaine, Négresse, Veuve de Joseph de Gorée en son vivant Maitre de Barque . . . Michel de Gorée, fils de Joseph de Gorée et de Marie Thereze Yaram Semaine" (Sainville 1972, 71).

Governor Devaulx (1733–34) and his advisory council raised the marital issue anew, contending that the company's regulations had not prevented sexual and commercial relationships and that sanctioning marriages might make clandestine commerce easier to control. They also invoked Christian precepts, arguing that Eurafrican women and girls would be saved from living in sin, since circumstances made Eurafricans dependent on whites for their livelihoods. That Eurafrican females were alleged to be dependent suggests that they—and their mothers—were held apart by Wolof society. Their condition was made all the more precarious by the company's practice of not permitting children to inherit property acquired by an employee, a policy that fostered so much ill will that it seems to have been abandoned a few years later (A. Delcourt 1952, 124 ff.). A communication concerning circumstances at Gorée in June 1736 indicated that the officials' practice was to allow children to inherit the property of their mothers (Searing 1993, 101). By 1749, ten of the thirteen private properties on Gorée belonged to Eurafricans, nine of whom were women (Knight-Baylac 1970b, 402–3).

Cohabitation and its consequences for the Compagnie du Sénégal were subjected to a searching critique by the noted French botanist Michel Adanson, who spent the years from 1749 to 1753 in Senegambia studying flora and fauna and collecting specimens. Adanson prepared a report for the minister for foreign affairs in 1763, when Gorée was returned to French control following the Seven Years' War (both Gorée and Saint-Louis were captured by the British in 1758). He excoriated the corrupt practices of officials associated with signares, which were grossly unfair to lower-ranked French employees. On the one hand, signares received double and triple rations and whatever else they desired, and their domestic slaves were fed with meat and millet at the company's expense. On the other hand, French workers, soldiers, sailors, and even officers of the lower grades were deprived while the "bloodsuckers" and their collaborators banqueted upon provisions diverted from their use. Furthermore, the signares' slaves who were hired in the firm's service engaged in trade on behalf of their mistresses and the high-ranking company officials who colluded with them, with the result that the signares obtained the choicest merchandise, including commodities not available to lower-level French employees. Adanson blamed these practices on the company's regulations forbidding employees to bring their wives from France; consequently, Frenchmen lavished on signares the housing and amenities that could have served European women. Adanson acknowledged that such behavior was not surprising and that, in a hot climate, men were especially vulnerable to women's charms—not least of all Frenchmen, who were always drawn to "a sex as dangerous as it is attractive" (Cariou n.d., 18–19).

Adanson's mémoire related that the male offspring of Frenchmen and signares were employed by the Compagnie des Indies as hired laborers and grumetes (or laptots, as they were known at Saint-Louis). They were not categorized as slaves even if their mothers had been slaves, which accorded with the Wolof practice regarding children of a female slave married to a freeborn man. The signares' daughters made alliances with Frenchmen in furtherance of their own interests. Adanson warned that the growing numbers of domestic slaves belonging to signares constituted an increasing drain on the company's resources (Cariou n.d., 18–19; Searing 1993, 108).

By the mid-eighteenth century, Senegal River trade was carried on by craft with crews of about twenty-five laptots and several officers who were usually *habitants*—freemen from Saint-Louis, some of whom were Christian converts. Over time, the term *laptot,* a gallicized form of the Wolof word for sailor, came to mean any African who worked with Europeans. The voyage to Galam was arduous: it took laptots manning tow ropes some fifty days to pull trading craft upriver against the flow of the Senegal River and the prevailing winds blowing from the northeast. Laptots were paid in trade goods and salt, enabling them to engage in remunerative trade while upriver. In 1755, a partial census of Saint-Louis enumerated the African male population, finding that it included 15 masters of boats, 15 mates, 36 sailors, 3 chief translators, 36 journeyman workers, 98 slaves belonging to the company, and 550 slaves belonging to other inhabitants. Apprentices were called *gourmets* (Curtin 1975, 114; Searing 1993, 101–2).

Adanson's distinction between the privileged and corrupt company officials associated with signares versus the lower-ranked employees and the soldiers and sailors who were cheated and deprived suggested a similar dichotomy concerning the women of Saint-Louis and Gorée who associated with Europeans. Compared to the few women who achieved the status of signare, there would have been many Eurafrican and African girls who—due to their youth, lack of resources, or slave or grumete status—could establish liaisons only with artisans, soldiers, and sailors. Girls and young women might hope thereby to acquire some European commodities for trade, besides learning a European language and European ways. After perhaps several liaisons curtailed by the deaths or departure of lovers, enterprising women might accumulate sufficient resources and experience to parlay a marriage with a privileged company official and become a signare. Such possibilities were problematic, however, for many European soldiers and sailors were brutal and undisciplined, their dissipation condoned if not encouraged by a ration of a bottle of brandy each Saturday (Knight-Baylac 1970b, 399–400). Avid for sexual partners, their companionship was more likely to diminish the prospects of women rather than enhance them. African women making such alliances could at least hope that any Eurafrican daughters conceived in their liaisons might be successful in contracting marriages.

The identities and social standing of the women described by Adanson and other authors are matters of speculation, since few sources recorded the name or the status of a woman. If the first names of females were mentioned, their surnames were not. Rare indeed were references to signares' relatives (whether parents, siblings, uncles, aunts, cousins, or nephews), numbers of whom doubtless participated in the illicit commercial ventures that cheated the Compagnie du Sénégal.

The hierarchy of Wolof and Lébou groups comprised the following: freeborn individuals (*jambor*); blacksmiths (*tega*), leather workers (*ude*), and bards/griots (*jewel*); and persons of slave descent (*jam*). Marriage across class lines was extremely rare. One exception occurred when a wealthy freeborn man, after marriage to several freeborn wives, married a jam woman (called a *tara*) whose beauty enthralled him. In such a case, the tara and her children were accorded freeborn status (Ames 1956, 156–57).

Many of the women who associated with European soldiers and sailors were jam. Apparently, most were very young—barely in their teens. Golberry rhapsodized on the beauty of Wolof, Fula, and Mandinka girls "thirteen to fourteen years of age" (Golberry 1802 2:431–34; cf. Lamiral 1789, 44). L. Prélong (1793, 299), who lived in Senegal from 1787 to 1789, stated that when a Frenchman married a slave, he granted her freedom at their wedding. Freeborn women at Gorée and Saint-Louis included the daughters of grumetes (or gourmettes, in French usage), but almost no information about them was recorded in European sources. In some communities in western Africa, wives probably belonged to the same societies as their husbands; in others, local women were taken as wives (Nardin 1966; Rodney 1970, 77, 79). Grumete males spoke Crioulo, "Black French," and "Black English," and their wives and children no doubt learned the lingua franca of the trading communities.

Antoine Edmé Pruneau de Pommegorge, whose experiences in western Africa extended over twenty-two years before he returned to France in 1765, provided a highly favorable opinion of signares in a book published in 1789, an account that was doubtless suffused with nostalgia:

The women on the island [of N'Dar] are, in general, closely associated with white men, and care for them when they are sick in a manner that could not be bettered. The majority live in considerable affluence, and many African women own thirty or forty slaves which they hire to the Compagnie. Each year the domestic slaves make the voyage to Galam engaged as sailors; they bring back to their mistresses fifteen, twenty, even up to thirty weight of gold for the sale of two hogsheads of salt which they are permitted to embark duty-free. The women have some of this gold made into jewelry, and the rest is used to purchase clothing, because they adore, as do women everywhere, fashionable clothing. Their mode of dress, characteristically very elegant, suits them very well. They wear a very artistically arranged white handkerchief on the head, over which they affix a small narrow black ribbon, or a colored one, around their head. A shift *à la française,* ornamented; a bodice of taffeta or muslin; a skirt of the same and similar to the bodice; gold earrings; anklets of gold or silver, for they will wear no others; red morocco slippers on the feet; underneath their bodice a piece of two ells of muslin, the ends of which dangle beneath the left shoulder—thus appareled when they go out in public, they are followed by one or two young girls who serve as their chambermaids, likewise well dressed, but somewhat more lightly and a little less modestly than is our own custom. . . . The women being escorted when they go out, they frequently encounter a *griot* [a type of man who sings someone's praises in return for money]; in such instances he does not lose the opportunity to precede them declaiming their praises with all the exaggerations he can think of, and some immodesties which they know, the women being so flattered that in the rapture excited by this adulation they often fling some of their garments to the singer when they have nothing left in their pockets to give him. Next to finery, the greatest passion of these women is their dances, or *folgars,* which they sometimes hold until daybreak, and during which one drinks a great deal of palm wine, *pitot* [a type of beer], and also wines from France, when they are able to procure them. The usual way to praise those who have excelled in dancing is to fling a cloth or handkerchief over them, which they return to the person who has thrown it, making a deep bow to thank him. Some of these women are married in church, others *à la mode du pays,* which in general consists of the consent of both parties and the relatives. It is remarked that the latter marriages are always more successful than the former; the women are more faithful to their husbands than otherwise the case. The ceremony which follows the latter form of marriage is not in fact as becoming as the good behavior of the women. The morning following the

> consummation of the marriage, the relatives of the bride come at daybreak and carry off the white cloth on which the couple have spent the night. Do they find the proof they search for? They affix the cloth at the end of a long pole, waving like a flag; they parade this all day long in the village, singing and praising the new bride and her chastity; but when the relatives have not in fact found such proof of the morning after, they take care to substitute for it as quickly as possible. (Pruneau de Pommegorge 1789, 3–7)

Pruneau de Pommegorge's observation that the women who married Frenchmen à la mode de pays were reputedly more faithful to their husbands than those married by a priest testified to the sanctions imposed by Wolof communities. *Or de Galam* (gold from Bambuk, purchased along the upper Senegal River) was a byword for quality and purity, and it was used by artisans in fabricating highly valued jewelry—conspicuous, portable wealth that could be readily negotiated to finance trading ventures or for other purposes or, as fashions changed, reworked into another ornament more à la mode. The gold and silver jewelry created for signares and Wolof and Lébou women by Wolof, Lébou, Moor, and Berber artisans was significantly influenced by the artistic traditions of the Muslim world (M. A. Johnson 1980, 1994). Such accessories contrasted sharply with the adornments of Luso-African women living along the Petite Côte and in Luso-African communities to the south, for they wore rosaries and crucifixes and asserted a Christian, Catholic heritage.

Griots, who were exclusively attached to leading families as praise-singers and entertainers in times past, manifestly adapted to changing circumstances, seizing opportunities to cater to affluent signares. Female bards were often hairdressers, an occupation that gave them privileged opportunities to learn and pass on gossip. They were also known for their lascivious dancing and for otherwise having an immoral influence on young women (Villeneuve 1814, 4:193–94; Gamble 1967, 45).

Adanson reported that "signare" was what women called themselves, while Poncet de Rivière, the commandant of Gorée in 1764, stated that women were given that designation more for their "Portuguese appearance" than for their origins, since they were of Franco-African descent (Adanson, cited in Cariou n.d., 18–19; Saulnier 1918, 344 n. 1). Golberry observed that "signare" was applied to all Eurafrican women, but only to those African women who were free and rich (Golberry 1802 1:156). The slave children purchased by signares were known as *rapaces* and *raparcilles,* from the Portuguese *rapaz* and *rapariga* (Villeneuve 1814, 4:55).

Nharas were now known as signares, but their patterns of dress remained much the same, except that the more affluent women could afford the most sumptuous fabrics for their garments, enhanced by gold and silver jewelry. The headpiece made of a single, white handkerchief as described by Pruneau de Pommegorge evolved into the elegant, cone-shaped turban artfully contrived from as many as nine colored kerchiefs—a distinguishing feature of the signares and a hallmark identification that seemingly derived from Serer and Luso-African women along the Petite Côte. Sources are mute concerning the likelihood that the flaunting of sumptuous garments and jewelry by signares aroused envy and angered the wives of rulers and elites, especially since those signares were former slaves or daughters of slaves and were accompanied by retinues of slaves and griots who addressed them with extravagant praise. Perhaps that is why signares apparently restricted their activities to the islands of Guet N'Dar and Gorée.

A distinctive feature of the signares' social life was the *folgar*. *Folgar* is a Portuguese and Luso-African word that passed into Franco-African usage as a general term for celebrations with music and dancing. Louis Moreau de Chambonneau, who lived at Saint-Louis and traded along the Senegal River during the 1670s, described folgars as gatherings organized by griot drummers that featured a sequence of wrestling matches, displays of martial skills, and dancing by young girls who were later joined by young men (C. Ritchie 1968, 326–28). In an entirely different context, Adanson wrote about a folgar associated with funerary ceremonies. During a visit to the Petite Côte in 1749, he described this folgar as a line dance that was held on three consecutive nights at Portudal following the interment of a young woman killed by a snakebite. To the music of two drummers and singing by participants and spectators, young men and women advanced and retreated with many diverse movements, and much beer was consumed (Adanson 1814, 623–24). At Saint-Louis and Gorée, signares transformed the folgar into a couples' dance in the confined spaces of their dwellings. These entertainments, similar to European balls, provided signares with the opportunity to display their beauty, social graces, splendid garments, and jewelry. An 1844 illustration by Edouard Auguste Nousveaux depicted a signare and a European man dancing to the beat of drummers, with numerous onlookers gathered around the room being served by female domestics (Frey 1890, 12–13; cf. mural in Gorée's *mairie*). What better opportunity for newly arrived or unattached Europeans to meet potential partners, perhaps through the introduction and manipulation of signares attached to the most influential men in a trading company or military garrison who acted as matchmakers, preceptors, and confidants for their daughters, female relatives, and friends? Such matchmaking involved promising commercial opportunities, especially regarding men with privileged access to merchandise, shipping, or other resources controlled by the Europeans in the community.

Folgars and other recreations arranged by the signares represented an admirable combination of pleasure and business, with a style and character far removed from the debaucheries associated with Europeans living in forts, factories, and settlements elsewhere in western Africa—excesses of all sorts that were precipitated by boredom, homesickness, poor health, and depression, all of which contributed to a mean and short-lived existence. Marriage to signares provided Europeans with a lifestyle and regimen that contributed much to their survival and well-being. A European living in a signare's household enjoyed the best possible circumstances in tropical Africa: an attractive companion who spoke his language and was familiar with European ways, a stable home life, regular and well-prepared meals, and sensible recreational outlets conducive to good health, both physical and psychological. And during inevitable periods of illness, he could rely on nursing and attentive care from the signare and her female domestics.

Many Crioulo words and Luso-African customs and practices persisted among Luso-Africans and Franco-Africans and their descendants, especially at Gorée and along the Petite Côte. These included Crioulo as the language of commerce and social intercourse, Christian practices modified by Luso-African usage, panos and turbans worn by women, and Luso-African domestic practices and cuisine.

During the Seven Years' War, British naval expeditions captured Saint-Louis in April 1758 and Gorée the following December. The Compagnie du Sénégal's resources at Saint-Louis were significantly diminished by the cumulative effects of a ruinous drought that extended from 1747 to 1758 and by the disaffection of Eurafricans and free Africans. When British vessels succeeded in crossing the bar at the mouth of the Senegal River, laptots blockaded the fort and refused to allow the French garrison to leave until their freedom and safety were guaranteed. The laptots' demands were incorporated in the articles of surrender drafted by company representatives and prominent individuals from the Eurafrican and free African communities; it was accepted by the British commanders on April 29, 1758 (Webb 1997, 49). The first article of captitulation stated that the employees of the Compagnie du Sénégal would be returned to France under safe conduct in an English vessel. The second article specified that "mulâtres" and "mulâtresses" and "nègres" and "négresses libres" would not be interfered with concerning the practice of religion and would not be deprived of any of their possessions (Jore 1965, 21–23). Having received these guarantees, Eurafricans and free Africans generally prospered during the following two decades of British rule.

Pruneau de Pommegorge's tribute to signares derived from personal experiences decades earlier, but his admiration of these women was shared by the Reverend John Lindsay, chaplain aboard one of the English vessels that captured Gorée in December 1758.

> As to their women, and in particular the ladies (for so I must call many of those in Senegal) they are in a surprising degree handsome, have very fine features, are wonderfully tractable, remarkably polite both in conversation and manners; and in the point of keeping themselves neat and clean (of which we have generally strange ideas, formed to us by the beastly laziness of slaves), they far surpass the Europeans in every respect. They bathe twice a day, . . . and in this particular have a hearty contempt for all white people, who they imagine must be disagreeable, our women especially. Nor can even their men, from this very notion, be brought to look upon the prettiest of our women, but with the coldest indifference, some of whom there are here, officers' ladies, who dress very showy, and who even in England would be thought handsome. You may, perhaps, smile at all this; but I assure you 'tis a truth. Negroes to me are no novelty; but the accounts I received of them, and in particular the appearance of the females on this occasion, were to me a novelty most pleasing. They were not only pretty, but in the dress in which they appeared, were even desirable. Nor can I give you any drapery more nearly resembling theirs, than the loose, light, easy robe, and sandal, in which we see the female Grecian statues attired; most of which were of exceeding white cotton, spun, wove into narrow slips of six or seven inches, and sewn together by themselves. Their hair, for it differs a little from wool, very neat and curiously plaited; and their persons otherways adorned, by earrings, necklaces, and bracelets, of the purest gold. And indeed I cannot help thinking, that it was to the benefit of the African company in general, and the happiness of those they sent abroad in particular; that, with such promising inhabitants, the French suffered no white women to be sent thither. (Lindsay 1759, 77–78)

There was, however, no easy fraternization, to the dismay of the British garrison. Lindsay took pains to describe the women's high reputation for chaste and respectable behavior. Wives defended their rights with fearsome weapons: women on Gorée kept sawfish blades in their dwellings to shred the flesh of rivals in any quarrel (Lindsay 1759, 80). A French resident living on Gorée later in the century mentioned an instance of an African woman using solanum (a plant of the nightshade family that grew on Gorée) to poison her former lover and the Eurafrican for whom he abandoned her (Prélong 1793, 275–76). Signares held no less potent a sanction over their European partners deriving from their invaluable role in shared commercial enterprises.

Reverend Lindsay related that a "Mr. Charles" functioned as pastor to Gorée's Christians, "the chief part of the inhabitants." Lindsay described him as follows:

> There is on the island a gentleman (although a negroe) of extraordinary good sense, a good education, and withal polite; and not from authority, so much as the knowledge of his honesty and other amiable qualities, has obtain'd such ascendancy over the minds of the inhabitants, that his voice is with them a law in every thing. On sundays, and other holidays, his house becomes a chapel, where a very decent and considerable community meet together, the gentleman himself officiating to them as pastor; so that Mr. Charles, for so he is call'd, may be truly stil'd their king, priest, and lawgiver. (Lindsay 1759, 76)

"Mr. Charles" was the Eurafrican trader Charles Thévenot, whom the British were constrained to recognize as "mayor" of Saint-Louis in 1764 (Hargreaves 1969, 82–83 n. 2).

Reverend Lindsay provided one of the few references to a woman of elite status who was married to a European—to wit, "Princess Pinetica," the wife of Estoupan Saint-Jean, the French commandant of Gorée when the British captured the island in 1758. She was the daughter of the former *brak* (ruler) of Waalo and niece of the current brak, and she lived in "a sort of palace" on Gorée and was attended by numerous slaves. When the British commandant Major J. M. Mason alienated the "princess" by commandeering one of her slaves without her permission (a cook trained in French cuisine), the lady's grievance united Gorée's inhabitants on her behalf; in Reverend Lindsay's words, this "alienat[ed] from our interest those we ought to cherish" (Lindsay 1759, 80, 89–91). A crisis was averted through the mediating skills of "Mr. Charles" (Lindsay 1759, 91).

Lindsay expressed both praise and unease concerning the "three hundred free Negroes" inhabiting the southern part of the island: "[They] live in a manner wonderfully neat and decent—the village itself is a curiosity for regularity. In their tempers they are sociable; in their genius, tractable to a miracle; and so sensible are they of a proper or improper behaviour us'd towards them, that they will become of service or disservice accordingly. By an easy and gentle treatment they are won to any thing, while the least insolent usage may endanger the throats of most of our soldiery, and render the lives of all irksome and miserable" (Lindsay 1759, 50). Lindsay was unique in expressing such concerns. Administrators and military men were reluctant to communicate apprehensions about problems they might not be able to control. Greatly outnumbered by Eurafrican and African inhabitants and commanding a debauched and unreliable soldiery, the successive commandants of Gorée and Saint-Louis were noteworthy for their accommodation to circumstances beyond their control.

The salient features of "signareship" were maintained during the eighteenth century and into the first decades of the nineteenth century. Europeans were constrained to contract traditional marriages, with all the responsibilities and obligations that entailed. Marriage à la mode de pays included paying bridewealth to the woman's parents, supplying a wedding feast, providing the woman with a dwelling, and adhering to accepted norms of marital practices, including sexual fidelity. Children bore their fathers' names, and a European was expected to purchase a slave for each child to provide for its support. When a husband died or returned to Europe, the signare was free to remarry, take the new husband's name, and raise another family along with any children of a previous marriage (who retained their father's name) (Golberry 1802, 1:156–57; Villeneuve 1814, 1, 68).

At Gorée, a signare's children inherited her possessions, following the Lébou custom that called for children to inherit from their mothers without interference from their fathers. Practices may have differed at Saint-Louis before the acceptance of Islam, since Wolof practiced double-descent, which affiliated individuals with some kin groups through the patralineal rule and with others through the matrilineal rule (Angrand 1946, 33; Gamble 1967, 60–61, 94). Inheritance practices were transformed during the 1760s and 1770s when French and British authorities conferred title deeds for house plots and Eurafricans registered marriages conducted by Christian clergy. Accumulating wealth in slaves, dwellings, and other possessions with successive husbands, signares might anticipate attracting more privileged partners with each marriage. Fortunate indeed was a European newly arrived at Saint-Louis or Gorée who could made an alliance with a signare possessing a large household, a skilled labor force dwelling in her compound, and established trade networks. And, for their part, wealthy signares could choose among trading company employees, ranking government officials, and military officers.

In contrast to the hybrid African-European fashions of signares, Eurafrican men wore European-style clothing (Villeneuve 1814, 1:69–70). Officials of trading companies and European traders at Saint-Louis and Gorée combined to curtail the opportunities and entrepreneurship of Eurafrican and African traders, but as the years passed, more and more of these individuals acquired trading craft and engaged in Senegal River trade and coastwise commerce.

The Treaty of Paris, concluded in February 1763, restored Gorée to France, but Britain retained Saint-Louis as part of an ill-conceived Senegambia federation (Langer 1958, 435). During the decades that followed, signares prospered as never before, both at British-ruled Saint-Louis and at French-ruled Gorée. So also did Eurafrican men, taking advantage of the changing circumstances.

Gambia-Cacheu-Casamance, 1710s–1750s

The Gambia River was a contested and dangerous commercial arena during the 1710s and 1720s. English independent traders competed with French and Dutch traders, and piratical craft sporadically raided vessels trading along the lower reaches of the river (Gray 1940, 152).

A number of private French traders had settled along the Gambia River during the closing years of the War of the Spanish Succession, and André Brüe, the director of the Compagnie du Sénégal, reestablished a factory at Albreda after the signing of the Treaty of Utrecht in April 1713. French traders formed alliances with Luso-African women and soon carried on an extensive trade, to the discomfiture of the Royal African Company's new chief agent, William Cooke, when he arrived on November 13, 1713. As reported by David Francis, chief agent in August 1715, the French factors were married to "the Chief women of the country, who having canoes and boats up the river, prevent the [African] merchants coming down [to James Island] with their trade." The directors of the Royal African Company were well aware of Luso-Africans' influence: one of Cooke's instructions was to contact Luso-African traders and "oblige them to your interest." Private English traders were to be treated as trespassers if the refused company employment. The independent traders—including John Snow, a former chief agent for the company (1706–9)—were not intimidated and continued to trade with English, French, and Dutch vessels belonging to private traders. (Gray 1940, 154, 157; Wright 1976, 182, and 1997, 132 n. 38).

Abandoned in 1709, the establishment on James Island was in such ruins by 1713 that Cooke negotiated with the Niumi ruler to construct a new fort at Juffure that would control access to the well. The negotiations failed, however, and as a result, the employees of the company lived on the store ship while the fort on James Island was slowly rebuilt, not to be ready for occupation until 1718

(Gray 1940, 151–52). Soon after Cooke's arrival in the Gambia, an expedition dispatched by the governor of the Azores entered the river with the mission of reasserting Portuguese influence. When the Portuguese commander attempted to persuade the Niumi ruler to collaborate against the Royal African Company, Cooke seized his vessel as a prize (Gray 1940, 26, 148, 153–54).

Whether due to the shifting of trade upriver or for other reasons, there was much conflict between Europeans and Mandinka in Niumi during this period. In January 1715, Niumi residents killed an English private trader named Nathaniel Bugby and pillaged his factory. Subsequently, two private French traders named Godiveau and du Buisson living near Albreda fled to the Compagnie du Sénégal's factory, leaving their goods in the hands of their assailants. As a consequence, in June 1716, all but one of the French factors were withdrawn from Albreda. The Europeans' relations with the people of Niumi worsened, and the last Frenchman abandoned Albreda in August 1717 after the Niumi ruler led fifty men to James Island in an unsuccessful attempt to assassinate chief factor William Cooke. Four months later, in December 1717, an agent for the Compagnie du Sénégal refused to reoccupy the factory at Albreda and instead established a factory at Bintang in the Banyun state of Foni. Only after the Niumi mansa made several appeals and pledged the safety of factors did André Brüe reopen the factory at Albreda in March 1718 (Cultru 1910, 175; Gray 1940, 155–57).

In May 1719, the English pirate Edward England raided the Gambia River and captured five vessels belonging to private traders and a sloop belonging to the Royal African Company. Another English pirate, Howel Davis, followed soon after, pillaged James Fort, and persuaded seven of the fourteen men at the garrison to sail with him (Gray 1940, 158–59). These losses caused the directors of the Royal African Company to institute a new regime in 1720, appointing Col. Thomas Whitney as governor and dispatching some 170 persons to the Gambia. After receiving gifts, the Niumi ruler expressed his willingness to have the company construct a fort at Juffure, but Whitney decided to rebuild James Fort instead. The large contingent of people sent to the Gambia experienced grievous losses: many died, including 19 of the 23 women and children, and some deserted to become pirates. Within a year, only 26 of the original 170 were left (Gray 1940, 160–71; Curtin 1975, 113).

Esperança (Hope) continued to be an invaluable ally for agents of the Royal African Company. Almost surely, she was the "Duchess" who "commanded" the village of Juffure and was credited in 1721 with giving "all possible Assistance" to the company's factory, doubtless much to her own advantage (Atkins 1735/1970, 57). Esperança's circumstances improved in 1723 with the arrival of Robert Plunkett as chief agent, previously the company's chief agent at Bunce Island. In November 1725, when James Fort's powder magazine blew up, killing Plunkett and ten other Englishmen, Esperança lost a leg. She was for ten years afterward paid a pension by the company because of her association with Plunkett (Gray 1940, 181, 191; Wright 1976, 190). What her associations may have been with other chief agents of the Royal African Company is not known, but the fact that four of them sought alliances with her attests to the surpassing role she and other nharas exercised in Gambian commerce. There is an intriguing postscript to this story. During the 1730s, the Royal African Company gave presents to a "Sra. England" living at Sika, some eight kilometers upriver from Albreda, including a contribution to repair her dwelling before the onset of the rainy season (Wright 1976,: 200, n. 39). Might "Sra. England" have been Esperança's daughter, who was born in England?

Another individual with influence concerning Niumi's ruler was Diogo Gomes, head slave of Mansa Alimaranta Sonko, who traded on his master's behalf. Following the mansa's death in 1725, Gomes continued to reside in the ruler's village of Essau and became a prosperous independent trader, doing business both with the French at Albreda and with the factors of the Royal African Company on James Island. According to Donald Wright, in 1730 the Royal African Company advanced Gomes goods for the trade season, to be repaid in slaves. Between 1733 and 1735 the company made three separate gifts to him, two more to his head wife, Sra Hannah Rodriguez of Juffure, one to help her get her crops planted and the other to his daughters. Yet, despite Gomes's prosperity, his *jongo* (slave) status did not change. A decade after Alimaranta Sonko's death, company accounts continue to refer to him as "the late King of Barra's head slave" (Wright 1976, 191; 1997, 124; 1999, 422).

Gomes's antecedents are uncertain. Possibly, he was the child of a Portuguese or Luso-African man and the female slave of a mansa, thereby being a *mansajong* by birth (Boulègue 1972, 67, cited in Wright 1976, 190). His wife Hannah Rodriguez had lived in Juffure while married to John Dias, a company linguist. When Dias died in 1734, the company gave her gifts (Wright 1976, 189). Wright described the challenges of delineating Luso-African relationships: "For every entry of gifts to 'Sra. Terezia Giar, wife of Valentine Mendez,' or to 'the Senhoras of Niumi on their going to the cry [wake] of Sr. Antonio Vos,' an obscure company writer recorded twenty more gifts to Eurafricans without including any suggestions as to their relations, their position in Gambian society, or their place of residence" (Wright 1976, 195–96).

A brief communication to the Royal African Company in June 1721 from the two chief traders—Henry Glynne (who had previously been a company employee and was later a private trader in Sherbro) and William Ramsey—was insightful concerning the role of Luso-African middlemen. Glynne and Ramsey reported that they had sold slaves to vessels from Bristol and the West Indies for fifty-five bars each, having purchased them from "Merchants" (meaning African traders) for thirty bars. They added, "Since [then we] have paid the Customary price of 40 Barrs per head of the Portuguese and lend 'em goods to trade with the Merchants" (Donnan 1930/1969, 2:283; Gray 1940, 161–62). Left unexplained is why Glynne and Ramsey advanced goods on credit to Luso-African middlemen instead of purchasing slaves upriver from African traders at significantly lower prices. From what was related thereafter, it seems that company factors found it prudent and personally more remunerative to accommodate to the interests of Niumi's rulers and Luso-African intermediaries.

Glynne, Ramsey, and other English factors used the term *merchants* to denominate African traders. The term derives from the Portuguese *mercador* (retail merchant, tradesman), which was Luso-African usage for a Mandinka *juula* (trader). English for a time used *mercadores* but then adopted the word *merchants,* expanding its usage to designate the Mande area extending eastward from the Gambia River as "the merchants' country" (Curtin 1975, 81). William Smith, a surveyor employed by the Royal African Company who visited the Gambia in 1726, acknowledged the importance of the Luso-Africans as middlemen but denigrated them as well: "This place was first discover'd and settled by the *Portuguese,* whose Progeny are still pretty numerous up in the Inland Country, and drive a very good Trade with the *English.* Tho,' to speak Truth, there is but little of the *Portuguese* to be found in them, beside the Language, being quite degenerated into Negroes, and having but very imperfect Ideas of Christianity. They think themselves sufficiently qualified for the Title of *Boon Christians,* if they distinguish themselves from the *Pagans,* &c. by wearing a little Crucifix about their Necks" (W. Smith 1744/1967, 25).

In 1722, the alcaide of Bintang permitted the Royal African Company to establish a factory, thereby granting English traders access to the Banyun trade route linking Ziguinchor and Cacheu. An attempt to open trade with Foni miscarried when a Luso-African dispatched with a present of brandy for the ruler, Faran Antony, found that the man had recently suffered a costly defeat in a conflict with Diolas, including the loss of nine members of his family. Not until sometime later did Foni's ruler permit the company to establish a factory at Brefet, the head of the Banyun trade route linking the Gambian River and the Casamance River. In the meantime, Royal African Company agents expanded trade southward, dispatching vessels to Cacheu, Bissau, and the Casamance and Nunez Rivers (Gray 1940, 178–79, 194; Donnan 1930/1969, 2:316).

Competition between the Royal African Company and the Compagnie du Sénégal escalated to conflict in December 1723 when the French factor at Albreda attempted to travel upriver to trade at Tankular in the Mandinka state of Kiang and Englishmen seized his canoa. Two months later, in February 1724, when the Royal African Company attempted to reestablish a factory at Portudal on the Petite Côte, Frenchmen seized a sloop. The vessel was subsequently released, but the Royal African Company drove French traders from Albreda and Bintang. In retaliation, a French warship sporadically fired on James Island for several weeks during September and plundered the Royal African Company's factories at Bintang and Brefet—but not at Geregia, where the Banyun ruler defended the premises (Gray 1940, 189–90).

Subsequently, agents for both companies negotiated an end to hostilities. English factors resumed trading at Portudal and Joal, and French factors returned to Albreda but not to Bintang, for from then on, the English prevented French vessels from passing upriver past James Island (Gray 1940, 193–94, 207–8). As Philip Curtin astutely observed, this situation created a natural alliance between French traders and Luso-Africans, the latter serving as an extension of the French trade diaspora into the interior. The Royal African Company, for its part, reversed its policy of paying premium prices to Luso-Africans, instead paying them 25 percent less than African traders (Curtin 1975, 100).

In 1726, the Rhode Island–built sloop *Ark*, under Captain Edmonson, was captured in the Gambia River, the last pirate vessel to threaten shipping in Senegambia (W. Smith 1744/1967, 10–12; Gray 1940, 194). With the upper reaches of the Gambia River closed to European rivals and with vessels engaged in coastwise trade safe from piratical craft, the following years were generally prosperous for the Royal African Company. Gov. Antony Rogers (1729–33) established a large number of out-factories along the Gambia River, even as far upriver as Fattatenda in the Mandinka state of Wuli on the north bank, and promoted trade at Portudal on the Petite Côte, in the Casamance River, and at Cacheu and Bissau. Rogers was suspected but not charged in the embezzlement of company goods for private trade in association with a "Senhora Angela." The company's directors promoted wax trade, sending out a London chandler named Joseph Bick in 1730 to refine beeswax prior to shipping (Gray 1940, 206–8). Thriving trade continued during the governorships of Richard Hull (1733–37) and Charles Orfeur (1737–45).

Niumi mansas enforced their privileges and prerogatives. The Royal African

Company paid annual customs to mansas for James Fort and the subfactories at Juffure and Colar, and most private traders entering the river paid some 120 bars in customs on the threat that they would be denied wood and water. Niumi's mansa also "made it no less than Slavery for any of his Subjects to serve as Linguisters on Board of any Vessels, but what pay his Customs and trade in his Country" (Moore 1738, 20–21, 67). Customs charged English traders almost quadrupled in the century after 1665, and, in addition, mansas extorted presents during their visits to James Island and by taking company employees hostage.

During the 1720s and 1730s, the Royal African Company employed numerous Luso-Africans. In 1729, for example, five of its seven linguists and messengers were Luso-Africans. In 1734, the company hired Philip Gomez, Emmanuel Vos (Vaz), and Barnaby Lopez to reside in villages in Niumi in order to purchase food for the residents of James Fort and to provision vessels. A Franco-African named Lemaigne was in charge of a factory upriver (Wright 1976, 189; rept1997, 123, 128). Seemingly, the influence of Luso-Africans was so pervasive during this era that employees of the Royal African Company accorded the titles "senhor" and "senhora" to Africans with whom they associated in commerce. This practice apparently explained the case of a "country [African] trader" whom Daniel Pepper, the demented chief agent, wounded with a sword at James Fort in 1729; the injured man was titled "Senor Alexander Jelloiff [Jolof-Wolof]" (Gray 1940, 205).

Two of the Luso-African daughters of the Portuguese trader António de Aguiar, mentioned in chapter 5, were prominent nharas residing in Sika, Juffure, and Albreda during the 1730s. Senhora Bring (Catarina?) Giar was a wife of Mansa Dusu Koli Sonko (r. 1727–36), who lived in Berending. She was mentioned in Royal African Company records as receiving gifts on several occasions. Senhora Terezia Giar was married to the Luso-African trader Valentine Mendez, who was characterized in 1731 as "the only brisk trader in the River" (Wright 1976, 193). Mendez regularly dispatched grumetes to the salt pans along the Atlantic coast north of Niumi, and he negotiated contracts with the Royal African Company to supply slaves, ivory, and gold at set prices. Prior to his death in 1738, he lived at Wallia in Niani and managed the company's factory at the Sami River, a tributary of the Gambia River that linked trade routes connecting the upper Senegal River (Wright 1976, 193–94; Galloway 1974, map on p. 331a).

In addition to Valentine Mendez, Wright identified two other prominent Luso-African traders named Mendez who were living in the 1730s and whose kinship affiliations are problematic. Simon Mendez was of such consequence in Niumi that he received gifts from the Royal African Company on five occasions in 1734. Bordering Niumi to the north and east was Saluum, where Luso-

Africans had exercised prominent roles in commerce for centuries. These included Tomba Mendez, son of a former bur of Saluum and a Luso-African woman, who lived at Joar, 160 kilometers upriver from Juffure, where his cousin was the *boumi,* a subordinate official of the reigning bur (Gray 1940, 14 n. 5; Wright 1976, 194).

Francis Moore, who arrived in the Gambia in November 1730, was first employed as a "writer" (that is, a clerk) and then worked as a factor trading along the Gambia River until his departure for England in May 1735. Three years later, he published a wonderfully informative account of his experiences. Moore identified the most important Luso-African communities along the Gambia as Sika ("Seaca") in Niumi, Tankular ("Tancrewall") in Kiang, and Geregia in Jagra. All three settlements had churches that were visited twice yearly by priests from São Tiago—in contrast to the situation in Coelho's time a century earlier, when there were no churches along the Gambia River and when priests from Cacheu visited at "wickedly long intervals" (Hair 1985, chap. 2: 32).

Cabo Verde–Gambian links were extensive during Moore's era. For instance, the Royal African Company dispatched vessels to the archipelago for salt, which was sold profitably along the Gambia River. In 1730, a company vessel carried artisans from São Tiago to repair James Fort, and mares from Cabo Verde were highly prized by Mandinka living along the Gambia, since Wolof horse dealers refused to sell mares. In 1733, when the inhabitants of São Tiago were afflicted by drought conditions, the Royal African Company bartered a schooner load of grain for goatskins, one of the archipelago's premium exports. Portuguese vessels were also occasionally permitted to visit the Gambia to exchange salt for lime (Moore 1738, 47–49, 55, 59, 63). Clandestine trade in panos, wine, aguardente, and other Cabo Verdean products was not mentioned but was very likely to have been pursued. The sale of panos to foreigners was expressly prohibited by a royal order in 1700, and the sentence for breaking the law was elevated to a death penalty by a judicial writ in 1721 (Carreira 1968, 43–44).

Commercial exchanges between Cabo Verde and the Gambia during these years served to reinforce Luso-African social links and cultural patterns. So did the Royal African Company's commercial links with the Casamance and its coastwise trade with Cacheu and Bissau. Indicative of English-Portuguese relations in this period, Moore related that, in 1731, a merchant at Cacheu named Mr. Verman (Vermão?) traveled overland to Geregia in Jagra and thence by water to James Fort to confer with the company's chief agent. English vessels transported so many cargoes of young slaves to Lisbon and Cádiz that the price of boys and girls was driven up and became almost equal to that of adults (Moore 1738, 45, 67, 78, 89).

Moore characterized Crioulo as the second most important language along the Gambia, after Mandinka:

> The most general Language is *Mundingoe* by which Name the Country and People are call'd; If you can speak that Language, you may travel from the River's Mouth up to the Country of *Joncoes* (alias Merchants;) so call'd from their buying every Year a vast Number of Slaves there, and bringing them down to the lower Parts of this River to sell to the White People. . . . The next Language mostly us'd here is call'd *Creole Portuguese,* a bastard Sort of *Portuguese,* scarce understood in *Lisbon;* but it is sooner learnt by *Englishmen* than any other Language in this River, and is always spoken by the Linguists, which serve both the separate Traders and the Company. The two foregoing Languages I learnt whilst in the River. (Moore 1738, 38–39)

Regarding Luso-Africans living along the Gambia, Moore appreciated the significance of the twice-yearly pastoral visits paid by Cabo Verdean priests: "[Portuguese] have cohabited with the *Mundingoes,* till they are now very near as Black as they are; but as they still retain a sort of a bastard *Portuguese* Language call'd *Creole,* and as they christen and marry by the Help of a Priest sent yearly over hither from *S. Jago,* one of the *Cape de Verd* Islands, they reckon themselves still as well as if they were actually White, and nothing angers them more than to call them *Negroes,* that being a Term they use only for Slaves, and their not understanding the true Meaning of the Word is the Reason of their being so very much affronted at it" (Moore 1738, 29).

Like the Luso-Africans, Royal African Company traders established in factories upriver lived under the supervision and protection of African landlords known either as *Toubaubo Mansas* (white man's kings) or, more generally, as *Alcades*—the latter name testifying to the progressive spread of Islam along the Gambia. Moore commented, "If a Factor does not take Care to keep in with the Alcade, he will seldom or never get Things done as they ought to be. The Alcade's is a very beneficial Place, for both the Company and separate Traders pay a Custom for every Slave they buy, sometimes one Barr per Head, sometimes not so much, but that is according to the Place you are at" (Moore 1738, 128).

Moore evocatively recounted the socially corrosive consequences of the intensification of the slave trade, most insidiously that any crime—even the most trifling of offenses—might be punished by enslavement. A man in Tumana along the south bank of the upper Gambia, for instance, was offered for sale because he had stolen a tobacco pipe. In the neighboring state of Cantora, also part of the Kaabu Empire, a man who had accidentally killed another while firing at a wild animal was condemned to enslavement by the mansa, as were his mother, three brothers, and three sisters. The Bur Saluum was notorious for capturing the inhabitants of his own state. Moore expressed admiration for Fula, who, in contrast to Mandinka, would redeem any one of their number who was captured and enslaved (Moore 1738, 32–33, 42, 66).

The foregoing notwithstanding, social norms along the Gambia protected domestic slaves from arbitrary sale into the Atlantic slave trade. Moore wrote: "Tho' in some Parts of *Africa* they sell their Slaves born in the Family, yet in the River *Gambia* they think it a very wicked thing; and I never heard of but one that ever sold a Family-Slave, except for such Crimes as would have made them to be sold had they been free. If there are many Family-Slaves, and one of them commits a Crime, the Master cannot sell him without the joint Consent of the rest; for if he does, they will all run away, and be protected by the next Kingdom, to which they fly" (Moore 1738, 43).

The corruption of judicial processes was exacerbated by the consequences of the droughts that caused bad harvests in 1729 and several years thereafter (Moore 1738, 75; Curtin 1975, app. 1: 4; Becker 1985, 169). The shortage of provisions was so acute that, in June 1736, factors at James Fort dispatched 113 slaves to South Carolina on the vessel of an independent trader, for otherwise "[they] must have perished, for it was with the greatest difficulty that we with short allowance could feed them and the Castle Slaves" (Littlefield 1981, 49–50). Agents of the Royal African Company were held to the same obligations for castle slaves as Gambian slaveholders were for their domestic slaves. Occasionally, castle slaves were exchanged with slaves from the Gold Coast to diminish the likelihood of escape (Curtin 1975, 115).

Moore discussed the chief centers of Luso-African trade. Siaka in Niumi had a church, and along with Geregia and Tancrowall, it was visited twice yearly by a priest from São Tiago (Moore 1738, 55). Bintang on Vintang Creek was the chief market in the Banyun state of Foni, where Luso-Africans and Mandinka were the principal traders. The latter had constructed a "handsome mosque" with an ostrich egg on the roof spire. In December 1730, the Royal African Company established a factory at Bintang to purchase beeswax and provisions (Moore 1738, 53, 74). Though acephalous, the Diola ("Floops") of Foni had devised effective means of defending themselves from Mandinka slave raiding: "In the Empire of *Fonia,* and but a little Way inland are a Sort of People call'd *Floops,* who are in a manner wild: They border close to the *Mundingoes,* and are bitter Enemies to each other. Their Country is of a vast Extent, but they have no King among them, each of their Towns being fortified with Sticks drove all round, and filled up with Clay: They are independant of each other, and under the Government of no one Chief; notwithstanding which, they unite so firmly, that all the Force of the *Mundingoes* (tho' so very numerous) cannot get the better of them" (Moore 1738, 35–36). A growth in Diola populations during the eighteenth and nineteenth centuries was indicated by Diola groups settling progressively eastward between the Gambia and Casamance Rivers.

Geregia, the principal market in Jagra, was two dozen kilometers along the twisting loops of Vintang Creek on the south bank at the head of the portage connecting the Songrougrou River. Moore described the Luso-Africans at Geregia as "very civil," as they were elsewhere along the Gambia. By contrast, he characterized the Banyun as "scarcely civilized," an opinion perhaps related to the incident in 1736 when the Banyun ruler seized a priest, who had to be ransomed by the Royal African Company. Previously, priests had visited James Island in 1733 and 1735 (Moore 1738, 51–52; Gray 1940, 14 n. 1). The company's factor at Geregia purchased cotton and great quantities of beeswax, much of which was from Cacheu, some three days' travel away. Company vessels were also sent to Cacheu by sea, though wax obtained at Cacheu was sometimes so adulterated as to entail a 20 to 30 percent loss (Moore 1738, 66).

The Royal African Company's factory at Geregia must be accounted a notable success, for João Carvalho, the capitão-mor of Cacheu, complained to the Conselho Ultramarino in August 1734 that traders at Ziguinchor were traveling to the Gambia, instead of trading at Cacheu. The council's feckless response, almost two years later, was to issue an edict forbidding such trade (Rodney 1970, 162). Eight years later, in 1744 , Chief Agent Charles Orfeur dispatched an Armenian named Melchior de Jaspas on an overland reconnaissance to Cacheu, but nothing was recorded about his journey. De Jaspas knew Arabic and had been hired by the company a decade earlier to accompany Ayuba Suleiman Diallo/Job ben Solomon to Bundu after his manumission in England. De Jaspas was killed the following year along with Governor Orfeur in a quarrel with the people of Niumi (Gray 1940, 210–13; Curtin 1967, 32–33).

Tankular in the Mandinka state of Kiang was an important market for caravans traveling along the south bank of the Gambia River, as well as the northern terminus of a trade route that connected the Gambia and the Futa Jallon via Mandinka markets at Sédhiou on the middle Casamance River, Farim on the upper Cacheu River, and Geba on the Geba River. Tankular consisted of two settlements, one Mandinka and the other comprising "a great many" Luso-Africans. The former lived in round dwellings, the latter in "square large houses." There was a church, and when a priest made one of the twice-annual visits, he said mass almost daily (Moore 1738, 50–51). Tankular's Luso-Africans sent craft upriver to trade once or twice yearly, "by which means," Moore commented, "they have made this Town a Place of great Resort, and the richest in the whole River." Foremost among the Luso-Africans was António Vaz (Moore 1738, 49–51):

> [Vaz] is reckon'd to be worth 10,000l. Sterling, and has got a vast Number of House-Slaves, (*viz.* Slaves which live with him as Servants, a Grandeur much used both by the *Portuguese* and *Spaniards*) which he keeps for Service and Breed, and are esteemed by him almost as much as his own Children. And as he has got a great many Canoas, he sends his own Men-Slaves with them to all Ports of Trade up the River, and by that Means engrosses a great deal of Trade; insomuch that he has commonly a great many Slaves, and good Quantities of Elephants Teeth and Bees-Wax by him, with which he turns a Penny with the separate Shipping, and is well skilled in his Way of bartering, he being thoroughly Master of the prime Cost, in *England,* of all sorts of Goods, taking always care to keep his Warehouse well stocked with Goods, and has the upperhand vastly of some of his Neighbours, who are sometimes obliged to stand still half a Year together for want of Goods to trade with. (Moore 1738, 50)

António Vaz's alleged (and perhaps much exaggerated) wealth begs comparison with the annual salaries of the Royal African Company's chief agent (200 pounds sterling) and factors (40 pounds), as well as the soldiers of the James Fort garrison (13 pounds) (Curtin 1975, 100). Of crucial importance to António Vaz's commercial success, evidently, was the fact that he was related to the Banyun ruler of Foni, a relationship that possibly dated to the time of Manuel Vas de Franco, the Portuguese representative in the Gambia River in the 1660s (Gray 1940, 14 n. 5, 78–79). He was reportedly a nephew of Bibiana Vaz, who lived in Niumi and had been fined for taking part in a revolt against the capitão-mor of Cacheu in 1684 . He was also probably related to Emmanuel Vos, who lived in Sika, and Chequo Vas, who persuaded the inhabitants of Cassan in Niani to attack a New England schooner in 1732 (Rodney 1970, 211, 215; Wright 1976, 195; Moore 1738, 102, 112–13). Wright speculated that António Vaz likely had kinship ties with the mansas of Kiang and Niumi. When Vaz died in 1736, Niumi's mansa and the company factor at James Island sent gifts to accompany a host of nharas who went to Tankular for the "cry" (wake; adopted from the Portuguese word *chorar*) (Wright 1976, 195–96). Perhaps due to the declining fortunes of Banyun in Jagra and Foni, which will be discussed in chapter 9, Vaz's relatives subsequently lost influence.

Moore's remarks concerning European males' relationships with Mandinka women along the Gambia River were generalized, without regard to the women's social standing. He noted that Luso-African women negotiated for marriages country-style:

> The Girls would have People think they are very modest, especially when they are in Company; but take them by themselves, and they are very obliging; for if you will give them a little Coral, or a Silk Handkerchief, you may take what Liberty you please with them: But those who pretend to be of the *Portuguese* Religion, and therefore call themselves Christians, they indeed are somewhat more reserved than the *Mundingoes* are. But notwithstanding their Religion and Christianity too, if any White Man has a Fancy to any of them, and is able to maintain them, they will make no Scruple of living with him in the Nature of a Wife, without the Ceremony of Matrimony. (Moore 1738, 121)

Left unstated were the multiple advantages of having Luso-African wives who could serve as interpreters, informants, and traders.

The 1730s marked a transition in Niumi and perhaps elsewhere along the Gambia River, as Muslims began to rival Luso-Africans for influence with rulers and elites. Wright explained:

> One can recognize the importance of Muslims in the trade of the lower Gambia in the 1730s from examination of records from James Island listing gifts and payments rendered in hopes of facilitating English trade. A portion of the Royal African Company's largess went to "Oil for the Mahometans," to the "Great Mohamedan priest of Sika, on having lost his slippers," and to the "great priest's son that is with the King." The same records show that Muslim clerics were retained by Niumi's rulers and most prominent traders to work as advisers and protectors: Company payments go to "Seca Scaroe, Bushreen [marabout] of Niumi," to "Bram Bojan to go to the great Priests to get their opinion for the best place for the new King of Niumi to make his town," and to "the Bishreen attendants of Sr. Antonio Vas." (Wright 1997, 125)

Power broker that he was, António Vas was not behind the times!

In Niumi and other places along the Gambia River where the two groups contended for influence, Muslims had significant advantages over Luso-Africans, who were accorded a marginal social status by Mandinka elites. Muslims who contracted marriages with Mandinka elites shed their stranger status, enabling their children to inherit their property. Competing for souls, marabouts offered protective charms comprising passages from the Koran encased in leather packets. These items were similar to the amulets that western Africans had long used, but Christian crucifixes and rosaries were not. Along the Gambia River and elsewhere, Luso-Africans contended with insurmountable difficulties. Of crucial importance, no Luso-Africans were trained and consecrated as priests. Consequently, their communities lacked educated religious leaders who could teach children reading and writing, inculcate and reinforce Catholic beliefs and practices, and contest Muslim marabouts concerning religious doctrines and things miraculous. Cabo Verdean priests were short-term, fee-taking visitors to the Gambia who contributed little to Luso-African communities besides saying mass, baptizing newborns, and, rarely, consecrating marriages and conducting funerals. Luso-Africans along the Gambia were bereft of literacy, bibles, religious literature, and, most important, resident clergy to champion their causes like the redoubtable Jesuits who, during the first decades of the seventeenth century, contested marabouts for souls and for influence with African elites.

Another disability for Luso-Africans was the insidious circumstance that the majority of Europeans trading along the Gambia were Protestant English who denigrated and demonized Luso-Africans' Catholic beliefs and disparaged their assertions that they were "Portuguese" and "whites." Frenchmen at Albreda provided some support for Luso-African coreligionists while depreciating the paucity of their knowledge of Catholicism and disdaining to accept them as fellow "Europeans." Thus, the Luso-African "identity" was both contested and defined by others. Along the Gambia and elsewhere, elites in stratified societies denied Luso-Africans the status of free persons and refused to allow them to become integrated into their groups. Refused acceptance by African groups, disparaged by Protestant Europeans, bereft of the advantages of resident Catholic clergy, Luso-Africans nonetheless stubbornly asserted that they were "Portuguese" and "whites" and displayed European garments, crucifixes, rosaries, dwellings, furniture, cuisine, and other cultural manifestations that set them apart from Africans.

In 1740, Gov. Charles Orfeur and Peter Felix David of the Compagnie du Sénégal negotiated a ten-year agreement to exchange slaves for gum that included a clause calling for neutrality in the event of war. This agreement was honored by both parties following the outbreak of the War of the Austrian Succession (1743–48)—but not by two vessels of the British navy that captured a French sloop and pillaged Albreda in May and June 1745. Orfeur was murdered later the same year by subjects of the mansa of Niumi, though whether or not this was in retaliation is unknown. Albreda was reoccupied by French factors in 1748 after the ratification of the Treaty of Aix-la-Chapelle (Gray 1940, 208–9, 213).

Niumi's mansas constantly played English and French factors against each other. As James Skinner complained in 1752: "The King of Barra comes 2–3 times each month to the Fort & demands spirits &c, which we always give him expecting he would turn the French out of the river, according to his promise. Instead he told the French at Albreda of his plan & likewise got more from them." When Skinner refused the mansa hospitality on his next visit, the ruler retaliated by seizing an Englishman and extorting five kegs of rum as ransom (Wright 1976, 251; 1997, 116). During 1754 and 1755, English and French traders competing for the trade of Niumi and Saluum engaged in hostilities, in the course of which the French comptoir at Albreda was burned in October 1755. Negotiations between Skinner and Estoupan de Saint-Jean, the French commandant on Gorée, achieved a return to the status quo before the outbreak of the Seven Years' War in 1756 (Machat 1906a, 103; Gray 1940, 224–27).

One Luso-African who prospered during the 1750s was Senhora Llena (Helena) of Juffure, who hired out grumetes and domestic slaves to European vessels to serve as sailors and linguists. Llena capitalized on her kinship affiliations, being a wife of Haly Sonko, a brother of Niumi's next mansa (Wright 1976, 182–83; 1997, 123). Due to the high death rates among European sailors, grumetes and linguists were essential for vessels trading upriver. Pruneau de Pommegorge, whose experience in western Africa extended from the 1740s to the 1760s, said that not a year passed without some English vessel losing an entire crew in the Gambia River (Pruneau de Pommegorge 1789, 89).

During the 1750s, English traders based in American ports carried on a growing commerce with western Africa. In 1752, a Rhode Island sloop owned by Robert Crook and commanded by William Brown loaded a cargo of slaves in the Sherbro River. The following year, Captain Brown sailed to Cacheu. Nicholas Owen related that Brown obtained a pilot to cross the dangerous bar and afterward moored close to the town, under the walls of the fort. Capitão-Mor Francisco Roque Sottomayor leased the vessel for 322 *moidores* (gold coins) to transport forty slaves and several tons of beeswax to Lisbon. The vessel returned to Cacheu with, remarkable to relate, forty soldiers whose accommodations can only be imagined. Subsequently, a leading Cabo Verdean trader, Pedro da Costa, leased the sloop to carry his slaves and entourage to São Tiago. Costa had lived in exile for fifteen years after killing a man but could now return home, having made his fortune (E. Martin 1930, 29, 32–35).

Captain Brown purchased panos in Cabo Verde and sailed to the Sherbro River, where he traded for a cargo of slaves; after selling the slaves in Barbados, he returned to Rhode Island with a cargo of rum. Owen recorded that a pano purchased in Cabo Verde for "3 bars or crowns" was worth 10 or 12 in western Africa (E. Martin 1930, 35–37). The following year, Owen participated in another voyage to Cabo Verde on a sloop belonging to Richard Hall, an English trader who had settled on York Island in Sherbro after spending almost four years in African captivity in the Bissagos Islands. Hall's sloop was principally manned by grumetes, who were paid wages of no more than two crowns/bars a month. En route to the Sherbro, Captain Hall sold panos to traders in the Sierra Leone estuary and the Plantain Islands (E. Martin 1930, 38–45). Portuguese officials profiting from prohibited trade enabled foreigners to compete against Cape Verdeans and Luso-Africans in markets they had previously monopolized. Sales of panos were monitored more closely during the era of the Companhia Geral do Grão-Pará e Maranhão (1755–77). So also was trade at the praças in Guinea. In 1755, when an English vessel from Barbados navigated the Casamance River to Ziguinchor without taking on a pilot—something Portuguese vessels always did—the navigational feat only added to the asperity of the dispatch written by Cacheu's capitão-mor, Francisco Roque Sottomayor (Rodney 1970, 242).

Geba-Grande, 1710s–1750s

During the half century following the 1701 abandonment of the fort built at Bissau by the second Cacheu company, French traders acquired most of the slaves sold in the Geba-Grande area. Nonetheless, Papel and Luso-Africans prevented the Compagnie du Sénégal from building a fort at Bissau and drove away French factors who established comptoirs. Portuguese interests in the Geba-Grande area were delegated to Luso-African traders living at Bissau and accorded the title *cabos de esquarda* (infantry squad leaders) under the (nominal) authority of the capitão-mor of Cacheu (Barreto 1938, 150; Rodney 1970, 244–45).

Following the War of the Spanish Succession (1702–13), André Brüe, who directed the Compagnie du Sénégal from 1714 to 1720, established a comptoir at Bissau. After trading for several years, the factor Pierre Mascon was beset by difficulties. In June 1720, he reported that the ruler and inhabitants stole goods belonging to the company, verbally abused him, and compelled him to pay whatever they demanded. When he lacked the merchandise they wanted, they took twice what they were owed, breaking open his storage chests and flinging the contents around the factory. Mascon asked to be relieved of his post until the company fortified the comptoir and provided a greater variety of merchandise (Sainville 1972, 68–70; Hall 1992, 33). What seems likely is that Luso-African traders colluded with Papel to dislodge a rival supplied by a well-funded company.

The governors of the Compagnie du Sénégal decided to construct a fortified comptoir at Bissau. However, when the expedition arrived in Senegal in February 1724, Julien Dubellay, the company's director from 1722 to 1725, canceled the project. According to one report, the capitão-mor of Cacheu had dispatched forty men to Bissau to assist the inhabitants in opposing the construction of a fort, and Dubellay was concerned about repercussions from the government of Portugal (Boulègue 1996, 94–95). In the circumstances, Bolama was considered as an alternative to Bissau. The island's strategic location in relation to the Geba and Grande Rivers had attracted the attention of many traders over the centuries. In 1724, proponents argued that a comptoir on Bolama would dominate Geba River commerce, attracting Luso-Africans to French protection and away from the oppressive Papel ruler of Bissau who "treat[ed] them like slaves." An additional consideration was that plantations on Bolama could produce sugar, cotton, cacao, tobacco, and anatta dye, as well as crops to feed slaves (Boulègue 1996, 95–97, 104).

Dubellay's successor, Nicolas Despres de Saint-Robert (who had the post in 1725), selected Rolland de la Combe to head the proposed comptoir on Bolama. De la Combe was an independent trader living at Geba who visited Bissau and other markets in his sixty-ton vessel. He had lived at Geba and Bissau for more than twenty years and was married to a (Luso-African?) woman with whom he had children. The Bolama project came to naught in June 1725, when the vessel dispatched on a reconnaissance mission was wrecked south of Cape Roxo. The crew were rescued and taken to Bissau, where the vessel's captain recorded the community's hostility to the idea of the French constructing a fort at Bissau. Captain Delorme was told that there were at least two hundred well-armed Luso-Africans at Bissau, not counting the Papel and "creolized" Africans, and his informants boasted that the French would have to kill all of them before they could construct a fort (Boulègue 1996, 100–101 n. 29). In the aftermath of the shipwreck, Captain Delorme quit the company's service and became an independent trader at Geba (Boulègue 1996, 101).

Setbacks ashore notwithstanding, the Compagnie du Sénégal aggressively pursued ship-borne trade in the Geba-Grande area. In 1731, the captain of one of the company's vessels, impatient to depart before the onset of the rainy season, outfitted thirty-eight pirogues carrying eight hundred men to raid the Bissagos

Islands and the Biafada along the Grande River (Mettas 1975, 354). Doubtless, Luso-Africans contributed many of the pirogues and fighting men.

Bijago captives were not highly prized by slavers. Numerous sources testified to the difficulties of holding Bijago warriors as prisoners awaiting shipment, of their fomenting rebellions aboard slave vessels, and of their suicides in the Americas, the latter promoted by the belief that their spirits would return home (Rodney 1970, 109–10; Mettas 1975, 354, 358).

Papel refused to concede a trade monopoly to any nation, and their demands and impositions became so unbearable to French traders established at Bissau in 1736 that the Frenchmen abandoned the comptoir, asserting that they would no longer remain "slaves of the people of the country" (Mettas 1975, 349). The Compagnie du Sénégal subsequently dispatched vessels from Senegal to engage in commerce along the rivers and islands of the Geba-Grande area during the trading season from November to May. Papel, Bijago, and Biafada were incited to raid each other's communities in war craft that carried fifty to sixty "extremely savage" warriors, and the French paid higher prices than their competitors for captives taken in these forays (Pruneau de Pommegorge 1789, 132–34; Rodney 1970, 244).

The Compagnie du Sénégal dominated European trade in the Geba-Grande area until the outbreak of the War of the Austrian Succession disrupted French and English commerce with western Africa. Seizing on this opportunity, Portuguese merchants lobbied the government to take new initiatives in western African trade. Portuguese commerce at Bissau improved significantly due to Luso-African influence and missionary blandishments, and in 1748, the Conselho Ultramarino was informed that the ruler of Bissau wished to be converted, that he desired new clothing, and that he was willing to have a fort constructed. Proponents of a new company to supply slaves to Brazil extravagantly claimed that English traders operating from Serra Leoa had obtained a thousand slaves at Bissau during the first five months of 1748. Nonetheless, the Conselho Ultramarino delayed action, and it was not until the accession of King José I (1750–77) and the appointment of the Marquis de Pombal as chief minister that new initiatives were undertaken concerning African trade and that Bissau's ruler received the gifts recommended a six years earlier by the capitão-mor of Cacheu (Barcellos 1899–1913, 3:3; Barreto 1938, 150; Rodney 1970, 244, 250).

In 1752, the cabo de esquarda at Bissau began preparations for the construction of a fort. The next year, the commandant of Cacheu, Francisco Roque Sottomayor, hoisted a Portuguese flag on Bolama and erected a *padrão* (stone marker) to confirm Portuguese sovereignty over the island (Rodney 1970, 244–

45; Barcellos 1899–1913, 4:252, 6:217–18; Hair 1996, 36 n. 24). Portuguese imperial initiatives were seconded by missionary endeavors. In 1752 (?), a Portuguese friar supposedly persuaded José Lopez, known as "King of Serra Leoa," to donate his alleged domain to the Portuguese Crown. No western African ruler possessed the authority to make such a cession of territory, and the archaic feudal gesture was inconsequential regarding both African landlords and Portugal's European rivals (Barcellos 1899–1913, 4:252; Iria 1964, 116; Hair 1996, 36–37 n. 24, 1997b, 9, and 2000c, 418–22).

A frigate carrying men and material to construct the new fort arrived at Bissau in February 1753, having stopped in Cabo Verde while en route to load additional laborers and soldiers. At first, Papel welcomed the members of the expedition, but when their purpose became evident, mistrust escalated to conflict. The warship's cannons inflicted numerous casualties, and Papel were compelled to cease hostilities. Reflecting Portugal's expanding economic ties with England, some of the supplies dispatched by the Conselho Ultramarino were transported in English vessels (Rodney 1970, 242, 242, 245).

Named to honor the Portuguese ruler, the Praça of São José de Bissau was sited on Intim territory, with Antula extending to the east and north and Bandim to the west and south. Crucial to Papel-Portuguese relations for two centuries to come, this praça had the same weakness as the praça at Cacheu and the English fort on James Island: African landlords controlled the Pidgiguiti Spring hundreds of meters west of the fort, the chief source of potable water along the brackish Geba estuary. During the 1750s, there was halting progress on the fort and a steady attrition of soldiers and laborers—the former comprising the dregs of the Portuguese army, the latter recruited in the Cape Verde Islands. The refusal of Papel to provide labor or foodstuffs contributed to the escalating human and financial costs of the project (Barreto 1938, 150–52; Rodney 1970, 245–47). Meanwhile, French trade continued in the Geba-Grande area. Estoupan Saint-Jean, the French commandant of Gorée during the 1750s, visited Bolama several times and endeavored to persuade the Compagnie du Sénégal to found a comptoir (Wadstrom 1794–95/1968, part 2, 143). The possibility that French and English traders might exploit Papel hostility was precluded by the outbreak of the Seven Years' War.

Portuguese military initiatives at Bissau were ably seconded by missionary endeavors. In 1758, the garrison's officers were so depleted by death, sickness, and desertion that one of the Franciscan priests, Padre Manuel de Vinhais Sarmento, became acting commandant. His leadership and the capabilities and fortitude of fellow Franciscans who acquired influence among Papel were of surpassing importance in sustaining Portugal's precarious foothold in the Geba-Grande region (Barreto 1938, 151–52). At Bissau and elsewhere in western Africa, crucifixes proved, time and again, to be more potent than forts and cannons and inestimably more cost effective.

Serra Leoa, 1710s–1750s

The Royal African Company reoccupied Bunce Island in 1713 as a subfactory, supervised by the chief agent residing at York Island in the Sherbro. When York Island's low-lying, swampy ground proved too unhealthy, Bunce Island was again made the company's headquarters, with factors dispatched to the Pongo and Nunez Rivers (Kup 1961, 105; Fyfe 1962, 4). During the 1710s and 1720s, pirates pillaged seafarers frequenting the coast and rivers of Serra Leoa. The expansion of the Fula almamate in Futa Jallon during the eighteenth century transformed Serra Leoa trade. As Fula conquered new territories, prisoners captured in wars were taken to the Nunez, Pongo, and other rivers for sale into the Atlantic slave trade. Slaves used as porters transported European goods and salt back to the Futa Jallon highlands.

No Catholic missionaries had resided in the Sierra Leone estuary since the Spanish Capuchins abandoned their mission in the 1680s. Except for sporadic visits by ships' chaplains and priests from Cabo Verde, Luso-Africans were bereft of spiritual guidance until 1715, when Signor Joseph settled along the south bank of the Sierra Leone River. Signor Joseph was an African who had lived in America and was schooled in England before visiting Portugal, where he converted to Catholicism and trained for the priesthood. He was one of many victimized by pirates: in 1718, the English pirate Captain Thomas Cocklyn seized Signor Joseph and his sloop and held him for ransom, demanding provisions and ammunition (Snelgrave 1734/1971, 197; Kup 1961, 68). Afterward, Signor Joseph and his followers abandoned their "clean, well-built Town" and moved some nine miles upriver to Kissy. Signor Joseph explained to the Royal Navy surgeon John Atkins that the reason for the displacement was the palavers regarding his people and grumetes, coupled with the higher prices he had to pay living with English as neighbors. Regarding the priest's mission, Atkins related that Signor Joseph had constructed "a little Oratory for his People's Devotions; erected a Cross; taught several of his Kindred Letters, dispersing among them little Romish Prayer-Books, and many of them are known by Christian Names." Atkins added that by means of trade, Signor Joseph supplied the needs of his relatives and the residents of villages under his care (Atkins 1735/1970, 51, 54–55). That he instructed people in reading and writing would have been invaluable for Luso-African traders. Reputedly, he lived until old age and died on one of the Banana Islands, the last Catholic priest to reside in Serra Leoa during the eighteenth century (Bane 1956, 103–4; Kup 1961, 68).

In 1719, pirates bombarded and captured Bunce Island, holding it for seven weeks (Kup 1961, 54–55). The island was pillaged again the following year by the pirate Bartholomew Roberts. Robert Plunkett, who subsequently was the company's chief agent at James Island in the Gambia, defended Bunce until the fort ran out of ammunition (W. Smith 1744/1967, 41–43). When a Royal Navy frigate caught Roberts's vessel off Cape Lopez in 1721, 45 of the 157 men captured or killed were Africans (Bolster 1998, 51).

In 1721, John Leadstone, the former Royal African Company employee who had turned pirate, settled at Whiteman's Bay on the south side of the Sierra Leone estuary. Leadstone acquired a number of African women, as did other brigands who joined his settlement, and preyed on Europeans and Africans alike (Snelgrave 1734/1971, 256–57, 287; Kup 1961, 52–53, 56). He and some thirty others living along the Sierra Leone estuary acted as intermediaries for allegedly respectable slave traders from Bristol and other English ports, to the considerable detriment of the Royal African Company factors upriver at Bunce Island. John Atkins, who visited the Sierra Leone estuary in 1721, described them as "loose privateering Blades, that if they cannot trade fairly with the Natives, will rob; . . . and with their Profits purchase from time to time, Strong-beer, Wine, Cyder, and such Necessities, of *Bristol* Ships, that more frequently than others put in there; of these, *John Leadstine,* commonly called *old Cracker,* is reckoned the most thriving" (Atkins 1735/1970, 40).

Atkins mentioned that the pirates hired male and female grumetes — the men to trade on their behalf in the rivers of Serra Leoa, the women to serve as domestics and concubines. "They all keep *Gromettas* (*Negro* Servants) which they hire from *Sherbro River,* at two *Accys* or *Bars* a Month. The Women keep House, and are obedient to any Prostitutions their Masters command. The Men-servants work in the Boats and Periagoes [pirogues], which go a trading in turns with Coral, Brass, Pewter Pans, Pots, Arms, *English* Spirits, &c. and bring back from the Rio *Nunes,* Slaves, and Teeth; and from *Sherbro,* Camwood for Dyers" (Atkins 1735/1970, 40).

Independent traders residing in the Banana and Plantain Islands traded in the Sherbro and northward in the Pongo, Nunez, and other Serra Leoa rivers, selling the captives they obtained to slave vessels passing down the coast. The Plantain Islands were located halfway between the Sierra Leone estuary and the

Sherbro, and they provided convenient anchorages for off-loading cargo into small craft that could more safely negotiate the shallow waters in the Sherbro. Slaves and camwood were the chief commodities traded in the Sherbro, but ivory and mats were also sought. Bullom were renowned for their beautiful matting made of stained grass. Bullom made annual expeditions to the upper reaches of the Sherbro River, where they cut camwood and hunted elephants, returning with the onset of the rainy season when the creeks were full. Camwood was transported in canoas; if a canoa overturned, the dense and heavy camwood would sink, to be retrieved during the next dry season (Matthews 1788/1966, 24–25; W. Smith 1744/1967, 92–93; Kup 1961, 101; Rodney 1970, 158–60).

Names and titles testify to continuing Luso-African influences in the Sherbro. A dispatch from Richard Smith, the Royal African Company agent at York in January 1714, indicated that an escaped slave had taken refuge with a *phydalgo* (from the Portuguese *fidalgo,* meaning a noble or grandee) and that it would cost more than the man's worth to retrieve him (Fyfe 1964, 68–69). Obviously, African elites retained Crioulo usage, despite the fact that Anglo-Africans had supplanted Luso-Africans. Richard Smith likewise related his difficulties in settling affairs in the Sherbro following the death of Henry Clark: "Mr Clark died October the 3rd Last [1714], and Left your Affairs in a great Confusion, he having no Will, but Verball which was to his Woman and her Friends. They together rifled all his Effects and several other things which was in the Fort as its reported by Sundryes. I found all things in great Distraction and the Country People coming daily with their Palavars which Mr Clark had made some time before his death" (Fyfe 1964, 67–68). Among the palavers was the grievance of a Sherbro ruler who was not invited to the "cry" along with other elites who attended the wake. In revenge, he seized company goods valued at 536 bars (Fyfe 1964, 68).

The "chief" of York Island was discredited and replaced in 1726 by his "speaker," a man named Maximo, when the Royal African Company moved its factory to Jamaica, a palisaded town protected by cannons belonging to Zachary Cumberbuss. Cumberbuss was the son of a former company employee named John Cumberbaitch, who, along with his brother Zachariah, was stationed at York Island in 1689. Despite having an English father, Cumberbuss was styled "Senior" (or, in Portuguese, "senhor"), a title conveying respect in Sherbro. Lynda R. Day speculated that Jamaica Town was the home of Zachary Cumberbuss's mother, enabling him to assert landlord privileges that could be combined with the trade connections derived from his father. Cumberbuss acted as the company's "ambassador" to Sherbro's ruler (W. Smith 1744/1967, 57–59, 76, 81, 87; Kup 1961, 107–8, 150; Day 1983, 100–101).

Although Portuguese and Luso-Africans were supplanted by English and Anglo-Africans, numerous words and names remained in use. In 1726, the company's Sherbro "linguist" was named António, a man who, under duress, acknowledged that he had "two Tongues; Tongue for white Man and Tongue for Black Man." In 1728, a "Senior Derby" was a mediator for traders in the Sherbro. The principal elders were called "Caboceroes" (from the Portuguese *cabeca,* meaning head or top, and *cabo,* meaning chief or commander). Smith also referred to a "grometto," described as "a Black Freeman who hires himself by the Week to work for any one, but chiefly for White Men, by whom many here are employ'd," and a "panyar" (from the Portuguese *apanhar,* to seize, entrap, or take unawares), who could steal people or anything else (W. Smith 1744/1967, 74–75, 87–88, 91, 99, 101–2; Atkins 1735/1970, 53, 58; Kup 1961, 108). Besides references to grumetes ("gremetoes"), Owens's journal listed numerous palavers—"pilavers, or black law" (E. Martin 1930, 38, 70, 74, 89, 101, 103). Luso-African names were maintained for generations: in 1755, a "black trader" named Berebosa (Barbosa) had a town comprising seven dwellings at the head of navigation on the Jong River (E. Martin 1930, 59 and pl. 11 facing p. 59). Numerous Portuguese and Crioulo words were permanently incorporated in Mande and West Atlantic languages, especially the latter, including some four dozen identified during the mid-twentieth century (Bradshaw 1965).

Especially damaging for the commerce of the Royal African Company were the experienced employees who deserted company service to become independent traders. William Smith, a surveyor for the company who visited the Banana Islands in November 1726, stated that two former employees named Pearce and Sanderson traded in sloops north to the Pongo and Nunez Rivers for slaves, ivory, and camwood, attracting vessels bound down the coast to stop at their establishments in the Bananas. The men were trading in the Pongo River when he visited, but Smith observed Pearce's wife and her female slaves busy stringing beads and counting cowries in her husband's absence (W. Smith 1744/1967, 54–55, 93–94). Doubtless, she and Sanderson's wife capably traded with visiting vessels when their husbands were gone. The women were daughters and relatives of elites, with ties that were invaluable for their own and their husbands' success in commerce (Kup 1961, 107).

Pirates' brigandage during the 1710s and 1720s inflicted great damage on the Royal African Company in the Sierra Leone estuary, but it was not pirates but Luso-Africans who ultimately drove the company from Bunce Island. In 1727 and 1728, Walter Charles, the chief factor at Bunce Island, parlayed with local rulers to eliminate the middleman role exercised by Luso-Africans. He castigated

Luso-Africans for insulting African rulers and behaving "tyranically" toward Africans generally. His detestation of Luso-Africans was recorded in his diary: "I will take effectual care while I stay in the country that no white black man shall make any figure here, above what the meanest natives do" (Rodney 1970, 213).

Charles's chief adversary and the acknowledged leader of Luso-Africans living dispersed in Serra Leoa was the elderly José Lopez de Moura, reputedly the grandson of a Mani ruler and possibly a son of Barnabé Lopez, the prominent Bissau trader. Moura, whose town was sited on a hill to the east of Fourah Bay, rallied the support of Bullom rulers hostile to the Royal African Company, along with resident independent traders, to boycott trade with Bunce Island. Moura contrived to subvert the grumetes and castle slaves on Bunce Island, and on the night of October 25–26, 1728, Charles and other English residents were driven off the island by a band led by Moura and Luso-Africans named Jerome and Thomâ/Tomé who burned the premises. Local Luso-Africans were joined by others who arrived "from the Rio Pongo, the Soussas and Scarcies, and from several places to the northward." Moura warded off a retaliatory attack by holding hostage Bunce Island's doctor and a trader (Kup 1961, 48, 84, 108–12; Hair 2000c, 415, 428 n. 40).

Lopez de Moura later posted a notice on a large sheet of paper at the watering place, proclaiming "the ships of all nations, English, French, Dutch, etc., shall have free liberty of trade in the river and the utmost safety, except those belonging to the Royal African Company of England." Rodney observed, "In effect, this was the Company's obituary." The Royal African Company's chief ally, Suphulo, a Bullom ruler along the Rokel River, was compelled to eat food placed at Lopes de Moura's feet (Rodney 1970, 214–15).

Following the company's loss of Bunce Island, a sister of Moura founded a settlement near Cape Sierra Leone along the Atlantic side of the Sierra Leone peninsula; it became known as "Seniora Maria's town." A Bullom woman, Maria organized salt production during the dry season, selling loads of salt in Port Loko Creek in exchange for rice. Seniora Maria had been an interpreter on Bunce Island, and she had relatives in Sherbro, where the company traded. Her husband, named Monday, had been hung as a traitor, but she had supported the company nevertheless, considering it more dependable than independent traders (Kup 1961, 133, 150–51; Fyfe 1962, 3; Rodney 1970, 19).

Subsequently, three London traders and malt makers—Alexander Grant, Richard Oswald, and John Sargent II—acquired Bunce Island and carried on Serra Leoa trade. In 1744 , Grant, Oswald and Company's title to the island was recognized by the British government, so that in 1751, Bunce Island, unlike other

Royal African Company properties, was not taken over by the Company of Merchants Trading to Africa (George 1904, 285–86, 289–90; Fyfe 1962, 7; Rodney 1970, 248–49; Hancock 1995, chap. 6). Meanwhile, Luso-Africans continued to dominate trade and politics in the Sierra Leone estuary. When Capt. John Newton visited in August 1752, the new ruler of Whiteman's Bay was "Seignor Don Pedro de Case," who was subordinate to "Seignor Don de Lopez, the undoubted king-maker of Sierra Leon" (Martin and Spurrell 1962, 66). This Lopez was presumably the Agostinho Lopez mentioned in the preceding Geba-Grande section who "donated" his domain to the king of Portugal in November 1752.

Nicholas Owen described the Plantain and Banana Islands in the mid-1750s. The principal island in the Bananas was inhabited by Bullom, some white traders, and "several malatos, tradeing men that lives upon the low grounds and lords it over the rest of the island." The island had high ground and fertile soils, but the anchorage was foul and full of rocks. The inhabitants paid annual customs to the ruler of Sherbro, who sent a canoa each year to collect the tribute. By contrast, the principal island in the Plantains was low and flat and covered with palm trees, and it produced little but rice; however, the harbor was good for small vessels, and there was a "considerable trade with shipping" (E. Martin 1930, 29–30, 47). An Englishman named Clow carried on trade with a Bullom woman whose name John Newton recorded as "P. I." because the sound of it was similar to the pronunciation of those letters. P.I. treated Newton with great enmity while Clow was absent on trading expeditions (B. Martin 1950, 54–59).

English traders established on the Plantain and Banana Islands ranged the coast and rivers of western Africa. In 1754, the crews on a vessel belonging to an English trader established at the Banana Islands and two vessels from the Carolinas acted so irresponsibly along the Petite Côte, even kidnapping inhabitants, that the Bur Saluum seized three men from one of the vessels and held them for ransom (Gray 1940, 224).

At midcentury, the slave trade of Serra Leoa was characterized as "prodigious" by a commission appointed to investigate English forts and factories. The growth in slave exports coincided with the expansion of Fula conquests under the leadership of Ibrahima Sory between c. 1751 and his death in 1791 (Rodney 1970, 237–38; Barry 1981b, 291–92).

A number of American slavers ventured to western Africa during this era. New England traders promoted a growing market for rum distilled from West Indian molasses, and an estimated eighteen vessels from Rhode Island visited West Africa each year from the 1730s onward (Hedges 1952, 70). Rum was one of the few commodities that could be traded alone for slaves. Consequently, from midcentury forward, Rhode Island vessels were laden almost entirely with rum, and their crews purchased slaves at lower prices than their English competitors. Indeed, molasses, rum, and slaves made the merchants of Newport prosperous during the second third of the eighteenth century; and "rum vessel" became synonymous with "slave ship" (Alison Jones 1981; Crane 1985, 14–15, 21; Chapter 2). Such was African consumers' preference for rum that in February and March 1750, Newton, to his frustration, was constrained to purchase two hogsheads of rum from the brig *Mermaid* of Rhode Island when he had a large supply of brandy unsold (Martin and Spurrell 1962, 38, 41). Keeping "assorted"—that is, keeping an assortment of goods on hand to meet the discriminating choices of African consumers—was always a challenge for European and American traders. For more than a century, New England rum and Virginia tobacco provided American traders a competitive advantage via-à-vis their European counterparts.

Visiting shipmasters, like resident traders, were constrained to submit to the demands of Sherbro landlords. Thus, Captain Keith, master of the *Mermaid,* returned a free boy who had been carried off on a previous voyage (Martin and Spurrell 1962, 38–39). Nicholas Owen reported a similar instance in May 1756, when free people were taken back from the Danish West Indies (E. Martin 1930, 72). Panyarring—the seizing of free Africans—by departing shipmasters disrupted the commerce of resident traders and endangered the lives of crews arriving on subsequent vessels. John Newton told of the consequences and acknowledged the forbearance of some victimized Africans: "A quarrel, sometimes, furnishes pretext for detaining, and carrying away, one or more of the natives, which is retaliated, if practicable, upon the next boat that comes to the place, from the same port. For so far their vindictive temper is restrained by their ideas of justice, they will not, often, revenge an injury received from a Liverpool ship, upon one belonging to Bristol or London" (Martin and Spurrell 1962, 106; cf. Wadstrom 1789, 17–21).

Like Owen, Newton related extensive dealings with Anglo-Africans in Sherbro as well as resident European traders. However, entries in November and December 1750 referred to commerce with "Maria's people," suggesting trade with a Luso-African nhara (Martin and Spurrell 1962, 20). Like Owen, Newton hired grumetes ("grimetars") to supplement his crew. In December 1750 at Shebar, he paid three bars a month for a grumete named John Cumberbach (Cumberbuss), who was related to "Jubly" James, the man who was second in command of Bunce Island and who, by 1758, had become a private trader (Martin and Spurrell 1962, 24; E. Martin 1930, 104).

The Caulkers, Tuckers, and other Anglo-Africans increasingly dominated trade in Sherbro, along the mainland extending north to the Sierra Leone estuary, and on the Banana and Plantain Islands (George 1904, 286, 293–94; Fyfe 1962, 10, 81). Walter Rodney astutely observed that Anglo-Africans in the Sherbro benefited from the heritage of the Mane, who conquered the area in the sixteenth century: "The Manes were accustomed to breaking up a patrimony, and setting up several village chiefdoms of approximately equal power, so that when a mulatto built a town he automatically had as much power as the average chief in the country. Indeed, the mulatto towns were usually stronger, often being protected by European cannon" (Rodney 1970, 221).

Both Newton and Nicholas Owen had extensive dealings with the Anglo-African Henry Tucker. While trading at Shebar River in December 1750, Newton wrote in his journal: "I depend more upon Mr. Tucker than any of them, or should not trust my boat an hour in the river, for I believe them to be all villains to a man except him." Two of the "villains" he named were William Cumberbatch and Joseph Tucker, who seized a French vessel and killed members of the crew. Three months later, Newton wrote, "I have found more dependance due [Henry Tucker's] word than any of the white men hereabouts." Decades later, Newton characterized Tucker as "the man with whom I had the largest connexion in business and by whom I was never deceived" (Martin and Spurrell 1962, 15, 24–25, 39–40).

In February 1757, Nicholas Owen and his brother Blayney left York Island to place themselves under the protection of Henry Tucker, "a malato who bears great sway in the country" (E. Martin 1930, 70). In a journal entry the following August, Owen described how Anglo-Africans acquired growing power and influence in Sherbro. Referring to Harry Tucker, he stated:

> He has been in England, Spain and Portugall and is master of the English tongue; he has 6 or 7 wives and a numerous ofspring of suns and daughters; his strength consists of his own slaves and their children, who has built a town about him and serves as his *gremetos* upon all occassions. This man bears the character of a fair trader among the Europeans, but to the contrary among the blacks. His riches set him above the kings and his numerous people above being surprized by war; almost all the blacks ows him money, which bring a dread of being stopt upon that acount, so that he is esteem'd and feared by all who has the misfortune to be in his power. He's a fat man and fair spoken, and lives after the manner of the English, haveing his house well furnish'd with English goods and his table tolarably well furnish'd with the country produce. He dresses gayley and commonly makes use of silver at his table, haveing a good side board of plate. (E. Martin 1930, 76)

The following year, in June 1758, Owen unburdened his frustrations in a journal entry concerning Anglo-African traders in Sherbro, his invective made more bitter by financial losses caused by commerce raiding during the Seven Years' War, by declining health, and by expenses incurred by "pilavers or black law" (E. Martin 1930, 80, 82, 101; see also 70, 74, and 89).

> I shall fill up today with the charectar of the mallatoes on this river. They are in a general way worse then the blacks and as they are given to trade, which leads them into the fashons of the English and shews them insight in the manner we trade with the black people, our proffit is not sufficent to satisfy them, but they make new extortions of thier own, which renders the poor blacks miserable a both sides. I have heard of some instances of thier cruelty, as that they have poyson'd thier own mothers by red watter, in order to get what slaves or affects they have in thier persesion. It's easey to consider our circumstances between the blacks and melatoes and our unhappy life, which we are obliged to lead all for the sake of riches, which at best we are not sure of in these times of wars and troubles at home and abroad. We are afread to move one way or other and so is miserable in both. (E. Martin 1930, 102)

Owen added that Harry Tucker "of all men bears the worst of charactars even with the blacks" (E. Martin 1930, 102). Owen, it may be noted, likewise recorded disgraceful and lawless activities by whites, such as the dastardly behavior of an English shipmaster who took advantage of a friend's misfortune to acquire his vessel and cargo of slaves (E. Martin 1930, 86–87). Anglo-Africans in Serra Leoa contrasted with Luso-Africans in a notable aspect: Anglo-Africans did not assert that they were "English" or "Christians."

Anglo-Africans were not the only intrusive group gaining influence in Sherbro. Nicholas Owen discussed the itinerant Mande marabouts who astounded Bullom and resident traders, himself included, by their ability to identify thieves and witches and foretell the future (E. Martin 1930, pl. facing p. 46, 55–57, 71, 81, 89–90, 95). Nonetheless, the Poro Society long maintained its ascendancy in local affairs, and the English-educated Anglo-African James Cleveland used membership in Poro to acquire a dominant position in Sherbro in the 1780s (E. Martin 1930, 48–49, 74–75; Martin and Spurrell 1962, 107; Fyfe 1962, 10).

Owen died at his Sherbro factory in March 1759. By that time, Newton had retired from the slave trade. He subsequently became an Anglican minister and a renowned opponent of the trade, persuading William Wilberforce and many other influential people to lobby Parliament for its suppression.

Despite the growing dominance of English and Anglo-African slave traders in the rivers of Serra Leoa, Luso-Africans maintained their coastwise commerce in kola. Trading in the Denby/Denbia (?) River in Sherbro in April 1756, Nicholas Owen wrote in his journal about the arrival of a canoa from Bissau: "This canno came down in order to purchase cole, or cola, a fruit that's esteem'd very much at Gambia and Catchew and serves for part of thier assortments in theer country trade for slaves and teeth [ivory tusks]." Owen added that kola was purchased "at easey rates," but he did not specify what was bartered in exchange, nor did he record the craft's size, owner, commander, or crew (E. Martin 1930, 69–70). His journal entry testified that notwithstanding English and French encroachments along the Upper Guinea Coast, Luso-Africans continued their annual voyages to Serra Leoa for the cargoes of kola that were crucial to maintaining their commercial networks in the Guinea-Bissau region and Senegambia. Indeed, Portuguese authorities at Bissau long maintained a supervisory responsibility. As late as March 1772, following the death of one Plínio Jorge, the commandant of Bissau appointed the Geba-born João Mendes Leão as *capitão-cabo* (headman) of the settlement at Rokupr ("Cubra") on the Kolente River (Rema 1982, 243; Hair 2000c, 427 n. 22).

Owen's mention of "assortments" referred to the crucial concern of all traders, especially shipboard traders, about maintaining a variety of merchandise to meet the demands of their African customers, who would otherwise trade with better-supplied rivals. Europeans were constrained to accept African modes of barter and reckoning of accounts. And bartering was a difficult and time-consuming process, especially frustrating when the haggling was conducted in another language through an interpreter or by means of signs. Thus, captains and supercargoes engaged in shipboard trade hired grumetes or "trade-men" to expedite exchanges, and they chafed at their inability to control or speed up calculations involving an African trader's demand for a wide-ranging assortment of goods for a single captive, tusk of ivory, or quantity of gold dust (Brooks 1970, 225–29).

Europeans vented their frustrations in widespread cheating. John Newton, who ultimately sought to expiate his guilt by preaching and writing against the slave trade, described how Africans were cheated "in the number, weight, measure, or quality of what they purchase, in every possible way." He noted that "not an article that is capable of diminution or adulteration is delivered genuine or entire. The spirits are lowered by water. False heads are put into the kegs that contain the gunpowder. . . . The linen and cotton cloths are opened, and two or three yards, according the length of the piece, cut off, not from the end, but out of the middle, where it is not so readily noticed" (Martin and Spurrell 1962, 106;

cf. Wadstrom 1794–95/1968, 26–28). Newton attested that English and Africans reciprocally considered each other consummate villains: "When I have charged a black with unfairness and dishonesty, he has answered, if able to clear himself, with an air of disdain, 'What! do you think I am a white man?'" (Martin and Spurrell 1962, 107). Eurafricans might engage in similar reprehensible practices, but dwelling as they did in African societies, they were answerable for their actions.

The spread of Islam from the interior to the Serra Leoa littoral was fostered by Mande and Fula marabouts, who founded Koranic schools that introduced the study of Arabic and Islamic law. In addition, Muslim immigrants transformed political institutions and commercial networks in the region (Fyfe 1962, 5–6; Skinner 1989, 92–94). As happened along the Gambia River, however, the spread of Islam proved incompatible with the interests of Luso-Africans. So too did the competition of the Anglo-African families founded in the Nunez and Pongo Rivers and the Iles de Los by English slavers. From the mid-eighteenth century on, therefore, Anglo-Africans contended with long-established Luso-African families for the expanding slave trade from Futa Jallon carried on by Susu and, increasingly, by Fula from the growing Fula almamate. Like Harry Tucker in Sherbro, Europeans and Eurafricans in the Pongo and Nunez acquired ever larger numbers of family members and dependents, and over time, they gained ascendancy over landlords in acephalous societies along the rivers.

During the Seven Years' War from 1756 to 1763, which disrupted English and French trade in western Africa, Luso-Africans in Serra Leoa benefited from a revival of Portuguese and Cabo Verdean commerce with western Africa, especially after the dictator Pombal organized the Companhia Geral do Grão-Pará e Maranhão to supply slaves to northeast Brazil.

CHAPTER 9
Senegambia
Luso-Africans Supplanted by Franco-Africans

> [At Saint-Louis], Gorée, Saluum, in the Gambia, and along the coasts as far as Cape Palmas, one encounters numerous mulattos and Africans with French, English, and Portuguese names.
>
> —GOLBERRY 1802, 1:157

THE LATTER DECADES OF THE EIGHTEENTH CENTURY were marked by significant growth in the Atlantic slave trade, with western African societies increasingly involved in warfare and slave raiding as predators and as victims. Their difficult circumstances were only exacerbated by the drought and famine of the c. 1630–c. 1860 dry period. The principal slave suppliers were the Mandinka state of Kaabu and the Fula almamate in Futa Jallon, both of which were involved in almost continuous raiding and pillaging of neighboring groups. While France and England fought the Seven Years' War (1756–63), the Companhia Geral do Grão-Pará e Maranhão, which functioned from 1755 to 1778, promoted a resurgence of Portuguese trade with western Africa. Founded by the Marquis de Pombal to supply slaves to northeast Brazil, the company brought considerable benefits to Luso-African middlemen and to Cabo Verdeans who were employed as seamen, clerks, and soldiers in the Cacheu and Bissau garrisons and dependent presidios. These developments reinforced Luso-African trading networks and expanded social and cultural ties with Cabo Verde, along with commercial relationships. The company was terminated following the dismissal of Pombal as chief minister, and the Portuguese Crown reassumed responsibility for the administration of Cabo Verde and the presidios and entrepôts of the Guinea-Bissau region.

Following the Seven Years' War, French and English traders again dominated western African trade until the renewed outbreak of hostilities brought on by the American War of Independence. The Treaty of Paris awarded Saint-Louis to Britain and restored Gorée to France. Breaking with the past, both countries instituted royal administration at their Senegambian entrepôts, dispatching governors and entourages of civilian administrators and military officers. In 1765, the British Parliament established an ill-conceived colony comprising Saint-Louis and James Island, separated by Gorée and French comptoirs along the Petite Côte and Albreda. The awkwardly bifurcated Province of Senegambia lasted until January 1779, when a French fleet captured Saint-Louis; James Island was surrendered the month following (Gray 1940, 228, 267–68; Curtin 1975, 104).

French administrative initiatives in the aftermath of the Seven Years' War were neither more rational nor more successful. The Compagnie des Indes and its subsidiary Compagnie du Sénégal were terminated in 1767; like the officers of the Royal African Company, the French administrators found it was financially impossible to maintain forts and garrisons in Africa in competition with independent traders unburdened with such expenses (Curtin 1975, 104). In principle, commerce was open to all French traders subject to payment of a tax, but up to the eve of the French Revolution, French commercial policy oscillated between the royal prerogatives of chartering monopolistic companies and merchants' demands for the end of mercantilist practices. A succession of chartered companies awkwardly coexisted with the declared royal policy of freedom of trade.

Monopolistic practices were reinstated in 1770 with the founding of the Compagnie de la Côte d'Afrique, which was succeeded in 1776 by the Compagnie de la Colonie Française de Guyane. In 1777, the latter was accorded an exclusive privilege to trade in slaves and a monopoly of trade with Gorée and the coast from Cape Verde to the Casamance River for five years. This company was superseded in 1784 by the Compagnie Nouvelle du Sénégal et Dépendances (Machat 1906a, 95; Sainville 1972, 77). In practice, collusion between company directors and royal officials in Senegal negated the proclaimed free trade for all Frenchmen. Nonetheless, French and Franco-African traders aggressively expanded their commerce southward to the Guinea-Bissau region, taking advantage of the demise of the Companhia Geral do Grão-Pará e Maranhão.

During the 1770s and 1780s, Luso-Africans' commercial networks were progressively circumscribed. Luso-Africans were excluded by Diola from trade routes connecting the Cacheu and Gambia Rivers and challenged by French and Franco-African traders in the Casamance River. English and Anglo-African traders dominated Serra Leoa trade, with factories in the Sierra Leone estuary, in the

Iles de Los, and in the Pongo and Nunez Rivers, and by the 1780s, these same traders were challenging Luso-Africans in the Grande and Geba Rivers. Competition was ruthless, with traders attacking rivals afloat and ashore.

Contending with English and Anglo-Africans advancing from the south and French and Franco-Africans from the north, Luso-African traders in the Guinea-Bissau region between the Casamance and Grande Rivers might have become subordinated as compradors to French and English traders. But that outcome was forestalled by the renewal of Anglo-French conflict between 1778 and 1783 during the American War of Independence, followed by the French Revolution and the Napoleonic Wars from 1791 to 1815. The ensuing treaties outlawing the slave trade transformed western African commerce, and Luso-African and Cabo Verdean traders turned these circumstances to their advantage.

The constriction of the Luso-African and Cabo Verdean commercial sphere to the Guinea-Bissau region increased and reinforced ethnic and cultural exchanges, with reciprocal and cumulative effects on the populations of both areas. During Portugal's long economic and political diminuendo, which extended well into the nineteenth century, Luso-Africans born in Guinea, together with Cabo Verdeans, almost entirely supplanted Portuguese traders, soldiers, and priests in Guinea's praças and trading communities.

The Companhia Geral do Grão-Pará e Maranhão, 1755–78

The resurgence of Portuguese commerce with western Africa owed much to Sebastião José de Carvalho e Melo, the Marquis de Pombal—first minister and de facto ruler of Portugal during the reign of José I (1750–77). Pombal promoted unprecedented investments in Portugal's colonies and overseas commerce, encouraged new industries and business enterprises, curtailed the influence of the Inquisition, and ended legal discrimination against New Christians. Although some of Pombal's initiatives had only limited success and others were repudiated by José I's successor, his policies achieved a great deal with respect to Portuguese and Luso-African interests in western Africa (Alden 1968, 7–13; Lang 1979, 168).

Pombal founded the Companhia Geral do Grão-Pará e Maranhão in 1755 for the purpose of supplying slave labor to spur the development of the sugar industry in the sparsely inhabited states of Pará and Maranhão in northeast Brazil—and for the profit of interested speculators, himself included. The company was organized by Francisco Mendonça Furtado, who was the governor of Pará and

Pombal's brother. Pombal was a major shareholder in his wife's name, and the pliant José I was induced to accord the Maranhão Company generous privileges, including a twenty-year monopoly of commerce with the Cabo Verde archipelago and the coast of West Africa from Cape Blanco to Cape Palmas, disregarding the protests of private Portuguese and Cabo Verdean traders. The Companhia Geral do Grão-Pará e Maranhão's twenty-year charter was to begin with the dispatch of its first vessel in April 1756, but the company did not formally undertake administrative responsibilities in Cabo Verde and Guinea until 1757; the implementation of the monopoly began one year later (Barcellos 1899–1913, 3:25; Carreira 1969, chap. 2; Rodney 1970, 246–47; Mettas 1975, 345).

Pombal's influence over José I ensured strong government support for launching the company, but it was the fortuitous outbreak of the Seven Years' War in 1756 that enabled the firm to become established before encountering concerted French and English competition in western Africa (Machat 1906a, 90–91; Mettas 1975, 350–51, 356). Portugal was endangered at the war's outset, when its alliance with Britain provoked an attack by Spanish and French forces. The invasion was repulsed with British assistance by the close of 1762, and Portugal was not thereafter threatened (Langer 1958, 454).

The Seven Years' War, which lasted until 1763, was the first Anglo-French "global" conflict. The British navy achieved mastery of South Atlantic shipping lanes, capturing Saint-Louis and Gorée in May 1758. With the British navy ascendant in West African waters, Portuguese vessels safely traded during the remaining years of the war. Since French trade was halted along the upper Senegal River, slave caravans were rerouted to the Gambia River and the Guinea-Bissau region. Many of the manufactured goods traded by Pombal's company were acquired from English trading firms established in Portugal (Rodney 1970, 248; Mettas 1975, 356). The initiatives taken by Pombal and his successors to diminish Portugal's dependence on Britain and promote Portuguese industries were undermined by French invasions during the Napoleonic Wars, which had the consequence of promoting renewed and increased dependence on Britain and new concessions to British commercial interests, particularly in terms of commerce with Brazil (Sideri 1970, 19–20).

The Companhia Geral do Grão Pará e Maranhão's objective of shipping large numbers of slaves to Brazil was largely achieved, and its subscribers reaped windfall profits. The more than twenty-eight thousand captives shipped to Pará and Maranhão between 1757 and 1777 were used in the large-scale cultivation of rice and cotton, and through their labor, they realized considerable wealth for the planters. Most of the slaves were embarked from Cacheu and, in even greater numbers, from Bissau; together, these ports supplied captives at a fairly steady rate of approximately one thousand a year during the second half of the eighteenth century (Boxer 1969, 192–93; Carreira 1969, 91; Rodney 1970, 247; Mettas 1975, 363; Lang 1979, 161–64).

Besides slaves transported to Brazil, the Maranhão Company's vessels carried to Portugal large quantities of ivory and beeswax, plus orchil from Cabo Verde. The inhabitants of Cabo Verde experienced both advantages and disadvantages during this period. On the positive side, agents of the company purchased panos, aguardente, foodstuffs, and other supplies. Weavers created new designs for panos; Carreira enumerated two dozen different patterns for barafulas exported from 1757 to 1782 (Carreira 1969, 237; Duncan 1972, 221–22). On the negative side, however, the drought and famine conditions prevailing in the archipelago during the 1750s and 1770s had dreadful consequences, even as they facilitated the company's recruitment of employees in Cabo Verde. The company's purchases of supplies only added to the food shortages and price inflation that contributed to the famine-induced deaths of thousands of the archipelago's destitute inhabitants (Barcellos 1904, 5–11; Patterson 1988, 306–8).

Cabo Verdeans hired as sailors on company vessels and as soldiers, laborers, and clerks for the praças and detachments in Guinea contributed to reinforcing Luso-African social and cultural patterns both in the archipelago and at trading establishments in western Africa. Traces of cultural diffusion are evidenced in an engraving by Alexis Noel (1792–1871) depicting people congregated at a well in Praia, São Tiago: two well-dressed women in the image are wearing turbans like those described for Luso-African women living in Senegambia (Santos 1995, book cover and fig. 3).

In June 1765, Desmesnagers, the first commandant of Gorée after its return by Britain, reported that Papel at Bissau sought the return of French traders and had refused to permit other traders to establish a factory on the plot of ground that had previously been allotted to the French traders. Desmesnagers likewise expressed interest in Bolama, "a very beautiful island, well-wooded where there is water and it is uninhabited" (Machat 1906a, 92–93). Bolama would have a strong attraction for French and English traders and proponents of African colonization for decades to come.

To preempt French initiatives to exploit Papel disaffection at Bissau following the Seven Years' War, the Companhia Geral do Grão-Pará e Maranhão was required to complete the praça of São José, to reinforce the garrison, and to enforce exclusive Portuguese trade (Mettas 1975, 345–46, 350). The fort was in effect refounded in January 1766 with the arrival of more than seven hundred

Portuguese and Cabo Verdean soldiers, stonemasons, carpenters, and laborers. Some fifteen hundred Papel were induced to work on the project, largely due to the missionary endeavors of the Franciscan Fr. Manuel de Vinhais Sarmento and his colleague Fr. Fernando (Barreto 1938, 152–53; Rema 1982, 241–42).

During the era of the Maranhão Company, Bissau gradually supplanted Cacheu as the principal place of slave exports because the bar at the entrance of the Cacheu River was dangerous, especially for larger vessels with deeper drafts, while the Geba estuary was easily navigable for even the largest sailing vessels if routine precautions were taken. An increasing number of slaves were obtained along the coast between Bissau and the Sierra Leone River due to the decline of French and English competition at Bissau with the assertion of the company's monopoly. The Fula almamate in Futa Jallon sent more and more slaves to the Nunez, Pongo, and other rivers where Luso-African middlemen competed with augmenting numbers of English and Anglo-African traders (Mettas 1975, 345–46, 351).

Vessels dispatched by the Companhia Geral do Grão-Pará e Maranhão sailed to the entrepôts of Bissau and Cacheu, rarely engaging in coastwise and riverine commerce. Such commerce was left to Portuguese, Cabo Verdean, and Luso-African traders who undertook trading voyages in sailing vessels and canoas manned by grumetes. Traders at Ziguinchor and Farim tapped the Banyun-Bak and Mande trade networks extending to the Gambia River and eastward across the Kaabu Empire. Traders at Geba linked with Mande traders from Kaabu. And to command markets south of the Geba River, traders from Bissau linked with Biafada and Luso-Africans established along the Grande River; with Susu, Fula, Luso-Africans, English, and Anglo-Africans sited along the Nunez and Pongo Rivers and on the Iles de Los; and with African traders along the Kolente and other rivers where kola was obtained.

The praça of São José de Bissau was not completed until August 1775, at great cost in term of both money and loss of life. The final decade of construction alone took the lives of 2,602 laborers and soldiers, principally Cabo Verdeans (Rodney 1970, 246–47). The spacious fort, with its high walls and four bastions surrounded by a moat, could be defended with a skeleton garrison—as indeed it was on a number of occasions but nearly always with the vital assistance of Luso-African traders and their retinues of armed grumetes. During the rainy season, the praça's garrison could store water in cisterns, and the moat surrounding the fort conserved rainwater. But as the dry season advanced, the garrison and the inhabitants of the settlement were dependent on the Pidgiguiti Spring, which was controlled by Papel until 1844, when the spring was captured and enclosed by a palisade extended from the fort (Barcellos 1899–1913, 5:40).

São José's massive stone walls were not vertical but were sloped inward at an obtuse angle in order to deflect cannonballs fired by European adversaries. Remarkably, the builders left large chinks between the stones, enabling vegetation to lodge and give purchase to a climber. Sparsely garrisoned with sick and dispirited convicts, the fort was vulnerable to any determined assault force possessing scaling ladders or felled trees, but such an event never occurred. São José's real defense lay in the commandants' payment of tribute exacted as part of landlord-stranger reciprocities, the desire of all parties for trade, the mediating role played by Franciscan priests, and, when conflict threatened, the preemptive distribution of liquor and other gifts by praça commanders. As a perceptive French visitor observed, the Portuguese survived by "acts of weakness" (Mollien 1820, 338–39).

The construction of the praça of São José de Bissau and the appointment of commandants of equal rank with those assigned to Cacheu's praça accorded official recognition to the long-standing commercial bifurcation of the Guinea-Bissau region. During the time of the Companhia do Grão-Pará e Maranhão and for many years thereafter, the praças at Bissau and Cacheu were garrisoned with the dregs of Portuguese regiments, including criminals and other undesirables, supplemented by men similarly recruited in Cabo Verde. The soldiers were frequently sick and unfit for duty, and they were rarely paid; what pay they did receive came in the form of *cedulas* (script) and tobacco and other imports from Cabo Verde. They also endured chronic shortages of rations, uniforms, and equipment and were subjected to despicable treatment by their officers. Not surprisingly, the soldiers malingered when not being openly mutinous. Few details about the situation were recorded in the sporadic dispatches sent to authorities in Portugal. The first report issued by a new commandant at Cacheu or Bissau might have related "for the record" the deplorable circumstances he found on taking command, but subsequent dispatches mentioned little or nothing concerning reforms or improvements (Brooks 1973, 304–10).

During the years between the end of the Seven Years' War in 1763 and the resumption of war between France and England in 1778, renewed French and British competition curtailed the Companhia Geral do Grão-Pará e Maranhão's trade and profits. At Bissau and elsewhere, there was extensive collusion between Portuguese, Cabo Verdean, and Luso-African traders and the traders of rival French and English companies, reportedly despite the efforts of officials of the Maranhão Company but more likely with their connivance. The seizure of a British schooner at Geba in May 1774 and the French vessel *Saint-Jean Baptiste* at

Ziguinchor in September of the same year doubtless represented a sporadic enforcement of the company's asserted monopoly of western African trade, for it is improbable that the shipmasters would have entered the Casamance and Geba Rivers, making themselves liable to reprisals, had there not been opportunistic collusion in previous years (Mettas 1975, 350–51). In 1775, in one of the numerous Franciscan demonstrations of support and loyalty to the Portuguese Crown, a priest at Cacheu declared excommunicated the residents who traded with a French vessel, presumably with the knowledge of the commandant (Rema 1982, 220; Hair 2000c, 411–12). The pervasive enmity between peninsula Portuguese and Luso-Africans was explicit in a 1777 dispatch sent by Francisco Martinez, an official of the Maranhão Company: Martinez characterized Luso-Africans as "monkeys" (Rodney 1970, 203).

The Companhia Geral do Grão-Pará e Maranhão was dissolved in 1778, the year after Pombal's dismissal as chief minister on the accession of the new ruler, Maria I (1777–1816). Opponents of the company argued the necessity of canceling monopolies in the hope, largely unrealized, that the debt-ridden government might obtain new revenues from customs duties. The company went into gradual liquidation in February 1778, and royal administration was reestablished over the Cabo Verde archipelago and the praças of Cacheu and Bissau (Rodney 1970, 248). The Companhia Geral do Grão-Para e Maranhão's affairs were only gradually phased out, with the firm continuing to ship a few slaves until 1786, mostly as freight in private vessels (Mattas 1975, 359, 361). Reportedly, Portuguese merchants sent only four or five pinques/pinks a year to Cacheu in 1784 and 1785, and of the one or two that came from Lisbon, the cargo usually belonged to English merchants. The others were small vessels dispatched from São Tiago, Madeira, or Terceira in the Azores (Labarthe 1802, 144).

Due to disastrous financial circumstances, the Portuguese government disbursed no funds for the administration of Cabo Verde and the praças in the Guinea-Bissau region; thereafter, needs in these areas were to be financed exclusively from customs duties—an impossibility that ensured their impoverishment and stagnation for decades to come. The praças were administratively attached to the governors-general residing at Praia, the chief port of São Tiago and the Cabo Verde archipelago. Governors-general could raise only derisory amounts of revenue in the best of times—that is, when the archipelago was not afflicted by its frequent periods of drought and famine conditions. Deprived of revenues and requisite military and naval forces, governors-general never visited the praças in Guinea. Thus, Luso-Africans, Cabo Verdeans, and the few Portuguese dwelling in Guinea exercised almost complete independence of action, trading slaves and commodities with traders of any nationality. Portuguese commerce and territorial claims in western Africa might have ceased had it not been for the resiliency of Luso-Africans and Cabo Verdeans—and for the successive reprieves afforded them by Anglo-French warfare and destructive commerce raiding in western Africa and elsewhere around the globe. It was Luso-Africans and Cabo Verdeans, not peninsula Portuguese, who, for a century following, sustained a "Portuguese presence" in western Africa in competition with the expanding French and Franco-African and English and Anglo-African commercial and imperial spheres.

The Province of Senegambia, 1763–78

Britain returned Gorée to France with the making of peace in 1763 but retained Saint-Louis as the headquarters of the governor of an ill-conceived Province of Senegambia. In addition, a lieutenant governor was stationed at James Fort and was responsible for overseeing English trade along the Gambia River. For all practical purposes, however, Saint-Louis and James Fort were independently administered, separated by French-occupied Gorée and French comptoirs along the Petite Côte and at Albreda on the north bank of the Gambia River. These awkward circumstances existed for two decades, until the rebellion of the American colonies ignited a new round of Anglo-French warfare and France recaptured Saint-Louis in January 1779.

The period from the 1760s to the 1780s was an era of advancement for Franco-Africans, females and males alike. English traders and military officers at Saint-Louis were as easily seduced and co-opted as Frenchmen on Gorée by the prospects of personal gain in partnership with enterprising signares and African women. What differed from previous circumstances was the growing importance of Franco-African men as commercial intermediaries and as community leaders on both islands. British and French authorities at Saint-Louis and Gorée found it expedient to recognize Franco-African men as "mayors" (*maires*) in order to secure their assistance in resolving conflicts with inhabitants and coping with populations that doubled between the 1760s and the 1780s. Mayors and other male Franco-African notables shared kinship and business ties with the signares married to the British and French government officials and military officers, forming an oligarchy of shared interests. The Franco-Africans' support of British and French rule was further promoted by the introduction of European legal systems that secured their rights in regard to house plots and dwellings, ownership of slaves, and inheritance laws. Nowhere else in western Africa did Eurafricans—or Africans—possess such rights and protections. In addition to instituting ownership and inheritance laws, French and British rule transformed Wolof and Lébou practices in numerous other ways, both obvious and subtle. These included the introduction of European-style dwellings and furnishings, house plots, street grids, wage employment, literacy and record-keeping, time-keeping and daily routines, and changing European fashions. Gorée and Saint-Louis were two hundred kilometers apart and were inhabited by different Europeans during the period of the Province of Senegambia; they also had different African groups as neighbors and separate spheres of trade. Yet the Eurafrican communities developed, in tandem, the same social practices, derived from their shared Luso-African heritage.

Saint-Louis during British Administration, 1758–79

The British capture of Saint-Louis in 1758 ended the commercial monopoly of the Compagnie du Sénégal and replaced it with trade that was open to all Englishmen. Prominent among the new traders were British military officers, who were authorized by the Board of Trade to barter goods in order to obtain necessary stores but forbidden to engage in "any private trade or traffick whatsoever on their own account further than may be absolutely necessary for the supply of mere personal wants" (E. C. Martin 1927/1970, 71). These two exculpatory provisos allowed officers and signares all the latitude they needed for commercial aggrandizement.

The character of the British military occupation of Saint-Louis from 1758 to the end of the Seven Years' War was revealed in a report prepared by John Barnes, who arrived to take charge of the settlement in December 1763. Barnes described the fort as a "dismal heap of ruins" and characterized the British garrison as "a set of the most mutinous, drunken, abandoned fellows I ever met with," which implied much the same about their officers. According to Barnes's estimates, Saint-Louis had about three thousand inhabitants, including a considerable number of nonindigenous Africans. Soldiers and sailors, together with Africans, drank and brawled in the numerous taverns on the island (Dodwell 1916, 274–75).

Franco-African boatmen had taken over the trade with Galam along the upper reaches of the Senegal River during the last years of the Compagnie du Sénégal, and incoming English traders did not interfere with their thriving commerce.

North-south trade across western Africa expanded following the establishment of two Fula almamates: the founding of the almamate in Bundu in the 1690s, which controlled the territory between the Falemé River and the upper reaches of the Gambia River, was followed by the founding of a second Muslim state in Futa Jallon during the 1720s. The two almamates dominated groups living between their territories, so caravans from Futa Jallon could transport kola and other goods to Galam without interference. English traders, for their part, controlled imports and exports. British rule of the Province of Senegambia opened the way for Anglo-Portuguese trade in Brazilian tobacco as well as Virginia-grown tobacco (Saugnier and Brisson 1792/1969, 295; Richardson 1979, 326 n. 46; Curtin 1975, 115, 229).

There is a dearth of information concerning the period of British control in Saint-Louis, principally attributed to the "over-mastering aversion to correspondence" of Gov. Charles O'Hara, whose tenure spanned the years from 1766 to 1776 (E. C. Martin 1927/1970, 76). Nonetheless, it is evident that Eurafricans and Africans had unprecedented roles in trade—as well as unprecedented influence—during the era of British rule. In 1764, the Eurafrican trader Charles Thévenot was reluctantly recognized as the spokesman for the Eurafrican and African community, styling himself "mayor." Thévenot had resided in Paris for several years, where he represented himself as an "African prince." He also officiated as a priest to the Catholic community and, in the words of a 1765 dispatch, "had arrogated to himself the Office of a civil Magistrate, without any authority from the Committee or their Officers" (Saugnier and Brisson 1792/1969, 179–80; Golberry 1802, 1:243–44; Hargreaves 1969, 82–83 n. 2). Manifestly, Governor O'Hara had reason to accommodate someone who had such recognition and stature when he recognized him as the community's spokesman. Philip Curtin put the development in perspective: "The operative word here is 'recognize,' not 'appoint' or 'create,' since the office paralleled the role of the Wolof *Jawdi mbul,* who represented the free-born lineages of Kajor" (Curtin 1975, 115).

A decade later, Charles Thévenot opposed Governor O'Hara in a petition incorporating twenty-three grievances that was sent to the British secretary of state and dated August 22, 1775. Among numerous arbitrary and high-handed acts, O'Hara was charged with selling free people into slavery; seizing three properties to house concubines named Gone Fall, Coumba Poole, and Silvia; and taking a house for his son. Thévenot's signature was followed by those of fourteen other men, including a John/Jean Thévenot, who may have been his brother or son (Hargreaves 1969, 76–83).

One of the grievances of Saint-Louis's inhabitants was that Governor

O'Hara, an Irish Protestant, sought to extirpate Catholicism, notwithstanding the terms of the French surrender of the island in 1758 that stipulated that Eurafricans and free Africans would not be molested in matters of religious observance. The tenacity of practicing Catholics and their duress under British rule was suggested by John Hargreaves: "In 1776, Governor McNamara [O'Hara's successor] appealed for Protestant clergy and teachers to stop 'the vile custom of going to Gorée daily for confession and marriage,' and lamented that after eighteen years of British occupation 'the Children of the English, even of my Council, are breeding up to the Popish faith'" (Hargreaves 1965, 180). One may suppose that the visitors to Gorée were attracted by social and commercial opportunities as well as religious observances.

Gorée and French Commercial Initiatives, 1763–79

France regained possession of Gorée on September 13, 1763. Pierre-Thomas-Guillaume Poncet de la Rivière, the first royal governor, was accompanied by an entourage that included 6 officers and 110 soldiers, 25 laborers, and 30 sailors — far too many people to be accommodated in the few dilapidated buildings surviving the two fires that had swept the island during the British occupation. Governor Poncet rented a house from Blaise de Saint-Jean (son of the former French commandant) and subsequently purchased it for a signare named Marie-Thérèse (Demanet 1767, 88–89; J. Delcourt 1982, 52). A Catholic African resident of Gorée named Antoine Kiaka was recognized as maire, succeeding another Catholic African named Kiémé. Joseph Bonnet, maire in 1778, was succeeded by other Franco-Africans (Jore 1965, 257; Knight-Baylac 1970b, 404).

The royal governor, officials, and military officers had few duties to perform on the small island, and they proved to be easily corruptible and preoccupied with acquiring illicit wealth (Machat 1906a, 88–89). Although freedom of commerce was proclaimed, successive governors succumbed to the blandishments of directors of the Compagnie du Sénégal and imposed regulations and edicts that restricted the activities of independent French traders and both Eurafricans and Africans (Knight-Baylac 1970a, 58–59). Indeed, Governor Poncet was relieved of his command in 1764 for, among other reasons, illicit collusion with the Bordeaux entrepreneur Abraham Grades, who aquired the exclusive contract to transport personel and supplies to Gorée.

In circumstances in which the entrepreneurship of Eurafrican and African males was inhibited, Eurafrican and African women flourished as the partners of company employees, royal officials, military officers, and soldiers in the garrison. Such was the welcome accorded the French newcomers by the island's females that the Abbé Demanet, Gorée's chaplain, denounced the employees of the Compagnie du Sénégal for abandoning themselves to idleness and the pleasurable association of women who were enriching themselves. According to Demanet, some (unidentified) women at Gorée, Saint-Louis, and in the Gambia—women who previously had no possessions whatsoever—accumulated fortunes of a hundred thousand livres (Demanet 1767, 116–17). Surely one successful signare was Catherine Baudet, who, by 1767, had married three husbands successively: the sieurs Porquet, Pépin, and Franciéro, the next-to-last the surgeon of the Compagnie du Sénégal. She also raised six children: Marie-Anne Porquet; Anne, Jean, and Nicholas Pépin; and Pierre and André Franciéro (Cariou 1950, 15). Evrard Duparel's 1776 map of Gorée showed that of eighteen compounds (or *tapades,* from the Portuguese word meaning fenced grounds) that belonged to the government, eleven were occupied by signares. During the English occupation from 1779 to 1783, more buildings were constructed of slabs of basalt bonded with lime mortar. Thatch roofs long remained a fire hazard, especially when desiccated by harmattan winds, but after the French reoccupied Gorée, the easily ignited thatch was gradually replaced by tile on stone dwellings on the island. In 1780, the only private stone dwelling belonged to Jeanne Gracia (or Gratia), one of the few signares who, by that date, retained a Luso-African name (Knight-Baylac 1970b, 385–86, 403–4).

Governor Poncet pursued an activist policy with respect to French commerce and territorial acquisitions. In 1763 and 1765, he negotiated treaties with the damel of Cayor to open a comptoir at Rufisque and cede land on the Cape Verde peninsula, including the watering place at Hann and the villages of Bin and Daccard (Dakar). Poncet sought to assure a supply of water for Gorée's inhabitants and passing vessels, firewood and other building materials, and pasture for livestock. However, the agreements were rejected by the Lébou inhabitants of Cape Verde, who continued to exact payments for water and firewood. Governor Poncet also made treaties with the rulers of Baol and Siin to reestablish comptoirs at Portudal and Joal in order to purchase slaves and obtain millet, rice, and livestock for Gorée's inhabitants. The treaties negotiated by Poncet fell into desuetude, as his successors were preoccupied with obtaining provisions for Gorée's burgeoning population. Insofar as French officials could estimate, there were more than one thousand inhabitants by 1767, and the population of the island continued to increase in spite of their attempts to check its growth (Machat 1906a, 84–85; Knight-Baylac 1970b, 402, 411–12).

During the 1760s, the Gambia was an arena of conflict. In 1758, during the Seven Years' War, Niumi's warriors had engaged English forces in defense of Albreda. In the years that followed, commerce along the Gambia changed significantly, to the detriment of the people of Niumi. English vessels from Liverpool and Bristol sailed upriver past Niumi, refusing to pay customary dues despite the efforts of the commander of James Fort to persuade them to comply with long-observed practice (Gray 1940, 232). Luso-Africans living upriver likewise experienced losses, their middleman role diminished by British shipboard and factory trade.

Thus, in September 1763, the inhabitants of Niumi welcomed the reestablishment of the French comptoir at Albreda, which fronted James Island, headquarters of the lieutenant governor of the newly created Province of Senegambia. To the dismay of the English, the mansa of Niumi permitted the factory to be enclosed by a palisade with cannons mounted in two bastions (Gray 1940, 229). Nonetheless, the English fort on James Island denied French traders access to the upper river, and the English factory at Juffure a few hundred meters upstream from Albreda exploited the advantage of being the first to engage leaders of caravans descending the north bank of the Gambia.

Abbé Demanet, Gorée's chaplain, accompanied Governor Poncet on a visit to the Petite Côte and the Gambia in July 1764; the abbé ostensibly wanted to save souls, but he did not overlook potential commercial opportunities. Demanet characterized the inhabitants of Joal as "mostly Catholics." He boasted that during his visit, he baptized approximately eight hundred persons of all ages and converted many Muslims to Christianity. The bourba Siin expressed his approbation, asserting that Christians were his best subjects, but declined conversion himself (Demanet 1767, 111–12). It is noteworthy that Abbé Demanet made no mention of efforts on his part to sanctify marriages, hear confessions, or recite masses for the souls of deceased members of the Luso-African community.

Demanet did mention the navigational hazards at the mouth of the Saloum River, without reference to the Niominka middlemen inhabiting the Djomboss Islands who controlled trade. Yet he reported that sometime previous to his visit, an English vessel that attempted to sail upriver was boarded by local people who killed the crew and seized the ship and that no English vessel had since entered the river. Following Demanet's visit, Captain Aussenac made a trading voyage to Cahone in 1764. His success may have been due to his association with Caty Louet/Louette, who was the richest signare on Gorée in 1767, owning forty-three domestic slaves and twenty-five trade slaves. She was also one of the few signares who signed her name to documents (Demanet 1767, 117, 152; Knight-Baylac 1970b, 402–3; Knight 1977, 44–45).

Abbé Demanet was favorably impressed by the ruler and people of Niumi, whom he characterized as "loving" the French and "hating" the English, notwithstanding their extensive commerce with English traders. According to Demanet, whose informants likely exaggerated considerably, more than fifty vessels traded in the Gambia each year, purchasing several thousand slaves (Demanet 1767, 120–22). He described the French comptoir at Albreda as surrounded with ditches, interlaced with palisades nine to ten feet high, and protected by four cannons. Niumi's ruler lived upstream in the midst of woods inland from the river, his village identifiable by two trees rising higher than the surrounding vegetation. The largest tree was known as the ensign ("pavilion") of the mansa, who was said to insist that passing vessels fire a salute; if they neglected to do so, he supposedly forbade trade and caused all the trouble he could (Demanet 1767, 126, 133–34).

Demanet's information concerning the influence of Luso-Africans in Niumi was reflected in the trade book entries of Capt. Ezek Hopkins of the Providence, Rhode Island, brigantine *Sally,* which arrived in Niumi several months after the abbé's visit. Besides recording the titles *fidalgo* (Portuguese for nobleman or lord), *linguister* (from the Portuguese word *língüista,* meaning linguist), and *geógrafo* (the Portuguese term for geographer), Hopkins's trade book testified to the artful procrastination of the mansa and his entourage. The *Sally* arrived in Niumi in November 1765, and during the following four months, Captain Hopkins disbursed large quantities of rum and other trade goods as presents; for customs dues; and for payments to "King Fodolgo Talko," his son, the alcaide, "fodolgo Ecorte" (from the Portuguese word *escolta, meaning* escort or bodyguard), the "linguister" and "geograff," and their retinues. Meanwhile, Hopkins acquired only one or two slaves at a time (Wax 1972, 175–76; Coughtry 1981, 120–21).

Abbé Demanet professed a high regard for the Christians in Niumi and asserted that Christianity was well implanted, despite the fact that allegedly no priest had visited the Gambia during the twenty years preceding his visit. He characterized the black "Portuguese" inhabitants of seven (unidentified) villages as "nearly all Christians," who, as "scrupulous observers of the faith," baptized all newborn children. Demanet consecrated a chapel at Albreda, and, accompanied by celebratory shots fired by the cannons of Fort François de Albreda, he boasted that he baptized more than seven hundred people, including some Muslims (Demanet 1767, 122–23). As in his account of the pastoral visit to Joal, he made no mention of sanctifying marriages, hearing confessions, or saying masses for deceased members of the community. Nor did he record that he distributed bibles or devotional literature, rosaries, crucifixes, or scapulars, which he could have publicly blessed and distributed to compete with animist and Muslim amulets. Evidently, such pastoral endeavors would have distracted him while he inquired about commercial opportunities.

Demanet was informed that the dangerous bar at the mouth of the Casamance River made it impracticable for large vessels. A Luso-African ("Nègre Chrétien") at Albreda had recently returned from a pioneering voyage to the Casamance in a large (Niominka?) pirogue and had traded with several villages and obtained captives, gold, ivory, wax, and rice at extremely favorable exchanges (five times more than he anticipated). The Diola inhabitants of the Casamance—possessing only small fishing dugouts with which they conveyed captives, wax, and foodstuffs for sale to Mandinka and traders from Bissau—said that they had never seen such a large pirogue. A handful of Luso-Africans lived on the north bank near the mouth of the Casamance, but for lack of merchandise, they traded with only a few neighboring villages. The informant asserted that people living in the Casamance would welcome French traders bringing gunpowder, lead, arms, and brandy, for which they would exchange captives, gold, ivory, beeswax, and rice. Demanet stressed his confidence in the Luso-African's veracity, having reminded the man that, as a Christian, he must tell the truth (Demanet 1767, 178–81).

It seems likely that the Luso-African's reconnaissance expedition to the Casamance River was sponsored by the French traders who had recently reoccupied Albreda. Who better to initiate trade in the Casamance than Luso-Africans who possessed large pirogues (manned by Niominka?), spoke Crioulo, and possibly shared kinship affiliations with Luso-Africans living along the lower Casamance? This may or may not have been the case in this instance, but during the years that followed, Luso-Africans living on Gorée and along the Petite Côte were recruited by French shipmasters to man vessels engaged in trade south of the Gambia River.

Abbé Demanet was informed (possibly by the same Luso-African at Albreda) that there were two "Portuguese" settlements along the Casamance. Guinguim (on the Rio Pequeno de São Domingos, a tributary of the Cacheu River) and Ziguinchor were described as being composed of miserable dwellings surrounded by tapades made of sticks and earth; the dwellings, he reported, were inhabited by a few wretched Luso-Africans ("Portugais") who formerly excluded foreigners from the Casamance River. The Luso-Africans conveyed local products in pirogues to "Sommers," a village on the "left bank" of the river, thence to Geregia ("Gereges"), and from there to the Gambia, where they would be sold to either French or English traders. Demanet was told that many "Portugais" had, in the past, lived along the Casamance River and traded six hundred to seven hundred slaves a year from the Mandinka state of Kaabu. Exaggerated numbers aside, a decline in the Casamance trade with Kaabu probably resulted from the shift in trade from Cacheu to Bissau during the era of the Companhia do Grão-Para e Maranhão. Demanet did not visit Bolama, but his book included an enthusiastic report on the island's agricultural potential and valuable timber. When he returned to Gorée, the abbé persuaded Governor Poncet to furnish two chaloupes for a reconnaissance expedition to the Casamance, but the venture was abandoned after Demanet fell ill and the governor was recalled to France (Demanet 1767, 178–83, 189–91, 211–15; cf. Wadstrom 1794–95/1968, 2:130–32).

Poncet proposed establishing French comptoirs at Bissau and Bolama, as did Desmesnagers, his successor as governor of Gorée. In a dispatch dated June 13, 1765, Governor Desmesnagers communicated that Bissau's ruler and people welcomed the return of French traders and refused to allow any foreigners to construct dwellings at the place formerly occupied by French traders. Reportedly, the "Portuguese" would not oppose the return of French traders, since they too appreciated the potential benefits. Desmesnagers also called attention to Bolama, characterizing the island as very beautiful, well wooded, possessing good water sources, and uninhabited (Machat 1906a, 92–93; Jore 1965, 47–48). The last assertion was untrue; Desmesnagers's informant evidently was unaware that Bijago cultivated rice on the southern part of the island during the rainy season. Poncet's and Desmesnagers's recommendations were not approved.

In 1764, English and French traders competing for the trade of Niumi and Saluum initiated a conflict that allied French traders with the Mandinka of Niumi and English traders with the Serer of Saluum. British warships arrived in March 1765 and compelled the French to remove the cannons from the comptoir at Albreda, which thereafter was to remain unfortified. The conflict between European and African traders continued. In April 1766, responsibility for English trade along the Gambia River passed from the Committee of Merchants to the British Crown when a detachment of troops from Saint-Louis, commanded by Lt. Gov. Joseph Debat, arrived to garrison James Island.

The Anglo-Mandinka dispute continued unresolved, with the English meanwhile relying on Luso-Africans as intermediaries for trade along the upper Gambia. In 1767, Niumi's mansa ordered the seizure of four Europeans and twelve slaves and cut off water and wood to James Island. In April 1768, soldiers from James Fort burned Albreda, taking thirty-nine prisoners, including the "queen" of Niumi. Niumi's boycott continued, and the English had to obtain water from Bintang along Vintang Creek. In May, Debat reported, "I pay for water as I do for wine" (Gray 1940, 229–30, 237, 240, and cf. 246; Curtin 1975, 123–24).

On July 14, 1768, Niumi's forces launched an unsuccessful surprise raid on James Island, allegedly with French complicity. Mandinka attacks on trading craft continued until May 1769, when the presence of British men-of-war constrained the people of Niumi to reestablish former trade relations. Besides their commerce at Albreda, French traders competed with English traders along the south bank at Bintang, Béréfil, and Dyarmé. The comptoir at Bintang was especially valued for the large quantities of beeswax which French traders obtained from Diola who carried it along routes linking the Casamance and Cacheu Rivers (Machat 1906a, 103, 109; Gray 1940, 240–43; Curtin 1975, 122–24).

An extraordinary episode associated with the expanding trade between the British colonies in North America and western Africa involved the courageous initiative of the female Gambian trader Penda Lawrence, who took passage to Charleston, South Carolina, in 1772 on the snow *New Brittania,* commanded by Stephen Deaux. Captain Deaux secured a court certificate to ensure her safety while in America. The certificate read, in part:

> [Penda] Lawrence a free Black Woman and heretofore a Considerable trader in the River Gambia on the Co[a]st of Africa hath voluntarily come to be and Remain for sometime in this province, and at the request of the said Stephen Deaux—these are therefore to certify and make Known to all whom it may concern that the said [Penda] Lawrence is a free woman and is therefore intitled to ever[y] Priviledge which by Law she aught to have in this province, and I do hereby permit the said [Penda] Lawrence to pass and Repass unmolested within the said Province on her Lawfull and necessary occations she Conforming to the Laws thereof. (Phillips 1969, 141–42)

Other information concerning Penda Lawrence was not provided. Possibly, she was a daughter of "Lawrence of Deal," the father of David Lawrence (c. 1775–1812), an Anglo-African trading in the Nunez River in the early 1790s (Mouser 1994, 109, "Lawrence"). One supposes that Penda Lawrence was of considerable assistance to Captain Deaux while he was trading along the Gambia.

Information concerning Luso-African trade during this period was recorded in a 1771 mémoire by a Captain Morel, reporting on his many years in African commerce. Morel remarked on the lucrative trade in salt that English and especially Luso-Africans ("Portugais") obtained in the Saloum River and sold in markets along the upper Gambia as far as Yanamarou ("Niani Mar"), the head of navigation for seafaring vessels. Luso-African pirogues transported ten, twelve, or even fifteen hogsheads ("barriques"), some trading upriver past Yanamarou a few kilometers down river from Kassang, the head of navigation for large sailing vessels. Both French and English traders knew that caravan routes linked Galam with its gold trade (Machat 1906a, 93–94; cf. Boulègue 1989, 76–77, 82 n. 28).

Morel did not identify the crews, but it is likely the pirogues were manned by Niominka employed by Luso-Africans. Further, English traders' wives participated in the upriver commerce. In 1776, Gov. Joseph Alexandre le Brasseur reported that the mansa of Niumi was angered by the loss of customs revenues due to the fact that slave caravans no longer went downriver to Gilifree and Albreda—so angered, in fact, that he had, for some time, contemplated sending a fleet of canoes upriver to apprehend the wives of the English traders and bring them back to Juffure. Le Brasseur asserted that it would be easy for aggressive French traders to supplant the English, especially with the support of Niumi's ruler and the "grand marabout Faude" (Machat 1906a, 103, 105). The last remark referred to the *falifo* at Juffure (termed *alquier* by the English) to whom Europeans paid customs. This lucrative position was monopolized by the Tall family, members of a Muslim commercial and clerical lineage from Futa Toro that settled in Niumi (Wright 1997, 85, 112, 124, 133 n. 51). By the 1760s, the Tall serving as falifo was an important marabout: the title "Fodé" designated a cleric who had mastered some of the most recondite Arabic texts (Wright 1997, 85, 112, 124, 133 n. 51). That Niumi's ruler appointed a marabout to be alquier was indicative of the increasing power of Muslims along the Gambia River and the declining influence of Luso-Africans professing Christianity.

Captain Morel's account of the deficiencies of French trade was corroborated by a British officer who visited Albreda around 1771. He reported meeting "only one French woman, all the men except her husband being dead, and he was gone up the river trading, and while I was there, she heard he was dead and all the white men with him, which was a very common case, for she had five husbands in three years" (Gray 1940, 243). This grisly anecdote testifies to the high death rates Europeans experienced in the Gambia River. Luso-African men continued to be hired to crew French trading craft, and a "Sinara Leaser" was sufficiently affluent to purchase 560 gallons of rum from an American vessel in November 1774 (Gray 1940, 245; Donnan 1930/1969, 3:280).

During the 1770s, if not previously, French vessels ventured into the Casamance River. The crews of Gorée-based vessels included Luso-Africans from Gorée and the Petite Côte and Lébou residing on the Cape Verde peninsula (Curtin 1975, 114). Luso-Africans pioneering this commerce doubtless used Crioulo to advantage and capitalized on cultural and social attributes shared with Luso-Africans living along the Casamance. The Portuguese response to the French intrusion in the Casamance came not from Cacheu but from Bissau. In September 1774, a schooner and four other vessels from Bissau captured a ship from Nantes, the *Saint-Jean Baptiste,* while it was trading at Ziguinchor. The capture led to contentious diplomatic exchanges between French and Portuguese officials during the months that followed, which included disagreement as to whether French traders had the right to trade in the Bissagos Islands (Machat 1906a, 108). Meanwhile, French vessels continued trading in the Casamance River.

French trade at Albreda—and expectations of its potential—oscillated during the 1770s. In 1773, a French report asserted that the quality of merchandise English traders offered along the upper Gambia was so inferior to French imports that Mandinka caravans descended the north bank of the river to trade at Albreda (Knight-Baylac 1970a, 90). The same year, Gov. Pierre-Louis de Rastel de Rocheblave contrasted circumstances in the Gambia with those in the Saloum and Casamance Rivers, where French initiatives had failed due to the hostility of Niominka middlemen and the opposition of Luso-Africans. Albreda, he contended, offered the best opportunities for French traders: living conditions were peaceful for the residents, and the ruler and his alquiers were accommodating and "more civilized" than others (Machat 1906a, 91). In 1774, Rocheblave's successor, Gov. Joseph Alexandre Le Brasseur, likewise expressed disappointment regarding French attempts to trade in the Saloum River, whence slave caravans from the interior were redirected to the English traders at Kau-ur on the Gambia who made generous presents to the Bur Saluum. French vessels attempted to trade in the Saloum River from time to time, but many were pillaged (Machat 1906a, 102–5; Becker and Martin 1977, 106–7).

In 1775, officials in France reviewed the rising costs of maintaining Albreda, Gorée, and the comptoirs along the Petite Côte, compared with the disappointing returns from their trade. As a consequence, the government ceased to supply the colony, instead tending a contract to the newly founded Compagnie de la Colonie Française de Guyane. This company was so incompetently managed that circumstances would worsen greatly (Cultru 1910, 218–19; Machat 1906a, 112). By 1776, French trade had declined to such an extent that Governor Le Brasseur reported that Africans living along the Gambia River were becoming convinced that France no longer possessed either resources or vessels (Knight-Baylac 1970a, 89). Two years later, outraged by unfulfilled promises, the ruler of Niumi resolved to eject the French from Albreda and welcome English traders, but he was persuaded to await new communications from France (Labarthe 1802, 246).

In a June 1778 mémoire compiled on his return to France, Governor Le Brasseur wrote that French traded at the village of Itou at the mouth of the

Casamance to the exclusion of competitors. Vessels from Gorée obtained abundant quantities of rice, and prospects were promising for expanding trade in captives, ivory, and wax. Le Brasseur dismissed the Luso-African inhabitants of Ziguinchor as slothful and impoverished, relying on goods obtained on credit from the agents of the Companhia Geral do Grão-Para e Maranhão at Cacheu. Having acquired merchandise the agents valued as worth two or three slaves, the Luso-Africans contrived to obtain twice as many, selling the remainder to foreign traders (Machat 1906a, 106).

As elsewhere in western Africa, the inability of Luso-Africans to amass capital compelled them to trade on credit. This handicap, plus the incapacity of the nearly defunct Maranhão Company to supply the needs of Luso-African clients, enabled French traders to realize considerable profits in Casamance trade. Le Brasseur anticipated that expanding trade upriver would attract large numbers of Mandinka, who were "very partial to French merchandise," bringing all the riches of the African interior. France, he argued, should undertake to supplant Portugal in the Casamance (Machat 1906a, 106–7; Becker and Martin 1977, 107–8). Such an eventuality was anticipated by informed Portuguese. During the American War of Independence, João da Costa, an employee of the Companhia Geral do Grão-Para e Maranhão, warned that once hostilities between France and England ceased, one or the other country might attempt to annex the Casamance to monopolize the large exports of wax and slaves. It was a matter of concern that, despite the fact that the garrison at Ziguinchor was a detachment of Cacheu's praça, the soldiers were effectively under the control of local *pretos,* that is, Luso-Africans (Barreto 1938, 156).

Signares and Their Households

Gorée's population increased from more than a thousand people in 1767 to half again as many by 1776 (Knight-Baylac 1970b, 402). Many of the island's inhabitants were domestic slaves belonging to signares. Signares who were successful in trade and marriages presided over large households, with enclosed compounds inhabited by their domestic slaves. Female slaves tended the signares and their families as cooks, washerwomen, and wet nurses and as the signares' personal maids and confidants. The compounds served as the workshops of male slaves who were skilled smiths, masons, carpenters, weavers, tailors, and sailors, the latter of whom the signares engaged to work on French vessels and trade on their behalf. As in other areas of western Africa, it was the older and more experienced signares, possessing large households of skilled domestic slaves and established commercial networks, who were sought as partners by the highest-ranking company employees (Prélong 1793, 285; Knight 1977, 45–47).

Domestic slaves lived in thatched dwellings ranged around the inside walls of the compounds. The growing number of domestic slaves on Gorée was a matter of concern for French authorities due to the unwillingness of signares to sell trade slaves after they had lived on Gorée a month or more and thereby had begun to acquire social ties (Knight-Baylac 1970b, 404). Once trade slaves "belonged" to a community, they could not be sold except as punishment for crimes or chronic misbehavior. Slave children were, from infancy, treated as members of the signares' extended families. Raised along with the signares' children, domestic slaves were regarded by others as fellow inhabitants of Gorée or Saint-Louis. During adolescence, the girls were taught domestic skills and the boys were apprenticed to learn useful trades such as weaving and tailoring, which they practiced in the compound, or were hired out to work as grumetes, stevedores, smiths, stonemasons, brick makers, carpenters, coopers, and wharf men and at other tasks to earn income for their owners (Villeneuve 1814, 70).

Domestic slaves were never sold into the Atlantic slave trade except in extraordinary circumstances, such as for threatening the life of a free person or displaying incorrigible social behavior. European slavers who pressured indebted slave owners to sell domestic slaves risked dire consequences (Saugnier and Brisson 1792/1969, 277–78; Pelletan 1800, 99–100; Villeneuve 1814, 70).

There was an additional consideration in play as well: the soldiers of the garrisons fraternized with female domestic slaves. When Gov. Jacques-Joseph Eyriès of Gorée sought to reduce the slave population of the island in 1770, the troops threatened to mutiny because each man claimed a lover among the island's domestic slaves (Knight-Baylac 1970b, 404–5; Curtin 1975, 116). British officers at James Fort were similarly stymied by the slave-soldiers in their garrison, as acknowledged in 1778: "The Castle Slaves are so closely connected with the People of the Country by Marriages and other Social Ties, that an Attempt to remove any of the former would infallibly occasion very great Disturbances and Insurrections among the Natives, and render the Safety of the Forts and Settlements highly precarious, as their Defense depends more on the Attachment of the Slaves than on the feeble force in Civil and Military Servants" (quoted in Wright 1997, 132 n. 38). Most of the slave-soldiers' children probably remained affiliated with their mothers' societies, but some doubtless found employment at James Fort and with English trading enterprises along the Gambia River.

The troops in Gorée's garrison were an undisciplined rabble, like the British soldiers sent to the Province of Senegambia and the soldiers dispatched from Portugal to the praças in Guinea. Shipped to Africa with little hope of returning to Europe, the men gave themselves up to debauchery fueled by the brandy that was issued as part of their rations. Governor Le Brasseur characterized the soldiers of Gorée's garrison as "ruffians collected from the slums of European cities, almost always from the refuse of [the port of?] Rochefort . . . the climate and idleness augment their vices" (Machat 1906a, 102 and n. 4).

To be sure, the troops were deplorably treated. Le Brasseur himself complained to the minister in January 1777 of the despicable rations supplied by the Compagnie de la Colonie Français de Guyane: as he put it, the wine was undrinkable and absolutely no one would touch it—they were reduced to drinking water—and the tobacco resembled fermented cabbage leaves. Le Brasseur's complaints notwithstanding, in April 1777, the Compagnie de Guyane was awarded the exclusive right to the slave trade and other commerce for fifteen years in return for paying Gorée's garrison and supplying the island's needs (Machat 1906a, 112–13; Cultru 1910, 219–20). When Le Brasseur departed for France, Gorée's inhabitants gave him a mémoire requesting his support in their fight against the Compagnie de Guyane. Of the thirteen signatories to the document, five were women: Cati Louet, Hélène Aussenac, Anne Casano, Anne Roussin, and Marie-Thérèse Rossignol, the last two of whom were householders. Of the eight men who signed, Antoine Kiaka and Etienne Jouga were African property holders (Knight 1977, 46–47).

Circumstances were comparable at the British garrisons at James Fort and Saint-Louis. During the 1770s, there was rancorous strife between the officers cooped up on James Island. The troops they commanded included convicted felons dispatched from the British garrison at Saint-Louis. Successive lieutenant governors victimized them by refusing to pay their wages in cash, instead foisting off grossly overvalued beads and iron bars in order to profit from the difference between the cost prices. Conditions at Saint-Louis were similarly deplorable: when Gov. John Clarke arrived at Saint-Louis in April 1777, he found the troops undisciplined, the government departments in a chaotic state, and "a very complicated scene of public fraud, embezzlement, and perjury" (Gray 1940, 235, 254–55, 257).

Anglo-French Warfare, 1778–83

The American War of Independence (1775–83) entangled Britain and France after February 6, 1778, when France concluded treaties of commerce and alliance with the rebellious British colonies in North America. American vessels opportunistically engaged in commerce raiding in western Africa: three vessels arrived at Gorée in March 1778, and others (or the same ones) cruised off the Gambia and Sierra Leone Rivers (Machat 1906a, 120; Allen 1913, 1:299–301). The residents of Saint-Louis and Gorée were distracted from warfare by a yellow fever epidemic that killed scores of Europeans and numerous inhabitants and slaves. During July and August 1778, sixty of the ninety-three whites on Gorée died (Lintingre 1966, 79; Knight 1977, 45; Searing 1993, 115).

French strategists had long awaited an opportunity to supplant English traders in western Africa. A fleet commanded by the Chevalier de Pontevez-Gien captured Saint-Louis in January 1779. When news of the arrival of the French fleet reached the Gambia, Africans pillaged English factories and seized trading craft along the length of the river. During this abdication of landlord responsibilities, it is likely that marauders victimized Luso-Africans and other Eurafricans unless their African relations opportunistically protected them. Luso-Africans living along the Gambia had already experienced difficulties prior to this outbreak of violence. Indeed, in a mémoire dated October 1777, Governor Le Brasseur described Luso-Africans as small in number, the greater part of them having been "empoissonnés" by the English or pillaged by African rulers (Machat 1906a, 109). That Englishmen would or could "poison" Luso-Africans must be accounted nonsense, but the import of Le Brasseur's statement is that English traders supplanted Luso-Africans.

The British garrison surrendered James Island on February 11, 1779, and the French demolished the fort, which was never to be rebuilt. The French fleet proceeded down the western Africa coast, destroying the English establishment on Bunce Island in the Sierra Leone estuary. An American privateer preceded the French vessels and pillaged English traders' factories in the Iles de Los (Machat 1906a, 117–20; Gray 1940, 266–68). Anticipating a British counterattack, officials transferred the French garrison on Gorée to Saint-Louis, and many of the island's inhabitants were transported across the Atlantic to the French colony of Guyane.

In May 1779, a British squadron seized Gorée, and five months later, a French squadron failed to recapture the island, whose inhabitants voluntarily assisted the British garrison (Cultru 1910, 221; J. Delcourt 1982, 56). The British soldiers were as undisciplined as the French soldiers they replaced. In 1782, Gov. Joseph Wall had three men flogged to death for alleged mutinous behavior. Wall afterward fled his command, to be tried and executed twenty years later (Gray 1940, 265).

Following the capture of Gorée in May 1779, English traders returned to the Gambia, gradually setting up factories along the river. By 1783, they were established at Bintang, Juffure, and Brefet along the lower river and at Nyanimaru in the upper river—all formerly places of extensive Luso-African trade. The treaty signed at Versailles on September 3, 1783, awarded France both Gorée and Saint-Louis, the latter occupation ending Britain's Province of Senegambia. Britain retained control of the Gambia River, although France held on to the right to maintain a comptoir at Albreda (Gray 1940, 269–70, 276–92).

Senegambia, 1783–92

The years between the 1783 Treaty of Versailles and the renewal of warfare between France and Britain in 1792 was a period of unprecedented commercial expansion in western Africa, encompassing not only slave trading but also commerce in palm oil, timber for ship construction, dyewoods, and other sylvan and vegetable commodities to meet the growing demand of European industries. These exchanges involved Africans in ever greater numbers, many of whom could, for the first time, acquire such commodities as European and Indian cotton textiles and American tobacco. And during these years, as never before in western Africa, French and English entrepreneurs attempted to found colonies, the English taking the initiative with settlements in the Sierra Leone estuary in May 1787 and on the island of Bolama in May 1792.

Following the reoccupation of Gorée on March 25, 1784, French trade and influence were quickly reestablished along the Petite Côte, at Albreda in the Gambia River, and in the Casamance River. Freedom of commerce was permitted all Frenchmen. During the 1780s, France invested considerable resources on its establishments at Saint-Louis and Gorée, and French traders associated with the Compagnie Nouvelle du Sénégal et Dépendances, in collaboration with Franco-African seamen and compradors, aggressively expanded French trade southward into the Guinea-Bissau region to compete with Luso-Africans and Cabo Verdeans. For the first time since the 1760s, French and Franco-Africans sought to trade at Cacheu and Bissau, challenging Luso-Africans in previously exclusive markets (Golberry 1802, 2:215–16; Knight-Baylac 1970a, 59).

Disbursements by the French government and the enterprise of the trading communities created a period of unprecedented prosperity for the inhabitants of Gorée and Saint-Louis. Charles Pierre Cornier was recognized as maire of Saint-Louis by the royal governor and served during the 1780s and 1790s. The maire functioned as an intermediary between the French commandant and two subordinates, who supervised the two wards of the town—north and south of the fort. The maire of Saint-Louis was paid a salary of 1,200 livres a year, his counterpart on Gorée 720 (Hargreaves 1967, 70; Curtin 1975, 115, 121). In 1785, Saint-Louis's population was estimated to be over six thousand inhabitants, and Gorée's was more than eighteen hundred (Golberry 1802 1:155, 2:60–61).

Luso-Africans living along the Petite Côte contrived to maintain their roles as middlemen and compradors for French and Franco-African traders as well as their identities as Luso-Africans, despite the expanding commercial and kinship links with resident French and Franco-Africans and those on Gorée. Abbé Coste settled on the Petite Côte in 1780, and was credited with much success evangelizing the inhabitants. He was buried at Joal when he died four years later (Boulègue 1989, 81). Trading on the Petite Côte in 1787, Geoffroy de Villeneuve characterized the inhabitants of Joal as conserving their Luso-African identities by "pretending" to be descended from Portuguese, by retaining their Portuguese family names, and by maintaining a semblance of Catholic practices. To his advantage and that of other Frenchmen, he acknowledged, whites were generally better treated at Joal than elsewhere (Villeneuve 1814, 1:104). Luso-Africans baptized their children with Portuguese names and buried their dead with Christian ceremonies. When they engaged in warfare, they hung large wooden crosses on their breasts and backs instead of wearing African amulets known as gris-gris (Villeneuve 1814, 3:82–83, cited in Boulègue 1989, 80).

Lacking priests and churches, Luso-Africans living along the Petite Côte traveled to Gorée for baptisms and funerals but, it seems, seldom or never for weddings. Knight reported two examples in 1787. The first was the baptism of Marie Goniès (Gomez?), the year-old daughter of Guillaume Goniès, described as a "Portuguese" from Joal, and Gracia Caffou, a resident of Gorée. The second was the interment on Gorée of Louison Commonil, "the illegitimate daughter of Fandet Goniés, 'Portuguese,' her father, and Maindoye, her mother, a Muslim, both inhabitants of Rufisque" (Knight 1977, 48).

French and Franco-Africans shipmasters hired sailors and compradors from the Petite Côte. Besides their combined Niominka and Luso-African seafaring heritage, their command of Crioulo and kinship affiliations indubitably were advantageous for their trading expeditions in the Casamance River and southward in the Guinea-Bissau region. Men from the Petite Côte may also have had greater resistance to malaria than the inhabitants of Gorée and Cape Verde, a significant advantage when navigating vessels in pestilential rivers.

During the 1780s, the French comptoirs at Rufisque, Portudal, and Joal were abandoned due to the small numbers of slaves traded. *Caboteurs* (coastwise traders sailing pirogues and other small craft) supplied Gorée with rice, livestock, poultry, and other provisions. In a major new initiative, Louis Le Gardeur de Repentigny, governor of Senegal from 1783 to 1785, took advantage of a falling-out between English traders and Serer that caused the latter to seize two vessels and kill many in the crews. English traders ceased to visit the Saloum River, and Bur Sandéné N'Dao made overtures to the French. Governor Repentigny visited the bur's residence at Cahone in February 1785, and in return for generous annual customs, the bur granted the French a monopoly of Saluum's trade, gave them permission to establish a comptoir in the large village of Kiawer where Mandinka caravans brought numerous slaves from the interior, ceded to France the island of Kasthiambee, and turned over three hostages (Saugnier and Brisson 1792/1969, 254; Golberry 1802, 2:106–31; Jore 1965, 81–82; Klein 1968, 27–28). Subsequently, some of Gorée's inhabitants, including Jean Saint-Jean, engaged in a remunerative commerce with Mandinka caravans and purchased inhabitants of Saluum captured by the bur's forces (Wadstrom 1794–95/1968, 13–15; Golberry 1802, 2:110–11; Durand 1806, 27–28).

French and Franco-Africans increasingly challenged Luso-African trade in the Casamance River. The intrusion of French and Franco-Africans in the Casamance was motivated by two factors: the need for rice to feed the burgeoning population of Gorée and for the purpose of buying slaves. By 1785, Gorée's population had increased to more than eighteen hundred people. Caboteurs brought millet and some rice from the Petite Côte, but the principal areas of rice cultivation extended from the Gambia River southward, and demand for rice increased whenever millet harvests were poor.

Jean P. L. Durand, the first director (1785–86) of the new Compagnie du Sénégal, advised his successor, M. Delaporte, to encourage shipmasters to obtain as much rice as possible in the Casamance, asserting that rice purchases would not interfere with trade for slaves, ivory, and wax. Durand added that rice purchased at Joal and in Casamance not only might be used to feed slaves but could also be sent to Europe on the company's vessels (AOFA, Q15, September 25, 1785). Joal was noteworthy for having pigs for sale, a Luso-African "trace element" (Golberry 1802, 2:110).

Gorée on the Eve of the French Revolution

In historical studies and literary accounts, a romantic aura is attached to the Gorée of the 1780s, especially with respect to the brief sojourn of Stanislas-Jean de Boufflers, the last royal governor before the French Revolution. The impecunious Chevalier de Boufflers forsook the sun-baked sands of Saint-Louis for the milder airs of Gorée, where he shared the companionship and commercial partnership of Anne Pépin, one of the islet's wealthiest signares. Nearly thirty years of age, she had been married before, perhaps more than once, had at least one child, and was the sister of Nicholas Pépin, a spokesman for Gorée's inhabitants. Mature and affluent signares such as Anne Pépin were sought as partners by the highest-ranking officials and officers. Nor were clergy impervious to Gorée's social ambiance: the parish priest Father Charbonnier, for instance, abandoned his vocation to marry a signare and father a child (Prélong 1793, 285; Cariou 1950, 15, and 1952, 40).

The population of Gorée continued to grow, requiring ever larger purchases of provisions along the Petite Côte and in the Casamance. There were more than one thousand people living on the island by 1767; half again as many by 1776, not counting transit slaves; and more than eighteen hundred by 1785 (Knight-Baylac 1970b, 411–12). The foregoing population estimates were calculated by households, for Gorée's inhabitants refused to permit dwelling-by-dwelling tabulations due to a concern that French authorities would implement their sporadic threats to expel "superfluous" population from the island. Silvain Meinrad Xavier de Golberry, a captain in the royal engineers and aide-de-camp to the Chevalier de Boufflers, delineated how Gorée's population was determined:

> According to a census made in 1785, its population amounted to one hundred and sixteen landed property owners, both free Africans and mulattos; assuming only three children to each dwelling, the number of free inhabitants of all ages and both sexes, comprising free resident Africans and those without property, amounted to five hundred and twenty two individuals; the number of domestic slaves . . . amounted to one thousand and forty-four persons; the total indigenous population, thus comprised fifteen hundred and sixty-six individuals; to which must be added two hundred slaves who circulated as articles of commerce and seventy to eighty men, including soldiers, officers, and employees, which elevated the total population of the island of Gorée to about eighteen hundred and forty individuals. (Golberry 1802, 2:60–61)

To accommodate the growing population, the island was transformed by the imposition of a rectilinear grid plan, with dwellings sited on streets crossing at right angles. French residents and free inhabitants lived in newly constructed square houses, while their domestic slaves remained in round dwellings. Possession of house plots was confirmed by title deeds, and legal ownership was reconfirmed following the British occupation of Gorée from 1779 to 1783. The institution of European private property rights was an important factor in convincing signares and other Eurafricans and free Africans to support French colonial rule (Knight-Baylac 1970b, 385; Knight 1977, 50–54; 1776 map by Evrard Duparel). For the first time in western Africa, Eurafricans and Africans could not only accumulate wealth, but also ensure that it was inherited by their children. The registration of Christian marriages raised questions concerning husbands' property rights: would Eurafrican men thereby gain legal access to houses, domestic slaves, trading vessels, and other forms of wealth belonging to their wives? In Senegal and elsewhere in western Africa, the introduction of European law gradually transformed prevailing African customs.

Literacy was essential for Franco-Africans in safeguarding their rights and interests, as well as engaging in commercial ventures. In 1779, the Saint-Louis parish register of a marriage that joined members of two noted Franco-African families showed that nine of the eleven signatories signed in French, including four women. The bride and groom were Jean-Jacques Thévenot, son of the former mayor Charles Thévenot and his wife Marie-Isabelle Baude, and Marie-Magdeleine Estoupan de Saint-Jean, natural daughter of Blaise Estoupan de Saint-Jean, the former governor of Gorée. Those who signed the register included Thévenot's widow, as well as Louison Kiaka, Jean Fermy, Louison Thévenot, Pierre DuBois, and Anne Cornier; Marguerite Roussin and Marie-Jeanne Thévenot made marks in lieu of signatures (Lintingre 1966, 137). Nicholas Pépin, brother of Anne and son of Catherine Baudet's second husband, Dr. Pépin, was well educated, and one may suppose that parents of others in his age cohort sought schooling for their children (Cariou 1950, 15). It is clear that the scions of leading families received some education, whether by priests, parents, or other literate residents of Gorée and Saint-Louis.

Although progressive "Europeanization" was ascribed to Gorée's inhabitants, there were countervailing influences as well. Citoyen Prélong, director of Gorée's hospital from 1787 to 1789, related that while the majority of the children on the island were baptized and inhabitants regularly attended mass, certain Islamic practices persisted. In 1788, two marabouts visited Gorée incognito and circumcised some twenty young Catholics, including a mulatto sixteen or seventeen years of age who worked at the hospital. On questioning the youth, Prélong learned that he was not entirely motivated by religious belief, having undergone the painful operation in order to please African women (Prélong 1793, 297–98).

The fact that the marabouts visited Gorée incognito was related to disputes between Muslims and French authorities. Two years previously, in January and February 1786, Saint-Louis was endangered by a spate of fires allegedly set in retaliation for the banishment of marabouts from the island. When the dispossessed inhabitants applied to French authorities for financial assistance, Boufflers promised aid only to those who would rebuild their homes with bricks (Magnieu and Prat 1875, 404–9).

The ground floors of the houses contained kitchens, pantries, storerooms, and cells for securing trade slaves. The signare and her family lived on the upper floor, which had high-ceilinged, airy rooms with louvered doors opening onto balconies facing the streets and verandas facing the compounds. Rooms were closed to sunlight during the day and were opened to the onshore sea breezes commencing in the late afternoon, which revitalized social activities and promoted a good night's sleep. The second-floor living quarters were not only cooler but also less accessible to snakes, scorpions, centipedes, and other insects, and they attracted companionable geckos—house lizards that patrolled walls and ceilings on suctioned footpads in pursuit of mosquitoes, moths, and flies and reputedly brought good fortune to a dwelling's inhabitants. Houses were enclosed by compounds with walls of the same material or by palisades of reeds. Inside the compounds were the dwellings of domestic slaves, palm and pawpaw trees, banana plants, and kitchen gardens.

The growing number of such dwellings was indicative of the mounting affluence of the inhabitants of Gorée and Saint-Louis in the 1770s and 1780s: on Gorée, that number increased from fewer than six in 1772 to more than fifty by 1789, all constructed with stone and lime mortar made of seashells (Prélong 1793, 285–86; Bennett and Brooks 1965, 65–66; Carnes 1852/1969, 40–41, 47–48). Several of these elegant houses survive to the present day (J. Delcourt 1982, illustrations on pp. 55, 69, and 71; Renaudeau 1978).

The earliest depiction of a signare appeared in a book published in 1789 by Dominique Harcourt Lamiral, who first arrived in Senegal in 1779 as agent for the Compagnie de la Guyane. Lamiral commenced his description, "Seeing the women in that country one infinitely regrets that they are not white" (Lamiral 1789, 44, 108). The picture was probably drafted according to Lamiral's instructions by a French artist unskilled in drawing Africans; however, except for European facial features, the portrayal corresponded to written descriptions and included the signare's distinctive turban (though not cone-shaped), her loose and flowing gown adapted from the French shift, and the female domestic slave carrying a parasol to shield her pale Eurafrican complexion from the sun's rays. One special feature of Lamiral's portrait is the signare's animated and forceful stance; this contrasts with artists' depictions of signares in the nineteenth century, which invariably (and improbably) presented lightly pigmented women in static postures with European facial features and passive expressions (Brooks 1980c). Passiveness in portraiture belied the passions exhibited by signares defending their reputations and interests (Sackur 1992, 76–78).

The apogee of the signares' wealth and influence was in the 1780s, after which they experienced a long diminuendo. Monopolistic trading companies were abolished at the time of the French Revolution, ending the remunerative illicit commerce that signares and company employees had opportunistically exploited. Yet for decades thereafter, signares continued to profit from the earnings of their domestic slaves, and newly arrived French traders, administrators, and military and naval personnel readily embraced the seductive lifestyle these women created and sustained. Many Luso-African social and cultural practices persisted among the descendants of Luso-Africans and Franco-Africans, especially at Gorée and along the Petite Côte, including Crioulo as the language of commerce and social intercourse, Christian practices modified by Luso-African usage, panos worn by women, and Luso-African cuisine and domestic practices. Among numerous Crioulo words in Senegambian languages is *Tougal,* the Wolof word for France, which was derived from *Portugal* (Angrand 1952, 97; Gamble 1992, 17).

Gambia Commerce, 1780s–1790s

Although French vessels and traders residing at Albreda were prevented from trading upriver past James Island, they remained active in markets along the lower Gambia during the 1780s (Gray 1940, 276–92). Remarkably, neither British nor French sources dating to the 1780s made reference to Luso-African traders residing along the upper Gambia, where they had prospered as middlemen for three centuries. The principal factors in Luso-Africans' "disappearance" seemingly were threefold: the fact that they were despoiled during conflicts, the progressive spread of Islam and Muslim traders, and the advent of English traders establishing factories along the upper river and supplanting Luso-African middlemen who had conveyed slaves and other commodities downstream to James Island and Albreda (Gray 1940, 14–15, 290–92). Most of the Luso-Africans who left the upper Gambia probably resettled in Ziguinchor, Farim, Cacheu, and Geba, reinforcing the Luso-African communities that will be discussed.

It is noteworthy that English and French slave exports from the Gambia

River markedly declined during the latter years of the eighteenth century. During the first two-thirds of the century, slave exports had averaged between 1,000 and 1,500 a year, but they diminished to about 800 per year during the 1770s, around 300 annually during the 1780s and 1790s, and as few as 150 per year during the first decade of the 1800s (Wright 1997, 145, derived from Curtin 1975, table 4.3 on p. 164). The extent to which this decline was associated with the departure of Luso-Africans, the redirecting of slave caravans to other rivers, or a combination of these and other factors remains to be determined.

Excluded from trade above James Island, French traders experienced ongoing difficulties engaging in commerce at Albreda (Gray 1940, 273). When Golberry, the aide-de-camp to the Chevalier de Boufflers, visited Niumi in April 1786, he was persuaded that the uncle acting as regent for a young and dissolute mansa was a friend of the French and a devout Muslim. Golberry negotiated a larger area for French traders and other privileges, and he exacted four children from leading families to be taken as hostages to Gorée (Golberry 1802, 2:160–63, 180–81). Significantly, Golberry's chapter on the Gambia made no mention of Luso-Africans. Golberry rented a compound at Albreda from a Franco-African named Feuillée, son of a former employee of the Compagnie des Indes (Golberry 1802, 2:170–71).

Europeans continued to experience difficulties trading in Niumi, complaining of extortionate duties exacted on vessels. The alquier of Juffure, who collected duties together with his entourage, made importunate and incessant demands on shipmasters for gifts (Park 1799/1971, 4; Durand 1806, 40; Anstey 1975, 20). J. G. Pelletan, director of the Compagnie du Sénégal in 1787 and 1788, characterized the comptoir at Albreda as having marginal value for French commerce and as a dangerous place for resident traders. Whether white, mulatto, or African, factors were subject to arbitrary pillages and personal violence, and several were murdered. Ship-borne trade in the Gambia was restricted to cabotage by inhabitants of Gorée and sporadic visits by French vessels that engaged pilots at Gorée and generally restricted their commerce to visiting English factories (Pelletan 1800, 33–35).

The falloff of slave exports from the Gambia River had devastating consequences for the Mandinka of Niumi, who were afflicted by progressive drought conditions beginning in the 1740s, rendering them increasingly dependent on food imports. Niumi's mansas attempted to maintain customary levels of expenditure for themselves and their entourages by imposing extortionary taxes on traders and by expropriating trade goods from resident Luso-Africans. These counterproductive policies, combined with occasional depredations by Niumi's warriors, drove Luso-Africans from Niumi after three centuries of profitable collaboration with Mandinka elites and traders (Wright 1997, 116–17, 128–29). Donald Wright contributed an epitaph:

> Niumi's rulers hurt the Luso-Africans, too, with their tendency to insist on customary rights of inheritance from foreigners dying on Niumi soil—and regardless of where they were born, the Luso-Africans remained a foreign group in this regard—or of all persons tied to the ruling lineages in relationships of dependence. As the latter half of the eighteenth century wore on, some Luso-Africans probably melded into Niumi's African population and disappeared from the record; some drifted off to areas of more promising trade south of the Gambia. By the late 1750s there are no longer Portuguese names in the English ledgers. Those who remained on Niumi soil into the 1760s and beyond clung to relationships with French traders in Albreda. . . . By the end of the century there no longer was a noticeable Luso-African presence in Niumi, unless, of course, one counts the cultural remains of square houses with white walls, *pirogues* carrying much of the trade goods along the lower Gambia, and a trade language of the region with many words rooted in Portuguese. (Wright 1997, 124)

Luso-Africans were likewise supplanted in other markets along the lower Gambia. Progressive drought conditions during the c. 1630–c. 1860 dry period contributed to the Mandinka conquest of the Banyun states of Jagra and Foni along the south bank of the river. Previously stymied by the wide, swamp-bordered Vintang Creek and Foni's tsetse-infested marshlands, Mandinka found their opportunities for making advances improved during the eighteenth century as Diola groups challenged Banyun hegemony and curtailed Luso-African and European travel between the Gambia and Casamance Rivers. During the second half of the eighteenth century, Mandinka supplanted Banyun as rulers of Jagra and Foni.

When the British explorer Mungo Park visited Niumi and Vintang in 1795, he did not record encountering any Luso-Africans. At Vintang, where sixty years earlier Francis Moore reported that Banyun and Luso-Africans were middlemen carrying on a thriving commerce and speaking Crioulo, Park reported that Diola trading beeswax were now dealing with Mandinka brokers who spoke some English and who schemed with Europeans to defraud them: "The [Mandinka] broker makes a bargain; and with the connivance of the European, receives a certain part only of the payment; which he gives to his employer as the whole; the remainder (which is very truly called the *cheating money*) he receives when the Feloop is gone, and appropriates to himself, as a reward for his trouble" (Park 1799/1971, 4–5). Besides selling great quantities of beeswax, Diola — whom Park's informants denigrated as "a wild and unsociable race of people" — supplied traders along both the Gambia and Casamance Rivers with rice, goats, and poultry at reasonable prices, keeping for themselves the honey they collected to make strong intoxicating liquor (Park 1799/1971, 5).

Along the upper Gambia River, Park was befriended by two hospitable Luso-African women. In December 1795, he rested at Jindey in the home of a woman whom he described as "a black woman, who had formerly been the *chere amie* of a white trader named Hewett; and who, in consequence thereof, was called, by way of distinction, *Seniora*" (Park 1799/1971, 31). At Tendacunda on his return journey in 1796, Park stayed at the house of "an aged black female called Seniora Camilla" who had lived at an English factory for many years (Park 1799/1971, 357–58). In both instances, Park referred to the women living in houses, and in relating the reaction of Karfa Taura, a slave trader ("slatee") who had befriended him, he indirectly described Camilla's house: "Everything [Karfa Taura] saw seemed wonderful. The furniture of the house, the chairs, &c. and particularly beds with curtains, were objects of his great admiration; and he asked me a thousand questions concerning the utility and necessity of different articles; to some of which I found it difficult to give satisfactory answers" (Park 1799/1971, 253, 357). Park paid a courtesy visit to Seniora Camilla in May 1805 during his final trip to the Gambia (Park 1815, 123–24). He made no mention of children, whether to spare the Englishmen's families or because he had not learned about any.

The "disappearance" of Luso-Africans from the Gambia reflected the changing circumstances in western Africa. Previously, Luso-Africans had dominated trade in kola and panos — commodities only political and commercial elites and their entourages could afford. But by the 1780s, increasing numbers of people in western Africa were able to purchase American leaf tobacco, an alternative indulgent to kola. Trading along the Petite Côte in the 1780s, Geoffroy de Villeneuve noted that coastal groups preferred Virginia tobacco to that grown in Galam, the former esteemed for having more flavor; indeed, Virginia tobacco was introduced to the Galam trade as well (Villeneuve 1814, 1:121; Saugnier and Brisson 1792/1969, 295, 324). Likewise, American rum increasingly competed with European brandy (Wright 1997, 121–22), and European and Indian cotton textiles became progressively less expensive than panos. American trading vessels carried dozens of European and especially Indian textiles to sell to discriminating western

African consumers (Brooks 1970, 56, 62–63). Between 1817 and 1850, the price of British textiles dropped by 75 percent, and during this era, both British and French traders offered African traders generous credit to induce them to purchase their goods (Wright 1997, 152–53). Nonetheless, panos long continued to be status markers flaunted by elites.

Regarding kola, Luso-Africans' coastwise routes were largely supplanted by Mandinka caravan networks linking markets across western Africa (Perinbam 1997, 200–207). The spread of Islam, with its prohibitions against the use of spirits, contributed to increased consumption of kola. In 1863, referring to Muslims living along the Gambia River, a British official asserted hyperbolically: "[A Muslim] is firmly attached to the belief that should he die with a portion of the cola-nut in his stomach, his eternal happiness is secure" (quoted in Gamble 1967, 39). With the expansion of commerce in hides, timber, palm oil, and other commodities, growing numbers of western Africans acquired the means to chew kola, smoke tobacco, take snuff, and wear imported textiles.

Gambia-Casamance-Cacheu, 1760s–1790s: Luso-African "Encapsulation" and "Indigenization"

During the latter decades of the eighteenth century, Luso-Africans in the Cacheu-Casamance-Gambia commercial sphere experienced a number of reverses. Diola blocked their access to trade routes linking the Cacheu and Gambia Rivers, and French and Franco-Africans encroached in Casamance markets, motivated by the demand for rice to feed the burgeoning population of Gorée as well as the need to acquire slaves. But this was also the era when the Luso-African inhabitants of Ziguinchor acquired increasing control over the settlement's affairs, after they and their predecessors had resided in the area for more than two centuries. From the 1760s forward, individuals bearing the names Alvarenga, Carvalho, and Carvalho-Alvarenga, together with their entourages of relatives and grumetes, came to dominate trade in the Ziguinchor area and supplant peninsula Portuguese in commanding and garrisoning the praça.

There were similar developments at Cacheu, where Luso-Africans' influence also significantly increased. The shift in trade from Cacheu to Bissau during the time of the Companhia do Grão-Pará e Maranhão due to the larger size of European vessels gradually reduced Cacheu to being an entrepôt subsidiary to Bissau, notwithstanding the fact that the commandants of Cacheu claimed the praça's seniority to that at Bissau. Cacheu retained as key assets the trade with

Ziguinchor and Farim, the latter being the principal entrepôt for slave trade with the Kaabu Empire.

During the eighteenth century, Diola dislodged Banyun and associated Luso-Africans from settlements and trade routes linking the Gambia, Casamance, and Cacheu Rivers. The last reports of Europeans or Eurafricans traveling the Vintang-Songrougrou route dated to the 1730s and 1740s, and two of the reports alluded to problems in transit (Gray 1940, 14, 209, 212). Most likely, displaced Banyun and Luso-Africans withdrew southward to congregate at Ziguinchor, to be joined by Luso-Africans supplanted by English and Anglo-Africans along the Gambia River. Luso-Africans established at Ziguinchor and their grumete compradors were restricted to trade along the Casamance and Songrougrou Rivers and their tributaries, with Diola controlling commerce along the riverine and caravan routes connecting Gambia markets. Such was the ongoing volume of trade along Vintang Creek and tributary streams that by the nineteenth century, English, French, and Portuguese became convinced that the Gambia and Casamance Rivers were connected; they portrayed the chimera on maps and tried to find the linking waterway (Brooks 1987, 300).

The increasingly dominant role of Luso-Africans in Ziguinchor's affairs derived from the ever larger number of resident Luso-Africans who possessed entourages of grumetes and slaves. From the 1760s, if not earlier, the most influential Luso-Africans replaced Portuguese as the officers at Ziguinchor's praça, and they recruited soldiers for the garrison from among their relatives and grumetes. The ascendancy of Luso-Africans at Ziguinchor was associated with Carlos de Carvalho Alvarenga. In 1766, when he was the capitão-cabo of the Forte de Nossa Senhora de Conceição da Praça de Ziguinchor, he took fifty-one slaves to Bissau to assist in the construction of the fort there (Barcellos 1899–1913, 3:48; Walter 1947, 11). One may suppose that possessing such an entourage of slaves enabled him to be independent from local landlords. His male descendants were recorded as officers commanding the bastions of the praça—including Manuel Carvalho Alvarenga (1753 or 1756–1827), who was appointed capitão-mor in 1787 and commandant in 1802 (AHU, Cx 16, February 5, 1802; Barcellos 1899–1913, 3:162–63). Those were challenging times for Luso-Africans; Manuel Carvalho Alvarenga testified that he fought in a war at Farim in 1775, assisted in the defense of Ziguinchor in 1787, and also participated in other conflicts (AHU, Cx 18, May 20, 1806).

When and to what extent Luso-Africans acquired landholding privileges in Ziguinchor are matters of speculation. The acquisition of residential plots in the trading community may have derived from marriages with Banyun, with whom

Luso-Africans had for centuries shared kinship and commercial relations. Yet Banyun were themselves strangers; their residence among Diola at Ziguinchor may have preceded the arrival of Portuguese lançados by only a century or two. Reportedly, it was not until the era of Manuel Carvalho Alvarenga, who, as mentioned, became commandant of Ziguinchor in 1802, that Luso-Africans acquired cultivable lands neighboring Ziguinchor that were free of obligations to African landlords and could be inherited and sold. It may be that Luso-Africans' predilection for planting orange and lemon trees was a factor in their acquisition of land-use privileges, inasmuch as African societies in the Guinea-Bissau region accorded ownership of fruit to whoever planted the trees (Bertrand-Bocandé 1849, 268, 309). Yet access to land and water, the role of ancestral spirits, and other matters continue to be contentious issues (Hesselink 1984; Slobbe 1984). And questions remain as to when and in what circumstances the inhabitants of Ziguinchor and other trading communities began practicing patrilineal descent, supplanting preexisting matrilineal patterns (Havik 2000, 2–3).

Circumstances at the praças at Cacheu and Bissau were different: it was principally Cabo Verdeans who supplanted Portuguese officers and soldiers following the dissolution of the Companhia do Grão-Para e Maranhão and the inauguration of the chimerical and destitute colony of Cabo Verde e Guiné. Commandants and other senior officers were sent from Portugal, but more and more Cabo Verdeans garrisoned the praças as junior officers. Renewed droughts and famines in the archipelago during the 1780s and 1790s impelled Cabo Verdeans to seek livelihoods in Guinea (Staunton 1799, 64–71; Barcellos 1899–1913: 3:115–16; Patterson 1988, 308). After 1801, when Portugal became disastrously involved in the Napoleonic Wars, replacements and supplies were dispatched only after long and unpredictable delays, with the consequence that Cabo Verdeans and indigenous Luso-Africans took control of the praças and the commerce of the region.

The ascendancy of Luso-Africans at Cacheu may be dated from the arrival of João Pereira Barreto, a Luso-African born on São Tiago, where he was ordained a priest. He was transferred to Guinea sometime during the 1770s (?), possibly because of his relationship with a slave woman who was the mother of his sons, João Pereira Barreto and António Teixeira Barreto. Information is lacking on their dates of birth and who was the elder. Padre Barreto acquired considerable influence in Cacheu, as evidenced by his serving as acting commandant in 1785. António Teixeira Barreto was appointed a captain of militias by the commandant of Cacheu, João Joaquim de Sousa Trovão (1802–3). His brother, João Pereira Barreto, was the capitão-mor of Cacheu in 1804, and in that year, it was recorded that he had been born in Cabo Verde, was twenty-nine years of age, and was married (but to whom is not mentioned). Barreto's alliance with Rosa de Carvalho Alvarenga enabled them to exercise growing influence in Cacheu and Ziguinchor and among neighboring African groups. No records have been located documenting a marriage or dating the births of their children—Maria Pereira Barreto (1808–?) and the renowned Honório Pereira Barreto (1813–59), the first and only Luso-African to be appointed governor of the colony of Guinea (Barcellos 1899–1913, 3:95, 224, and 6:156; Walter 1947, 11; Brooks 1990, 56–57; Havik 2000, 8–12).

The concentration of growing numbers of Luso-Africans and grumetes in a few communities and seasonal trading settlements in the Cacheu-Casamance area had pervasive social and cultural ramifications. Preeminent among them was the reinforcement of Luso-Africans' sense of identity, as evident from the increasing prominence of "family" names and marital affiliations (although the latter were rarely consecrated by priests). The marital status of a Luso-African man or woman recorded in a document was almost invariably *solteiro* or *soltiera* (single, unmarried), with an "X" marked in lieu of a signature. Cabo Verdean officers and traders anticipated returning to Cabo Verde with sufficient wealth, however earned, to contract advantageous marriages (Brooks 1973, 308–10).

CHAPTER 10

Geba-Grande and Serra Leoa

Luso-Africans Challenged and Supplanted by Anglo-Africans

[On the Anglo-African James Cleveland] To sum up his Character in a few Words: With a White Man he is a White Man, with a Black Man a Black Man.

—FYFE 1964, 101–2

Africans consider *"all white man witch,"* they also believe that *"all white man rogue."* There is no species of cheating, or deceit, or of treachery, of which they did not think a white man capable.

—BEAVER 1805, 294

DURING THE EIGHTEENTH CENTURY, the armies of the Fula almamate expanded their conquests in the Futa Jallon massif and extended Fula suzerainty over neighboring areas. Non-Muslim Fula and Susu (Mande) who refused to convert to Islam were conquered and enslaved, either confined to slave communities or sold into the Atlantic slave trade. Many Susu fled to coastal areas, while others (the "Jalonke" or "Yalunka") took refuge in the eastern ranges of the massif. Muslim Susu and traders from other Mande groups who remained in the almamate suffered liabilities, for the state-controlled caravan traffic was administered to the advantage of Fula elites. The almamate's expansion was spearheaded by Labé, the most powerful *diwal* (province). In order to eliminate middlemen and engage in direct trade with Eurafricans and Europeans, Fula armies imposed contested suzerainties over Susu along the Pongo River and Nalu and Landuma along the Nunez River.

Some non-Muslim Fula migrated north into the Guinea-Bissau region, joining others arriving from Senegambia. Ongoing desiccation made the area of the Kaabu Empire increasingly suited to pastoralism, and Mandinka found it to their advantage to entrust cattle to the care of Fula herders. Landlord-stranger relations became progressively strained during the long conflict between Kaabu and the Fula almamate, beginning in the latter decades of the eighteenth century and continuing until Kaabu's destruction in the 1860s.

European and Eurafrican slave traders engaged in fierce competition for the commerce of the Fula almamate and Kaabu Empire. By the 1780s, slavers made unprovoked attacks on rival vessels caught unawares in the Geba and Grande estuaries and the waters of the Bissagos archipelago. Luso-Africans were hard-pressed to sustain the competition of better-supplied rivals with recourse to warships. Had the French Revolution and the Napoleonic Wars not intervened, Luso-Africans would have been subordinated to English and Anglo-English slave traders.

Geba-Grande, 1770s–1790s

At the time the Companhia Geral do Grão-Pará e Maranhão was dissolved in 1777 and the administration of Guinea's praças and presidios devolved on royal officials, João da Costa, an official of the company, provided a description of the circumstances in the Geba-Grande area. He reported that Bissau's praca had a garrison of 190 soldiers, and the settlement comprised some 700 black Catholics (that is, Luso-Africans and grumetes) but lacked a priest. A small chapel outside the fort could hold barely 40 persons. There were some 1,000 Christians at Geba, but as in other trading communities scattered as far south as the Sierra Leone estuary, they had not been visited by a priest for a half-dozen years, notwithstanding an agreement between the company and the clergy residing at Bissau (Barcellos 1899–1913, 3:78–79).

Bernardino António Alvares de Andrade, who also served in Guinea during the 1760s and 1770s, completed a manuscript in 1796 that provided additional details concerning Geba as a flourishing community with a large population. Andrade almost surely exaggerated in reporting that the Christian inhabitants of the parish in 1775 possessed eighteen hundred dwellings (*fogos*), which were interspersed with eight hundred Soninke dwellings. There was a parish priest sent by the bishop of Cabo Verde and a lay brother from Porto who maintained a hospice for the sick. The capitão-cabo (who was not named) was a Luso-African appointed by the commandant of Bissau's praça.

Of particular note in Andrade's account is the reference to numerous Fula pasturing their herds in the area neighboring Geba. La Courbe had made no mention of Fula herdsmen in his writings a century earlier, so their presence in Andrade's time testified to the advancing desiccation of the c. 1630–c. 1860 dry period and the expansion of the Fula almamate. Andrade extolled the bountiful crops grown along the extensive floodplain following the rainy season. Some of the harvest was bartered with Fula herders for pastoral products, in a symbiotic relationship that was widespread across western Africa (Peres 1952, 56–59). The large numbers of Luso-Africans, Soninke, and Fula dwelling at Geba indicated that a thriving commerce was carried on along caravan routes linking the Kaabu Empire and the Fula almamate in Futa Jallon. Luso-African residents likely included some individuals who had been dislodged from the upper Gambia and traveled along the overland kola-slave caravan routes linked to Geba.

Frenchmen were, time and again, attracted to the possibilities of slave trading with the inhabitants of the Bissagos Islands, despite having information about the dangers of navigation and of dealing with the Bijago. A report on the Bissagos Islands in 1784 characterized the inhabitants as wanting only arms, iron, and brandy, disdaining manufactures and luxury goods for which they had no use (Knight-Baylac 1970a, 91). A French warship dispatched on the reconnaissance voyage in 1784 recruited a pilot at Gorée whose skill in navigating among the Bissagos Islands was assured by "everyone"—testimonies belied when the vessel was nearly shipwrecked near the island of Jatte, whose inhabitants attacked a landing party and killed an officer (Labarthe 1802, 127–29).

At Bissau, the ship's company encountered Constantin, a French sailor whose vessel had wrecked on Yoko/Uno? Island eleven years earlier; the members of the crew were either killed or made slaves. Constantin reported that the Luso-African trading sphere extended to the Nunez River. Small craft from Bissau dispatched by "Portuguese" (that is, Luso-Africans) to the Bissagos archipelago competed with craft sent by English traders from the Iles de Los. According to Constantin, Luso-Africans used every means at their disposal to drive off rivals. The French captain was no doubt daunted by the sailor's warnings and by much self-serving advice from members of Bissau's trading community concerning the difficulties of navigating to Bolama and the possibility of attacks by Bijago in large war dugouts. Consequently, the captain circumnavigated the Bissagos archipelago and set a course for the Iles de Los (Labarthe 1802, 127–33, 137, 140).

In March 1786, Governor Boufflers dispatched his aide-de-camp, Silvain Meinrad Xavier de Golberry, to undertake a survey of western African commerce. After the visit to Niumi described earlier, Golberry bypassed the Guinea-Bissau region, sailing to the Iles de Los and Sierra Leone River. The information he recorded on the littoral between the Gambia River and the Iles de Los derived from two Portuguese shipmasters with many years of experience in western African trade, both of whom had become naturalized French citizens and were living at Nantes when he interviewed them after his return to France in 1788. According to the ship captains, a Lisbon firm with considerable English investment held a monopoly on trade between Cape Saint Mary and Cape Verga—apparently a reference to the Sociedade do Comércio das Ilhas de Cabo Verde e Guiné, which was organized in January 1783 and declared bankrupt in December 1786 (Faro 1959, 232–33). The English used a private landing place at the mouth of the creek east of the fort at Bissau (in the Impernal Channel), and English traders shared some of the profits of "Portuguese" (Luso-African) factories along the Grande River.

According to Golberry, Luso-Africans engaged in "intrigues" and "foul play" in order to maintain their influence with the "very savage" and "very ferocious" African groups in the area; Golberry's words evidently referred to Bijago, since he coupled them with a reference to navigational difficulties. He related that in 1784, Maréchal de Castries, the minister of marine and colonies, briefly contemplated planting a settlement on Bolama. Golberry considered the project an excellent idea and recommended establishing a factory on the eastern shore of Bolama, with subsidiary places of trade on Canhabaque Island and Menterre—the mainland to the southeast of Bolama, which he believed was another island (Golberry 1802, 2:214–16, 221, 223–26, 231–32; Mota 1950, 149).

Golberry was informed by the Portuguese shipmasters that Nunez River trade comprised slaves, wax, ivory, hides, and a little gold and that the descendants of Portuguese were so mixed with Africans as to be Africans themselves. The shipmasters also told him (erroneously) that there were no Portuguese establishments south of Cape Verga. Regarding the Pongo River, Golberry was informed that Fula and Susu living along the upper river had numerous contacts with Timbo. In addition, he learned that English traders purchased many slaves, ivory, ebony, timber, hides, and foodstuffs. He was told nothing concerning Luso-Africans living in the Pongo. Nor, in enumerating products traded between Cape Verga and the Sierra Leone River, did his Portuguese informants mention kola (Golberry 1802, 1:227–29, 241).

In 1788, Governor Boufflers's successor, Col. François Emilie Blanchot, undertook a reconnaissance voyage on the schooner *La Cousine.* At Crawford's Island in the Iles de Los, Blanchot encountered a French trader named Ancel who helped him secure the services of Charles Wilson ("Wilsum"), an experienced black pilot who claimed to be an American. Wilson successfully piloted the *Cousine* through the Bissagos archipelago, but Blanchot decided that Tamara Island in the Iles de Los was more suitable for a French comptoir — an objective that was not achieved before war between France and Britain was renewed (Jore 1965, 112–13). Pelletan, director of the Compagnie du Sénégal in 1787 and 1788, publishing after Blanchot's reconnaissance, wrote that the area between the Gambia and Sierra Leone Rivers was infrequently visited by French traders because Luso-Africans resorted to force to drive away foreign rivals (Pelletan 1800, 37, 40).

During the following years, Bissau's safer anchorage and navigation for large seafaring vessels attracted more slavers than Cacheu. Mettas noted that more than three out of every five slave ships (thirty-two out of fifty) were loaded at Bissau from 1788 to 1794. Slave trading extended through the dry season, from December to July (Mettas 1975, 347–48).

The English naval officer Philip Beaver, whose intrepid role in the ill-fated English colony on Bolama in 1792 and 1793 will be discussed, reported what he learned observing Bissau's commercial affairs during an annual trading cycle. He said that Portuguese commerce was limited to four vessels laden with articles for the slave trade. These ships stopped en route at São Tiago to procure panos ("in great estimation as an article of trade"); loaded some two thousand slaves at Bissau, who were then sold in Brazil; and returned to Portugal with sugar, tobacco, rice, and other tropical products (Beaver 1805, 321–22). He summarized what he learned concerning Bissau's commerce:

> The merchants of Bissau procure this number of slaves by means of a class of natives called grumetas, who have generally been brought up from infancy in their houses, and who are in general an honest, industrious, and faithful class. They navigate all their small craft, whether canoes, or decked schooners and sloops; and carry on, for their principals, all the commerce of the country. The merchant, who seldom quits his own habitation, sends them with goods to the value of a certain number of slaves, either to [Ziguinchor], Cacheo, Geba, or any other place; where they make their purchases, and then return to their employers, who are seldom cheated, or deceived, by them; never, I believe, if their own conduct has been to them upright and just. Most of these slaves are procured from the Mandingoes at Geba; some from the Cacheo and Casamanza rivers; very few from the Biafaras, or Bijugas, but many from the Naloos. All these, however, would not supply their demand, if they had not found out means of procuring a great number from the Papels, on whose island they are fixed. (Beaver 1805, 322)

Regarding Papel captives, Beaver was informed that Ilha de Bissau was "governed by no less than 13 kings, who are seldom, if ever, altogether at peace. These petty wars, instigated and cherished by the Portuguese, furnish them with a considerable number of slaves" (Beaver 1805, 322).

Serra Leoa, 1760s–1790s

During the second half of the eighteenth century, Luso-Africans contended with growing numbers of English and Anglo-African traders attracted by the expanding slave trade of the Fula almamate in Futa Jallon. The Iles de Los were particularly favored by English traders for their relatively salubrious environment and their convenient location for trade in the neighboring rivers, which attracted Fula caravans during the dry season. English traders who established factories in the Pongo and Nunez Rivers married women from influential Susu, Baga, Landouman, and Nalu families and acquired entourages of grumetes and slaves armed with cutlasses and guns, all of which enabled them to assert increasing influence in African communities.

By the 1780s, English and Anglo-Africans had expanded their trade northward to the Grande and Geba Rivers, both by vessels and by a redirection of commerce from the Grande River via an overland route that connected with Kakundy along the upper Nunez River. Among the few Luso-Africans who retained significant influence in Serra Leoa were William Settel Fernandes and his descendants, who controlled trade in the Dembia River south of the Pongo River, and Signior Domingo in the Sierra Leone estuary, who, along with local Temne rulers, contended with the inhabitants of the English colony founded in May 1787.

During the 1780s, Fula conquests greatly expanded the almamate's territories, and the captives acquired were settled in slave villages (*dune*) or sold into the Atlantic slave trade. Politics in the almamate, which comprised nine provinces known as *diwe* (the singular is *diwal*), were polarized between Timbo and Labé, the two most powerful diwe, both of which were renowned as centers of commerce and Islamic scholarship. Labé, the largest diwal, expanded territorially to the north and west. Its rulers dispatched large armed caravans to coastal Serra Leoa, principally to the upper reaches of the Nunez River where Fula hegemony was imposed over Landuma and Nalu who were compelled to pay an annual tribute. Timbo achieved intermittent domination over Susu along the upper Pongo River, while at the same time expanding its trade with Eurafricans and Europeans in other rivers along the coast of Serra Leoa. Fula statecraft favored multiple outlets to the Atlantic coast, but traders generally resorted to Kakundy in the uplands along the upper Nunez River in preference to the more malarial lowlands along the Pongo River.

Fula traders engaged in riverine commerce were required to travel in caravans and pay a portion of their profits to the state officials who supervised external commerce. Caravans departed after the rainy season ended in October, when paths were dry and streams fordable. Ravines and large streams were traversed by skillfully crafted vine bridges. War captives were used to transport rice, hides, and ivory to the coast; many of these captives would be sold to slavers, but others would return to the Futa Jallon highlands carrying firearms, ammunition, textiles, and other European goods, as well as large quantities of salt for Fula cattle herds.

Fula overlords sought to impose their choice of rulers for subordinate groups by negotiating with leaders of the Simo society, which exercised wide powers. Fula dominance was impossible, for with the onset of the rainy season, Fula caravans withdrew to the highlands of Futa Jallon. Tributary groups in the Nunez and Pongo opportunistically contested the almamate's hegemony whenever Fula were distracted by slave revolts or struggles between claimants to rulership, but following such interludes, the almamate's forces reimposed hegemony over riverine groups (Winterbottom 1803/1969, 170–72; Rodney 1968, 280–82; A. Andrade 1970, 192–93; Mouser 1973, 46–54, 1975, 428–30, and 2000; Barry 1981b, 292–93; Robinson 1984, 53, 56–57; McGowan 1990, 28; Botte 1991, 1413–18).

Westward expansion of the Labé diwal challenged the Kaabu Empire's hegemony in the savanna-woodland zone, occasioning intermittent warfare that began in the latter part of the eighteenth century. Fula-Mandinka conflict generated numerous captives from the ranks of the combatants and from inhabitants of contested areas; these individuals were sold into the Atlantic slave trade. Meanwhile, riverine and coastal groups preyed upon by Fula and Mandinka were incited by Eurafrican and European traders to engage in internecine slaving. The ongoing desiccation of western Africa during the latter part of the long c. 1630–c. 1860 dry period contributed to the Fula-Mandinka conflict. Fula pastoralists from Senegambia and Futa Jallon migrated into Kaabu territory in growing numbers, intermingling with Mandinka cultivators who, as landlords, ruled and taxed the newcomers. As Fula became more numerous, Kaabu elites sought to intimidate them by means of extortionate taxation and arbitrary violence, practices that caused victimized Fula to seek redress by collaborating with raiding parties dispatched from the Fula almamate. More and more animist Fula living in Kaabu responded to the preaching of Muslim clerics, as did some Mandinka cultivators. Kaabu's Mandinka elites, for their part, disdained the blandishments of marabouts, despising them as socially inferior. Warfare between Kaabu and the Fula almamate continued for decades, culminating in the defeat of Kaabu in the mid-nineteenth century (Sidibe 1974, 15–16).

Mandinka and Fula marabouts infiltrated riverine and coastal societies in ever greater numbers. John Matthews, an unemployed naval officer who managed the Liverpool Company's factories in the Sierra Leone estuary and Iles de Los during the mid-1780s (Fyfe 1962, 7), asserted that Muhammad himself could not have wished for more zealous propagators of Islam than the Mandinka Muslims he encountered.

> Fully sensible of what importance it is to have the conscience in keeping, they neglect no means of policy to spread their religious doctrines—where they are strong they use coercive measures; and where they are not in a capacity to exert those means, they use every art that human subtilty can suggest. In the villages of the tribes around them they erect schools, and teach their youth gratis, to read and write Arabic; and their missionaries, by temporizing with the prevailing follies and foibles of the different nations they visit; by assuming to themselves the sanctity and authority of the servants of God; by abstaining from all strong liquors; and, above all, by pretending to have power over every species of witchcraft; and by their trade in charms, do so insinuate themselves into the confidence of the chiefs and principal people; that I never visited a town in this part of Africa where I did not find a Mandingo man as prime minister, by the name of *bookman,* without whose advice nothing was transacted. (Matthews 1788/1966, 68–69)

Between 1790 and 1793, one Laye-Salou, a self-styled Mahdi reportedly from Bambuk, greatly alarmed and victimized European and Eurafrican traders. He acquired a following of thousands of Susu and Mandinka in the Scarcies-Kolente region through his military prowess and vaunted claims to being invulnerable to bullets and sword wounds. Africans were coerced to supply provisions for his growing army and European and Eurafrican traders were compelled to contribute trade goods. The Mahdi came to a violent end when his lieutenants, fearful of his arbitrary behavior and executions of whomever he thought disloyal, clubbed him to death. His followers incorporated his teeth, bones, and hair into amulets; allegedly, such were the supernatural powers attributed to his relics that a single tooth was valued at two slaves (Zachary Macaulay's journal entry for June 30, 1793, in Fyfe 1964, 87–88; Winterbottom 1803/1969, 250; Rodney 1970, 234; Person 1971, 688; Schwarz 2000, 20).

Contemporaneous accounts about Luso-Africans living in Serra Leoa indicated that most were in difficult circumstances. By the 1770s, those living along the Pongo and Nunez Rivers were unable to compete with English traders and their agents for the purchase of slaves and ivory. One Portuguese official disparaged them as almost indistinguishable in their lifestyle from local Africans, notwithstanding the fact that they claimed to be Christians and seized the opportunity to make confessions, take communion, and baptize their children whenever priests visited (A. Andrade 1970, 192–93). That such opportunities were indeed rare was attested by João da Costa, an employee of the Companhia Geral do Grão-Pará e Maranhão, who reported that no priest had visited the Nunez during the preceding eighteen years, with the consequence that only a few residents retained a "memory" of the Catholic religion (Barreto 1938, 156). When Matthews visited the Nunez River in 1785, he noted the ruins of a Portuguese settlement some fifty kilometers upriver (presumably Kakandé), where only vestiges of dwellings and a chapel remained (Matthews 1788/1966, 10–11; Hair 2000c, 427 n. 30).

The American War of Independence entangled Britain and France in yet another conflict involving global commerce raiding. In February 1778, France signed a treaty of alliance with the United States, entering the war against Britain (Langer 1958, 436, 521). A month later, three American privateers arrived at the French-held island of Gorée, then sailed down the coast to raid a factory in the Iles de Los managed by Miles Barber for the Liverpool firm of Barber and Bolland, known in western Africa as the Liverpool Company. The following year, when a French squadron captured Saint-Louis, American vessels from Boston preceded the squadron down the coast to pillage English traders in the Iles de Los before the French sacked Bunce Island and demolished the premises in March 1779. American privateering ceased after June 1779, when a British squadron captured Gorée and reasserted naval supremacy in western African waters (Golberry 1802, 1:236–40; Machat 1906a, 120–24; Gray 1940, 266–68; Rodney 1970, 251; Brooks 1970, 16–17; Mouser 1996, 85–86).

The Treaty of Paris signed on September 3, 1783, which granted American independence, restored Gorée and Saint-Louis to France (Langer 1958, 436). Saint-Louis once again became the headquarters of the newly organized Compagnie du Sénégal, whose directors were committed to an activist policy to reestablish French commerce southward along the coast of western Africa, with the Casamance River specifically targeted for French penetration. The decade between the Treaty of Paris and the renewal of warfare between France and Britain in 1792 was marked by an intensified slaving that destabilized Serra Leoa's coastal and riverine groups as never before. A slave rebellion in the Sumbuya/Moria region lasted nearly a decade, during which numerous war captives were sold to pay for arms purchases (Mouser 2000).

During the 1780s, there was unprecedented collaboration between European slave merchants. In January 1785, the Liverpool Company concluded an agreement to supply slaves to the Bacheler, Forbisson, and Carmichel Company of Le Havre, and it made similar contracts with commercial houses in Nantes in 1787 and 1788. Bunce Island, which was managed by the London firm of John and Alexander Anderson from 1785 on, supplied Danish vessels and made large shipments to British islands in the West Indies (Golberry 1802, 2:280, 282, 273; Fyfe 1962, 7; Rodney 1970, 251–52). When Golberry visited Serra Leoa in April and May 1786, he was greatly impressed by the English establishments in the Sierra Leone estuary and the Iles de Los. He extolled the well-organized premises on Factory Island in the Iles de Los, where numerous skilled craftsmen, both free and slave, built and repaired vessels of twenty to one hundred tons, manned principally by African pilots and some two hundred grumetes who traded between Cape Verga and Cape Palmas. Besides communications conveyed on vessels, messages were sent by African couriers via an overland route that linked Bunce Island and the Iles de Los (Golberry 1802, 1:43–44, 57–58, and 2:237–40, 280–82; Searing 1993, 95).

On Bunce Island, seafaring grumetes ("pull away boys," in local usage) and skilled artisans lived with their families in a separate village known as Adam's Town, named for their headman, Bai Adam, a man so well regarded that annual ceremonies are still conducted at his grave (Corry 1807/1968, 4–5; Fyfe 2000, 20–21 and n. 20). English traders living on Bunce Island had reason to treat grumetes with circumspection, for many were sons of village heads in acephalous societies. John Matthews, who engaged in the slave trade in Serra Leoa during the 1780s, explained: "The family of a deceased king, or head man, lay no claim to superiority over their countrymen from their office, but fill that station only in which their wealth or connexions place them; it very often happens that the son of a deceased chief, a few days after his father's death is necessitated to hire himself as a gremeta, or sailor, to a European trader for subsistence" (Matthews 1788/1966, 78). Excluded from leadership positions, such individuals nonetheless retained links to their communities, kinship networks, and power associations, all of which were of considerable value to English traders.

In another passage describing slavery in Serra Leoa, Matthews distinguished between "labouring" and "house" slaves (that is, trade and domestic slaves); only the latter were allowed to become grumetes: "The former is as it were fixed to the soil, and held in no higher estimation than any other animal that contributes to its cultivation; but the latter is in some respect considered as a branch of the family, assumes his master's name, and calls him father; yet these are hired out as sailors or labourers, not only to Europeans, who are settled, or come to trade there, but also to each other; and their masters receive the wages of their labour. They are also obliged to attend their masters in their wars and predatory excursions" (Matthews 1788/1966, 150).

Miles Barber furthered the interests of the Liverpool Company by dispatching the sons and daughters of employees to England "to learn Sense and get a good Head" by studying reading, writing, and mathematics; he also hired them as compradors on their return. Other European and Eurafrican traders did likewise. In 1789, there were some fifty boys and girls in schools in Liverpool, and others were studying in London and Bristol. One of the Anglo-African girls educated in England was Betsy Heard, who returned to Bereira in the Bereira River to manage a slave factory (Fyfe 1962, 11; Mouser 1983, 321–24, and 1996, 86–87; Debbasch 1988, 209, 211).

In 1788, John Matthews was called to testify to a committee of the Privy Council concerning British trade with Africa. He submitted a paper relating how a number of African and Anglo-African children educated in England had behaved following their return to western Africa. Two of these, John and James Cleveland, were the sons of William Cleveland (d. 1758), who had settled in the Banana Islands and married a granddaughter of Thomas Caulker. Following John's early death, James Cleveland prospered in trade, and exploiting his membership in the Poro power association, he acquired unsurpassed influence in the region (Fyfe 1962, 10; Day 1983, 91–92). Matthews characterized James Cleveland as a "capital Trader" residing in the Banana Islands:

> His Manner of living is as nearly conformable to the European Custom, as Circumstances will admit: His House is also furnished in the English Style; but built (though upon a larger Scale) in the Country Manner. What his private Opinion on religious Subjects may be, I know not; but from his outward Practice he appears to coincide with the Belief which the Natives have in the Power and Efficacy of Charms and Witchcraft. In conversing with him on the Subject, he would sometimes join in the Laugh at their ridiculous Superstition; but when seriously asked his Opinion, he would never give a direct Answer, but strenuously assert, that the Predictions of the Conjurors and

> Sandcasters were often verified. In his Dealings and Transactions with the Europeans he is governed by his Interest: By this I would only infer, that as he lives not under the Protection of European Laws, so he is not governed by them, further than as a Merchant it is in his Interest to do so. To sum up his Character in a few Words: With a White Man he is a White Man, with a Black Man a Black Man. (Fyfe 1964, 101–2)

James Cleveland traded extensively during the 1780s with vessels dispatched from Liverpool by Robert Bostock. The latter vented his frustration concerning Cleveland's chronic indebtedness and his habit of prevailing on shipmasters to advance cargoes and await the collection of slaves, the classic pattern of Africans and Eurafricans trading on others' capital (Mackenzie-Grieve 1941/1968, 71–72). In his relations with Africans, Cleveland was notorious for enslaving people who failed to pay their debts and for raiding villages and selling the inhabitants. No less despicable was Charles Corker, Cleveland's relative on his mother's side, who was reputed to serve people alcohol, render them helplessly drunk, and then secure them in chains and sell them to waiting slave vessels (Wadstrom 1794–95/1968, 2:75–76, 84–85; Day 1983, 93).

Gambia Island—located at the mouth of the Bunce River, which flows into the Sierra Leone estuary—had a negligible role in the slave trade, but it was noteworthy in regard to Anglo-French competition and also for the role its Senegalese employees played in the spread of Islam among neighboring African groups. In 1772, a Frenchman named J. L. Hannibal, who arrived in the Sierra Leone estuary on a Danish vessel, established a factory on the low-lying island surrounded by swamps. He was joined in 1780 by another Frenchman, P. Ancel. After Hannibal died one year later, Ancel continued the business. In January 1785, a French naval officer, the Marquis de la Jaille, negotiated with the Temne subchief Panabouré Forbana, called "King Tom" by the English, to fortify the island and leave a small garrison of soldiers. When Golberry visited Gambia Island in April 1786, he criticized the location and the premises but decided it was preferable to maintain the factory rather than allow the English to monopolize the slave trade of the region (Golberry 1802 1:44, and 2:251–68, 284–85; Cultru 1910, 223; Fyfe 1962, 7, 19; Botte 1991, 1418).

The deplorable circumstances on Gambia Island were described by the redoubtable Anna Maria Falconbridge, who spent several days there in June 1791 when the factor was a Monsieur Renaud. The French soldiers stationed on the island had been so rapidly depleted by deaths that no replacements were dispatched from Senegal. Renaud resorted to his skills as a magician to ward off potential Temne predators, showing visitors "strange legerdemain tricks." Falconbridge was unsparing in her account:

> It is small and low, not two miles in circumference, situated in the midst of swamps and marshes, from whence a continued stench comes sufficient to choak a carrion crow—'tis wonderful how any human beings could pitch on such a place to live in. The Europeans there have all complexions as if they were fed on madder and saffron. Their manner of living is slovenly and hoggish, though they seem to have plenty of fresh stock, and provisions of almost every kind—they are very inactive and indolent, which I am not astonished at, for such must ensue from the lassitude produced by the unhealthiness of the place. The buildings are of mean and disrespectable appearance, being a pile of grass and sticks clumsily put together. They have a factory ship, and few goods are kept on shore, from a fear of being suprised and robbed by the natives. (Fyfe 2000, 50–51)

Apparently, Golberry had good reason to anguish over his decision in regard to maintaining the factory or abandoning the site!

Golberry returned to France in 1788 and submitted a detailed report of his findings to the Ministry of Marine. The following year, the Assemblée Nationale established the principle of equal trading rights, but it did not abolish the Compagnie du Sénégal—a move that Golberry would strongly recommend in a 1791 "lettre" addressed to the assembly deputies responsible for manufactures and trade. Recounting the lack of initiative and the stifling effect of the exclusive trading privileges accorded the Compagnie du Sénégal, Golberry asserted that British trade in western Africa was three times greater than that of France and that even Portuguese trade was slightly larger, and he exhorted the assembly to abolish the company (Golberry 1791; 1802, 2:214).

In an attempt to compete with English traders in the Sierra Leone estuary, the Compagnie du Sénégal introduced "Bundukus," that is, Muslim Tukulor from Bundu along the upper Senegal River who were dispatched as compradors among Temne and neighboring groups. Renaud abandoned Gambia Island in October 1794 after a French squadron pillaged Granville Town, but Bundukus remained and prospered, and together with their descendants, they introduced Islam among neighboring communities. One Bunduku married a daughter of Naimbana, the paramount Temne ruler, and became an important chief. Another gained control of the Mafonda chiefdom south of the Scarcies River (Labarthe 1802, 150–55; Fyfe 1962, 65; Wurie and Hurst 1968, chap. 1; Rodney 1970, 251–52).

European and Eurafrican slavers with armed retinues of grumetes and slaves arrogated increasing authority among African societies in Serra Leoa. Casting off landlord-stranger obligations and restraints, they behaved arbitrarily and treated people in their power ruthlessly, which made them detested and feared. Defeated and intimidated by Fula from the Futa Jallon almamate, Africans living along the Pongo and Nunez Rivers were especially victimized, as Fula and slavers combined to supplant landlords as commercial intermediaries.

Traders from Bissau continued to voyage to the Kolente River for cargoes of kola (Matthews 1788/1966, 60; Winterbottom 1803/1969, 77). During the 1780s and 1790s, resident Luso-African traders were most successful in the maze of rivers and tidal creeks between the Pongo and Dubréka Rivers; meanwhile, English and Anglo-African traders dominated commerce in the Pongo and Nunez Rivers, which attracted most of the Fula trade from the Futa Jallon almamate. Around midcentury, William Settel Fernandez, reputedly a "white Portuguese" but most likely a Luso-African, traveled from Bissau to settle in the Dembia River southeast of the Konkouré River (Mouser and Sarro 1999, 40, map 3). Fernandez married the daughter of a Baga leader of Bramaya/Konkouré and became "chief" of Bramaya in the 1780s after a war during which he and other strangers and their entourages, armed with guns and fighting together with Baga allies, defeated the Bankélé Susu. Three of Fernandez's children survived to adulthood to maintain dominance in the area: William Jelloram, Gabriel, and Maria (Kup 1961, 126, and 1967, 138; Rodney 1970, 215–16; Mouser 1971, 22–23, and app. B on p. 310).

Another successful Luso-African trader from Bissau was Emmanuel Gomez Sr., who traded in the Bakia River, a tributary of the lower Pongo. He leagued with William Settel Fernandez during the Baga-Susu war and gained control of the Bramaya chieftaincy. Appreciating the changing circumstances in western Africa, Gomez sent his son, Emmanuel Jr., to England for schooling. Other factories near Bakia in the 1780s were those of Gaspar (Gospar?) and Englishmen named Tool and John Holman. The latter arrived from England in the 1760s, settled along the Dembia River, and acquired considerable wealth in the slave trade. In 1791, Holman transported his slave woman Elizabeth, their children, and a number of slaves to a plantation he purchased in South Carolina. His oldest son, John Jr., who was educated in England, remained in Africa as a slave trader, as did a half brother, William Holman (Kup 1967, 115, 159, 31v: n. 2; Mouser 1971, 36, and 1973, 53; Koger 1985, 110–15).

The settlements of Luso-Africans from Bissau in the Pongo promoted priestly visitations. A scornful John Matthews related that clerics from Bissau visited "once or twice" yearly:

> The natives are originally Suzeés, but the principal people call themselves Portuguese, claiming descent from the colonists of that nation who were formerly settled here, though they do not retain the smallest trace of European extraction; but having had a white man once in the family, is sufficient to give them the appellation. They also profess the Roman Catholic religion; and are visited once or twice a year by a priest from the Portuguese settlement at Bassou, who baptizes their children, and receives their confession of faith according to his dictates; yet the most enlightened of them are merely nominal Christians. Their religion principally consists in repeating a *Pater Noster,* or an *Ave Maria,* and in wearing a large string of beads round their neck, with a cross, or crucifix, suspended. In every other respect they follow the customs and ceremonies of their pagan countrymen; but generally exceed them in treachery and revenge. The black merchants who bring slaves and ivory down to this river, and the adjoining one of Dembia, bring also large herds of cattle, goats, and sheep, which form an article of traffic with the neighbouring countries. (Matthews 1788/1966, 13–14)

Similar to other reports, Matthews's writings made no mention of priests sanctifying marriages or saying masses for individuals who had died since the last visit. Yet mass and communion would surely follow the hearing of confessions. Lamentably, neither Matthews nor anyone else described the crucifixes and rosaries, recorded their provenance, or indicated by whom these objects were purveyed. Likely, they were European imports and a lucrative source of income for the priests. Pieces produced by African smiths skilled in jewelry making might have surpassed the quality of imports, but priests would have disdained to consecrate such products. It is possible that some counterfeits circulated. At times, commercial enterprise were coordinated with religious endeavors, as exemplified by the sloop belonging to Bissau's priests that sailed for Serra Leoa in September 1780 to purchase slaves and kola (Rema 1982, 247–48).

John Ormond Sr. (d. 1791), an English slaver from Liverpool, was notoriously successful. Arriving in Serra Leoa in 1759 as a cabin boy, Ormond was employed by the slavers on Bunce Island before settling at Boké in the Nunez River around 1760. Three years later, he moved to Bashia along the Fatala branch of the Pongo River when warfare between Fula and Susu of Sulima provided slavers with large numbers of captives (Mouser 1979, map on p. 129). Ormond married the daughters of Susu and Baga chiefs along the Fatala and Bangalan Rivers. Called "Mongo John," he became renowned for his ruthlessness and his capricious and sadistic depravities. Although he himself was illiterate, he sent his son,

John Ormond Jr., to England for his education (Wadstrom 1794–95/1968, 87–88; Kup 1961, 113, 191n; Mouser 1971, 35, 1973, 52, and 1994, xiii and 111 n. 36).

David J. Lawrence, established at Kissassi in the Nunez (Mouser 1994, map A), also had a factory at Dominguia along the right bank of the middle Pongo; there, he employed a Luso-African named Anthony and a Eurafrican named Cooper Cummings, who subsequently operated his own factory at Ventura, so named for a "Portuguese" who resided in the area. Louis Gomez, characterized by Adam Afzelius as "a white Portuguese a villain," had a factory between Bashia and Karara on the Fatala River branch of the Pongo during the 1790s. So did the Englishmen Sam Perry and a Mr. Wilkinson. Afzelius expressed a strong dislike of Luso-Africans: "The Portuguese Blacks are full of pride and vanity. The call themselves Gentlemen, and give all the others name(s) of brutes and savages. For this reason they also insist on getting more in trading with [Englishmen]" (Kup 1967, 105, 112, 123, 132; Mouser 1971, 35, 37, and 1973, 52). John Irving, an Englishman, and William Skelton, an American, settled at Kissing in the 1780s. Skelton sent his son and successor, William Jr. (b. 1794), to England for his education (Mouser 1971, 34, 318).

Some half dozen English and Anglo-African traders had factories along the Nunez River upstream from the Sacred Grove at Kakundy. The most successful was James Walker, formerly a surgeon on a slave vessel, whose compound "Walkeria" was a magnet for Fula traders until his death in 1796 (Mouser 1994, 116, note). When James Watt visited the Nunez in February 1794 en route to Timbo, he encountered hundreds of Fula (Mouser 1994, 4–8). Neither Watt nor Joseph Hawkins, the supercargo on the American ship *Charleston* who traded for slaves in May 1795, mentioned Luso-African traders along the upper Nunez. Watt reported several Anglo-Africans, and at Timbo, he learned about the visit of an Anglo-African trader named Johnstone who had passed himself off as a white man and a relation of the king of England. While Hawkins traded in the Nunez, he made the acquaintance of "John Stone," and he subsequently co-opted his oral account of travel in Futa Jallon in the book he published in 1797 (Mouser 1994, 32, 34, and annotations in the index).

The *Charleston* traded successively in the Pongo and Nunez Rivers, arriving in the latter in mid-May (Hawkins 1797/1970, 14–15). Joseph Hawkins described the dissolute lifestyle of the slave traders living along the upper Nunez:

> Here the factors of European nations have established a settlement, and lead a life of heedless extravagance and dissipation. The American and European

> traders to this country, supply them with all the luxurious produce of the world, with wines, jewellery and costly clothing. The produce of their gardens, uniting the productions of every climate, by being maintained at a great expence of negro labor, is obtained in great perfection by a few, and in abundance by all. . . . Every individual, even of moderate property, supports his own establishment, of house, gardens, horses, and slaves. (Hawkins 1797/1970, 151–52)

Hawkins and the *Charleston*'s captain were treated to unstinting hospitality from the resident traders. Hawkins's observations of the factors' extravagant lifestyle dated to the beginning of the rainy season, after the Fula caravans had returned to Futa Jallon. This was a leisurely time of indulgence and celebration—a drunken spree for sailors at the close of the trading season, before the breeding of mosquitos endangered their lives with renewed malarial infection and, most feared of all, one of the sporadic yellow fever epidemics that decimated European residents in western Africa. Hawkins was unsparing in his description of the loutish behavior of his hosts, men whose retinues of armed slaves enabled them to acquire dominance over their landlords—a reversal of circumstances that landlords in stratified societies in Senegambia never permitted:

> I need not remark on the customary plurality of women in the domestic establishment, but will only observe that the whites adopt this fashin of the country in all its extent; the morning beverage of Madeira or Lisbon wines, spiritious liquor, or the more palatable LIQUEURS of the BELLE NATION, circulate during the forenoon, which is devoted to visiting from house to house. The hour of dinner is that which fixes company to a point, as all keep open and ample boards; . . . The board is scarcely spread, and the guest seated when the DEBAUCH begins; . . . They come to the table nearly intoxicated, and before dinner is completed, they become downright drunk; the vacancy which marks the uncultivated mind, affording no room here for useful conversation or agreeable hilarity, folly and wantonness supply their place. The coarse jocularity of destroying their apparel or wasting their food, is their amusement; while the most exquisite viands are wasted without utility, and the appetite being palled by superabundance loses all its value but that which gratifies the vanity of the provider, by indulging the waste and absurdity of his guests. After the wine has circulated freely, the meats are even occasionally dashed about the heads of the best humored, or most patient of the company, and the empty dishes, plates, and tables are demolished to shew the spirit of

> the party, and the lengths to which they could carry A JOKE. . . . At the conclusion of their debauches, the black wives who know their duty, attend and convey each exemplary master to his own house. This, with the simple variation of hunting, shooting, and giving parties, at particular seasons, giving orders for the management of their gardens, their meals, and occasionally their traffic, is the round of life the white people lead in this settlement. (Hawkins 1797/1970, 155–58)

Hawkins mentioned that one of the traders had acquired considerable wealth with the intention of returning to Europe to spend the remainder of his life but added that the man "confessed that he did not think he could be COMFORTABLE any where else, and had determined to stay where he was" (Hawkins 1797/1970, 158–59). Hawkins resolved to join the resident traders but failed in his attempt to leave the ship. During the *Charleston*'s voyage across the Atlantic, he was afflicted with blindness from a disease that spread among the slaves and crew of the vessel. Disabled at the age of twenty-three, Hawkins, with the help of friends, published an account of his voyage to earn money (Hawkins 1797/1970, 177). He expanded his narrative with exotic details of a fictional visit to Futa Jallon, almost certainly derived from conversations with the engaging "Nova Scotian" James Johnson, who had visited Timbo (Beaver 1805, 162, 195, 213, 215; E. Wilson 1976, 143; Mouser 1994, 107–8).

The despicable behavior of slavers in their private lives was complemented by their ruthless treatment of competitors, Luso-Africans included. Having displaced Luso-Africans in the Nunez River, English and Anglo-African traders expanded northward into the Grande and Geba Rivers. The first Englishman to found a factory along the Grande River was probably the Liverpool slaver John Ormond Sr., who established an Anglo-African named John Bootle there during the latter years of the 1780s. Bootle and his brother William had spent their youth along the Grande River and in the Iles de Los and in 1788 had attended school near Liverpool (Mouser 1983, 323). It appears that Bootle and the people associated with his factory were protected from Luso-African retaliation by Ormond's fearsome reputation. Ormond died in the Iles de Los early in 1791, soon after learning that rebellious slaves had killed the son he left in charge and destroyed his premises. Following Ormond's death, Bootle departed the Grande River. When he returned more than a year later, as will be related, he was murdered by grumetes associated with a Bissau trader named Galvão ("Gavine") (Mouser 1973, 52; Beaver 1805, 95–96, 472).

The "Province of Freedom"

For centuries, European advocates of colonization had proposed founding settlements in western Africa for commercial entrepôts and to establish tropical plantations using African slave labor. The English colony founded along the estuary of the Sierra Leone River in 1787 was motivated by new concerns that were to have a profound impact on western Africa during the nineteenth century: the return of freed Africans to the African homeland; the Christian evangelization of the peoples of Africa; and the suppression of the slave trade, to be replaced by commerce in agricultural and sylvan products that were in growing demand in Europe and America.

The "Province of Freedom" was conceived for the settlement of "Black Poor"—Africans liberated by Lord Chief Justice William Murray Mansfield's ruling in 1772 that a slave could not be returned to his owner in the Caribbean. Few freedmen were able to find employment in England, and their poverty and destitution motivated a group of philanthropists, headed by Granville Sharp, to return them to Africa. Yet of thousands of Africans living in England, only 411, including 41 women, availed themselves of the opportunity to return to Africa, accompanied by some 70 English women and 36 officials, craftsmen, and clergy. Among the Black Poor were destitute *lascars*—East Indian sailors who spoke Portuguese and were Catholics, discharged in English ports by vessels of the East India Company and British men-of-war. Information is lacking concerning whether the lascars became affiliated with Luso-Africans and what influence they may have had. One of the lascars, appointed a "corporal" among the Black Poor, was subsequently imprisoned for slave dealing; he later escaped and joined the French who pillaged Freetown in 1794 (Fyfe 1962, 98; Braidwood 1994, 32–33, 63–64, 148, 187).

The vessels transporting the expedition arrived in the Sierra Leone estuary in May 1787, the month the rainy season begins. Following negotiations with some but not all of the Temne leaders with territorial claims on the Sierra Leone peninsula, the expedition's leaders purchased a tract of land extending from the watering place to Gambia Island and inland for some twenty English miles. Granville Town was founded on the south bank of the estuary overlooking the watering place that European vessels had resorted to for centuries. Not far upriver from this settlement for free people were the English and French slave factories on Bunce and Gambia Islands (Fyfe 1962, 13–20).

During the rainy season, a third of the Black Poor died from malaria and dysentery. Many abandoned the settlement to seek livelihoods elsewhere, including employment by slave traders. The death in mid-1788 of "King Tom," the local Temne landlord, occasioned a dispute that was unanticipated by the colonists: European tenancy agreements were made with an individual landlord, and when that individual died, it was necessary to negotiate a new agreement with his successor (Fyfe 1962, 19, 22, and 1976, 175).

In December 1789, Granville Town was destroyed by Temne. The disaster was precipitated by crewmen on an American slave vessel who kidnapped several Temne while trading in the Sierra Leone River, unleashing a sequence of retaliation and retribution. Temne responded, as was customary in Serra Leoa, by taking revenge on a vessel from the same nation, killing and plundering a crew from the next American ship that entered the river. A British naval officer, informed of the incident but not of the kidnapping perpetrated by the previous American vessel, destroyed a Temne village in retaliation. Because some of the residents of Granville Town had collaborated with the British captain, Temne expelled the inhabitants and burned their dwellings (Fyfe 1962, 20–25; Peterson 1969, 25–26).

The colony was resettled in the spring of 1791 after the arrival of a relief vessel. In June, the colony's sponsors organized themselves as the Sierra Leone Company and obtained a charter from Parliament. The chairman of the company's board of directors was Henry Thornton, a businessman and a leading member of the so-called Clapham Sect, an influential group of Evangelical activists. Company employees were forbidden to engage in the slave trade or to possess slaves; the articles of commerce sought were ivory, beeswax, and camwood, some of which were acquired as far away as Bissau. The settlement required large quantities of rice, much of it paid for with American rum. In August 1793 and January 1794, the colony's directors were constrained to purchase the cargoes of American slavers in order to procure supplies of rum (Brooks 1970, 53–54). Zachary Macaulay recorded in his journal, "Without . . . rum . . . we must shortly starve. There is half a ton of rice consumed in the colony every day, and for the purchase of a ton of rice among other articles, about 20 gallons of rum are wanted in the Sherbro, and on the Bullam Shore, even in the rice season 40 gallons" (Schwarz 2000, 47). Ironically, slaving in the Sierra Leone estuary increased during the early 1790s, with large Fula caravans arriving from Futa Jallon. In January 1794, a slave ship captain estimated that fifteen hundred captives had been brought for sale. Until 1808, the slave trade was carried on legally, side by side with the settlement of free people (Kup 1961, 90; Fyfe 1962, 25–28).

The two main groups of settlers brought to Freetown, as the new settlement was named, were from America. In February and March 1792, British vessels landed more than eleven hundred "Nova Scotians." These men and women were formerly slaves in the American South but had abandoned their masters during the American War of Independence in response to General Sir Henry Clinton's promise of "freedom and a farm" for those enlisting in the British cause. After Britain failed to suppress the American revolt, most of the freed slaves were transported to Nova Scotia, where the majority subsisted unhappily until the opportunity arose to settle in Sierra Leone. A later group of immigrants, some 550 "Maroons," were former slaves taken from Jamaica in 1796 and transported to Nova Scotia. No more reconciled to the climate than their predecessors, the Maroons petitioned to be removed to Sierra Leone, to arrive in Freetown at the close of September 1800 when they helped subdue Nova Scotians made rebellious by unfulfilled promises (Fyfe 1962, 31–37, 79–80, 85–86).

Freetown became a lodestar for wage employment, especially for Kru living along the Malaguetta coast more than five hundred kilometers to the south. Beginning in 1793, Kru began paddling dugouts to Freetown to seek employment with the colony's residents and as seamen aboard ships (Fyfe 1962, 54–55, 78; Brooks 1972, 4–13). Temne and European and Eurafrican slavers residing in neighboring rivers opportunistically sold rice and other foodstuffs to the colony, and they sent their sons to Freetown's schools for education; some of their offspring intermarried with children of the settlers. Anna Maria Falconbridge addressed their motives, purportedly quoting local opinion: "They seem desirous to give education to their children, or in their own way of expressing it, 'Read book, and learn to be *rogue* so well as white man'; for they say that if white men could not read or wanted education, they would be no better rogues than *black gentlemen*" (Fyfe 2000, 45).

The schooling and evangelizing undertaken by Protestant missionaries and their converts in Freetown and in the rivers north of the colony inaugurated a new era in Serra Leoa. During the decades that followed, English-literate and Protestant-oriented Africans, Anglo-Africans, and Luso-Africans supplanted Luso-Africans adhering to a Catholic heritage that was only sporadically reinforced by priests visiting from Bissau and Cabo Verde. The momentum grew as Protestant converts raised churchgoing children who attended schools in the colony. Less evident but also of growing influence was the pervasive diffusion of Islam and Muslim practices disseminated by Mandinka and Fula marabouts

As the years passed, Temne living along the Sierra Leone estuary were increasingly frustrated and angered by the behavior of the settlers and the English officials. Following the initial land purchase, no rent was paid to the Temne landlord, nor was he allowed to interfere in the colony's affairs. Aware of simmering disputes ("palavers") between settlers and Temne landlords concerning property rights and other matters, the Anglo-African William Cleveland, nephew of James Cleveland (who died in 1791), was anxious to claim sovereignty over the Banana Islands "from hereditary right" (Day 1983, 94; Fyfe 2000, 80–81). Mounting distrust between Temne and settlers engendered conflicts in 1801 and 1802 (Fyfe 1962, 74, 89–90; Peterson 1969, 34–35).

One Luso-African who was prominently involved in the colony's affairs during this era was "Signior Domingo" (Domingues), the elderly chief of the village of Royema, to the east of Granville Town. He engaged the colony's inhabitants in the long-standing Luso-African roles of interpreter and intermediary. Signior Domingo's antecedents were not recorded in colonial accounts, but it is likely that he was educated by priests on São Tiago, for he read Portuguese, wore a rosary given him by a priest, and said prayers morning and night. Domingo had been an agent for John Ormond Sr. at Port Loko. He had captured and tortured to death an English ship captain who was responsible for the death of one of his sons. Made regent over the Koya Temne, Domingo was known as "Pa Potoo," the latter word originally meaning Portuguese and applied to all Europeans. Signior Domingo had a younger brother who was involved in a murder trial that was observed by several residents of the colony. In the course of the proceedings, Domingo had his rosary beads ("Portuguese Grigris") placed alongside the Temne "Grigris," for he considered the latter insufficiently potent, and then he harangued the man accused of killing his brother's slave (Butt-Thompson 1926, 59–60; Fyfe 1962, 44, and 2000, 19–22; Kup 1967, 24, 28, 89–90 n. 63r 1, 91 n. 89r 1).

Gov. John Clarkson characterized Domingo as "a shrewd and designing man." Domingo applied to have a schoolmaster sent to his village, and he sent his son Antony to be educated in England. When Domingo threatened to shoot a resident of Granville Town who he claimed had taken "liberties" with one of his wives, Clarkson persuaded him not to incite warfare. Living adjacent to the colony of free people, Domingo continued to engage in the slave trade, though he told acting governor Zachary Macaulay in June 1793 that he was thinking of quitting, saying "I am old; I ought to think only of heaven." Since no priests had visited his settlement for some years, Signior Domingo instructed his relatives that, when he died, they were to send two slaves to São Tiago to be given to a priest in return for saying masses for the repose of his soul (Fyfe 1962, 54; Kup 1967, 89–90 n. 63r 1; Clifford 1999, 134–35). In a treaty concluded in July 1807, Temne ceded Signior Domingo's town to the colony, promising to compensate him. Domingo died a few months later (Fyfe 1962, 96). His death coincided with the suppression of slaving along the Sierra Leone estuary. The following year, the British government outlawed the slave trade, and the Royal

Navy made Freetown its base of operations during the suppression of the slave trade.

The Calamitous English Settlement on Bolama

The chief organizer of the Bolama colonization scheme was Henry Hew Dalrymple, who had been an officer in the British garrison on Gorée during the 1780s. While serving on Gorée, Dalrymple heard favorable reports about Bolama, presumably from individuals familiar with the island. Selected to be governor of Sierra Leone but dismissed after disagreements with the directors of the Sierra Leone Company, Dalrymple broadcast glowing reports about Bolama's suitability for European settlement, invoking arguments that complemented those of Andre Brüe a century earlier. Such was the English public's enthusiasm for colonization schemes that a joint-stock company formed in November 1791 was quickly oversubscribed by investors and prospective settlers. Two vessels were fitted out and sailed in April 1792 with 275 colonists aboard: 153 men, 57 women, and 65 children (Wadstrom 1794–95/1968, 130–36; Beaver 1805, chap. 1; Hair 1960; Fyfe 1962, 35; Curtin 1964, chap. 4; Galli 1996).

Members of the Bolama expedition were informed that the island was uninhabited, and hence, they took no heed of African territorial claims or their own responsibilities as strangers to negotiate with African landlords. Nine days after the first vessel anchored off Ponta Oeste on May 25, a Canhabaque war party struck without warning, killed or wounded 10 men, carried off 6 women and children, and took 60 guns and quantities of powder and ammunition. The women and children were subsequently ransomed, but the unexpected attack so terrorized the remaining colonists that most decided to abandon the settlement and return to England via the Sierra Leone colony. Only 86 of them (48 men, 13 women, and 25 children), plus 4 seamen and a ship's boy, chose to remain on Bolama under the leadership of Philip Beaver, a furloughed Royal Navy lieutenant with an indomitable determination to make the colony a success (Beaver 1805, 2, chaps. 3 and 4, and app. 4). But as Beaver remarked, "the irrational confidence of the colonists was now converted into the most groundless fears" (Beaver 1805, 52). The disaster at Bolama proved to have far-reaching ramifications. Some of the refugees returned to England via Granada, conveying yellow fever. "Bulam fever," as it was known, spread rapidly in the West Indies and in coastal North America as far north as Philadelphia (Hair 1960, 381; Curtin 1964, 183–84).

The arrival of the English colonists occasioned much interest and concern on the part of Africans, Luso-Africans, and the Portuguese authorities at Bissau. When Beaver and Dalrymple visited Bissau early in June to seek assistance in ransoming the women and children taken captive by Bijago, the Papel ruler of Bissau sent a written message that was conveyed and translated by T. (Thomas?) Birchall, the captain of an English slave sloop; in it, the Portuguese authorities were disparaged and the colonists were welcomed to settle at Bissau. Dalrymple's letter in reply tactfully declined the invitation to avoid offending the Portuguese authorities (Beaver 1805, 56–57). Beaver did not record the name of the acting commandant, Domingos da Veiga Escórcio, whose authority was being challenged by Papel. One of the persons advising the Papel was the resident Cabo Verdean priest, António Sanches Gama, who had been appointed vigário of Bissau by the bishop of Cabo Verde. Described by Escórcio as a "preto" (black), Father Gama was more likely a "pardo," or Luso-African. He was estranged from the Portuguese authorities, who claimed that he was in league with the Papel in fomenting a revolt (Rema 1982, 248).

Birchall's motives as a go-between were dubious. He was employed as the captain of the schooner *Hannah* by a trader in the Banana Islands. Beaver subsequently learned that Birchall had been imprisoned by one of the Bijago rulers of Canhabaque for cheating him and was nearly put to death, "which he richly deserved" (Beaver 1805, 56–57, 70, 295–96). Birchall's despicable behavior occasioned a digression in Beaver's book concerning European (and Eurafrican) slave traders: "It has frequently been remarked that the Africans consider '*all white man witch,*' they also believe that '*all white man rogue.*' There is no species of cheating, or deceit, or of treachery, of which they did not think a white man capable, nay, they even thought those the predominant traits of his character; and, when we consider that those Europeans with whom they had hitherto had any intercourse, were probably among the lowest and basest of their colour, this ought not so much to surprize us" (Beaver 1805, 294).

Echoing John Newton's remarks concerning his experiences a half century earlier, Beaver reflected on a year's observations: "I need not mention the various modes which Europeans also take to over-reach [Africans] in trade, by light weights, short measure, and diminished capacity, &c. all of which are now as well known to the natives as to us; and therefore, as before observed, they consider us as a compound of treachery and deceit. There is nothing degrading, nothing base, nothing infamous, but what they consider to form part of the white character" (Beaver 1805, 297).

Following Dalrymple's departure for Sierra Leone with the majority of the colonists, Beaver negotiated agreements to purchase Bolama from both Bijago and Biafada, first from the rulers of Canhabaque—Bellchore and Jalorem—and later from Matchore and Niobana residing at Guinala in the Biafada state on the north bank of the Rio Grande. The latter two expressed a strong interest in attracting English traders and agreed to cede a large tract of land on the mainland opposite Bolama. Bellchore was renowned as the greatest of all Bijago warriors; among his exploits, he had once pillaged Bissau and set fire to the community (Beaver 1805, 71–73, 101–9, 339, 474). Lieutenant Beaver was greatly impressed by Bijago weaponry: "Europeans can scarcely form an idea of the order in which these savages keep their arms. Their cutlasses I can compare only to razors. They try the edge of them on the back of the nail, as we do razors in Europe. . . . The blades are about four feet long, and Solingen is marked on them all" (Beaver 1805, 51 n. *).

Many colonists succumbed to disease, and some deserted the settlement. The greater part of the toil involved in clearing land, planting crops, and constructing dwellings and a blockhouse was done by hired African grumetes. One of Beaver's concerns was to demonstrate the efficacy of employing Africans as free laborers. Beaver stated that *grumeta* was the word used for a hired African in "the language of the country": "[Grumeta] is particularly applied to those natives who Trade for Europeans in canoes; but it is generally applicable to all those who labour, for others, for wages. Many Portuguese words are incorporated into all the African coast languages, indeed a kind of Portuguese patois is almost every where spoken in it" (Beaver 1805, 143 and n. *). In appendix 15 of his book, Beaver recorded the names of the 196 grumetes ("grumetas, or free natives") he had hired from October 1792 to October 1793. Nearly all had Portuguese names. Most of the men were recorded by both surnames and first names, whereas surnames were given for only two of thirteen females (Beaver 1805, 490–93). The fact that Africans seeking employment used Portuguese names is evidence of the social and cultural influences sustained for centuries in the Guinea-Bissau region by Portuguese and Luso-Africans.

For help in obtaining grumetes, for needed supplies, and for many acts of assistance, the colonists were greatly indebted to José da Silva Cardoso, a Cabo Verdean trader at Bissau affiliated with the Lisbon firm of Pedro Nolasco Gaspar e Irmãos. Cardoso mediated on behalf of the colonists with successive commandants of Bissau, who, together with the majority of the resident traders, were hostile to the settlement and resentful of its commerce with neighboring Africans. Doubtless, they also questioned Cardoso's motives, inasmuch as he acquired English goods for his trading operations (AHU, Cx 15, October 15, 1793; Beaver 1805, 43, 55–60, 113–14).

In May 1793, José António Pinto arrived to take command of Bissau. Mandated to enforce Portuguese commercial regulations and check the expansion of foreign competitors, Pinto found customs records and other government documents either missing or in a state of great disarray (Barcellos 1899–1913, 3:123). Endeavoring to establish cordial relations with Pinto, Lieutenant Beaver returned a Portuguese soldier who had escaped to Bolama. The man confirmed what grumetes had told Beaver—that if they were given refuge, all the soldiers in the garrison would desert to Bolama (Beaver 1805, 228, 239–40).

Pinto's tenure in command was brief. He forbade foreign vessels from trading at Bissau and incarcerated Capt. Francisco Corrêa Gomes, a leading Luso-African trader, and James Johnson, a Nova Scotian who had purchased a longboat from Beaver to engage in commerce. In June, a month after Pinto's arrival, the soldiers of the garrison mutinied, and Pinto fled Bissau to the detachment at Fá, a hundred kilometers up the Geba River on the left bank. Details were not recorded, but one may suppose that the trading community, together with Papel rulers, were responsible for Pinto's expulsion from Bissau (Barcellos 1899–1913, 3:154–55; AHU, Cx 18, Gouvea to Visconde de Anadia, April 29, 1805).

By the latter part of 1793, the number of colonists on Bolama had dwindled to a handful, and Britain's involvement in a war with France precluded the colony receiving substantial reinforcements and supplies from England. Beaver sold the blockhouse and remaining supplies and trade goods to Francisco Corrêa Gomes, who was deputized by José da Silva Cardoso and the acting commandant of Bissau, Domingos da Veiga Escórcio. Gomes was the leading Luso-African trader in the Geba-Grande area. Born in the neighborhood of Geba, he was part Mandinka on his mother's side, owned many trading craft, had sailed numerous times to Cabo Verde, and had visited Portugal. By 1802 if not earlier, Gomes was Geba's sargento-mor. Known as "Capitano Corrêa," he favorably impressed Lieutenant Beaver: "He speaks very good Portuguese, is dressed in the European fashion, has considerable property, reads and writes, can ascertain the latitude by the sun's altitude, and appears to be a very intelligent man." At the end of November 1793, Beaver and five remaining males departed Bolama and sailed for Sierra Leone, stopping en route at Kakundy in the Nunez River to trade plantation tools for ivory. Two weeks later, a ship arrived from England, bringing supplies but no additional settlers (AHU, Cx 15, October 15, 1793; AHU, Cx 18, May 2, 1806; Beaver 1805, 275–83, 407; Hair 1960, 377).

In contrast to the settlement along the Sierra Leone estuary, where the Temne adhered to long-standing landlord-stranger reciprocities and accommodated the English colonists until they became too numerous to expel, the prospects of the

Bolama colony were ruined at the outset by the aggressive response of Bijago to intruders ignorant of their obligations as strangers. By killing and capturing a number of colonists and driving away most of the remainder, the Bijago at the same time helped preserve Luso-African commercial interests in the Geba-Grande area. Already, competition from English and Anglo-African traders had reached a critical juncture, as observed by Lieutenant Beaver.

Beaver's journal during his residence on Bolama from July 1792 to November 1793 incorporated much information concerning competition for the trade of the Geba-Grande area. English and Anglo-African traders residing as far distant as the Sierra Leone estuary and Banana Islands sent trading craft, as did English slaving vessels anchored along the coast of Serra Leoa. Entries in Beaver's journal described ruthless competition, with Luso-African and Portuguese traders allegedly resorting to poisoning and "cutting-off" their rivals by unprovoked attacks on trading craft caught unawares or poorly manned, their crews being murdered or enslaved.

One instance of cutting off a dangerous rival involved the return to the Grande River of the Anglo-African John Bootle following the death of John Ormond. Sr. Bootle may have been encouraged to return to the Grande River by the presence of the English settlement on Bolama and the treaty that Beaver had negotiated with the Biafada rulers of Guinala. When Bootle returned to Bolala in August 1792 to obtain slaves for the Liverpool slaver *Fisher,* lying in the Nunez River, a Bissau trader named Galvão ("Galvine") attempted unsuccessfully to incite the Biafada to seize Bootle's vessel. Subsequently, when Bootle sailed the *Fisher*'s schooner to Jeta Island west of Bissau, Galvão's grumetes seized the vessel and killed Bootle and Ashley, the *Fisher*'s third mate, along with two grumetes and three slaves. Galvão's men brought the schooner to Bissau, where, in February 1793, it was recaptured by a boat belonging to the ship *Nancy* of Liverpool, commanded by William C. Moore. As the trustee of John Ormond Sr.'s estate, Captain Moore had the invidious task of attempting to collect large debts owed to Ormond by Bissau traders, plus many owed himself, amounting to some £2,000 altogether. Moore confided to Beaver that he had made "three fruitless attempts" to recover the debts (Beaver 1805, 95–96, 166, 194, 472–75).

Bootle's violent death notwithstanding, English and Anglo-Africans continued to trade in the Grande River. Among the latter was David James Lawrence, son of an English slaver from Deal. His principal place of trade was at Kissassi along the upper Nunez, and he also had a factory at Dominguia in the Pongo River (Mouser 1973, 53). Lawrence gave considerable assistance to the English settlers on Bolama, and Beaver recorded that Lawrence took the schooner *Wil-*

liam and the pinnace *Jane* into the Grande River in October 1793 (Beaver 1805, 262). Lawrence's son David, after attending school in England, succeeded him in trade along the Grande River, living at Bolale during the 1820s (Owen 1833, 2:151–52).

Given the ruthless treatment of competitors in the Geba-Grande area, one may speculate as to whether English and Anglo-Africans retaliated against trading craft undertaking the annual kola voyages. They might have realized a considerable profit from supplying kola to markets in the Guinea-Bissau region, but apparently, they concentrated on the more lucrative slave trade. Beaver's journal made reference to numerous Nalu craft passing Bolama to trade at Bissau (Beaver 1805, 319–20 n.). Beaver did not have an opportunity to observe what the Nalu were transporting, but it may be that they and other Africans were supplanting Luso-Africans and grumetes in kola commerce. Significantly, Beaver did not mention Bijago molesting Nalu craft, which stood in contrast to Bijago predations against Biafada. The situation may be explained by the long-standing bonds between the two groups. Bijago men selected for community leadership had to go to Nalu territory for initiation ceremonies (Scantamburlo 1991, 49–50).

The French Revolution engendered renewed conflict between France and Britain. European commerce raiding preceded the declaration of war in Europe by nine months. On April 30, 1792, four British vessels destroyed a French trader's establishment in the Bight of Benin (Gaffarel 1908, 53). Hostilities officially began on February 1, 1793, when France declared war on Britain, Holland, and Spain. During the two decades of European warfare that disrupted French and English commerce in western Africa, Anglo-African and English traders consolidated their dominance in Serra Leoa commerce. Meanwhile, Luso-Africans were able to reestablish ascendancy in the Cacheu-Casamance and Geba-Grande trade networks. They would be challenged anew—and more aggressively—by French and Franco-Africans and English and Anglo-Africans during the decades following the making of peace in 1815.

Eurafrican traders encountered an unprecedented challenge when Britain abolished the slave trade in 1808 and dispatched naval vessels to western African to suppress slave trading. A decade later, France followed Britain's initiative. Ever opportunistic and entrepreneurial, many Eurafricans pioneered in the transition from slave trading to commerce in palm oil, peanuts, and timber. Successful traders and cultivators of export crops sent their children to the growing number of mission schools—some to become Protestant and Catholic clergy, many to have careers in Eurafrican and European commercial firms, and others to enter colonial administration or serve in the military. Eurafricans were indispensable subalterns prior to the systematic use of malaria prophylaxis and the promotion of sanitation programs that encouraged Europeans to venture to western Africa in ever greater numbers. For Eurafricans, especially Franco-Africans and Anglo-Africans, the first two-thirds of the nineteenth century constituted their "golden age."

References

Abbreviations

A	*Africa*
AA	*African Arts*
AAS	*Asian and African Studies*
AE	*American Ethnologist*
AEH	*African Economic History*
AES	*Archives Européenes de Sociologie*
AESC	*Annales Economies Sociétés Civilisations*
AFG	*Africana Gandensia*
AG	*Annales de Géographie*
AHR	*American Historical Review*
AHU	Arquivo Histórico Ultramarino, Lisbon
AL	*Anthropological Linguistics*
ALR	*African Language Review*
ALS	*African Language Studies*
AN	*American Neptune*
ANAF	*Annales Africaines*
ANYAS	*Annals of the New York Academy of Sciences*
AOFA	Afrique Occidentale Française Archives, Dakar, Senegal
ARB	*Africana Research Bulletin*
AS	*African Studies*
BAHC	*Boletim do Arquivo Histórico Colonial*
BAPH	*Boletim, Academia Portuguesa da História*
BCGP	*Boletim Cultural da Guiné Portuguesa*
BIFAN	*Bulletin,* Institut Français d'Afrique Noire/Institut Fondamentale d'Afrique Noire
BSGL	*Boletim da Sociedade de Geografia de Lisboa*

BSGM	*Bulletin de la Société de Géographie de Marseille*
BSGP	*Bulletin de la Société de Géographie de Paris*
BSOAS	*Bulletin of the School of Oriental and African Studies*
BUASCWP	Boston University African Studies Center Working Papers
CEA	*Cahiers d'Etudes Africaines*
CJH	*Canadian Journal of History*
CSSH	*Comparative Studies in Society and History*
E	*Ethiopiques: Revue Socialiste de Culture Négro-Africaine*
EEH	*Explorations in Economic History*
EHISTR	*English Historical Review*
EHR	*Economic History Review*
FO	*France Outre-Mer*
G	*Geographica*
G-A	*Genève-Afrique*
GR	*Geographical Review*
HA	*History in Africa*
HAHR	*Hispanic American Historical Review*
IJAHS	*International Journal of African Historical Studies*
IJSLS	*International Journal of Sierra Leone Studies*
IUASPWPS	*Indiana University African Studies Program Working Papers Series*
JAH	*Journal of African History*
JEH	*Journal of Ecclesiastical History*
JHSN	*Journal of the Historical Society of Nigeria*
JICH	*Journal of Imperial and Commonwealth History*
JRA	*Journal of Religion in Africa*
JSA	*Journal de la Société des Africanists*
JWP	*Journal of World Prehistory*
L-F	*Liberia-Forum*
LSJ	*Liberia Studies Journal*
NA	*Notes Africaines*
NG	*National Geographic*
NH	*Natural History*
P	*Paideuma*
PARCM	*Portugal em Africa: Revista de Cultura Missionaria*
PHSL	*Proceedings of the Huguenot Society of London*
PRO	Public Record Office, London
RA/EG	*Recherches Africaines/Etudes Guinéennes*
RALF	*Réalités Africaines et Langue Française*
RFBC	*Review of the Fernand Braudel Center*
RFHOM	*Revue Française d'Histoire d'Outre-Mer*
RHCF	*Revue Historique des Colonies Françaises*
RHMC	*Revue d'Histoire Moderne et Contemporaine*
RUC	*Revista da Universidade de Coimbra*
SA	*Slavery and Abolition: A Journal of Comparative Studies*
SAL	*Studies in African Linguistics*

SLBR	*Sierra Leone Bulletin of Religion*
SLGJ	*Sierra Leone Geographical Journal*
SLS	*Sierra Leone Studies*
SREG	*Soronda: Revista de Estudos Guinéenses*
T&C	*Technology and Culture*
WAJA	*West African Journal of Archaeology*

Manuscript Collections

England

London, Public Record Office (PRO)
T70 African Companies

Portugal

Lisbon, Archivo Histórico Ultramarino (AHU)
Guiné, Caixas 15–18

Senegal

Dakar, Afrique Occidentale Française Archives (AOFA)
Q Commerce et Compagnie du Sénégal, 1782–1793

Unpublished Sources

Bardwell, R. L. 1974. "The Governors of Portugal's South Atlantic Empire in the Seventeenth Century: Social Background, Qualifications, Selection, and Reward." Ph.D. diss., University of California, Santa Barbara.

Cariou, P. A. N.d. "Promenade à Gorée."

Crowley, E. L. 1990. "Contracts with the Spirits: Religion, Asylum, and Ethnic Identity in the Cacheu Region of Guinea-Bissau." Ph.D. diss., Yale University.

Frinsel, H. 1990. Personal communication.

Fyfe, C. 2000. Personal communication.

Galloway, W. F. 1974. "A History of Wuli from the Thirteenth to the Nineteenth Century." Ph.D. diss., Indiana University.

———. 1980. "A Working Map of Kaabu." Colloque International sur les Traditions Orales du Gabu. Dakar, Senegal, May 19–24, 1980.

Hair, P. E. H. 2000. Personal communication.

Hesselink, E. 1984. Personal communication.

Johnson, M. A. 1980. "Black Gold: Goldsmiths, Jewelry, and Women in Senegal." Ph.D. diss., Stanford University.

Kaba, L. 1978. Seminar presentation, Indiana University, March 1, 1978.

Knight-Baylac, M-H. 1970a. "Gorée et 'La Petite Côte': Origines et développement—

Les rélations commerciales avec les pays du sud (jusqu'au Rio Grande), 1677–1789." Treatise, Université de Paris, Sorbonne.

McCall, D. F. 1989. Personal communication.

———. 2000. Personal communication.

Mark, P. 2000. "Marginal Mande and Peripheral 'Portuguese': Trade and Identity in Seventeenth Century Gambia." African Studies Association meeting, Nashville, Tenn., November 16–19.

Mouser, B. L. 1971. "Trade and Politics in the Nunez and Pongo Rivers, 1790–1865." Ph.D. diss., Indiana University.

———. 2000. Personal communication.

Sackur, A. 2000. "Cultural Change and Creole Identities in Eighteenth-Century Senegambia." African Studies Association meeting, Nashville, Tenn., November 16–19.

Slobbe, E. van. 1984. Personal communication.

Wright, D. R. 1976. "Niumi: The History of a Western Mandinka State through the Eighteenth Century." Ph.D. diss., Indiana University.

———. 2000. Personal communication.

Published Sources

Adanson, M. 1759. A Voyage to Senegal, the Isle of Gorée, and the River Gambia. London.

———. 1814. "A Voyage to Senegal." In *A General Collection of the Best and Most Interesting Voyages and Travels in All Parts of the World,* edited by John Pinkerton, 598–674. 17 vols. London: Longman, Hurst, Rees, and Orme, 1808–14.

Albuquerqe, L. de, and M. E. M. Santos, eds. 1988. *História geral de Cabo Verde: Corpo documental.* Vol. 1. Lisbon: Institute de Investigação Científica Tropical.

Alden, D. 1968. *Royal Government in Colonial Brazil.* Berkeley: University of California Press.

Alldridge, T. J. 1910/1970. *A Transformed Colony: Sierra Leone.* Westport, Conn.: Negro Universities Press.

Allen, G. W. 1913. *A Naval History of the American Revolution.* 2 vols. Boston: Houghton Mifflin.

Almada, A. A. c. 1594/1964. "Tratado breve dos rios de Guiné do Cabo Verde." In *Monumenta missionaria Africana: Africa Ocidental (1570–1600),* edited by A. Brásio, 3: 229–378. Lisbon.

Alvares, M. c. 1615/1990. *Etiópia Menor e descripção géografia da Província da Serra Leoa,* translated and edited by P. E. H. Hair. Liverpool: University of Liverpool.

Ames, D. W. 1956. "The Selection of Mates, Courtship, and Marriage among the Wolof." BIFAN 18, 1–2: 156–68.

Amselle, J.-L. 1977. *Les négociants de la savana.* Paris: Anthropos.

———. 1998. *Mestizo Logics: Anthropology of Identity in Africa and Elsewhere.* Stanford: Stanford University Press.

Andrade, A. A. 1970. "Bernardino Alvares de Andrade, um 'Guineense' esquecido." BCGP 25, 98: 177–215.

Andrade, F. d'. 1582/1964. "Relação de Francisco de Andrade sobre as ilhas de Cabo

Verde." In *Monumenta missionaria Africana: Africa ocidental (1570–1600),* edited by A. Brásio, 3: 97–107. Lisbon: Agencia-Geral do Ultramar.

Angrand, A-P. 1946. *Les Lébous de la presqu'île du Cap-Vert.* Dakar, Senegal: La Maison du Livre.

———. 1952. *Manuel-Français-Ouolof.* Dakar, Senegal: La Maison du Livre.

Anstey, R. 1975. *The Atlantic Slave Trade and British Abolition, 1760–1810.* London: Macmillan.

Appia, B. 1965. "Les forgerons du Fouta-Djallon." JSA 25, 2: 317–52.

Archer, F. B. 1906/1967. *The Gambia Colony and Protectorate: An Official Handbook.* London: Frank Cass.

Arcin, A. 1911. *Histoire de la Guinée française.* Paris: Augustin Challamel.

Astley, T., ed. 1745–47/1968. *A New General Collection of Voyages and Travels.* 4 vols. London: Frank Cass.

Atkins, J. 1735/1970. *A Voyage to Guinea, Brazil, and the West Indies.* London: Frank Cass.

Azevedo, J. L. d'. 1921. *História dos cristãos novos portugueses.* Lisbon: Livraria Classica Editora.

Azevedo, W. L. d'. 1962. "Some Historical Problems in the Delineation of a Central West Atlantic Region." ANYAS 96, no. 2: 512–58.

———. 1989. "Tribe and Chiefdom on the Windward Coast." LSJ 14, 2: 90–116.

Baião, A., ed. 1940. *O manuscrito Valentim Fernandes.* Lisbon: Academia Portuguesa da História.

Bane, M. J. 1956. *Catholic Pioneers in West Africa.* Dublin: Clonmore and Reynolds.

Barbot, J. 1732. *A Description of the Coasts of North and South Guinea, In Six Books.* London: Awshan and Churchill.

Barcellos, C. J. de S. 1899–1913. *Subsidios para a história de Cabo Verde e Guiné.* 7 vols. Lisbon: Academia das Ciências.

———. 1904. *Cabo Verde: Algumas apontamentos sobre as fomes em Cabo-Verde desde 1719 à 1904.* Lisbon: Tipógrafo da Cooperativa Militar.

Barreto, J. 1938. *História da Guiné, 1418–1918.* Lisbon: Ediçao do Autor.

Barry, B. 1981a. "Economic Anthropology of Precolonial Senegambia from the Fifteenth through the Nineteenth Centuries." In *Uprooted of the Western Sahel,* edited by L. G. Colvin, et al., 27–57. New York: Praeger.

———. 1981b. "Senegambia from the Sixteenth to the Eighteenth Century: Evolution of the Wolof, Sereer, and 'Tukuloor.'" In *Africa from the Sixteenth to the Eighteenth Century,* edited by B. A. Ogot, 262–99. Berkeley: University of California Press.

———. 1988. *La Sénégambie du XV au XIX siècle.* Paris: L'Harmattan.

———. 1998. *Senegambia and the Atlantic Slave Trade.* New York: Cambridge University Press.

Barry, B., and L. Harding. 1992. *Commerce et commerçants en Afrique de l'ouest: Le Sénégal.* Paris: L'Harmattan.

Baum, R. M. 1999. *Shrines of the Slave Trade.* New York: Oxford University Press.

Baumann, H., and D. Westermann. 1962. *Les peuples et les civilisations de l'Afrique.* Paris: Payot.

Bazin, J. 1985. "A chacun son Bambara." In *Au coeur de l'ethnie,* edited by J.-L. Amselle and E. M'Bokolo, 87–127. Paris: Editions la Découvert.

Beaver, P. 1805. *African Memoranda: Relative to an Attempt to Establish a British Settlement on the Island of Bulama, on the Western Coast of Africa, in the Year 1792.* London: C. and R. Baldwin.

Becker, C. 1972. "A propos d'un plagiare: Le père Gaby." NA 133: 17–21.

———. 1985. "Notes sur les conditions écologiques en Sénégambie aux 17 et 18 siècles." AEH 14: 167–216.

Becker, C., and V. Martin. 1977. "Détails historiques et politiques, mémoire inédit (1778) de J. A. LeBrasseur." BIFAN 39, 1: 81–132.

Belinfante, J. C. E., Edward van Voolen, David P. Cohen Paraira, Jaffa Baruch-Sznaj, Julie-Marthe Cohen. 1991. *The Esnoga: A Monument to Portuguese-Jewish Culture.* Amsterdam: D'Arts.

Bennett, N. R., and G. E. Brooks, eds. 1965. *New England Merchants in Africa: A History through Documents, 1802 to 1865.* Boston: Boston University Press.

Berlioux, E.-F. 1874. *André Brüe ou l'origine de la colonie française du Sénégal.* Paris: Guillaumin.

Bertrand-Bocandé, E. 1849. "Notes sur la Guinée portugaise ou Sénégambie méridionale." BSGP 11: 265–350, map on p. 92; 12: 57–93.

Biasutti, A. 1982. *Kriol-purtugîs (esboço-proposta de vocabulário).* Bafatá, Guinea-Bissau: Missão Católica.

Bird, C. S. 1970. "The Development of Mandekan (Manding): A Study." In *Language and History in Africa,* edited by D. Dalby, 146–59. New York: Africana Publishing Corp.

Blackburn, R. 1997. *The Making of New World Slavery: From the Baroque to the Modern, 1492–1800.* London: Verso.

Blake, J. W. 1977. *West Africa: Quest for God and Gold, 1454–1578.* London: Curzon Press.

Blussé, L., and F. Gaastra, eds. 1981. *Companies and Trade.* Leiden: Leiden University Press.

Bodiel, T. 1950. "La coiffure 'Gossi' et les bijoux qui lui sont assortis." NA 45: 9–11.

Bolster, W. J. 1998. *Black Jacks: African American Seamen in the Age of Sail.* Cambridge: Harvard University Press.

Botte, R. 1991. "Les rapports Nord-Sud, la traite négrière et le Fouta Jaloo à la fin du XVIII siècle." AESC 6: 1411–35.

Boulègue, J. 1972. *Les Luso-Africains de Sénégambie XVI–XIX siècle.* Dakar, Senegal: Université de Dakar, Département d'Histoire.

———. 1973. "Trois anciens points de traite de la Petite Côte sénégalaise: Palmeirinha, Punto Sereno, Porto Novo." NA 137: 16–22.

———. 1977. "Lat-Sukaabe Fal." In *Les Africaines,* edited by C.-A. Julien, 9: 169–93. Paris.

———. 1981a. "Les pays wolof et seerer et le monde mande au moyen age." E 28: 168–73.

———. 1981b. "Un empire peul dans le Soudan occidentale au début du XVII siècle." In *Le sol, la parole, et l'ecrit: Mélanges en hommage à Raymond Mauny,* 2: 699–706. Paris: Société Française d'Histoire d'Outre-Mer.

———. 1987. *Le Grand Jolof, xiii–xvi siècle.* Blois, France: Karthala.

———. 1989. *Les Luso-Africains de Sénégambie XVI–XIX siècle.* Lisbon: Ministério da Educação/Instituto de Investigação Científica Tropical.

———. 1993. "Cacheu, les rivières de Guinée et le royaume du Kaabú, vus de Gorée, à la fin du XVIII siècle." In *Mansas, escravos, grumetes, e gentio: Cacheu na encruzilhada de civilizações,* edited by C. Lopes, 55–64. Bissau, Guinea-Bissau.

———. 1996. "Un projet d'établissement français a Bolama et son échec (1724–1725)." In *Bolama: Entre a generosidade da natureza e a cobiça dos homens,* edited by C. Cardoso, 91–105. Bissau, Guinea-Bissau.

———. 2001. "Contribution des sources françaises à la connaissance de l'actuelle Guinée-Bissau à la fin du XVII siècle." HA 28: 43–51.

Boulègue, J., and R. Marquet. 1971. "Le voyage de Richard Rainolds en Sénégambie (1591)." BIFAN 33, 1: 1–13.

Boulègue, J., and B. Pinto-Bull. 1966. "Un prêtre sénégalais au XVI siècle." NA 109: 27–29.

Boxer, C. R. 1969. *The Portuguese Seaborne Empire, 1415–1825.* London: Hutchinson.

Bradshaw, A. T. von S. 1965. "Vestiges of Portuguese in the Languages of Sierra Leone." SLR 4: 5–37.

Braidwood, S., Jr. 1994. *Black Poor and White Philanthropists: London's Blacks and the Foundation of the Sierra Leone Settlement, 1786–1791.* Liverpool: Liverpool University Press.

Brásio, A., ed. 1955. *Monumenta missionaria: Africa ocidental (1611–1621).* Vol. 4. Lisbon: Agencia-Geral do Ultramar.

———. 1958. *Monumenta missionaria: Africa ocidental (1342–1499).* 2nd ser., vol. 1. Lisbon: Agencia-Geral do Ultramar.

———. 1963. *Monumenta missionaria Africana: Africa ocidental (1500–1569).* 2nd ser., vol. 2. Lisbon: Agencia-Geral do Ultramar.

———. 1964. *Monumenta missionaria Africana: Africa ocidental (1570–1600).* 2nd ser., vol. 3. Lisbon: Agencia-Geral do Ultramar.

———. 1968. *Monumenta missionaria Africana: Africa ocidental (1600–1622).* 2nd ser., vol. 4. Lisbon.

Brooks, G. E. 1970. *Yankee Traders, Old Coasters, and African Middlemen: A History of American Legitimate Trade with West Africa in the Nineteenth Century.* Boston: Boston University Press.

———. 1972. *The Kru Mariner in the Nineteenth Century.* Newark, Delaware: Liberian Studies Association.

———. 1973. "Notes on Research Facilities in Lisbon and the Cape Verde Islands." IJAHS 6, 2: 304–14.

———. 1976. "The Signares of Saint-Louis and Gorée: Women Entrepreneurs in Eighteenth-Century Senegal." In *Women in Africa: Studies in Social and Economic Change,* edited by N. J. Hafkin and E. G. Bay, 19–44. Stanford: Stanford University Press.

———. 1980a. "Perspectives on Luso-African Commerce and Settlement in the Gambia and Guinea-Bissau Region, 16th–19th Centuries." BUASCWP, no. 24.

———. 1980b. "Kola Trade and State-Building—Upper Guinea Coast and Senegambia, 15th–17th Centuries," BUASCWP, no. 38.

———. 1980c. "Artists' Depictions of Senegalese Signares: Insights Concerning French Racist and Sexist Attitudes in the Nineteenth Century." G-A 18, 1: 75–89.

———. 1984. "The Observance of All Souls' Day in the Guinea-Bissau Region." HA 13: 1–34.

———. 1985. "Western Africa to c. 1860 A.D.: A Provisional Historical Schema Based on Climate Periods." IUASPWPS, no. 1. Bloomington.

———. 1986. "A Provisional Historical Schema for Western Africa Based on Seven Climate Periods (ca. 9,000 B.C. to the 19th Century)." CEA 101-102: 43-62.

———. 1987. "Historical Perspectives on the Guinea-Bissau Region, Fifteenth to Nineteenth Centuries." In *Vice-Almirante A. Teixeira da Mota: In Memoriam,* 2 vols., 1: 277-304. Lisbon: Academia de Marinha/Instituto de Investigação Científica Tropical.

———. 1989. "Ecological Perspectives on Mande Population Movements, Commercial Networks, and Settlement Patterns from the Atlantic Wet Phase (ca. 5500-2500 B.C.) to the Present." HA 16: 23-40.

———. 1990. "Notas genealógicas de proeminentes famílias Luso-Africanas no século XIX na Guiné." SREG 9: 53-71.

———. 1993a. "Cacheu: A Papel and Luso-African Entrepôt at the Nexus of the Biafada-Sapi and Banyun-Bak Trade Networks." In *Mansas, escravos, grumetes, e gentio: Cacheu na encruzilhada de civilizações,* edited by C. Lopes, 173-97. Bissau, Guinea-Bissau: Instituto Nacional de Estudos e Pesquisa.

———. 1993b. *Landlords and Strangers: Ecology, Society, and Trade in Western Africa, 1000-1630.* Boulder, Colo: Westview Press.

———. 1996 "Bolama: Cynosure of African, European, Eur-African, and American Imperialisms." In *Bolama: Entre a generosidade da natureza e a cobiça dos homens,* edited by C. Cardoso, 135-74. Bissau, Guinea-Bissau: Instituto Nacional de Estudos e Pesquisa.

———. 1998. "Climate and History in West Africa." In *Transformations in Africa: Essays on Africa's Later Past,* edited by G. Connah, 139-59. London: Leicester University Press.

Bühnen, S. 1992. "Place Names as an Historical Source: An Introduction with Examples from Southern Senegambia and Germany." HA 19: 45-101.

Butt-Thompson, F. W. 1926. *Sierra Leone in History and Tradition.* London: H. F. & G. Witherby.

Cardoso, C. 1996. *Bolama: Entre a generosidade da natureza e a cobiça dos homens.* Bissau, Guinea-Bissau: Instituto Nacional de Estudos e Pesquisa.

Cariou, P. A. 1950. "La rivale inconnue de Madame de Sabran dans l'ile de Gorée." NA 45: 13-15.

———. 1952. "Costumes d'autrefois à Gorée." FO 270: 38-42, 118.

Carlos, A. M. 1994. "Bonding and the Agency Problem: Evidence from the Royal African Company, 1672-1691." EEH 31: 313-35.

Carlos, A. M., and J. B. Kruse. 1996. "The Decline of the Royal African Company: Fringe Firms and the Role of the Charter." EHR 49, 2: 291-313.

Carnes, J. A. 1852/1969. *Journal of a Voyage from Boston to the West Coast of Africa: With a Full Description of the Manner of Trading with the Natives on the Coast.* New York: Negro Universities Press.

Carney, J. 1996. "Landscapes of Technology Transfer: Rice Cultivation and African Continuities." T&C 37, 1: 5-35.

Carreira, A. 1947. *Vida social dos Manjacos.* Bissau, Guinea-Bissau: Centro de Estudos da Guiné Portuguesa.

———. 1961. "Símbolos, ritualistas, e ritualismos ânimo-feiticistas na Guiné Portuguesa." BCGP 16, 63: 505–39.
———. 1966. "Crises em Cabo Verde nos seculos XVI e XVII." G 6: 35–46.
———. 1968. *Panaria Cabo-Verdiano-Guineense: Aspectos históricos e sócio-económicos.* Lisbon: Junta De Investigações do Ultramar.
———. 1969. *As companhias pombalinas de navigação, comércio, e tráfico de escravos entre a costa africana e o nordeste brasileiro.* Bissau, Guinea-Bissau: Centro de Estudos da Guiné Portuguesa.
———. 1972. *Cabo Verde: Formação e extinção de uma sociedade escravocrata, 1460–1878.* Lisbon: Agência Geral do Ultramar.
———. 1984. *Os Portuguêses nos rios de Guiné (1500–1900).* Lisbon: Litorafia Tejo.
Carvalho, F. P. de. 1635/1970. "Le Routier de la Côte de Guinée." Translated and edited by G. Thilmans and N. I. de Moraes. BIFAN 32, 2: 343–69.
———. 1635/1974b. Translated and edited by P. E. H. Hair. ARB 5, 1: 47–56.
Chauveau, J.-P. 1986. "Une histoire maritime africaine est-elle possible?" CEA 101–102: 173–235.
Church, R. J. H. 1980. *West Africa: A Study of the Environment and of Man's Use of It.* 8th ed. London: Longman.
Cissoko, S. M. 1969. "Traits fondamentaux des sociétés du Soudan occidental du XVII au début du XIX siècle" BIFAN 31, 1: 1–30.
Clifford, M. L. 1999. *From Slavery to Freetown: Black Loyalists after the American Revolution.* Jefferson, N.C: McFarland & Co.
Coelho, F. de L. 1684/1953. *Duas descriçoes seiscentistas da Guiné.* Edited by D. Peres. Lisbon: Academia Portuguesa da Historia.
———. 1684/1985. *Francisco de Lemos Coelho. Description of the Coast of Guinea (1684).* Translated and edited by P. E. H. Hair. Liverpool: Department of History, University of Liverpool.
Collier, et al. 1824. *West African Sketches: Compiled from the Reports of Sir G. R. Collier, Sir Charles MacCarthy, and Other Official Sources.* London: L. B. Seeley and Son.
Colvin, L. G. 1986. "The *Shaykh*'s Men: Religion and Power in Senegambian Islam." AAS, 20: 61–71.
Corry, J. 1807/1968. *Observations on the Windward Coast of Africa.* London: Frank Cass.
Costa, M. A. N. 1953. "Dom António e o trato inglês da Guiné." BCGP 8, 32: 683–797.
Coughtry, J. 1981. *The Notorious Triangle: Rhode Island and the African Slave Trade, 1700-1807.* Philadelphia: Temple University Press.
Crane, E. F. 1985. *A Dependent People: Newport, Rhode Island, in the Revolutionary Era.* New York: Fordham University Press.
Crone, G. R. 1937. *The Voyages of Cadamosto and Other Documents on Western Africa in the Second Half of the Fifteenth Century.* London: Hakluyt Society.
Cultru, P. 1910. *Histoire du Sénégal du XV siècle à 1870.* Paris: E. Larose.
———, ed. 1913. *Premier voyage du Sieur de la Courbe fait à la coste d'Afrique en 1685.* Nendeln, Liechtenstein: Kraus Reprint.
Curtin, P. D. 1964. *The Image of Africa: British Ideas and Action, 1780–1850.* Madison: University of Wisconsin Press.

———. 1967. *Africa Remembered: Narratives by West Africans from the Era of the Slave Trade.* Madison: Unversity of Wisconsin Press.

———. 1969. *The Atlantic Slave Trade: A Census.* Madison: University of Wisconsin Press.

———. 1975. *Economic Change in Precolonial Africa: Senegambia in the Era of the Slave Trade.* Madison: University of Wisconsin Press.

Daget, S. 1988. *De la traite à l'esclavage.* Paris: L'Harmattan.

Dalziel, J. M. 1948. *The Useful Plants of West Tropical Africa.* London: Crown Agents for the Colonies.

Dantzig, A. van, and A. Jones, eds. 1987. *Pieter de Marees: Description and Historical Account of the Gold Kingdom of Guinea (1602).* Oxford: Oxford University Press.

Dapper, O. 1686/1951. See Duarte, 1951.

Davies, K. G. 1957. *The Royal African Company.* London: Longmans, Green.

Day, L. 1983. "Afro-British Integration on the Sherbro Coast, 1665–1795." ARB 12, 3: 82–107.

Debbasch, Y. 1988. "L'Espace du Sierra-Leone et la politique française de traite." In *De la traite à l'esclavage,* 2 vols., edited by Serge Daget, 1: 209–12. Paris: L'Harmattan.

Delcourt, A. 1952. *La France et les établissements français au Sénégal entre 1713 et 1763.* Dakar, Senegal.

Delcourt, J. 1975. *L'ile de Gorée.* Dakar, Senegal: Clairafrique.

———. 1976. *Histoire religieuse du Sénégal.* Dakar, Senegal: Clairafrique.

———. 1982. *La turbulente histoire de Gorée.* Dakar, Senegal: Clairafrique.

———. 1984. *Gorée: Six siècles d'histoire.* Dakar, Senegal: Clairafrique.

Demanet, M. l'Abbé. 1767. *Nouvelle histoire de l'Afrique françoise.* Paris: Veuve Duchesne.

Dias, A. J. 1945. "Crencas e costumes dos indígenas da ilha de Bissau no século XVIII (segundo manuscrito inédito)." PARCM 2, 9–10: 159–65, 223–29.

Dodwell, H. 1916. "Le Sénégal sous la domination anglaise." RHCF 4: 267–300.

Donelha, A. 1625/1977. *Descrição da Serra Leoa e dos rios de Guiné do Cabo Verde (1625). An Account of Sierra Leone and the Rivers of Cape Verde (1625).* Edited by A. T. da Mota and P. E. H. Hair. Lisbon: Junta de Investigaçoes Científicas do Ultramar.

Donnan, E. 1930/1969. *Documents Illustrative of the Slave Trade to America.* 4 vols. New York: Octagon Books.

Dorjahn, R. V., and C. Fyfe. 1962. "Landlord and Stranger: Change in Tenancy Relations in Sierra Leone." JAH 3, 3: 391–97.

Duarte, F. 1951. "Os Rios da Guiné no livro do geógrafo flamengo D.O' Dapper: Descrição da Africa, século XVII." BCGP 6, 23: 711–43.

Dubiez, F. J. N.d. *The Sephardi Community of Amsterdam.* Amsterdam: Esnoga Synagogue.

Duchemin, M. G.-J. 1949. "La République Lébou et peuplement actuel." In *La Presqu'île du Cap Vert: Etudes sénégalaises.* Dakar, Senegal: IFAN.

Duncan, T. B. 1972. *Atlantic Islands: Madeira, the Azores, and the Cape Verdes in Seventeenth Century Commerce and Navigation.* Chicago: University of Chicago Press.

Dupire, M. 1985. "A Nomadic Caste: The Fulani Woodcarvers." *Anthropos* 80: 85–100.

Durand, J. B. L. 1806. *A Voyage to Senegal.* London: J. G. Barnard.

Emmer, P. 1998. *The Dutch in the Atlantic Economy, 1580–1880.* Ashgate, UK: Variorum Collected Studies Series.

Encyclopedia Britannica. 1926. 13th ed. London.

Esteves, M. L. 1988. *Gonçalo de Gamboa de Aiala, capitão-mor de Cacheu, e o commércio negreiro espanhol (1640–1650).* Lisbon: Centro de Estudos de História e Cartografia Antiga.

Ethnologische Zeitschrift Zürich 1990. 1.

Fage, J. D. 1987. *A Guide to Original Sources for Precolonial Western Africa Published in European Languages.* Madison: Unversity of Wisconsin African Studies Program.

Faro, J. 1958. "A aclamação de D. João IV na Guiné." BCGP 13, 52: 490–515.

———. 1959. "O Movimento commercial do porto de Bissau de 1788 à 1794." BCGP 14, 54: 231–58.

Fernandes, V. 1506–1510/1951. *Description de la côte occidêntale d'Afrique (Sénégal au Cap de Monte Archipels).* Translated and edited by T. Monod, A. T. de Mota, and R. Mauny. Bissau, Guinea-Bissau: Centro de Estudos da Guiné Portuguesa.

Fisher, H. 1977. "Review of G. Innes, *Kaabu and Fuladu.*" BSOAS 40, 3: 658–60.

Frey, H. N. 1890. *Côte occidentale d'Afrique.* Paris: C. Marpon and E. Flammarion.

Froger, F. 1699. *Relation d'un voyage fait en 1695, 1696, et 1697, aux côtes d'Afrique.* Amsterdam: Chez les Héritiers D'Antoine Schelte.

Fyfe, C. 1962. *A History of Sierra Leone.* London: Oxford University Press.

———. 1964. *Sierra Leone Inheritance.* London: Oxford University Press.

———. 1976. "Freed Slave Colonies in West Africa." In *The Cambridge History of Africa,* edited by J. E. Flint, 5: 170–99. Cambridge: Cambridge University Press.

———, ed. 2000. *Anna Maria Falconbridge: Narrative of Two Voyages to the River Sierra Leone; with Alexander Falconbridge: An Account of the Slave Trade on the Coast of Africa.* Liverpool: Liverpool University Press.

Gaffarel, P. 1908. *La politique coloniale en France de 1789 à 1830.* Paris: F. Alcan.

Gaillard, G., ed. 2000. *Migrations anciennes et peuplement actuel des côtes guinéenes.* Paris: L'Harmattan.

Galli, R. E. 1996. "Eighteenth Century Images of Bolama and its Colonization." In *Bolama: Entre a generosidade da natureza e a cobiça dos homens,* edited by C. Cardoso, 107–34. Bissau, Guinea-Bissau: Instituto Nacional de Estudos e Pesquisa.

Gallop, R. 1936. *Portugal: A Book of Folk-Ways.* Cambridge: Cambridge University Press.

Gamble, D. P. 1967. *The Wolof of Senegambia.* London: International African Institute.

———. 1992. *Early Published Vocabularies of the Wolof Language.* Brisbane, Calif.: D. P. Gamble.

Gamble, D. P., and P. E. H. Hair., eds. 1999. *The Discovery of River Gambra (1623)* by Richard Jobson. London: Hakluyt Society.

Garlake, P. 1990. *The Kingdoms of Africa.* New York: Peter Bedrick Books.

George, C. 1904. *The Rise of British West Africa.* London: Houlston & Sons.

Glanville, R. R. 1930. "Salt and the Salt Industry of the Northern Province." SLS 16: 52–56.

Golberry, S. M. X. de. 1791. *Lettre a mm les députés des manufactures et du commerce de France.* Paris: Devaux.

———. 1802. *Fragmens d'un voyage en Afrique, fait pendant les années 1785, 1786, 1787.* 2 vols. Paris: Treuttel et Würtz.

———. 1808. *Travels in Africa.* 2nd ed. 2 vols. London: Jones and Bumford.

Gomes, D. 1456/1959. *De la première découverte de la Guinée.* Edited by T. Monod, R. Mauny, and G. Duval. Bissau, Guinea-Bissau: Centro de Estudos da Guiné Portuguesa.

Goody, J. R. 1971. *Technology, Tradition, and the State in Africa.* London: Oxford University Press.

Goucher, C. L. "Iron Is Iron 'til It Is Rust: Trade and Ecology in the Decline of West African Iron-Smelting." JAH 22, 2: 179–89.

Gray, J. M. 1940/1966. *A History of the Gambia.* London: Frank Cass.

Greenberg, J. H. 1963. *The Languages of Africa.* Bloomington: Indiana University.

Gruvel, A. 1908. *Les pécheries des côtes du Sénégal et des rivières du sud.* Paris: Augustin Challamel.

Hair, P. E. H. 1960. "Beaver on Bolama." BCGP 15: 360–83.

———. 1961. "Notes on the Early Study of Some West African Languages." BIFAN 23, 3–4: 683–95.

———. 1964. "Sierra Leone and Bulama 1792–4: Further Notes." SLBR 6, 1: 26–31.

———. 1966a. "The Use of African Languages in Afro-European Contacts in Guinea 1440–1560." ALR 5: 5–26.

———. 1966b. "The Spelling and Connotation of the Toponym 'Sierra Leone' since 1461." SLS 18: 43–58.

———. 1967a. "Ethnolinguistic Continuity on the Guinea Coast." JAH 8, 2: 247–68.

———. 1967b. "An Ethnolinguistic Inventory of the Upper Guinea Coast before 1700." ALR 6: 32–70.

———. 1969a. "Some French Sources on Upper Guinea, 1540–1575." BIFAN 31, 4: 1030–34.

———. 1969b. "The Text of Valentin Fernandes' Account of Upper Guinea." BIFAN 31, 4: 1035–38.

———. 1969c. "Early Sources on Religion and Social Values in the Sierra Leone Region: (1) Cadamosto 1463." SLBR 11: 51–64.

———. 1970a. "Sierra Leone in the Portuguese Books of Complaint, 1567–1568." SLS 26: 2–10.

———. 1970b. "Protestants as Pirates, Slavers, and Proto-Missionaries: Sierra Leone 1568–1582." JEH 21, 3: 203–24.

———. 1974a. "Sources on Early Sierra Leone: (1) Beaulieu 1619." ARB 4, 4: 41–50.

———. 1974b. "Sources on Early Sierra Leone: (2) Andrade (1582), Ruiters (1623), Carvalho 1632[5]." ARB 5, 1: 47–56.

———. 1974c. "Early Sources on Religion and Social Values in the Sierra Leone Region: (2) Eustache de la Fosse 1480." ARB 4, 3: 49–54.

———. 1974d. "Barbot, Dapper, Davity: A Critique of Sources on Sierra Leone and Cape Mount." HA 1: 25–54.

———. 1975a. "Sources on Early Sierra Leone: (3) Sandoval (1627)." ARB 5, 2: 78–92.

———. 1975b. "Sources on Early Sierra Leone: (4) Ruiters (1623)." ARB 5, 3: 52–70.

———. 1975c. "Early Sources on Sierra Leone: (5) Barreira (letter of 23. 2. 1606)." ARB 5, 4: 81–118.

———. 1975d. "Sources on Early Sierra Leone: (6) Barreira on Just Enslavement, 1606." ARB 6, 1: 52–74.

———. 1975e. "From Language to Culture: Some Problems in the Systematic Analysis of the Ethnohistorical Records of the Sierra Leone Region." In *The Population Factor in African Studies,* edited by P. M. Rowland and R. J. A. R. Rathbone, 71–83. London: Unversity of London Press.

———. 1976a. "Sources on Early Sierra Leone: (7) Barreira, Letter of 9. 3. 1607." ARB 6, 2: 45–70.

———. 1976b. "Sources on Early Sierra Leone: (8) Bartolomeu André's Letter, 1606." ARB 6, 3: 34–60.

———. 1976c. "Sources on Early Sierra Leone: (9) Barreira's 'Account of the Coast of Guinea,' 1606." ARB 7, 1: 50–70.

———. 1977a. "Sources on Early Sierra Leone: (10) Schouten and Le Maire, 1615." ARB 7, 2: 56–75.

———. 1977b. "Sources on Early Sierra Leone: (12) The *Livro* of the 'Santiago' 1526." ARB 8, 1: 28–49.

———. 1978a. *The Atlantic Slave Trade and Black Africa.* London: The Historical Association.

———. 1978b. "Hamlet in an Afro-Portuguese Setting: New Perspectives on Sierra Leone in 1607." HA 5: 21–42.

———. 1978c. "Sources on Early Sierra Leone: (13) Barreira's Report of 1607–1608: The Visit to Bena." ARB 8, 2–3: 64–108.

———. 1978d. "Sources on Early Sierra Leone: (14) English Accounts of 1582." ARB 9, 1–2: 67–99.

———. 1979. "Sources on Early Sierra Leone: (15) Marmol 1573." ARB 9, 3: 70–84.

———. 1981a. "A Note on Jean Barbot (1655–1713)." PHSL 23, 5: 295–308.

———. 1981b. "Sources on Early Sierra Leone: (17) Alvares at Mitombo." ARB 11, 1–2: 92–140.

———. 1981c. "Sources on Early Sierra Leone: (18) Barbot 1678." ARB 11, 3: 46–60.

———. 1981d. *Sierra Leone and the English in 1607: Extracts from the Unpublished Journals of the Keeling Voyage to the East Indies.* Freetown: Institute of African Studies, University of Sierra Leone.

———. 1982. *André de Faro's Missionary Journey to Sierra Leone in 1663–1664: A Shortened Version, in English Translation.* Freetown: University of Sierra Leone.

———. 1983. "Sources on Early Sierra Leone: (19) Barreira's Report 1607–1608; the Deeds of King Pedro, alias Tora." ARB 13, 1–2: 55–97.

———, trans. and ed. 1984a. *André Alvares de Almada's Brief Treatise on the Rivers of Guinea.* Liverpool: Department of History, University of Liverpool.

———. 1984b. "Sources on Early Sierra Leone: (21) English Voyages of the 1580s: Drake, Cavendish, and Cumberland." ARB 13, 3: 62–88.

———. 1984c. "The Falls of Félou: A Bibliographical Exploration." HA 11: 113–30.

———, trans. and ed. 1985. *Francisco de Lemos Coelho: Description of the Coast of Guinea (1684).* Liverpool: Department of History, University of Liverpool.

———. 1986. "Material on Africa: Samuel Purchas, 1613–1626." HA 13: 117–59.

———. 1987a. "The Abortive Portuguese Settlement of Sierra Leone 1570–1625." In *Vice-Almirante A. Teixeira da Mota: In Memoriam,* 2 vols., 1:171–208. Lisbon: Academia de Marinha/Instituto de Investigação Científica Tropical.

———. 1987b. "The Task Ahead: The Editing of Early European-Language Texts on Black Africa." P 33: 29–51.

———. 1987c. "Colonial Freetown and the Study of African Languages." A 57 4: 560–65.

———. 1988. "The Spanish Capuchins in Sierra Leone." In *Sierra Leone Studies at Birmingham,* edited by Adam Jones, Peter K. Mitchell, and Margaret Peil, 21–24. Birmingham: Centre of West African Studies, University of Birmingham.

———, trans. and ed. 1989. *Jesuit Documents on the Guinea of Cape Verde and the Cape Verde Islands, 1585–1617.* Liverpool: Department of History, University of Liverpool.

———, trans. and ed. 1990. *Manuel Alvares: Ethiopia Minor and a Geographical Account of the Province of Sierra Leone (c. 1615).* Liverpool: Department of History, University of Liverpool.

———. 1996. "Some References to Bolama, 1450–1870." In *Bolama: Entre a generosidade da natureza e a cobiça dos homens,* edited by C. Cardoso, 27–40. Bissau, Guinea-Bissau: Instituto Nacional de Estudos e Pesquisa.

———. 1997a. "'Elephants for Want of Towns': The Interethnic and International History of Bulama Island, 1456–1870." HA 24: 177–93.

———. 1997b. "Christian Influences in Sierra Leone before 1797." JRA 27: 3–14.

———. 1997c. *African Encountered: European Contacts and Evidence, 1450–1750.* Aldershot, UK: Variorum Collected Studies Series.

———. 1998a. "Heretics, Slaves, and Witches as Seen by Guinea Jesuits c. 1610." JRA 28: 131–44.

———. 1998b. "Aspects of the Prehistory of Freetown and Creoledom." HA 25: 111–18.

———. 1999. "Attitudes to Africans in English Primary Sources on Guinea up to 1650." HA 26: 43–68.

———, ed. 2000a. *Hawkins in Guinea, 1567–1568.* Leipzig, Germany: Unversity of Leipzig Papers on Africa.

———. 2000b. "Portuguese Documents on Africa and Some Problems of Translation." HA 27: 91–97.

———. 2000c. "Franciscan Missionaries and the 'Donation of Sierra Leone.'" JRA 30: 408–32.

Hair, P. E. H., and R. Law. 1998. "The English in Western Africa to 1700." In *The Origins of Empire: British Overseas Enterprise to the Close of the the Seventeenth Century,* edited by N. Canny, 1: 241–63. Oxford: Oxford University Press.

Hair, P. E. H., and P. K. Mitchell. 1970. "Historical Toponymy of the Scarcies Area." SLGJ 14: 31–37.

Hair, P. E. H., A. Jones, and R. Law, eds. 1992. *Barbot on Guinea: The Writings of Jean Barbot on West Africa, 1678–1712.* 2 vols. London: Hakluyt Society.

Hakluyt, R., ed. 1904. *The Principal Navigations, Voyages, Traffiques, and Discoveries of the English Nation.* 12 vols., 1903–1905. Vol. 7. Glasgow: J. MacLehose and Sons.

Hall, G. M. 1992. *Africans in Colonial Louisiana: The Development of Afro-Creole Culture in the Eighteenth Century.* Baton Rouge: Louisiana State University Press.

Hamelberg, E. 1964. "The Jesuits in Sierra Leone, 1605–1617." SLBR 6: 1–8.

Hancock, D. 1995. *Citizens of the World: London Merchants and the Integration of the British Atlantic Community, 1735–1785.* Cambridge: Cambridge University Press.

Hanson, C. A. 1981. *Economy and Society in Baroque Portugal, 1668–1703.* Minneapolis: University of Minnesota Press.

———. 1983. "The European 'Renovation' and the Luso-Atlantic Economy, 1560–1715." RFBC 6, 4: 475–530.

Hargreaves, J. 1965. "Assimilation in Eighteenth Century Senegal." JAH 6, 2: 177–84.

———. 1967. *West Africa: The Former French States.* Englewood Cliffs, N.J: Prentice Hall.

———, trans. and ed. 1969. *France and West Africa: An Anthology of Historical Documents.* London: Macmillan.

Havik, P. 1994. "Women and Trade in the Guinea-Bissau Region." *Studia* 52: 83–120.

———. 1997. "Comerciantes e concubinas: Sócios estratégicos no comércio atlântico na costa da Guinéa." In *A dimensão atlântica da Africa,* edited by Fernando Albuquerque Mourão and Maria Odete Ferreira, 2: 161–79. São Paulo: CEA-USP/SDG-Marinha/Capes.

———. 2001. "Matronas e mandonas: Parentesco e poder feminino nos rios de Guiné (século XVIII)." In *Entre Africas e Brasis,* edited by Selma Pantoja, 13–34. São Paulo: Livraria Nobel S. A.

Hawkins, J. 1797/1970. *A History of a Voyage to the Coast of Africa and Travels into the Interior of That Country.* London: Frank Cass.

Hawthorne, W. 2001. "Nourishing a Stateless Society during the Slave Trade: The Rise of Balanta Paddy-Rice Production in Guinea-Bissau." JAH 42, 1: 1–24.

Haywood, D., and J. Oguntoyinbo. 1987. *Climatology of West Africa.* Totowa, N.J.: Barnes and Noble.

Hedges, J. B. 1952. *The Browns of Providence Plantations: Colonial Years.* Cambridge: Harvard University Press.

Henige, D. P. 1970. *Colonial Governors from the Fifteenth Century to the Present.* Madison: University of Wisconson Press.

Hopkins, A. G. 1973. *An Economic History of West Africa.* New York: Columbia University Press.

Hopkins, J. F. P., and N. Levtzion, eds. 1981. *Corpus of Early Arabic Sources for West African History.* Cambridge: Cambridge University Press.

Horta, J. da S. 2000. "Evidence for a Luso-African Identity in 'Portuguese' Accounts on 'Guinea of Cape Verde' (Sixteenth-Seventeenth Centuries)." HA 27: 99–130.

Horton, R. 1985. "Stateless Societies in the History of West Africa." In *History of West Africa,* 3rd ed., edited by J. F. A. Ajayi and M. Crowder, 1: 87–128. Burnt Mill, UK: Harlow, Essex, Longman.

Iria, A. 1964. "Auto-determinação da Serra Leoa, que desejava continuar portuguesa em 1722—Documentos inéditos." BAPH: 115–17.

Israel, J. I. 1989. *European Jewry in the Age of Mercantilism, 1550–1750.* 2nd ed. Oxford: Clarendon Press.

Jackson, S. P. 1961. *Climatological Atlas of Africa.* Pretoria, South Africa: Government Printer.

Jobson, R. 1623/1968. *The Golden Trade.* London: Dawson's of Pall Mall.

Johnson, J. W. 1986. *The Epic of Son-Jara (Sunjata): An Analytical Study of a West African Tradition.* Bloomington: Indiana University Press.

Johnson, M. 1977. "Cloth Strips and History." WAJA 7: 169–78.

Johnson, M. A. 1994. "Gold Jewelry of the Wolof and the Tukulor of Senegal." AA 27, 1: 36–49, 94–95.

Jones, Adam. 1983a. *From Slaves to Palm Kernels: A History of the Galinhas Country (West Africa), 1730–1890.* Wiesbaden, Germany: F. Steiner.

———. 1983b. *German Sources for West African History, 1599–1669.* Wiesbaden, Germany: F. Steiner.

———. 1983c. "The Kquoja Kingdom: A Forest State in Seventeenth Century West Africa." P 29: 23–43.

———. 1985. *Brandenburg Sources for West African History, 1680–1700.* Stuttgart, Germany: F. Steiner.

———. 1986. "Sources on Early Sierra Leone: (22) The Visit of a Dutch Fleet in 1625." ARB 15, 2: 43–64.

———. 1987. *Raw, Medium, Well Done: A Critical Review of Editorial and Quasi-Editorial Work on Pre-1885 European Sources for Sub-Saharan Africa, 1960–1986.* Madison: University of Wisconson African Studies Program.

———. 1989. "The Earliest German Sources for West African History (1504–1509)." P 35: 145–54.

———. 1990. "Decompiling Dapper: A Preliminary Search for Evidence." HA 17: 171–209.

Jones, Adam, and P. E. H. Hair. 1977. "Sources on Early Sierra Leone: (11) Brun 1624." ARB 7, 3: 52–64.

———. 1984. "Sources on Early Sierra Leone: (20) Von der Gröben 1682." ARB 13, 1 and 2: 78–116.

Jones, Alison. 1981. "The Rhode Island Slave Trade: A Trading Advantage in Africa." SA 2: 227–44.

Jore, L. 1965. *Les établissements français sur la côte occidentale d'Afrique de 1758 à 1809.* Paris: Société Français d'Histoire d'Outre-Mer.

Joucla, E. 1937. *Bibliographie de l'Afrique occidentale française.* Paris: Société d'Editions Géographiques, Maritimes, et Coloniales.

Kimble, G. H. T., trans. and ed. 1937. *Esmeraldo de Situ Orbis by Duarte Pacheco Pereira.* London: Haklyut Society.

Klein, M. A. 1968. *Islam and Imperialism in Senegal: Sine-Saloum, 1847–1914.* Stanford: Stanford University Press.

———. 1992. "The Impact of the Atlantic Slave Trade on the Societies of the Western Sudan." In *The Atlantic Slave Trade,* edited by J. E. Inikori and S. L. Engermann, 25–47. Durham, N.C.: Duke University Press.

———. 2001. "The Slave Trade and Decentralized Societies." JAH 42, 1: 49–65.

Klein, M., and P. E. Lovejoy. 1979. "Slavery in West Africa." In *The Uncommon Market: Essays in the Economic History of the Atlantic Slave Trade,* edited by H. A. Gemery and J. S. Hogendorn, 181–212. New York: Academic Press.

Knight, M-H. 1977. "Gorée au XVIII siècle: L'appropriation du sol." RFHOM 64, 234: 33–54.

Knight-Baylac, M-H. 1970b. "La vie à Gorée de 1677 à 1789." RFHOM 57, 209: 377–420.

Koger, L. 1985. *Black Slaveowners: Free Black Slave Masters in South Carolina, 1790–1860.* Jefferson, N.C.: McFarland and Company.

Kup, P. 1961. *A History of Sierra Leone, 1400–1787.* Cambridge: Cambridge University Press.

———. 1963a. "Jesuit and Capuchin Missions of the Seventeenth Century." SLBR 5: 27–34.

———. 1963b. "Early Portuguese Trade in the Sierra Leone and Great Scarcies Rivers." BCGP 18: 107–24.

———, ed. 1967. *Adam Afzelius: Sierra Leone Journal, 1795–1796.* Uppsala, Sweden: Almqvist & Wiksells.

Labarthe, P. 1802. *Voyage au Sénégal, pendant les années 1784 et 1785, d'après les mémoires de Lajaille, ancien officier de la marine française.* Paris: Dentu.

Labat, J-B. 1728. *Nouvelle relation de l'Afrique occidentale.* 5 vols. Paris: Giffart.

La Courbe, M. J. de. 1685/1913. See Cultru, ed., 1913.

Lacroix, J.-B. 1986. *Les Français au Sénégal pendant la compagnie des Indes, 1719 à 1758.* Vincennes: Service Historique de la Marine.

La Fleur, J. D., ed. 2000. *Pieter van den Broecke's Journal of Voyages to Cape Verde, Guinea, and Angola (1605–1612).* London: Hakluyt Society.

La Fosse, E. de. 1479-1480/1949. "Voyage à la côte occidentale d'Afrique (1479-1480)." Edited by R. Mauny. BCGP 14: 181–95.

Lamiral, D. H. 1789. *L'Affrique et le peule affriquain.* Paris: Dessenne.

———. 1791. *Mémoire sur le Sénégal.* Paris: Impremerie du Postillon.

Lang, J. 1979. *Portuguese Brazil: The King's Plantation.* New York: Academic Press.

Langer, W. L., ed. 1958. *An Encyclopedia of World History.* Boston: Houghton Mifflin.

Law, R. 1993. "The Royal African Company of England's West African Correspondence, 1681-1699." HA 20: 173–84.

Laye, C. 1954. *The Dark Child.* New York: Farrar, Straus, and Giroux.

Lespinay, C. de. 1987. "La disparition de la langue Baynunk: Fin d'un peuple ou processus réversible?" In *Contributions à l'histoire du Sénégal,* edited by J. Boulègue, 23–29. Paris.

———. 1996. "Baynunk et Beafad dans l'ensemble guinéen: Parentés et alliances anciennes (15–20 siècle)." In *Bolama entre a generosidade da natureza e a cobiça dos homens,* edited by C. Cardoso, 67–89. Bissau, Guinea-Bissau: Instituto Nacional de Estudos e Pesquisa.

———. 2000. "Un lexique Bagnon-Floupe de la fin du XVII siècle: Apport à l'histoire du peuplement de la Casamance." In *Migrations anciennes et peuplement actuel des Côtes Guinéennes,* edited by G. Gaillard, 191–213. Paris.

Levtzion, N. 1971. "Patterns of Islamization in West Africa." In *Aspects of West African Islam,* edited by D. F. McCall and N. R. Bennett, 31–39. Boston: Boston Unversity African Studies Center.

———. 1973. *Ancient Ghana and Mali.* London: Methuen.

———. 2000. "Islam in the Bilad al-Sudan to 1800." In *The History of Islam in Africa,* edited by N. Levtzion and R. L. Pouwels, 74–90. Athens: Ohio University Press.

Linares, O. F. 1981. "From Tidal Swamp to Inland Valley: On the Social Organization of Wet Rice Cultivation among the Diola of Senegal." *Africa* 51, 2: 557–95.

———. 1987. "Deferring to Trade in Slaves: The Jola of Casamance, Senegal in Historical Perspective." HA 14: 113–39.

Lindsay, J. 1759. *A Voyage to the Coast of Africa, in 1758.* London: S. Paterson.

Lintingre, P. 1966. *Voyages du Sieur de Glicourt à la côte occidentale d'Afrique pendant les années 1778 et 1779.* Dakar, Senegal: Afrique Documents.

Little, K. L. 1948. "The Poro as an Arbiter of Culture." AS 7, 1: 1–15.

Littlefield, D. C. 1981. *Rice and Slaves: Ethnicity and the Slave Trade in Colonial South Carolina.* Baton Rouge: Louisiana State University Press.

Livermore, H. V., ed. 1963. *Portugal and Brazil: An Introduction.* Oxford: Clarendon Press.

———. 1969. *A New History of Portugal.* Cambridge: Cambridge University Press.

Lombard, J. 1970. "Le Sénégal et la Mauritanie." In *Histoire générale de l'Afrique noire,* edited by H. Deschamps, 1: 237–52. Paris: Presses Universitaires de France.

Lopes, C., ed. 1993. *Mansas, escravos, grumetes, e gentio: Cacheu na encruzilhada de civilizações.* Bissau, Guinea-Bissau: Instituto Nacional de Estudos e Pesquisa.

Lovejoy, P. E. 1981. "Kola in the History of West Africa." CEA 77–78: 97–134.

———. 1982. "The Volume of the Atlantic Slave Trade: A Synthesis." JAH 23, 4: 473–501.

Ly, A. 1958. *La Compagnie du Sénégal, 1673–1695.* Paris: Présence Africaine.

———. 1964. *Un navire de commerce sur la côte sénégambienne en 1685.* Dakar, Senegal: Institut Fondementale d'Afrique Noire.

MacCormack, C. P. 1979. "Sande: The Public Face of a Secret Society." In *The New Religions of Africa,* edited by B. Jules-Rosette, 27–37. Norwood, N.J.: Ablex Publishing Corp.

———. 1980. "Proto-Social to Adult: A Sherbro Transformation." In *Nature, Culture, and Gender,* edited by C. P. MacCormack, 95–118. Cambridge: Cambridge University Press.

McCall, D. F. 1971a. "The Cultural Map and Time-Profile of the Mande-Speaking Peoples." In *Papers on the Manding,* edited by C. Hodge, 27–98. Bloomington.: Africa Series Vol. 3, Indiana University.

———. 1971b. "Islamization in the Western and Central Sudan in the Eleventh Century." In *Aspects of West African Islam,* edited by D. F. McCall and N. R. Bennett, 1–30. Boston: Boston University African Studies Program.

McGowan, W. 1990. "The Establishment of Long-Distance Trade between Sierra Leone and Its Hinterland, 1787–1821." JAH 30, 1: 25–41.

McNaughton, P. R. 1988. *The Mande Blacksmiths.* Bloomington: Indiana University Press.

Machat, J. 1906a. *Documents sur les établissements français de l'Afrique occidentale au XVIII siècle.* Paris: Augustin Challamel.

———. 1906b. *Guinée française: Les rivières du sud et le Fouta-Diallon.* Paris: Augustin Challamel.

Mackenzie-Grieve, A. 1968. *The Last Years of the English Slave Trade, Liverpool, 1780–1807.* New York: A. M. Kelley.

Magnieu, E., and H. Prat, eds. 1875. 2nd ed. *Correspondance inédite de la Comtesse de Sabran et du Chevalier de Boufflers, 1778–1788.* Paris: E. Plon.

Mane, M. 1978. "Contribution a l'histoire du Kaabu, des origines au XIX siècle." BIFAN 40, 1: 87–159.

Marees, P. de. 1602/1987. *Description and Historical Account of the Gold Kingdom of Guinea (1602).* Edited by A. van Dantzig and A. Jones. Oxford: Oxford University Press.

Mark, P. 1985. *A Cultural, Economic, and Religious History of the Basse Casamance since 1500.* Stuttgart, Germany: F. Steiner.

———. 1992. *The Wild Bull and the Sacred Forest: Form, Meaning, and Change in Senegambian Initiation Masks.* Cambridge: Cambridge University Press.

———. 1995. "Constructing Identity: Sixteenth- and Seventeenth-Century Architecture in the Gambia-Geba Region and the Articulation of Luso-African Ethnicity." HA 22: 307–27.

———. 1996. "'Portuguese' Architecture and Luso-African Identity in Senegambia and Guinea, 1730–1890." HA 23: 179–96.

———. 1999. "The Evolution of 'Portuguese' Identity: Luso-Africans on the Upper Guinea Coast from the Sixteenth to the Early Nineteenth Century." JAH 40, 2: 173–91.

———. 2000. "Les 'Portugais' de la Sénégambie et de Bissau: Identité et architecture." In *Migrations anciennes et peuplement actuel des Côtes Guinéennes,* edited by G. Gaillard, 467–85. Paris: L'Harmattan.

Markham, C., ed. 1878/1970. *The Hawkins Voyages.* New York: Burt Franklin.

Marques, A. H. O. 1976. *History of Portugal.* 2nd ed. 2 vols. New York: Columbia University Press.

Martin, B. 1950. *John Newton: A Biography.* London: Heinemann.

Martin, B., and M. Spurrell, eds. 1962. *The Journal of a Slave Trader (John Newton), 1750–1754.* London: Epworth Press.

Martin, E., ed. 1930. *Nicholas Owen: Journal of a Slave-Dealer.* London: Routledge and Sons.

Martin, E. C. 1927/1970. *The British West African Settlements, 1750–1821.* New York: Negro Universities Press.

Massing, A. 1980. *The Economic Anthropology of the Kru (West Africa).* Wiesbaden, Germany: F. Steiner.

Matthews, J. 1788/1966. *A Voyage to the River Sierra-Leone: 1785, 1786, and 1787.* London: Frank Cass.

Mauny, R. 1949. "Eustache de La Fosse: Voyage à la côte occidentale d'Afrique (1479–1480)." BCGP 14: 181–95.

———. 1952. *Glossaire des expressions et termes employés dans l'ouest africain.* Dakar, Senegal.

———, ed. 1956. *Esmeraldo de Situ Orbis: Côte occidentale d'Afrique du sud marocain au Gabon par Duarte Pacheco Pereira (vers 1506–1508).* Bissau, Guinea-Bissau: Centro de Estudos da Guiné Portuguesa.

———. 1961. *Tableau géographique de l'ouest africain au moyen age.* Dakar, Senegal: IFAN.

Mauro, F. 1959. "Types de navires et constructions navales dans l'Atlantic portugais aux XVI et XVII siècles." RHMC 6, 2: 181–209.

Mbiti, J. S. 1970. *African Religions and Philosophies.* Garden City, NY: Anchor Books.

Meintel, D. 1984. *Race, Culture, and Portuguese Colonialism in Cabo Verde.* Syracuse: Africa Series XLI, Syracuse University.

Mercier, P., and G. Balandier. 1952. *Les pêcheurs Lébou: Particularisme et évolution.* Saint-Louis, Sénégal: Centre IFAN-Sénégal.

Mettas, J. 1975. "La traite portugaise en haute Guinée, 1758–1797: Problèmes et méthodes." JAH 16, 3: 343–63.

Mollien, G. T. 1820. *Travels in Africa to the Sources of the Senegal and Gambia in 1818.* London: Sir R. Phillips and Co.

Monod, T., A. T. da Mota, and R. Mauny, trans. and eds. 1951. *Description de la côte occidentale d'Afrique (Sénégal au Cap de Monte, Archipels par Valentim Fernandes (1506–1510).* Bissau, Guinea-Bissau: Centro de Estudos da Guiné Portuguesa.

Monod, T., R. Mauny, and G. Duval, trans. and eds. 1959. *Diogo Gomes: De la première découverte de la Guinée.* Bissau, Guinea-Bissau: Centro de Estudos da Guiné Portuguesa.

Moore, F. 1738. *Travels into the Inland Parts of Africa.* London: E. Cave.

Moraes, N. I. de. 1969. "Sur les prises de Gorée par les Portugais au XVIIe siècle." BIFAN 31, 4: 989–1013.

———. 1972. "Le commerce des peaux à la Petite Côte au XVIIe siècle (Sénégal)." NA 134: 37–45, 136, 111–16.

———. 1973. "Le commerce des tissus à la Petite Côte au XVIIe siècle (Sénégambie)." NA 139: 71–75.

———. 1978. "La campagne négrière du *Sam-António-e-as-Almas* (1670)." BIFAN 40, 4: 708–17.

———. 1993. *A la découverte de la Petite Côte au XVII siècle (Sénégal et Gambie).* Vol. 1, *1600–1621.* Dakar, Senegal: IFAN.

———. 1995. *A la découverte de la Petite Côte au XVII siècle (Sénégal et Gambie).* Vol. 2, *1622–1664.* Dakar, Senegal: IFAN.

———. 1998. *A la découverte de la Petite Côte au XVII siècle (Sénégal et Gambie).* Vol. 3, *1664–1672,* Vol. 4, *1672–1679.* Dakar, Senegal: IFAN.

Morgan, W. B., and J. C. Pugh. 1969. *West Africa.* London: Methuen.

Mota, A. T. da. 1950. *Topónimos de origem portuguesa na costa ocidental de Africa.* Bissau, Guinea-Bissau: Centro de Estudos da Guiné Portuguesa.

———. 1951. "Contactos culturais Luso-africanos na 'Guiné do Cabo Verde.'" BSGL 69, 11–12: 659–67.

———. 1954. *A Guiné portuguesa.* 2 vols. Lisbon: Agência Geral do Ultramar.

———. 1969a. "A viagem do navio *Santiago* á Serra Leoa e rio de S. Domingos em 1526." BCGP 24, 95: 529–79.

———. 1969b. "Un document nouveau pour l'histoire des Peuls au Sénégal pendant les XV et XVI siècles." BCGP 24, 96: 781–860, 816–17.

———. 1970. "Fulas e Biafadas no Rio Grande no século XV." *Mémorias da academia das ciencias de Lisboa: Classe de ciencias* 14: 259–77. Lisbon.

———. 1972. *Mar, Além Mar.* Lisbon: Junta de Investigaçôes do Ultramar.

———. 1974a. "Actividade marítima dos Bijagos nos séculos XVI e XVII." In *Memoriam António Jorge Dias,* 3: 243–77. Lisbon: Instituto de Alta Cultura.

———. 1974b. *As viagens do Bispo D. Frei Vitoriano Portuense á Guiné e a christianização dos reis de Bissau.* Lisbon: Junta de Investigaçôes Cientificas do Ultramar.

———. 1978. *Some Aspects of Portuguese Colonization and Sea Trade in West Africa in the 15th and 16th Centuries.* Bloomington: Indiana University African Studies Program.

Mota, A. T. da, and P. E. H. Hair, eds. 1977. *André Donelha: Descrição da Serra Leoa e dos rios de Guiné do Cabo Verde (1625)* (An account of Sierra Leone and the rivers of Guinea of Cape Verde [1625]). Lisbon: Junta de Investigaçôes Cientificas do Ultramar.

Mouser, B. L. 1973. "Trade, Coasters, and Conflict in the Rio Pongo from 1790 to 1808." JAH 14, 1: 45–64.

———. 1975. "Landlords-Strangers: A Process of Accommodation and Assimilation." IJAHS 8, 3: 425–40.

———. 1979. *Guinea Journals: Journeys into Guinea-Conakry during the Sierra Leone Phase, 1800–1821.* Washington, D.C.: University Press of America.

———. 1980. "Accommodation and Assimilation in the Landlord-Stranger Relationship." In *West African Cultural Dynamics,* edited by B. K. Swartz and R. Dumett, 495–514. New York.

———. 1983. "Women Slavers of Guinea-Conakry." In *Women and Slavery in Africa,* edited by C. C. Robertson and M. A. Klein, 320–39. Madison: University of Wisconsin Press.

———, ed. 1994. *Journal of James Watt: Expedition to Timbo, Capital of the Fula Empire in 1794.* Madison: African Studies Program, University of Wisconsin.

———. 1996. "Iles de Los as a Bulking Center in the Slave Trade, 1750–1850." RFHOM 83, 313: 77–90.

Mouser, B. L., and R. Sarro, eds. 1999. *Travels into the Baga and Soosoo Countries in 1821 by Peter McLachlan.* Leipzig, Germany: University of Leipzig Papers on Africa.

Murdock, G. P. 1959. *Africa: Its People and Their Culture History.* New York: McGraw-Hill.

Nardin, J-C. 1966. "Recherche sur les 'gourmets' d'Afrique occidentale." RFHOM 190–91: 215–44.

Nicholas, F.-J. 1958. "Le bouracan ou bougran: Tissu soudanais du moyen âge." *Anthropos* 53: 265–68.

Nyerges, A. E. 1996. "Ethnography in the Reconstruction of African Land Use Histories: A Sierra Leone Example." A 66, 1: 122–44.

Oliver, P., trans. and ed. 1897. *The Voyages Made by the Sieur D. B. to the Islands Dauphine or Madagascar and Bourbon or Mascarenne in the Years 1669, 70, 71, & 72.* London: David Nutt.

Opala, J. A. 1987. *The Gullah: Rice, Slavery, and the Sierra Leone-American Connection.* Freetown, Sierra Leone: USIS.

Owen, W. F. W. 1833. *Narrative of a Voyage to Explore the Shores of Africa, Arabia, and Madagascar.* 2 vols. New York: J. & J. Harper.

Park, M. 1799/1971. *Travels in the Interior Districts of Africa in the Years 1795, 1796, and 1797.* New York: Arno Press.

———. 1815. *Journal of a Mission to the Interior of Africa in the Year 1805.* 2nd ed. London: John Murray.

Parrinder, G. 1969. *West African Religion.* London: Epworth Press.

Patterson, K. D. 1988. "Epidemics, Famines, and Population in the Cape Verde Islands, 1580–1900." IJAHS 21, 2: 291–313.

Paulme, D. 1939. "Parenté à plaisanteries et alliance par le sang." A 12: 433–44.

———. 1968. "Pacte de sang, classes d'âge, et castes en Afrique noire." AES 9, 1–2: 12–33.

Pelletan, J-G. 1800. *Mémoire sur la colonie française du Sénégal.* Paris: Ve Panckoucke.

Pereira, D. A. 1993. "A fundação da Companhia de Cacheu, 1671–1676." In *Mansas, escravos, grumetes, e gentio: Cacheu na encruzilhada de civilizações,* edited by C. Lopes, 199–247. Bissau, Guinea-Bissau: Instituto Nacional de Estudos e Pesquisa.

Pereira, D. P. c. 1506–1508/1937. *Esmeraldo de Situ Obrbis.* Translated and edited by G. H. T. Kimble. London: Hakluyt Society.

———. c. 1506–1508/1956. *Esmeraldo de Situ Obrbis.* Edited by R. Mauny. Bissau, Guinea-Bissau: Centro de Estudos da Guiné Portuguesa.

Peres, D., ed. 1952. *Planta da praça de Bissau e suas adjacentes por Bernardino António Alvares de Andrade.* Lisbon: Academia Portuguesa da História.

———, ed. 1953. *Duas descrições seiscentistas da Guiné de Lemos Coelho.* Lisbon.

Perinbam, B. M. 1980. "The Julas in Western Sudanese History: Long-Distance Traders and Developers of Resources." In *West African Culture Dynamics,* edited by B. K. Swartz and R. E. Dumett, 455–75. The Hague: Mouton.

———. 1997. *Family Identity and the State in the Bamako Kafu, c. 1800–c. 1900.* Boulder, Colo.: Westview.

Person, Y. 1968. *Samori: Une revolution dyula.* Dakar, Senegal: IFAN.

———. 1971. "Ethnic Movements and Acculturation in Upper Guinea since the Fifteenth Century." IJAHS 4, 3: 669–89.

———. 1984. "The Coastal Peoples: From Casamance to the Ivory Coast Lagoons." In *Africa from the Twelfth to the Sixteenth Century,* edited by D. T. Niane, 301–23. Berkeley: University of California Press.

Peterson, J. 1969. *Province of Freedom: A History of Sierra Leone, 1787–1870.* Evanston, Ill.: Northwestern University Press.

Phillips, U. B. 1969. *Plantation and Frontier, 1649–1863.* New York: B. Franklin.

Porter, R. 1968. "The Crispe Family and the African Trade in the Seventeenth Century." JAH 9, 1: 57–77.

Prélong, Citoyen. 1793. "Mémoire sur les îles de Gorée et du Sénégal." *Annales de chimie,* 1: 241–309.

Pruneau de Pommegorge, A. E. 1789. *Description de la Nigritie par M. P. D. P.* Paris: Chez Maradan.

Purchas, S., ed. 1613/1905. *Hakluytus Posthumus or Purchas His Pilgrimes.* Vol. 6. Glasgow: J. MacLehose and Sons.

Rainolds, R. 1591/1904. "The Voyages of Richard Rainolds and Thomas Dassel." In *The Principal Navigations, Voyages, Traffiques and Discoveries of the English Nation,* edited by R. Hakluyt, 7: 90–99. Glasgow: J. MacLehose and Sons.

Rediker, M. 1987. *Between the Devil and the Deep Blue Sea: Merchant Seamen, Pirates, and the Anglo-American Maritime World, 1700–1750.* Cambridge: Cambridge University Press.

Rema, H. P. 1982. *História das missões católicas da Guiné.* Braga, Portugal: Editorial Franciscana.

Renaudeau, M. 1978. *Gorée.* Périgueux, France: Pierre Fanlac.

Richard-Molard, J. 1956. *Afrique occidentale française.* Paris: Editions Berger-Levrault.

Richardson, D. 1979. "West African Consumption Patterns and Their Influence on the Eighteenth-Century English Slave Trade." In *The Uncommon Market: Essays in the Economic History of the Atlantic Slave Trade,* edited by H. A. Gemery and J. S. Hogendorn, 303–30. New York: Academic Press.

Ritchie, C. I. 1968. "Deux Textes sur le Sénégal (1673-1677)." BIFAN 30, 1: 289–353.

Ritchie, R. C. 1986. *Captain Kidd and the War against the Pirates.* Cambridge: Harvard University Press.

Robinson, D. 1984. *The Holy War of Umar Tal: The Western Sudan in the Mid-Nineteenth Century.* New York: Oxford University Press.

———. 2000. "Revolution in the Western Sudan." In *The History of Islam in Africa,* edited by N. Levtzion and R. L. Pouwels, 131–52. Athens: Ohio University Press.

Roche, C. 1976. *Conqête et résistance des peuples de Casamance (1850–1920).* Dakar, Senegal: Nouvelles Editions Africaines.

Rodney, W. 1965. "Portuguese Attempts at Monopoly on the Upper Guinea Coast, 1580-1650." JAH 6, 3: 307–22.

———. 1967. "A Reconsideration of the Mane Invasions of Sierra Leone." JAH 8, 2: 219–46.

———. 1968. "Jihad and Social Revolution in Futa Djalon in the Eighteenth Century." JHSN 4, 2: 269–84.

———. 1970. *A History of the Upper Guinea Coast, 1545 to 1800.* Oxford: Clarendon Press.

Rodrigues, R., ed. 1988. *"Cacheu cidade antiga" 1588–1988: IV centenário da sua fundação.* Braga, Portugal: Universidade do Minho.

Rougé, J-L. 1986. "Uma hipótese sobre a formação do crioulo da Guiné-Bissau e da Casamansa." *Soronda* 2: 28–49.

Roussier, P. 1935. *L'établissement d'Issiny, 1687–1702.* Paris: Larose.

Roussin, A. R. 1819. *Mémoire sur la navigation aux côtes occidentales d'Afrique, depuis le Cap Bojador jusqu'au Mont-Souzos.* Paris: Imprimerie Royale.

Rouzaud, A. 1884. "Voyage au Rio-Cacheo (Guinée portugaise)." BSGM: 349–54.

Ruiters, D. 1623/1974. See Hair, 1974b, 1975b.

Sackur, A. 1992. "The French Revolution and Race Relations in Senegal, 1780–1810." In *People and Empires in African History: Essays in Memory of Michael Crowder,* edited by J. F. A. Ajayi and J. D. Y. Peel, 69–87. London: Longman.

Sainville, L. 1972. *Histoire du Sénégal depuis l'arrivée des Européens jusqu'à 1850.* Dakar, Senegal.

Samb, D., ed. 1997. *Gorée et l'esclavage.* Dakar, Senegal: IFAN.

Sanneh, L. O. 1979. *The Jakhanke: The History of an Islamic Clerical People of the Senegambia.* London: International African Institute.

———. 1989. *The Jahanke: Muslim Clerics.* Lanham, Md.: University Press of America.

Santos, M. E. M. 1978. *Viagems de exploração terrestre dos Portugueses em Africa.* Lisbon: Centro de Estudos de Cartografia Antiga.

———. 1993. "Lançados na costa da Guiné: Aventureiros e commerciantes." In *Mansas, escravos, grumetes, e gentio: Cacheu na encruzilhada de civilizações,* edited by Carlos Lopes, 64–78. Bissau, Guinea-Bissau: Intstituto Nacional de Estudos e Pesquisa.

———. 1994. "Mulatos, sua legitimação pela chancelaria régia no século XVI." *Studia* 53: 237–46.

———, ed. 1995. *História geral de Cabo Verde* Vol. 2. Lisbon: Centro de Estudos de História e Cartografia Antiga/Praia: Instituto Nacional da Cultura de Cabo Verde.

Sapir, J. D. 1981. "Leper, Hyena, and Blacksmith in Kujamaat Diola Thought." AE 8: 526–43.

Saugnier, F., and P. R. de Brisson. 1792/1969. *Voyages to the Coast of Africa by Mess. Saugnier and Brisson.* New York: Negro Universities Press.

Saulnier, M. 1918. "Une réception royale à l'île de Gorée en 1831." RHCF 339–48.

Saunders, A. C. de C. M. 1982a. "The Depiction of Trade as War as a Reflection of Portuguese Ideology and Diplomatic Strategy in West Africa, 1444–1556." CJH 17, 1: 220.

———. 1982b. *A Social History of Black Slaves and Freedmen in Portugal, 1441–1555.* New York: Cambridge University Press.

Scantamburlo, L. 1981. *Gramática e dictionário da língua criol da Guiné-Bissau.* Bologna, Italy: Editrice Missionaria Italiana.

———. 1991. *Etnologia dos Bijagós da ilha de Bubaque.* Lisbon: Instituto de Investigação Científica Tropical.

———. 1999. *Dicionário do Guineense.* Lisbon: Edições Colibri/FASPEBI.

Schwarz, S., ed. 2000. *Zachary Macaulay and the Development of the Sierra Leone Company, 1793–4,* pt. 1. Leipzig, Germany: University of Leipzig Papers on Africa.

Searing, J. F. 1993. *West African Slavery and Atlantic Commerce: The Senegal River Valley, 1700–1860.* Cambridge: Cambridge University Press.

Sideri, S. 1970. *Trade and Power: Informal Colonialism in Anglo-Portuguese Relations.* Rotterdam, the Netherlands: Rotterdam Unversity Press.

Sidibe, B. K. 1974. *A Brief History of Kaabu and Fuladu, 1300–1930: A Narrative Based on Some Oral Traditions of the Senegambia.* Banjul, The Gambia: The Gambia Cultural Archives.

Siegmann, W. 1980. *African Sculpture from the Collection of the Society of African Missions.* Tenafly, N.J.: SMA Fathers.

Silva, M. da G. G. N. da. 1970. "Subsídos para o Estudo dos 'Lançados' na Guiné." BCGP 25, 97: 25–40, 98: 217–32; 99: 397–420; 100: 513–60.

Skinner, D. 1989. "Sierra Leone Relations with the Northern Rivers and the Influence of Islam in the Colony." IJSLS, 1: 91–113.

Smith, D. G. 1974. "Old Christian Merchants and the Founding of the Brazil Company, 1649." HAHR 54: 233–59.

Smith, W. 1744/1967. *A New Voyage to Guinea.* London: Frank Cass.

Snelgrave, W. 1734/1971. *A New Account of Some Parts of Guinea.* London: Frank Cass.

Staunton, G. 1799. *An Authentic Account of an Embassy from the King of Great Britain to the Emperor of China.* 2 vols. Philadelphia.

Stein, R. 1979. *The French Slave Trade in the Eighteenth Century: An Old Regime Business.* Madison: University of Wisconsin Press.

Stone, T. G. 1924. "The Journey of Cornelius Hodges in Senegambia, 1689–90." EHISTR 39, 153: 89–95.

Tamari, T. 1997. *Les castes de l'Afrique occidentale: Artisans, et musiciens endogames.* Nanterre, France: Société d'Ethnologie.

Teixeira, C. da S. 1950. "Companhia de Cacheu, rios e comércio da Guiné" BAHC 1: 85–132.

Thilmans, G. 1968. "Sur l'existence, fin XVI, de comptoirs néerlandais à Joal et Portudal." NA 117: 17–18.

———. 1971. "Le Sénégal dans l'oeuvre d'Olfried Dapper." BIFAN 33, 3: 508–63.

———. 1976. "La relation de François de Paris (1682–1683)." BIFAN 38, 1: 1–51.

Thilmans, G., and N. I. de Moraes. 1970. "Le routier de la côte de Guinée de Francisco Perez de Carvalho (1635)." BIFAN 32, 2: 343–69.

———. 1972. "La description de la côte de Guinée du père Baltasar Barreira (1606)." BIFAN 34, 1: 1–50.

———. 1973. "La 'gouvernanate' de Rufisque (1664–1697)." NA 138: 36–39.

———. 1977. "Les passages à la Petite Côte de Pieter van den Broecke (1606–1609)." BIFAN 39, 3: 471–92.

Thilmans, G., and J. P. Rossie. 1969. "Le 'Flambeau de la Navigation' de Dierick Ruiters." BIFAN 31, 1: 106–19.

Thornton, J. 1992. *Africa and Africans in the Making of the Atlantic World, 1400–1680.* New York: Cambridge University Press.

Torrão, M. M. F. 1995. "Rotas commerciais, agentes económicos, meios de pagamento." In *História geral de Cabo Verde,* vol. 2, edited by M. E. M. Santos, 2: 17–123. Lisbon: Centro de Estudos de História e Cartografia Antiga/Praia: Instituto Nacional da Cultura de Cabo Verde.

Trimingham, J. S. 1959. *Islam in West Africa.* Oxford: Clarendon.

———. 1962. *A History of Islam in West Africa.* London: Oxford University Press.

Unger, R. W. 1987. "Portuguese Shipbuilding and the Early Voyages to the Guinea Coast." In *Vice-Almirante A. Teixeira da Mota: In Memoriam,* 2 vols., 1: 229–49. Lisbon: Academia de Marinha/Instituto de Investigação Científica Tropical.

Unwin, R. 1960. *The Defeat of John Hawkins: A Biography of His Third Slaving Voyage.* London: Allen and Unwin.

Valdez, F. T. 1861. *Six Years of a Traveller's Life in Western Africa.* 2 vols. London: Hurst and Blackett.

———. 1864. *Africa ocidental: Notícias e considerações.* 2 vols. Lisbon: No Escriptorio de Francisco Arthur da Silva.

Van-Chi-Bonnardel, R. 1967. "La pêche sur la Petite Côte (Sénégal)." BIFAN 29, 3–4: 739–79.

———. 1969. "Les problèmes de la pêche maritime au Sénégal." AG 25: 25–57.

Van der Drift, R. 2000. "Birds of Passage and Independence Fighters: An Anthropological Analysis of Balanta Migration to Southern Guinea-Bissau and Mobilisation for the Liberation War (1890–1964)." In *Migrations anciennes et peuplement actuel des Côtes guinéennes,* edited by G. Gaillard, 151–64. Paris: L'Harmattan.

Van Geertruyen, G. 1976. "La fonction de la sculpture dans une société africaine: Les Baga, Nalu, et Landuman." AFG 1: 63–117.

Verlinden, C. 1970. *The Beginnings of Modern Colonization.* Ithaca, N.Y.: Cornell University Press.

Vicente, J. 1993. "Quatro séculos de vida Cristã em Cacheu." In *Mansas, escravos, grumetes, e gentio: Cacheu na encruzilhada de civilizações,* edited by C. Lopes, 99–134. Bissau, Guinea-Bissau: Instituto Nacional de Estudos e Pesquisa.

Villault de Bellefond, E. 1666/1968. "Abstract of a Voyage to the Coast of Africa and Guinea in 1666." In *A New General Collection of Voyages and Travels,* edited by T. Astley, 2: 374–87. London: Frank Cass.

Villeneuve, R. G. V. de. 1814. *Afrique, ou histoire, moeurs, usages, et coutumes des Africains.* 4 vols. Paris: Napveli.

Wadstrom, C. B. 1789. *Observations on the Slave Trade, and Description of Some Part of the Coast of Guinea, during a Voyage Made in 1787 and 1788.* London: J. Phillips.

———. 1794–95/1968. *An Essay on Colonization Particularly Applied to the Western Coast of Africa.* New York: A. M. Kelley.

Walter, J. 1947. *Honório Pereira Barreto.* Bissau, Guinea-Bissau: Centro de Estudos da Guiné Portuguesa.

Warburton, E. 1849. *Memoirs of Prince Rupert and the Cavaliers.* 3 vols. London: R. Bentley.

Wax, D. D. 1972. "The Browns of Providence and the Slaving Voyage of the Brig *Sally,* 1764–1765." AN 32: 171–79.

Webb, J. L. A. 1995. *Desert Frontier: Ecological and Economic Change along the Western Sahel, 1600–1850.* Madison: University of Wisconsin Press.

———. 1997. "The Mid-Eighteenth Century Gum Arabic Trade and the British Conquest of Saint-Louis du Sénégal, 1758." JICH 25, 1: 37–58.

Webster, D. 1999. "Pirates of the *Whydah.*" NG 195, 5: 64–77.

Wilkinson, W. 1690. *Systema Africanum, or a Treatise Discovering the Intrigues of the Guiney Company.* London: [S.N.]

Williamson, J. A. 1927. *Sir John Hawkins: The Time and the Man.* Oxford.

———. 1969. *Hawkins of Plymouth.* 2nd ed. New York.

Willis, J. R. 1974. "Introduction: Reflections on the Diffusion of Islam in West Africa." In *Studies in West African Islamic History.*Vol. 1, *The Cultivators of Islam,* edited by J. R. Willis, 1–39. London: Frank Cass.

Wilson, E. G. 1976. *The Loyal Blacks.* New York.

Wilson, W. A. A. 1962. *The Crioulo of Guiné.* Johannesburg, South Africa: University of Witwatersrand Press.

Winius, G. D. 1981. "Two Lusitanian Variations on a Dutch Theme: Portuguese Companies in Times of Crisis, 1628–1662." In *Companies and Trade,* edited by L. Blussé and F. Gaastra, 119–34. Leiden, the Netherlands: Leiden University Press.

Winterbottom, T. 1803/1969. *An Account of the Native Africans in the Neighbourhood of Sierra Leone.* London: Frank Cass.

Wright, D. R. 1977. *The Early History of Niumi: Settlement and Foundation of a Western Mandinka State in Gambia.* Athens: Ohio University Press, Center for International Studies.

———. 1979. *Oral Traditions from the Gambia.* Vol. 1, *Mandinka Griots.* Athens: Ohio University Press, Center for International Studies .

———. 1985. "Beyond Migration and Conquest: Oral Traditions and Mandinka Ethnicity in Senegambia." HA 12: 335–48.

———. 1997. *The World and a Very Small Place in Africa.* Armonk, N.Y.: M. E. Sharpe.

———. 1999. "'What Do You Mean There Were No Tribes in Africa?': Thoughts on Boundaries—and Related Matters—in Precolonial Africa." HA 26: 409–26.

Wurie, A. 1953. "The Bundukas of Sierra Leone." SLS N.S. 1: 14–25.

Wurie, A., and E. Hirst. 1968. *Rassin.* London: Unversity of London Press.

Wylie, K. C. 1977. *The Political Kingdoms of the Temne: Temne Government in Sierra Leone, 1825–1910.* New York: Africana Publishing Company.

Zook, G. F. 1919/1969. *The Company of Royal Adventurers Trading into Africa.* New York: Negro Universities Press.

Index

Page numbers in *italics* indicate maps.